BATTLESHIP
DUKE OF YORK

BATTLESHIP DUKE OF YORK

An Anatomy from Building to Breaking

IAN BUXTON & IAN JOHNSTON

Seaforth
PUBLISHING

First published in Great Britain in 2021 by
Seaforth Publishing
An imprint of Pen & Sword Books Ltd
47 Church Street, Barnsley
S Yorkshire S70 2AS

www.seaforthpublishing.com
Email info@seaforthpublishing.com

British Library Cataloguing in Publication Data
A CIP data record for this book is available from the British Library

ISBN 978-1-5267-7729-4 (Hardback)
ISBN 978-1-5267-7730-0 (ePub)
ISBN 978-1-5267-7731-7 (Kindle)

Pen & Sword Books Limited incorporates the imprints of Atlas, Archaeology, Aviation, Discovery, Family History, Fiction, History, Maritime, Military, Military Classics, Politics, Select, Transport, True Crime, Air World, Frontline Publishing, Leo Cooper, Remember When, Seaforth Publishing, The Praetorian Press, Wharncliffe Local History, Wharncliffe Transport, Wharncliffe True Crime and White Owl.

Typeset and designed by Mousemat Design Limited
Printed in China by 1010 Printing International Ltd

Contents

Dedication

The authors would like to dedicate this book to the memory of British shipyard workers and in particular, the thousands of men and women who built HMS *Duke of York* at John Brown's shipyard in Clydebank.

Introduction

THE INTENTION BEHIND this book is to offer a unique insight into the battleship *Duke of York*, making use of photographs, plans and various documents referring to and retrieved from the ship herself and the shipyard that built her. The photographs cover her construction from keel laying to acceptance, and her ultimate disposal in an act of recycling which has always been the fate of ships that had not otherwise been lost, given the intrinsic value of their materials.

The definition of a ship in visual form lies in the final set of plans drawn up on her completion, As Fitted plans supplied to the Admiralty, which represent a miniscule proportion of the ones required during the construction process but which summarise succinctly and with clarity what the ship is and how she can be worked and fought. In this instance the plans represent the ship as completed late in 1941 and again in early 1945 on completion of the only major refit which this ship would receive.

In taking this somewhat abstract view of the ship as object, no attempt has been made to discuss the design of the *King George V* class beyond that which is written below as this has been well covered elsewhere. For similar reasons the operational career of *Duke of York* is not part of this study, although one might note that had a British battleship been preserved, *Duke of York* would have been in contention not least for her role in the Second World War and in the action against the German battleship *Scharnhorst* in December 1943.

Like all things man-made, warships become obsolete and do not last. *Duke of York* had a short life which happened to span the period when battleships were eclipsed as the ultimate expression of power afloat. Conceived from a mindset that believed the battleship to be all-powerful, this view was rapidly disabused following tumultuous events at sea during the war years which saw the rise of the aircraft carrier and air power in general. After the war, there was limited discussion about what might be done with the *King George V* class regarding modernisation and conversion to other roles but neither the public purse nor the operational requirements were capable of being so stretched and the ideas were dropped. *Duke of York* and her three sisters eventually languished as features in lochs and creeks until the inevitable decision to release their value was made and the ships sent to the breakers, after a life of only about 16 years.

The origin of the class is best described by the man responsible for their design, the Director of Naval Construction (DNC), Stanley V Goodall who, in a letter to Henry Markham, a Principal Secretary at the Admiralty, on 9 March 1937, wrote:

> Since Nelson and Rodney were built, 60 different designs of capital ships have been prepared. We commenced working in earnest on the design from which the King George V emerged when the 14" gun was adopted for the main armament. Eighteen designs of 14" gun ships were considered']KGV Class Covers 0094]

The adoption of the 14in gun in 1935 was the single fighting characteristic of the *King George V* class that would define them and at the same time relegate them in the eyes of some, given the adoption of the 15in gun and above by every other battleship-building nation. There is a certain irony that the navy that did more than most to develop the battleship as a type should prosecute the Second World War with battleships armed with the smallest-calibre main armament of that era's designs.

Nevertheless, given the rush to rearmament, from that point onwards the final design of the ships was put into production in the drawing offices, platers' sheds and engineering shops of the British shipbuilding industry, then recovering from long years of depression. Every bit as important were the related industries where the key components of the battleship were manufactured: armour and armament. Both of these industries, especially the armament manufacturers, would determine how much hardware could be made and when, and effectively circumscribe the building programmes of succeeding years.

The British armour and armament industries, as they stood in 1937 after the rationalisation of the 1920s, had significantly reduced capacity compared to the final years of the First World War. Capacity limitations therefore necessitated a drawn-out process of construction which came under increasing pressure after the start of the Second World War in September 1939 when urgent demands on materials, labour and other resources were understandably made. This would result in individual build times of between four and over five years for the five *King George V* class. While all five were laid down in 1937, *King George V* and *Prince of Wales* in January followed by *Duke of York* in May, *Howe* in June and *Anson* in

July, completion would be a different matter with *King George V* in December 1940 and the last, *Howe*, in August 1942. Primarily for this reason the succeeding *Lion* class, of which there would have been four 16in-gunned ships, simply could not be built despite laying the keel of the first two, such was the pressure on materials and labour.

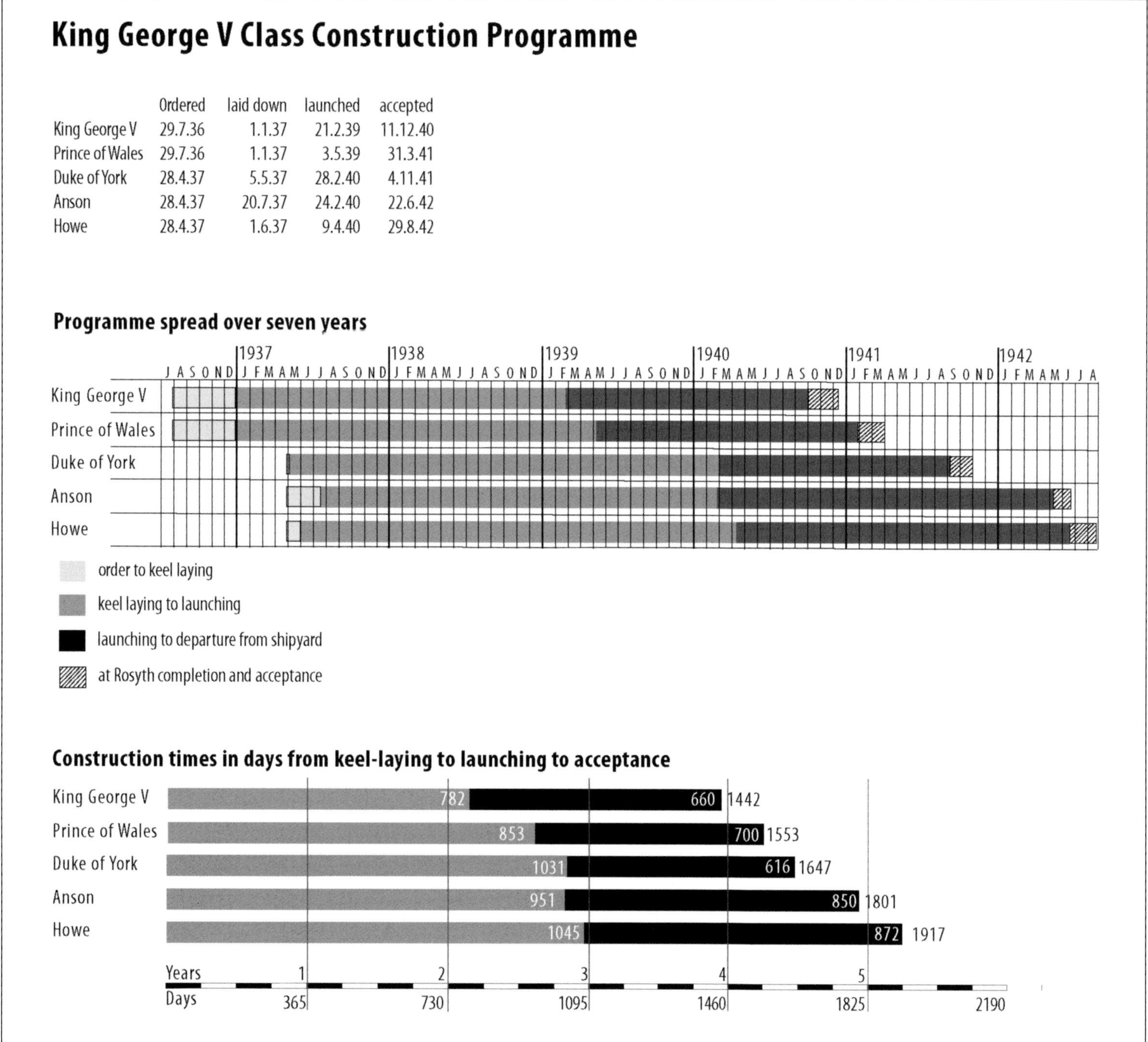

King George V Class Construction Programme

	Ordered	laid down	launched	accepted
King George V	29.7.36	1.1.37	21.2.39	11.12.40
Prince of Wales	29.7.36	1.1.37	3.5.39	31.3.41
Duke of York	28.4.37	5.5.37	28.2.40	4.11.41
Anson	28.4.37	20.7.37	24.2.40	22.6.42
Howe	28.4.37	1.6.37	9.4.40	29.8.42

Programme spread over seven years
1937
1938
1939
1940
1941
1942
J A S O N D J F M A M J J A S O N D J F M A M J J A S O N D J F M A M J J A S O N D J F M A M J J A S O N D J F M A M J J A S O N D J F M A M J J A
King George V
Prince of Wales
Duke of York
Anson
Howe
order to keel laying
keel laying to launching
launching to departure from shipyard
at Rosyth completion and acceptance
Construction times in days from keel-laying to launching to acceptance
King George V
782
660
1442
Prince of Wales
853
700
1553
Duke of York
1031
616
1647
Anson
951
850
1801
Howe
1045
872
1917
Years
1
2
3
4
5
Days
365
730
1095
1460
1825
2190

The building times of individual ships does not indicate the relative speed of construction by one shipbuilder over another. Many factors combined to delay progress, chiefly the wartime pressure on armour and armament companies who had to respond to evolving and urgent requirements and the removal of labour to work on emergency war work being the main examples. For the first reason work on *Anson* and *Howe* was suspended in May 1940 for a period of three months for the former and six months for the latter.

The launch of *Duke of York* was delayed for a period of six months at Admiralty request because of delays in main armament manufacture. Although work did not stop completely, there was a limit to what could be done while the ship was still on the building berth with launch weight being a critical factor. Her fitting-out period subsequently proved to be the shortest of the class partly because men were transferred from the suspended *Howe* and the loss of *Hood* in late May which applied additional pressure to have *Duke of York* in service as early as possible.

The choice of *Duke of York* as the subject of this book is principally because of the excellent visual record of her construction at the John Brown shipyard at Clydebank on the River Clyde where over 600 negatives were exposed during her construction. The building of this ship was accompanied by a series of monthly progress reports which describe the process-of-construction as well as some of the wider events that affected the pace of construction over two war years. These reports have been reproduced which, together with the progress of construction photographs, provide a unique insight not just into the building of a British battleship but a glimpse into the way in which ships were built when riveted construction was the norm. To that end, in some respects it could represent any large warship built in any major shipyard in Britain at that time, such was the similarity of approach and the techniques used.

Shipbuilding was a major industry employing in the region of 180,000 people in 1939, concentrated at sites around the country, most notably Clydeside, the North East Coast, Barrow, Belfast and Birkenhead. This industry, sometimes referred to as an assembly industry, was connected to scores of other industries that manufactured not only the basic materials used in construction but thousands of components large and small, simple and complex. This greatly increased the number of persons working directly and indirectly in shipbuilding and marine engineering. Manufacturing capacity in the UK at that time was extensive and there are few things if any that were beyond the capability of industry, unlike today.

The photographs of *Duke of York* are concerned with work that took place outside in the shipyard, almost exclusively on the ship herself. There are no photographs of the sizeable proportion of work that was undertaken in the offices and workshops. To get a complete picture of ship construction in the shipyard, photographs depicting work in the drawing offices, mould loft, engine and boiler shops, foundries, joiner and engineer workshops would have been necessary but these areas were rarely visited by the photographer, even under the auspices of such a visually-aware company as John Brown's at Clydebank.

Some of the detailed practices used in constructing *Duke of York* are difficult to describe and beg the question how did they actually do it? Many of these craft-based rule-of-thumb methods and techniques have slipped into history, even though riveted ship construction was widespread until comparatively recent times. Although welding was well known as a means of joining metal, at this time it was not sufficiently developed or trusted and its introduction into British shipyards was gradual and it was used only in less critical areas where the resulting structure was not subjected to great stress. Although there was a significant amount of welding in *Duke of York*, she was, as with all vessels of the period, essentially of riveted construction.

Other technical procedures are unique to warships, such as planing the steel surfaces on which gun mountings weighing many hundreds of tons must rotate and do so with great accuracy. Photographs in this book highlight this rarely seen activity and show a massively constructed barbette planing machine, specifically designed and built for this purpose.

Finally, John Brown's, like all shipyards, was full of energy and purpose as up to 10,000 persons from various trades and backgrounds converged daily working to a common purpose. Noisy, at times hazardous but always visually exciting, workers had to contend with climatic conditions not always favourable to outside working as thousands had to do at the building berths. In the era to which this book refers, building ships was considered to be a hard industry. Nevertheless, despite the hardships, it instilled a great sense of pride in shipyard workers, something easily understood as the photographs in this book bring *Duke of York* to life on her berth adjacent to the towering bulk of the Cunard liner *Queen Elizabeth*.

DUKE OF YORK

The Shipyard

JOHN BROWN & CO was one of the most important and well-known British shipyards, which could trace its history back to the early days of shipbuilding on the Clyde as J&G Thomson & Co (established 1847) and to Sheffield where John Brown began his involvement with steel products (c.1838), leading to the company that would bear his name. As shipbuilding in Britain became a major industry buoyed by the world's largest merchant and naval fleets, the Clyde became an epicentre for invention, methods and skilled workers. In 1871 Thomson's, under pressure from the rapidly expanding city of Glasgow with its requirement for ever more port facilities, were forced to relocate, fortuitously doing so to a greenfield site at what became Clydebank. The site was adjacent to the mouth of another river, the Cart, and although not then obviously an asset, this would later allow very large ships to be launched in an otherwise relatively narrow River Clyde. From here, the shipyard known locally invariably as 'Tamsons', 'Broons' or just Clydebank, would launch more nationally significant vessels than any other British yard throughout its life.

Founded mainly to construct merchant and passenger vessels, the build-up of the Royal Navy from the 1890s onwards proved irresistible to the company and the inclusion of warship contracts began to assume a growing proportion of ships built. With the Royal Dockyards unable to meet demand and somewhat behind the rapidly growing technical curve of ship construction, the private armaments companies began to equip for naval work. To do this, they acquired shipbuilding yards as a means of securing output of armour plate and gun mountings, additionally benefitting from having the ability to complete warship contracts within their own works.

In 1899 John Brown & Co Ltd acquired the Clydebank company although in doing so they stopped short at that time of adding gun-mounting capacity, unlike Armstrong and Vickers before them who had such capacity. Not long after this acquisition, the company secured the order to build the Cunard express Atlantic liner *Lusitania*, followed two years later by the battlecruiser *Inflexible*. At this point, with no decline in the demand for warships, John Brown & Co entered into an agreement with shipbuilders Cammell Laird and Fairfield to acquire the Coventry Ordnance Works and thus enter the market for gun mountings. Under this agreement large works were built at Scotstoun on the Clyde in 1907 to supplement those at Coventry and here mountings destined for the Clyde yards were manufactured.

The company strove to maintain the dual strategy of simultaneous construction of a major passenger and naval vessel, which they did through the contract for the *Aquitania* and a string of capital ships, *Australia*, *Tiger* and *Barham*. While the First World War put paid to further liners, it did result in *Hood*, probably the best-known British warship of the twentieth century. The years following the war did not match expectations and the signing of the Washington Treaty stopped the building of further capital ships in the UK with the exception of *Nelson* and *Rodney*, until the *King George V* class battleships including *Duke of York*, the subject of this book. Innovation, such as it was in British shipyards throughout this period, was often restricted to propulsion such as with Charles Parsons' great development of the turbine in the 1890s. Less well known was the Clydebank firm's development of the Brown Curtis turbine from 1907 onwards, resulting in its selection for hundreds of warships including *Tiger*, *Repulse*, *Barham* and *Hood*.

The 1920s and early 1930s were blighted by very poor trading conditions and the Depression, despite which the company pulled off the contracts to build the giant liners *Queen Mary* and *Queen Elizabeth*, having just built the *Empress of Britain* for Canadian Pacific in the late 1920s. It was during the construction of the *Queen Elizabeth* (1936–40) that the keel for *Duke of York* was laid down. The Second World War was a very interesting period for the John Brown shipyard as at one point no fewer than five capital ships were contracted for, if not all built: *Duke of York*, *Indefatigable*, *Conqueror*, *Vanguard* and *Malta*. This level of construction together with sister vessels to be built elsewhere was hugely optimistic and well beyond the capacity of the armament and steel-making industries to supply. Lack of manpower was another significant issue which never reached the levels of the First World War.

In terms of plant and facilities, the shipyard, one of the largest single-site yards in the UK, was well equipped to build vessels of all types and sizes. The depressed years of the 1920s and 1930s already mentioned had supressed profits, discouraging investment in new facilities, and the shipyard that built *Duke of York* between the years 1937–41 was little different to the one that built *Hood* in 1916–20. However, not much had changed in the intervening years with welding making a slow and gradual presence but not rivalling riveting as the principal method of construction. The fully up-to-date John Brown

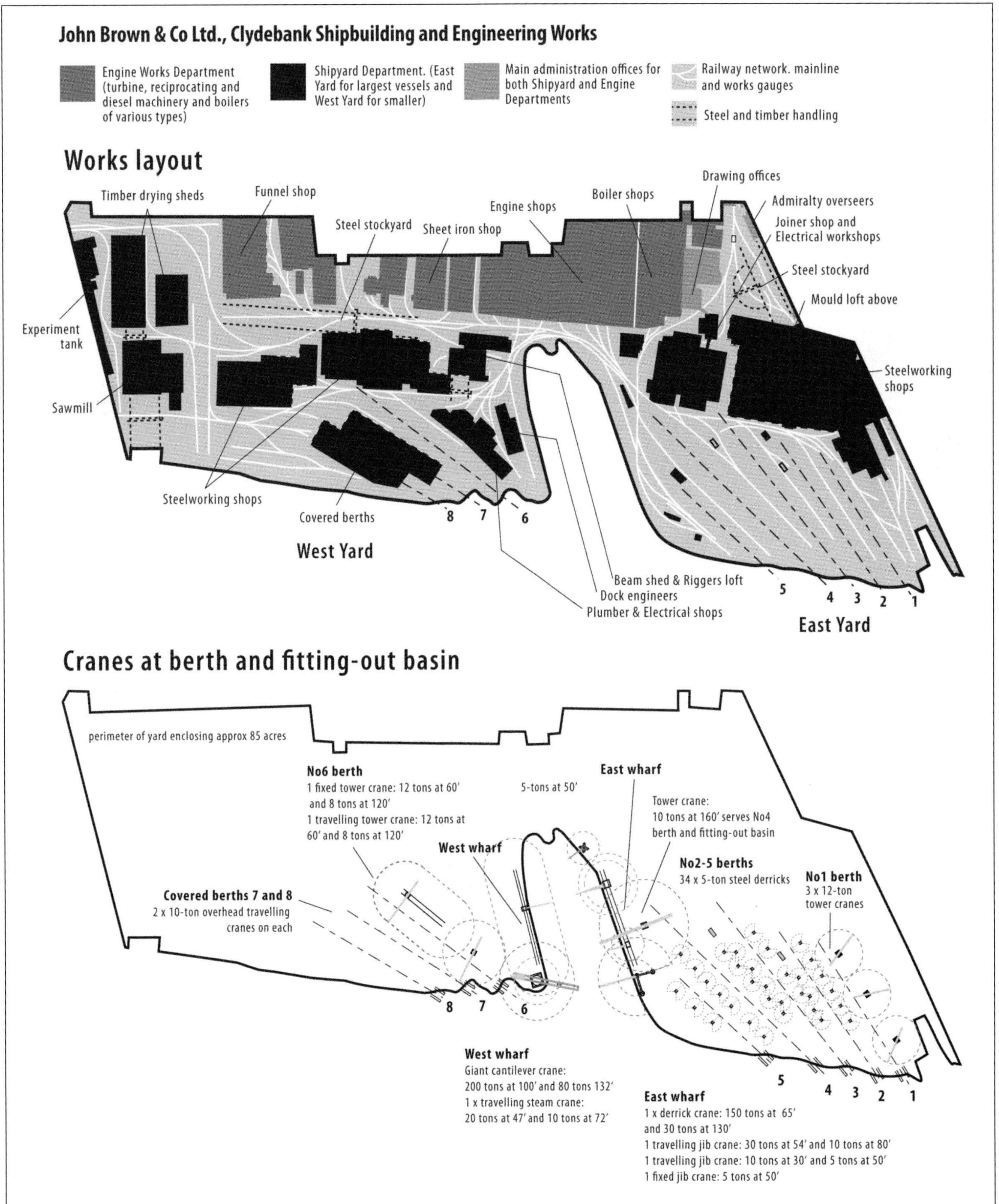
John Brown & Co Ltd., Clydebank Shipbuilding and Engineering Works
Engine Works Department (turbine, reciprocating and diesel machinery and boilers of various types)
Shipyard Department. (East Yard for largest vessels and West Yard for smaller)
Main administration offices for both Shipyard and Engine Departments
Railway network. mainline and works gauges
Steel and timber handling
Works layout
Timber drying sheds
Funnel shop
Steel stockyard
Sheet iron shop
Engine shops
Boiler shops
Drawing offices
Admiralty overseers
Joiner shop and Electrical workshops
Steel stockyard
Mould loft above
Steelworking shops
Experiment tank
Sawmill
Steelworking shops
Covered berths
8 7 6
West Yard
Beam shed & Riggers loft
Dock engineers
Plumber & Electrical shops
5 4 3 2 1
East Yard
Cranes at berth and fitting-out basin
perimeter of yard enclosing approx 85 acres
No6 berth
1 fixed tower crane: 12 tons at 60' and 8 tons at 120'
1 travelling tower crane: 12 tons at 60' and 8 tons at 120'
5-tons at 50'
East wharf
Tower crane:
10 tons at 160' serves No4 berth and fitting-out basin
West wharf
No2-5 berths
34 x 5-ton steel derricks
No1 berth
3 x 12-ton tower cranes
Covered berths 7 and 8
2 x 10-ton overhead travelling cranes on each
8 7 6
5 4 3 2 1
West wharf
Giant cantilever crane:
200 tons at 100' and 80 tons 132'
1 x travelling steam crane:
20 tons at 47' and 10 tons at 72'
East wharf
1 x derrick crane: 150 tons at 65' and 30 tons at 130'
1 travelling jib crane: 30 tons at 54' and 10 tons at 80'
1 travelling jib crane: 10 tons at 30' and 5 tons at 50'
1 fixed jib crane: 5 tons at 50'

Opposite: Taken loosely, the term 'shipyard' refers to the shipyard and engine works, the latter where engines and boilers were manufactured including steam turbines and reciprocating machinery and diesels under licence. The shipyard included East and West Yards, separated by the fitting-out basin. The works were connected by an extensive railway network linked to the main lines which allowed for the easy transportation of material. A 400ft-long experiment tank was built in 1903 to give the works access to design information in the ongoing development of hull hydrodynamics. As a single integrated works, John Brown & Co, often simply referred to as Clydebank, was among the largest in the United Kingdom.

Below: An RAF reconnaissance photograph taken of the John Brown shipyard on 11 July 1940. *Duke of York* is at the east wharf of the fitting-out basin bows out with the depot ship *Hecla* and the destroyer *Nizam* at the west wharf. Barely visible tucked in at *Duke of York*'s stern is the destroyer *Nerissa*. The East Yard shows the cruiser *Bermuda* on No 1 berth, *LC 8* salvage vessel on No 2 berth, the monitor *Roberts* on No 3 berth and the fleet carrier *Indefatigable* on No 4 berth. Furthest from the camera in the West Yard on No 6 berth is *Hororata*, a refrigerated cargo vessel for the New Zealand Shipping Co. The destroyers *Onslow*, *Paladin*, *Blankney* and *Avon Vale* are hidden from view in the covered berths.

The launch of RMS *Queen Elizabeth* on 27 September 1938 drew an audience of tens of thousands to witness the largest and longest vessel in the world enter the water at a then record 39,000 tons launch weight. This photograph shows the ship having left No 4 berth with the hull of *Duke of York* to the left and tugs standing off to the right.

shipyard of 1920, with investment mostly concentrated on the West Yard, was not seriously out of date by 1937. The possible exception was the berth cranes in the East Yard which were limited to a lift of 5 tons. These cranes dated from the period before and during the First World War. By the 1920s, most of the large British yards had moved to berth cranage with a lifting capacity of 10 tons and above. Lifting capacity at the berth dictated what could be produced in the steel-working shops where riveted assemblies were restricted to the 5-ton limit i.e. a single plate or frame. This had an obvious implication for steel throughput. If John Brown & Co made the decision to stick with 5-ton berth cranes, they made up for this, at least in part, by saturating the building berths with them. Building times were as good as any and where delay occurred, as with *Duke of York*, it was invariably the fault of circumstances beyond the yard's control.

The way in which ships were built would not undergo major change until the advent of welded fabrication where initially units of 20 to 40 tons became possible but this did not take place in the UK until the late 1940s and early 1950s and then only gradually because of full order books. After the war, there were many intermediate passenger liners to be built, passenger cargo vessels, the Royal Yacht *Britannia* and a trickle of naval orders including *Tiger*, *Hampshire* and finally *Intrepid*. The possibility of a major warship order in the form of the aircraft carrier CVA01 did not materialise due to cuts imposed by the Defence Review of 1966.

The rest of the story for the Clydebank works, British shipbuilding and a major chunk of industry in Britain is dismal. Although significant sums were spent at Clydebank, especially on the West Yard which was completely renewed to build ships up to 100,000 tons during the 1950s, it was too little, too late and in any case the mindset and attitudes then prevailing did not offer much hope of survival. With the decline of the Navy and the merchant marine, coupled with the advent of containerisation, the industry was all but finished, a sequence of events that took just a few decades to unfold. For Clydebank its last great achievement was the building of the Cunarder *Queen Elizabeth 2* (1965–9), albeit at a loss. Far from benefitting from having built the most prestigious vessel in the world, it seemed, paradoxically, as if its

The Clydebank shipyard site in 2018 looking east past the mouth of the fitting-out basin and the 200-ton crane, from a similar angle to the photo on pp172–3. The former East Yard is now home to West College Scotland and a leisure centre. The cantilever crane now has the highest level of protection that society can offer as an A-listed structure. It serves as a reminder of what once happened here and as a tourist attraction with an elevator and staircase added to enable visitors to reach the top safely and quickly.

construction hastened the fate of the yard. In 1966 the John Brown group of companies was restructured which meant at Clydebank that the Engine Works and Shipyard were separated, facilitating the closure of either should the trends which were then apparent continue. In 1968, with financial support and encouragement from the Government, British shipyards were grouped where possible in an effort to reduce costs and withstand intense competitiveness from overseas yards. On the Clyde this resulted in the formation of two groups, Scott Lithgow Ltd on the lower Clyde and Upper Clyde Shipbuilders Ltd on the upper reaches. The John Brown yard was part of the latter. The trajectory of Upper Clyde Shipbuilders Ltd was brief and volatile resulting in liquidation in 1971 despite a full order book. The campaign to save the yards gained great publicity and support in the UK and beyond and while elements of the original group survived as Govan Shipbuilders Ltd, the Clydebank yard was sold off to the US-based Marathon Shipbuilding Co (UK) Ltd to become an oil rig fabrication yard. By this time the engine works had been transformed into John Brown Engineering Ltd (JBE), manufacturers of gas turbine power systems in collaboration with the American General Electric Co. In 1980 the oil rig yard was acquired by UiE, part of the French Bouygues Group. In 1996 JBE was acquired by Kvaerner Energy. By the end of the century both the former engine and shipyard businesses were up for sale with no likely buyers other than developers who saw potential in the 85-acre site by the river Clyde. Over the course of 2001–2 the entire site was cleared, leaving only the fitting-out basin and the 200-ton Sir William Arrol giant cantilever crane to mark the site of this great shipbuilding and marine engineering works.

Management at Clydebank

In the mid- to late 1930s management at John Brown's continued to build on the outstanding reputation that Sir Thomas Bell had achieved for the shipyard during his period as managing director (1909–34). The contract for *Duke of York* followed hard on the heels of the two largest ships in the world, *Queen Mary* and *Queen Elizabeth*. The contract for the latter ship ran in parallel with *Duke of York* for a time and with other merchant and naval contracts, an organisational achievement for such complex vessels of the first order particularly by today's standards where all manner of digital calculations and numerically-controlled machine tools are available.

Once vacated by *Duke of York*, No 3 berth would then see the construction of Britain's last battleship, *Vanguard*, while in the adjacent No 4 berth, the fleet aircraft carrier *Indefatigable* was taking shape. After *Indefatigable*'s launch, No 4 berth was reserved for the very large aircraft carrier *Malta*, a contract that was cancelled at the end of the war.

This great, unparalleled shipbuilding achievement that directed thousands of workers was overseen by Stephen Pigott, Managing Director; Donald Skiffington, Shipyard Manager; Tom Crowe, Engine Works Manager and James McNeill, Naval Architect.

DUKE OF YORK

Labour

THE DEARTH OF shipbuilding orders in the late 1920s had been offset at Clydebank with the contract to build the Cunard liner *Queen Mary* in December 1930. Further deterioration of the financial climate forced the suspension of this contract and by the beginning of 1932 the yard was at a standstill with most employees paid off. A trickle of small Admiralty contracts then offered some employment and when *Queen Mary* was restarted in the spring of 1934, several thousand were immediately re-employed. Securing the contract for *Queen Elizabeth* in October 1936 brought the numbers in the shipyard up to almost 4000 with a further 2000 in the engine and boiler shops. Orders for merchant vessels followed along with that for the cruiser *Southampton* as rearmament began. With the contract for *Duke of York* awarded in 1937, employment in the shipyard and engine works grew to a total of over 10,300 in December 1939 peaking again at much the same level in September 1941.

Work on Ship No 554, originally named *Anson*, began before the keel was laid on 5 May 1937 with many hundreds employed in various departments, most notably the drawing offices, mould loft and steelworking shops, the latter preparing parts of the keel and double bottom. At the same time shipwrights and riggers would have been responsible for preparing the berth and setting out the keel blocks. Thereafter, from 5 May onwards erection on the berth started with the numbers of steelworkers growing steadily.

Surviving data concerning labour comes primarily from the activities of the Time Office and the Counting House and is associated with calculating pay from hours worked. Records were kept on each employee on a daily basis by the Time Office where a timekeeper – there would typically be a dozen or so spread across the Works – checked every man off, recording name, number, hourly rate, hours worked and on what contract. This applied to 'time workers', men working at a fixed hourly rate, and 'pieceworkers' where the incentive lay in more pay for more work completed. The timekeeper also marked off work done by men on piecework in calculating pay to ensure it was not counted twice. This was done using paint, some of which can be seen in some of the construction photos, typically marking off riveting.

By the end of 1937, about 700 people were working on No 554. Numbers were allocated on being sufficient to bring the ship to launching condition by 16 September 1939, a date selected well in advance to fit in with material deliveries and high tides. By then numbers had risen to about 1300, mostly steelworkers, all of whom worked directly on this contract. Other support workers amounting to several hundred such as managers, foremen, draughtsmen, tracers, typists, accounts clerks, modelmakers, experiment tank staff, canteen staff etc were not booked to each contract but were regarded as overheads included in establishment charges.

Holidays

In peacetime holidays included spring and autumn holidays, normally two days in April, one day in September. The summer holidays known as the Glasgow Fair, later the Clydebank Fair, lasted ten working days and the New Year holiday five days. Christmas Day was not a holiday in Scotland and it was not until the late 1950s and in some cases the early 1960s that it became one. In the summer of 1940, because of the war, the Summer Fair holiday was replaced with what were termed rest periods lasting five days and staggered across the various ships under construction. In this way the Works remained open throughout the holiday period. In 1941 the normal Summer Fair holiday was reinstated although work continued on *Duke of York* throughout, with holidays taken later for those involved.

Interruptions

The first issue to affect progress on the ship was the decision taken by the Admiralty to postpone the scheduled launch for a period of five months. This was taken because of the delay in manufacturing and delivering the 14in mountings to the yard. Numbers were reduced over this period to about 300 which allowed a small amount of additional work to continue on the hull. In January 1940 labour was again ramped up prior to the new launch date on 28 February 1940. This date was two days after the departure of the *Queen Elizabeth* which created significantly more space in the fitting-out basin as well as freeing up fitting-out trades.

Essential wartime repairs inevitably disrupted workflow in the yard and this happened most notably when the fleet carrier *Illustrious* arrived on 24 July 1940, followed on 27 July by the Clydebank-built cruiser *Fiji*. Although both vessels were repaired over the course of the next two weeks, the work required significant labour which had to be taken from vessels building in the yard including No 554. A shipyard report from July 1940 notes that 'These emergency repairs greatly disturbed work in yard'. This accounts for the drop in numbers on No 554 at the end of July. The unfortunate *Fiji* would soon return for further repairs lasting from September 1940 to February 1941 after being torpedoed in the North Sea. From the beginning of 1941 numbers were gradually worked up, ensuring that the ship looked all but complete by the time the last main armament mounting arrived in July. The loss of *Hood* in May probably did not alter the speed at which this contract was worked, as there were too many long-lead items, in particular gun mountings, that were being delivered late, but it would have underlined the urgency of getting this ship into service. On delivery of the last 14in mounting in July, workers peaked at over 4000 in a major drive to complete the ship. This included about 1800 subcontractors fitting specialised equipment such as auxiliary machinery, weapons and ventilation systems, plus some 200 supervisory and Admiralty staff. After she left Clydebank on 7 September, the number of shipyard workers allocated to her dropped to between 50 and 180, probably manufacturing minor fittings or working on the ship at Rosyth to help complete installation of various items.

The blitzing of Clydebank on the nights of 13 and 14 March 1941 resulted in severe damage to the town of Clydebank but with limited damage to the shipyard. Out of 12,000 homes in Clydebank, 4300 were completely destroyed with 448 lives lost. The day after the raids ended, only 500 workers turned up at the yard to resume employment, with many workers bombed-out and transport completely dislocated. A shipyard report dated 29 March noted that in the shipyard 'the shops affected were Brass Shop, Engine Shop Tool Room, Shafting Shops where gearing hobbers and shafting lathes are being reconditioned. Biggest problem is feeding our workers as all canteens in Clydebank were destroyed.' Employment was nearly back at normal levels, approximately 9300, by the end of the month, however, and work on *Duke of York* was little delayed. A further air raid on 7 April destroyed the Mould Loft while on 7 May two land mines fell on the East Yard not far from *Duke of York*, causing damage to the yard but none to the battleship.

Employment Data

Although it is known that women worked in the yard during the Second World War from 1941 onwards, it is not clear how many. The heavy nature of some trades within shipbuilding precluded the introduction of women employees, the exception in peacetime apart from office workers (admin and tracers) being polishers employed in the joinery department. Women were employed at Clydebank during both World Wars and typically these roles would have been as semi-skilled or unskilled such as in the electrical department where cables were pulled through hulls and the wiring of components. Little else could be expected with such brief periods of training beforehand. However, the trade unions were reluctant to permit too many of such 'dilutees', fearing for job prospects after the war.

The charts which follow covering the period of *Duke of York*'s construction show a breakdown of labour in the Clydebank shipyard which was typical of many shipyards at that time. The employment figures after 1937 show the dramatic increase in overall numbers as the nature of the war translated into manning the existing programme of construction plus emergency war construction and repairs. The biggest changes in the make-up of the labour force was the increase in the outfitting trades over the steelworkers (from 40 per cent of the shipyard total to 53 per cent), and big increases in electricians and engineers (up about 260 per cent) as warship weapons and equipment became ever more complex to install. Welder numbers trebled while riveters fell, as the proportion of welded structure increased. Journeymen (time served tradesmen) made up over half of *Duke of York*'s labour force, with apprentices who served typically five years, making up about one-fifth of skilled men. The rest of the workforce was semi-skilled or unskilled.

Shipyard Trades

The list below gives a brief description of the main trades involved in shipbuilding at Clydebank. These trades were typical of most shipyards in UK at the time of *Duke of York*'s construction, although some variation in job titles existed from yard to yard. Most trades had a percentage of apprentices (the intake of which was controlled by the unions to preserve wage rates), boys (young men used for menial tasks who might later start apprenticeships), helpers (semi-skilled), and labourers (unskilled). Each trade had one or more foremen who organised the day-to-day work and the men required, and often had hire and fire authority.

In the Drawing Offices
Naval Architects (ship designers) and Cost Estimators
Draughtsmen: Steelwork, Outfit, Electrical. As well as drawing plans, they also ordered material.
Tracers (the draughtsmen often prepared drawings in pencil on paper for speed and ease of correction which were then traced in Indian ink on translucent linen by women tracers, suitable for reproduction).

Receipt of drawings from Admiralty and sub-contractors. Preparation of drawings for mould loft. Development of drawings for various production departments. A multitude of drawings had to be reproduced and sent to every corner of the yard, as well as to the shipowner and regulatory bodies for approval. In December 1939 there were in the shipyard, including apprentices, 117 ship and 24 electrical draughtsmen and 68 tracers. In the engine works there were 68 draughtsmen plus 37 tracers, a total complement of 290.

Loftsmen
: Scaled up the small scale lines plan and transferred the lines full size to the mould loft floor for fairing. Then prepared wooden templates for each frame, shell plate etc., for the steelworking shops and for the shipwrights (from whom they were recruited).

Shipwrights or Carpenters
: Shipwrights were responsible for setting-out and ensuring correct alignment of the structure, ranging from wooden keel blocks to frames and shell plates etc. Where platers had 'screwed up' shell plates, shipwrights checked alignment, a process known as fairing-off. Shipwrights positioned frames and beams in readiness for the riveter, ensuring they were square to the keel despite the ship being built on a slope. They also laid the launchways and wood decks.

Riggers
: Riggers were responsible not just for rigging the ship's masts and derricks but fixing up all manner of structures where ropes were involved such as staging down the side of the ship. They were also used for slinging loads to be lifted by crane and for handling mooring lines.

Anglesmiths or Frame Turners
: Bent frames and beams to shape and worked angle iron either cold or heated red hot to shape and punched for riveting. Angle iron (actually steel) was used both as stiffeners to plates as well as the means by which sections of riveted steelwork could be joined together, e.g. bulkhead to deck. Some were on piecework, a price being agreed for a batch of frames.

Shipsmiths or Blacksmiths
: Made smaller metal items such as guard rail stanchions, usually by forging.

Platers
: In the steelworking shops platers marked out and prepared each frame or plate to the required dimensions including punched rivet holes and bent plates (in plate rolls) to shape where required. At the berth platers fixed plates to the frames using bolts to hold them in place temporarily, a process termed 'screwing-up'. Platers worked in squads, typically shell, frame, beam, bulkhead and deck.

Borers or Drillers
: Bored holes in for rivets in plates and sections or openings of all kinds e.g. for pipes and cables.

Riveters
: Riveted sub-assemblies in the steelworking shops, steelwork at berth including joining plates, frames and beams. Riveters worked in squads comprising in the case of hand riveting a left- and right-handed riveter for synchronised riveting to drive the point of the red-hot rivet down, a 'holder on' who worked behind the steelwork being riveted holding the rivet head in place with a heavy dolly and a rivet boy who managed and passed the rivets in the rivet heating brazier. Where machine riveting was employed, a practice that started before the First World War, only one riveter in place of two hand riveters was required to operate the pneumatic rivet gun, using compressed air. Hydraulic riveting used water pressure in a U-shaped device which squeezed both ends of the rivet simultaneously. Most riveters were on piecework.

Caulkers
: Used hand tools or pneumatic caulking guns to close every plate joint to ensure watertightness, for which they tested compartments.

Welders
: Although already in use for specialised purposes such as oil-tight work and in non-load bearing areas of the structure, welding was gaining wider use as it reduced weight and required only one man to make a joint. X-ray machines could be used to check the quality of the weld. Employment of welders increased threefold during the Second World War.

Pattern Makers
: Made the wooden moulds for castings such as hawse pipes and bollards. Larger castings like stern frames would be contracted out.

Engineers or Fitters
: Were responsible for installing mechanical equipment, such as deck machinery, pumps and valves.

Plumbers
: Worked with pipes (usually steel or galvanized steel) of all diameters from water supply to accommodation and galleys (kitchens) to transfer systems for salt and fresh water and for oil tanks. Coppersmiths could be used for non-ferrous metal piping.

Electricians
Fitted electrical cables, junction boxes and tested electrical equipment.

Joiners
Made and fitted all interior woodwork, especially in accommodation. Polishers, often women, finished decorative work.

Sheet Iron Workers
Made fittings of thin gauge metal such as ventilation trunking and lockers.

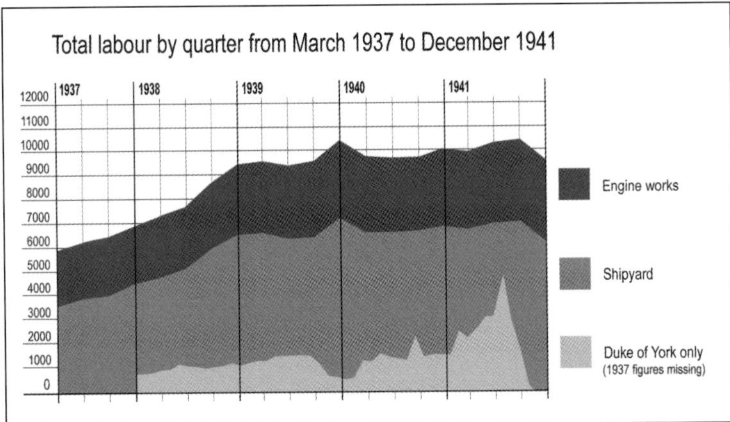
Total labour by quarter from March 1937 to December 1941
12000
11000
10000
9000
8000
7000
6000
5000
4000
3000
2000
1000
0
1937
1938
1939
1940
1941
Engine works
Shipyard
Duke of York only
(1937 figures missing)

This chart shows the total number of employees in the shipyard and engine works over the period of *Duke of York*'s construction. The steady rise in numbers on No 554 throughout 1941 indicates the effort required to finish the ship ready for transfer to Rosyth for final completion.

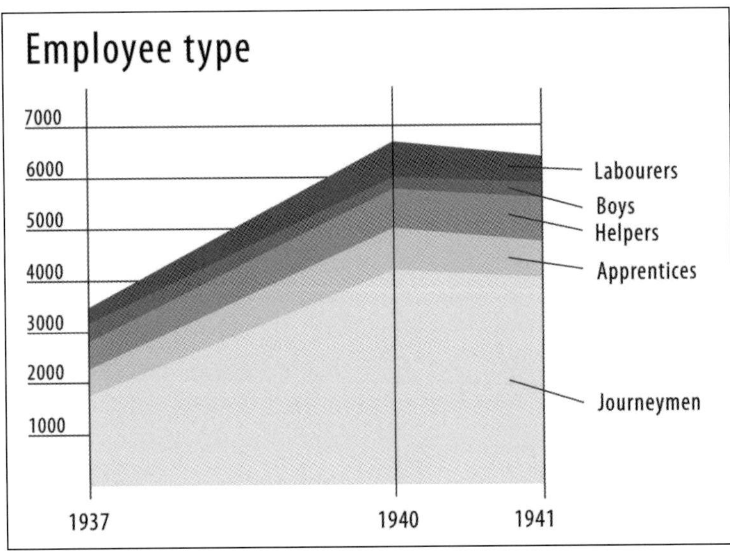
Employee type
7000
6000
5000
4000
3000
2000
1000
Labourers
Boys
Helpers
Apprentices
Journeymen
1937
1940
1941

This shows the type of shipyard employee with journeymen (more than doubling) and apprentices accounting for three-quarters of the total.

Painters
For both outside and inside the hull. The less skilled ones were called redleaders, working on undercoats.

Turners
Primarily in the engine works, turners operated lathes, mills, boring machines and other machines in making parts of engines.

Ancillary Workers
A host of other personnel were required to maintain the shipyard, its plant and employees. Timekeepers to keep track of employees and their work effort, plant maintenance staff (which included millwrights), storekeepers, wage and cost clerks, typists, canteen staff, photographers, first aid personnel and even 'detectives' (as Clydebank called their security staff) to stop pilfering – a problem with shipyards building passenger ships with large amounts of desirable fittings.

Sub-contractors
Various specialised areas such as interiors in the case of high class passenger vessels could be contracted out if required by the shipowner. In building *Duke of York* the principal sub-contractors were for installing the many items of armament, electrical and navigation equipment, steering gear, generators, air conditioning and ventilation.

Trials Crew
This would be drawn from the relevant trades, mostly finishing, including engine works fitters, both to operate the ship and to fix minor problems before handover.

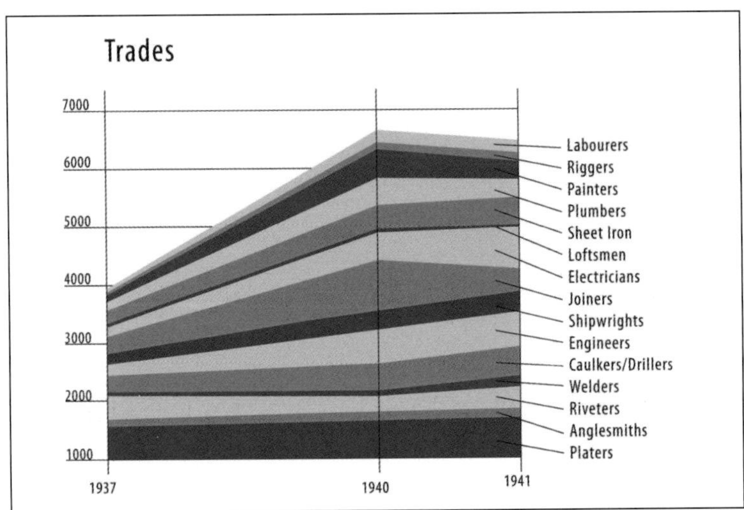
Trades
7000
6000
5000
4000
3000
2000
1000
Labourers
Riggers
Painters
Plumbers
Sheet Iron
Loftsmen
Electricians
Joiners
Shipwrights
Engineers
Caulkers/Drillers
Welders
Riveters
Anglesmiths
Platers
1937
1940
1941

This shows a breakdown of the main types of employee in the shipyard and the growth in total numbers from June 1937 to January 1940 to May 1941. Labourers for specific trades, such as joiners, are included under that trade.

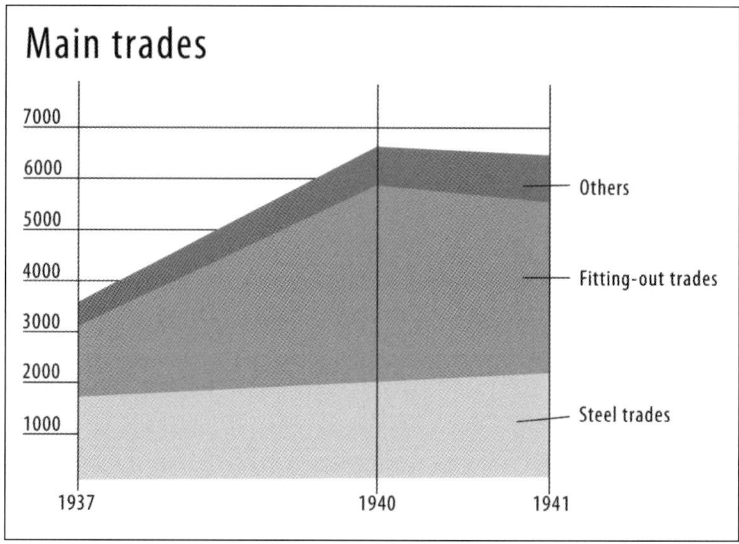
Main trades
7000
6000
5000
4000
3000
2000
1000
Others
Fitting-out trades
Steel trades
1937
1940
1941

From a similar number of employees in 1937, the requirement for the fitting-out trades in complex warships and liners accounts for the great rise of these trades over the steel trades by 1940. The peak in January 1940 is accounted for by joiners, plumbers and painters completing *Queen Elizabeth*.

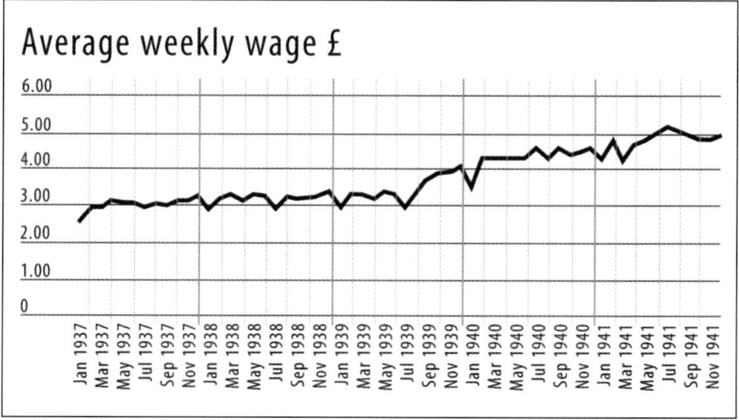
Average weekly wage £
6.00
5.00
4.00
3.00
2.00
1.00
0
Jan 1937
Mar 1937
May 1937
Jul 1937
Sep 1937
Nov 1937
Jan 1938
Mar 1938
May 1938
Jul 1938
Sep 1938
Nov 1938
Jan 1939
Mar 1939
May 1939
Jul 1939
Sep 1939
Nov 1939
Jan 1940
Mar 1940
May 1940
Jul 1940
Sep 1940
Nov 1940
Jan 1941
Mar 1941
May 1941
Jul 1941
Sep 1941
Nov 1941

The slow rise of wage increases pre-war increased significantly after the start of the war in September 1939.

Average weekly wage bill £

60000
50000
40000
30000
20000
10000
0

Jan 1937, Mar 1937, May 1937, Jul 1937, Sep 1937, Nov 1937, Jan 1938, Mar 1938, May 1938, Jul 1938, Sep 1938, Nov 1938, Jan 1939, Mar 1939, May 1939, Jul 1939, Sep 1939, Nov 1939, Jan 1940, Mar 1940, May 1940, Jul 1940, Sep 1940, Nov 1940, Jan 1941, Mar 1941, May 1941, Jul 1941, Sep 1941, Nov 1941

The upper line shows total wage bill for the shipyard and engine works, the lower line number of employees. Higher wage and material costs elevated the total wage bill for the works from £15,000 per week to £40,000 per week over the period.

Trades	June 1937	Jan 1940	May 1941
Platers	641	732	786
Anglesmiths & Shipsmiths	144	168	188
Riveters	529	355	486
Welders	78	143	208
Caulkers & Borers	326	519	586
Engineers	198	507	687
Shipwrights	241	388	403
Joiners & Polishers	346	1191	495
Electricians	204	542	785
Loftsmen	70	82	75
Sheet Iron Workers	260	474	554
Plumbers	158	534	349
Painters	139	593	391
Riggers	73	147	160
Labourers & others	96	272	257
Total	**3503**	**6647**	**6410**

This table which applies to the shipyard side of the Clydebank Works, shows the fluctuation in numbers by trade over the period of *Duke of York*'s construction. Having the required number of each trade in place to match workload was a perennial problem for shipyard management. With over twenty trades in total, it was not until union amalgamations from the 1960s onwards that these numbers were reduced, leading to fewer demarcation disputes. By then, however, the industry was facing problems of an altogether greater magnitude.

Costs

SHIPYARDS KEPT EXTENSIVE cost records, at that time usually in the form of handwritten ledgers. Some related to individual ships, some to suppliers, some to wages, some to cash and bank payments and some to overall accounts. These were required not only as business and statutory records, but also for cost control and for recording all costs associated with particular contracts. The figures can be multiplied by about 60 to give equivalent 2021 values. In the case of John Brown, these included (with archive series reference):

- Hull Costs (UCS1/80/16-17) recording by dates many categories of material and labour costs. There was probably a similar ledger for machinery costs, but it appears not to have survived.
- Wages Costs (UCS1/83/2).
- Contract Costs Registers (UCS1/76/4-5).
- Managers Progressive Costs (UCS1/77/264) monthly.
- Estimated vs. Actual Costs (UCS1/86/128-129) broken down by labour and material.
- Progress Payments Received from Admiralty (UCS1/61/4).
- Finished Costs (UCS1/85/27) monthly summary for hull, engines and boilers, plus cumulative totals.

The latter two are the most useful for extracting income and expenditure on No 554. The Progress Payments ledger shows when each of some 250 building instalments were received, and can be linked to the Hull and Machinery Instalments Schedule part of the Admiralty contract (UCS1/107/161). Each 'milestone' triggered a payment as a percentage of the contract price for Hull and Electrical (£2,499,250) and for Machinery (£906,486). Examples include:

Hull No. 16: 1% when 20% of the structural steel bars, plates, rivets by weight is worked into the ship. £24,992 received on 25.11.37.

Hull No. 42: 1% when all the side armour below the lower deck is fitted in place and fastened. £24,992 received on 23.10.39.

Hull No. 75: 1% when the supports are complete and seatings machined ready to receive four of the twin 5.25" turrets. £24,992 received on 25.1.41.

Hull No. 91: 1% when all cabin furniture and upholstery is complete and in place and all stores have been provided and stowed as required by the contract. £24,992 received on 7.9.41.

Machinery No. 47: 1½% when the port outer set of turbines and gearing is erected on the engine maker's premises and shop tests completed. £12,597 received on 7.9.39.

Machinery No. 94: ½% when all the boilers are complete and ready for fitting on board. £4532 received 27.11.39.

Machinery No.119: ½% when the funnels are fitted on board. £4532 received 19.5.41.

Costs continued to be incurred after delivery (4 November 1941), for example for guarantee claims and for late modifications for the Admiralty. Payments also continued to be claimed for Extras or Rebates (refunds to the Admiralty e.g for curtailed trials). Although such trickles continued right up to 1947, showing the totals as at March 1942 gives a good overall picture. All costs do of course exclude Admiralty Supply Items (ASIs) such as armament and armour.

Item	**Actual £**	**% total**	**Estimated £**	**% difference**
Hull materials	911,487	28.98	891,754	2.21
Hull labour	937,726	29.81	745,800	25.73
Hull charges	435,503	13.85	462,370	-5.81
Hull total	2,284,716	72.64	2,099,924	8.80
Engines materials	393,031	12.50	386,569	1.67
Engines labour	154,426	4.91	129,150	19.57
Engines charges	78,347	2.49	80,073	-2.16
Engines total	625,804	19.90	595,792	5.04
Boilers materials	132,885	4.22	110,200	20.59
Boilers labour	67,465	2.14	53,350	26.46
Boilers charges	34,553	1.10	33,077	4.46
Boilers total	234,903	7.47	196,627	19.47
Machinery total	860,707	27.36	792,419	8.62
Ship Total	**3,145,423**	**100.00**	**2,892,343**	**8.75**
Total materials	1,437,403	45.70	1,388,523	3.52
Total labour	1,159,617	36.87	928,300	24.92
Total charges	548,403	17.43	575,520	-4.71
Total costs	3,145,423	100.00	2,892,343	8.75

Hull costs included electrical. Charges were overheads in

modern parlance, general costs shared across all contracts such as power (electricity and coal), insurance, plant maintenance, senior staff, subscriptions (including the Shipbuilding Conference trade association), London office etc.

The estimated costs were prepared for the tender of 15 February 1937, so had to make some allowance for expected wage and other cost increases over the next four years. The table shows that for materials plus charges the estimate was only 1 per cent different from the final, but for labour there was a 25 per cent difference. Some of this may have been for unanticipated work (such as fitting new Admiralty equipment) or rework (remedying defects) but most would have been due to wage increases. As shown on p23 average weekly wages increased from £3.00 in 1937 to £4.75 in 1941, more than anticipated due to wartime inflation. However, the profit margin in the contract price allowed most of such increases to be absorbed. While no final profit and loss statement on the contract has been found, one can be estimated from the total of Admiralty payments as at March 1942, namely £3,378,937. This suggests that the final profit was about £233,500, or 7.4 per cent, virtually the same as the profit margin of about 7 per cent that the Admiralty allowed on wartime contracts which were based not on tenders or fixed prices but on costs incurred.

As well as totals, the cost ledgers reveal some specific figures:

Steering gear (Brown Bros, Edinburgh) £14,401.
Forward capstans (Napier Bros, Glasgow) £14,277.
Turbo-generators (W H Allen, Bedford six at 300kW each) £32,270.
Fresh water distilling machinery (Caird & Rayner, London) £12,739.
Steel (probably including D quality) total invoiced 15,534 tons £193,675 (£12.47/ton) plus 75 tons from stock. Floating steel would be less, because of cutting off 'green' material (plates were ordered slightly oversize to allow for working), holes etc.
Rivets total 494.6 tons £9530 (£19.2/ton, 3.2% of steel).
Deck timber £11,717 total. Teak £2.50 per cuft (Borneo about half that).
Decorating launch platform £189.
Photography £4161.
Hire of planing machine £579.

Admiralty records give a figure of £7,426,000 for the final price of *Duke of York* including ASIs, indicating that John Brown's share was about 45 per cent. The Admiralty supplied all the armament, its total cost being about £2,250,000, almost the same as the hull price. The balance of the total cost to the Admiralty of about £1,800,000 was mostly armour plus specialist items like fire-control equipment, aircraft equipment, radar and radio, anchors and cables, boats, salvage pumps, bulletproof plating, telephone system, engine room fans and medical equipment.

It is interesting to compare the costs of US-built battleships of similar size. Figures were published in *The Shipbuilder* for June 1943 for *Massachusetts* and *South Dakota* completed in private yards in 1942. Their hull and machinery costs, i.e. excluding armour and armament, averaged $44.4 million or £11 million each at the official exchange rate of £1 = $4.03; over three times *Duke of York*. US shipbuilding wage rates were about three times higher than UK.

	US			***Duke of York***		
	$M	**£M**	**%**	**£M**	**%**	**US/DOY**
Materials	15.8	3.92	35.6	1.44	45.7	2.72
Labour	19.6	4.86	44.1	1.16	36.8	4.19
Charges	9.0	2.23	20.3	0.55	17.5	4.06
Total	44.4	11.01	100.0	3.15	100.0	3.50

Procurement

THE NORMAL PROCESS for ordering British warships in the 1930s was:

- Naval Staff perceive a need for a new (class of) warship, to meet new threats or to replace old ships.
- After internal Admiralty departmental discussions, a Staff Requirement is sent to the Director of Naval Construction (DNC) to prepare sketch designs.
- Designs reviewed by the Controller (Third Sea Lord, in charge of materiel) and Staff with approximate costs.
- If acceptable to the Admiralty Board and affordable after Treasury approval, detailed design prepared with estimated costs included in forthcoming Navy Estimates presented to Parliament each March.
- Tenders issued to suitable shipbuilders on Admiralty list, together with design drawings and specifications.
- Tenders received by Admiralty (typically one to two months later), reviewed by DNC, Director of Contracts and Engineer-in-Chief, including a check that prices looked reasonable.
- Recommendation via Controller to Board of Admiralty on shipbuilder(s) selected.
- Orders placed with shipbuilder and machinery builder. Sometimes phased to give a regular pattern of expenditure throughout the financial year.

The contract covered the hull and machinery only, as the Admiralty placed separate orders for the armament, armour plating and other ASIs such as fire-control equipment. The contract (Agreement) took a broadly similar form for all warship types, full of long unpunctuated legalistic sentences for such things as late delivery (£200 per day), arbitration, insurance and failure of the contractor. It included the contractor's name, contract price for hull and for machinery and for electrical work, and the delivery date. It was accompanied by 'Schedules' which were in effect the specifications, divided into:

First: General Conditions.
Second: Specifications of Hull, Electrical, Machinery, Auxiliary Machinery, Naval Stores, Materials etc.
Third: List of plans of hull and machinery.
Fourth: List of ASIs.
Fifth: Movement of vessel for trials and seaworthiness.
Sixth: Hull and electrical instalment payments.
Seventh: Machinery instalment payments.

The Admiralty would appoint an Overseer (a member of DNC's department) to each shipyard, who would inspect materials and equipment, approve stages of construction and tests, and sign off progress reports. Progress payments (instalments) would be made according to the schedules, after the shipyard had submitted a claim for work done at each 'milestone', a percentage of contract price. Despite the bureaucracy, the shipyards liked this system as the payments received roughly matched expenditure on materials and labour, thus minimising work in progress to be financed by the shipbuilder.

As the build period was usually several years, the Admiralty would inevitably require 'extras' to be added to the ship such as installing new equipment. Sometimes there would be 'rebates' (credits) if items were removed. Thus the final price paid by the Admiralty to the shipbuilder would be the contract price (assuming a fixed price) plus extras and minus rebates, after allowing for any increases in wages or other costs permitted under the contract. There would also be an adjustment for major items of auxiliary machinery such as steering gear, generators and distilling machinery (fresh water evaporators) as only a token sum was included in the shipyard's tender. To maintain uniformity across ships ordered at the same time, the Admiralty would agree with the shipbuilders who would be the manufacturer of each of those items on the basis of tenders submitted by approved suppliers. At the contract stage, that decision had not been made, so that only a token cost of such auxiliary machinery was included (£62,032 for *Duke of York*), with the final figure determined after the appropriate sub-contracts had been placed and delivered.

Particularly during wartime, the Admiralty would make many additions during the build period, reflecting experience from ships in service, so that it would take a year or two after delivery to negotiate all these extra payments before agreeing a final price (although of course the shipbuilder had been receiving regular payments from the contract throughout the build period). In the case of *Duke of York*, Admiralty cost adjustments continued until 1947.

In order to arrive at their tender figures, the cost estimators at the shipyard and engine works would use pro-forma sheets with standard headings to build up the costs for bought-in materials (steel, timber, pipe etc) based on estimated quantities and unit price, for labour costs (usually by shipyard trade e.g. riveters, based on previous costs or man-hours and wage rates for similar ships), and establishment charges (overheads) consisting of those costs not attributable to any one ship but incurred across the whole business, such as insurance and plant maintenance. They would have to make some allowance for likely wage and material price increases over the build period, contingencies and any likely delay in delivery of sub-contract items and ASIs. The company directors would then decide what profit margin to apply to the estimated costs before submitting their tender price.

In the case of the five planned *King George V*-class battleships, the Admiralty recognised that by 1936 there were only six British shipbuilders left who could undertake the construction of their hulls and machinery. While Harland & Wolff were keen to build a battleship, the Admiralty preferred to keep them for aircraft carriers and cruisers and they did not have a crane which could lift the 200-ton 14in gun mounting turntable. In order to speed delivery of these long-awaited ships, the Treasury agreed that competitive tendering need not be undertaken for the 1936 battleships. The Admiralty was able to indicate to each of the other five shipbuilders that they could expect one battleship each (this also spread employment), either from the 1936 Programme (two ships) or the 1937 Programme (three), subject to a satisfactory tender price being submitted later and judged affordable and reasonable. Vickers-Armstrongs were allocated *King George V* (hull from their Tyneside yard, machinery from Barrow) and Cammell Laird *Prince of Wales*. With one east coast and one west coast yard, that matched the supply of their 14in gun mountings, with Vickers-Armstrongs' Elswick works on the Tyne supplying *King George V* and their Barrow works *Prince of Wales*. For the 1937 Programme, John Brown was selected for *Anson* (later renamed *Duke of York*), Swan Hunter & Wigham Richardson on the Tyne for *Jellicoe* (later renamed *Anson*) with machinery from their subsidiary Wallsend Slipway & Engineering and Fairfield on the Clyde for *Beatty* (later renamed *Howe*). It had been indicated to John Brown in November 1936 that they were likely to get one of the 1937 battleships, so they were able to start preparatory work such as piling No 3 berth and ordering steel.

John Brown's tender was requested on 21 December 1936 and submitted on 15 February 1937, for £3,409,000: £2,270,000 for hull, £233,000 for electrical and £906,000 for machinery. Its make-up is shown in the Appendix. The Admiralty accepted it and ordered the ship on 28 April, but the actual contract was not signed until 10 July. The contract price for hull was £2,266,250, electrical £233,000 and machinery £906,486, totalling £3,405,736. This was about 45 per cent of the total ship cost to the Admiralty. Delivery was to be on or before 15 January 1941. What the Admiralty was not fully aware of at that time was that the main warship builders were operating a price-fixing scheme. Merchant shipbuilding was very competitive during the 1930s, so builders were often faced with the prospect of accepting a contract at a loss or going out of business. A Warship Builders Committee was formed by their trade association The Shipbuilding Conference to ensure that loss-making tenders were not submitted for British warships. The Committee reviewed the tenders which the various builders were about to submit, placed them in price order and then added what they regarded as an adequate profit margin to each. The prices submitted were thus in a competitive order but high enough to offset some of the losses they had been making on merchant-ship contracts. By so doing they were inadvertently maintaining a core of warship building skills and capacity which would be desperately needed once war came. The likelihood of collusion is evident from Swan Hunter's tender for *Jellicoe*/*Anson* at the same date; almost identical at £2,283,000, £229,500, £911,200 totalling £3,423,700.

The Admiralty later discovered that high profit margins often resulted, an investigation showing a range from a low of less than 10 per cent of hull and machinery cost to a high of over 70 per cent on submarines, with an average of 28 per cent. With the press of wartime construction, they recognised that requesting competitive tenders simply delayed delivery; it was more important to place orders where the capacity existed. In 1942 a system of cost-plus contracts was brought in, i.e. paying the shipyard its actual costs plus a modest profit margin of about 7 per cent. The investigation had revealed that on *Duke of York*, the profit margin (on cost) for the hull was 20.4 per cent and machinery 8.3 per cent, or 17.3 per cent on the total, i.e. about £500,000. As a result of these generous amounts, the builders of the *King George V* class agreed to forego claiming most extras, absorbing them within the original contract price. However, these figures must have been interim ones before all John Brown costs had been recorded and agreed, as the actual figures on p25 suggest a profit at March 1942 of under £250,000 or 7.4 per cent on the £3,145,000 actual cost, not an unreasonable figure.

As well as ASIs already mentioned, there was a list of over 100 other items including boats, two cranes for boats and aircraft, aircraft catapult, capstans, compasses, searchlights and even potato peelers.

Shipbuilders were requested when placing orders for materials and smaller sub-contracts to do so in a way that spread work around, especially in areas of high unemployment.

2

Notice.—This Contract involves obligations of secrecy and confidence and attention is drawn to the provisions of the Official Secrets Acts, 1911 and 1920, and particularly to Section 2 of the first-named Act.

This Indenture made the tenth day of July in the year of our Lord one thousand nine hundred and thirty seven **between** Messrs. John Brown and Company Limited, Clydebank hereinafter called "the Contractors" of the one part and the Commissioners for executing the office of Lord High Admiral of the United Kingdom of Great Britain and Ireland (for and on behalf of His Majesty His Heirs and Successors) hereinafter called "the Admiralty" of the other part **WITNESSETH** that it is hereby mutually covenanted and agreed by and between the Contractors which expression shall herein be taken to include as well the said Messrs. John Brown and Company Limited as* their assigns and the Admiralty as follows that is to say :—

* *Add* here if a firm or individual "their and each of their (or 'his') heirs, executors, administrators and assigns," or if a company "their assigns."

1. The Contractors will at their own cost in a proper and workmanlike manner and of the best materials and with the best workmanship and to the satisfaction of the Admiralty BUILD LAUNCH UNDOCK and DOCK from time to time as may be considered necessary by the Admiralty AND COMPLETE in all respects a BATTLESHIP for His Majesty's Service and will provide the said vessel with main machinery of the aggregate power stated in the Specification and with boilers auxiliary machinery spare gear tools fittings and things as referred to in the relative Specifications and with such fixtures and fittings as are usual for similar vessels in His Majesty's Navy and will fix on board the armour armament and all fixtures and fittings in connection therewith also all first fitting stores and other articles which have been and may be delivered to them by the Admiralty to be permanently fitted or placed in the vessel and will deliver the same complete as aforesaid safely afloat at the nearest open water to the port of construction into the charge of such person or persons as the Admiralty may appoint to receive the same.

The first page of the contract to build *Duke of York*, at that time called *Anson*, dated 10 July 1937.

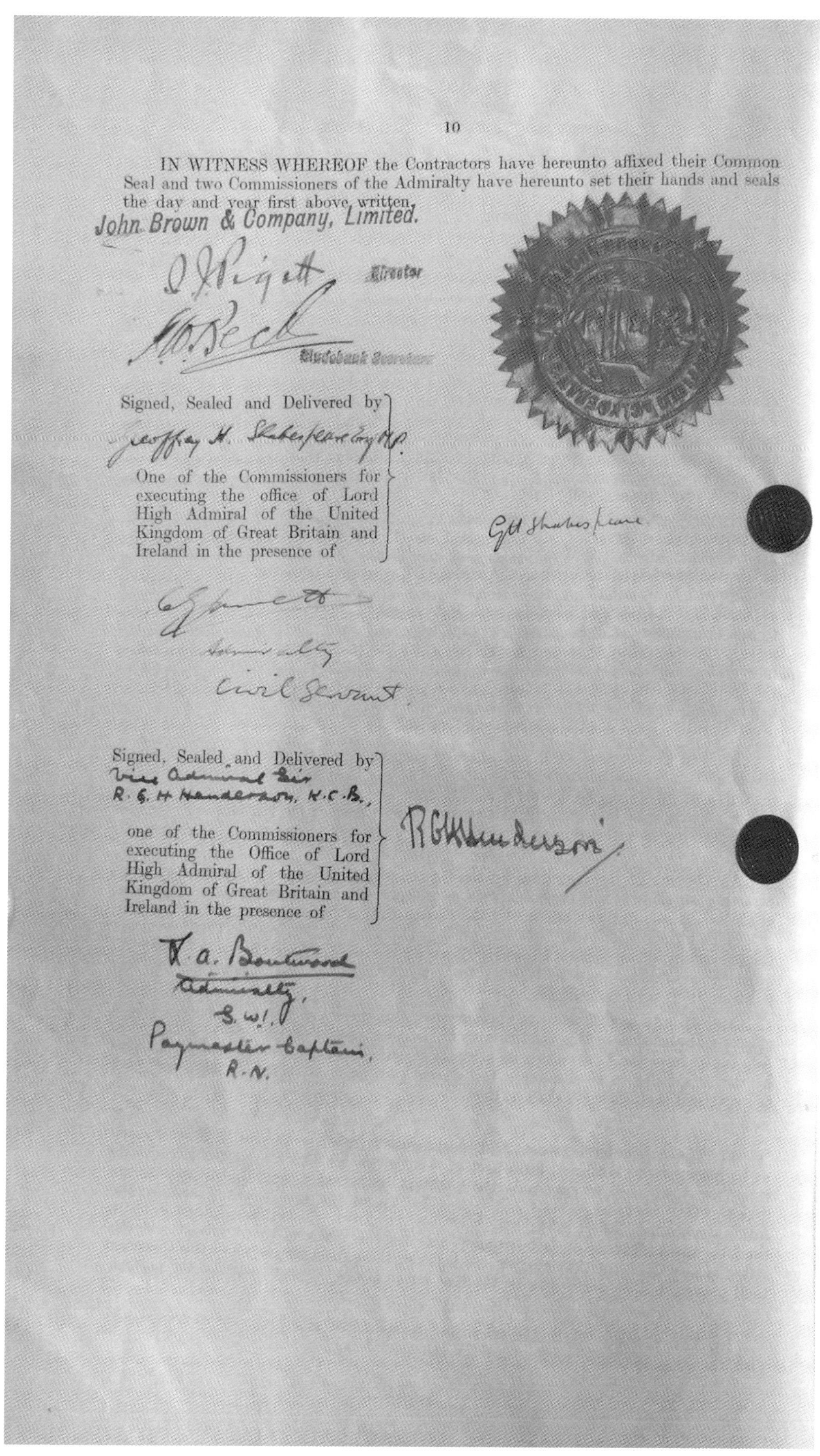

10

IN WITNESS WHEREOF the Contractors have hereunto affixed their Common Seal and two Commissioners of the Admiralty have hereunto set their hands and seals the day and year first above written.

John Brown & Company, Limited.

Director

Secretary

Signed, Sealed and Delivered by Geoffrey H. Shakespeare Esq M.P. One of the Commissioners for executing the office of Lord High Admiral of the United Kingdom of Great Britain and Ireland in the presence of

Admiralty Civil Servant.

Signed, Sealed and Delivered by Vice Admiral Sir R. G. H. Henderson, K.C.B., one of the Commissioners for executing the Office of Lord High Admiral of the United Kingdom of Great Britain and Ireland in the presence of

Admiralty, S.W.1. Paymaster Captain, R.N.

The last page of the contract bears the signatures of S J Pigott, John Brown's managing director, J W Beck, company secretary, Geoffrey H Shakespeare MP, Parliamentary and Financial Secretary to the Admiralty and Vice Admiral Sir R G H Henderson, Controller of the Navy.

Contract and Specification Conditions

THE OFFICIAL DOCUMENTS run to over 600 pages, but only a selection of the more interesting items are paraphrased here.

General Conditions

No foreign employees or visitors allowed in the shipyard except by consent of the Admiralty.

Official Secrets Act 1911 and 1920 to apply. References to 'prohibited place', 'munitions of war' [includes ships], penalties for spying, unauthorised possession of documents, wrongful communication of information.

Prevention of Corruption Act 1906 applies. No inducements etc to be offered to show favour to any person in relation to his principal's business.

No Member of Parliament to have any share in this contract [a hangover from the nineteenth century].

Economy of weight is of the utmost importance. [The Admiralty wished to ensure that the 35,000 tons standard displacement was not exceeded.]

Quarterly progress reports to be made to the Admiralty with a statement regarding dates for laying down, launching, trials and completion [but no mention of progress photographs].

Drawings, patterns and arrangement details to be the property of the Admiralty. [This enabled the Admiralty to pass them on to builders of sister-ships.]

No new contrivances unusual in Admiralty work to be introduced without Admiralty sanction.

A minimum of two months' notice to be given to the Admiralty of the proposed launch date. The formalities used in His Majesty's Service to be observed at the launching. Early notice of the name of the lady to perform the ceremony to be given for approval.

After launch, the ship to be in a safe berth always afloat.

Fair wages to be paid. The rates to be not less favourable than those in the trade and district. Admiralty to have the right to inspect wage books [but not other company books].

Title to the vessel as [partly] constructed and materials bought to vest in the Admiralty after payment of first instalment.

Admiralty may terminate the contract and complete the ship in certain cases [e.g. bankruptcy]. The Admiralty may then complete the work, either at that yard or removed to another.

Maintenance and efficiency of the main and auxiliary machinery to be guaranteed for 12 months after vessel proceeding to sea in full commission.

Shipbuilder to provide warehouse accommodation for guns, gun mountings, boats and first fitting stores supplied by the Admiralty, maintained in good condition, lubricated, painted and protected from the weather.

Admiralty to pay cost of carriage of items supplied by them, if by sea vessel to be British and British manned.

Inspecting officers and overseers to be appointed by Admiralty and provided with accommodation and access to the work. Powers to reject materials and workmanship.

Contractor not to sub-let or re-assign any part of the contract without Admiralty approval.

Admiralty to do their best to provide a drydock at a Royal Dockyard prior to trials, at a rent of £130 per 24 hours.

Hull Specification

All materials and articles whether for hull, machinery, gun mountings, stores or equipment must be weighed before they are placed on board and reported to Admiralty.

Standardisation of fittings: it is desired that the fittings shall be as uniform as practicable in all vessels of this class.

The vessel is to be so laid off that the main castings – sternframe, rudder and shaft brackets – are interchangeable between the several vessels of the class.

It is desired that electric welding be used as extensively as possible. Riveting is to be retained for D quality plating and important parts of the structure [the Admiralty was not yet sure how welded structures would stand up to high stresses in key parts of the hull]. Each of the welders to be subject to a proficiency test.

Watertight subdivision: it is of the utmost importance that the watertightness of the separate compartments indicated on the drawings shall be preserved intact. No watertight doors or other openings are to be cut in the bulkheads at stations [22 listed frames] below the middle deck.

Bulkheads below the lower deck not to be pierced apart from shafts and steam pipes.

Steel plates generally to be not less than 36ft long, angles 42ft.

Deck planking to be Borneo white hardwood with teak nosing. Planks generally 2½in thick, 7in wide in 24ft lengths. Secured by screwed studs welded to the deck.

Main, middle and lower decks laid with 4.5mm thick linoleum or approved composition.

Masts, spars and rigging: proposals to be worked out on a model of scale ⅛in to the foot before drawings are prepared and submitted. Masts of 20lb D quality tubular steel. Foremast 24in diameter, mainmast 12in.

Rivets and bolts: rivets to thoroughly fit holes, size of hole drilled no more than 1/32in larger than rivet diameter in all main structure, 1/16in elsewhere.

Rivet spacing: oiltight 4½ diameters, watertight 5, non-watertight 7-8.

Countersunk heads [i.e. flush]: outer bottom plating below waterline, plating behind deck or side armour [see drawing on p67 left].

Pan heads: generally outside above areas.

Snap heads: non-watertight in accommodation spaces [neat appearance].

Joggling in frames, beams and bars to avoid liners [to accommodate the step in plate thickness where riveted overlaps] [see drawing on p77].

To provide against damage by lightning to men working under the ship while building, there is to be a thorough metallic connection by wire rope between several points of the ship's steel hull and the water adjacent to the ship.

Pumping, flooding and drainage: each main transverse compartment to be independent. Fourteen 350 ton/hour self-priming electric submersible pumps to be provided by Admiralty, piping by shipbuilder.

Key compartments to be flooded in less than 15 minutes: magazines, shell rooms, bomb room, petrol compartment, spirit [rum] store, [in]flammable store.

Spraying system for weather deck and ready use magazines, ammunition cases, hangar.

The final cleaning of fresh water storage tanks is to be carried out by healthy men of clean habits, wearing clean overalls and rubber shoes.

Ventilation: fans and electric motors supplied by Admiralty, fitted by shipbuilder [a 17½in diameter fan served a 2ft^2 vent trunk].

Fan supply, natural exhaust: living and sleeping spaces, magazines, offices, galley, most stores.

Natural supply, fan exhaust: washplaces, WCs, petrol compartment, hangar.

Fan supply and fan exhaust: engine rooms, action machinery room, harbour machinery room, diesel generator compartments.

Air filtration system [against gas]: fire control rooms, conning tower, telephone exchange, switchboard room.

Supply intakes and exhausts to be well separated.

Seamen's cooking apparatus capable of cooking for about 1550 men, steam and oil fired types.

Ablution cabinets are to be built for the treatment of venereal disease.

Hammock berth hooks 21in apart, 10½-12ft long.

Anchors: 3 stockless 180 cwt, 1 sheet 60 cwt, 1 kedge 16 cwt, Admiralty supply.

Cable: 200 fathoms [1200ft] of 2⅞in diameter for each main anchor.

These anchors and cables not to be used in launching the ship.

Aircraft equipment: bogies and tracks suitable for maximum weight of 12000lb.

Searchlights: six 44in main, four 20in and four 10in signalling projectors.

The following boats are to be carried: three 45ft motor picket boats, one 45ft motor launch, three 25ft fast motor boats, two 32ft sailing cutters, two 27ft whalers, one 16ft motor dinghy, two 14ft dinghies, one 13½ft balsa raft. All Admiralty supply.

Materials

To use only the best materials and workmanship of British manufacture.

Names of manufacturers of materials to be submitted for approval.

Material test pieces to be selected by Overseer and testing machines approved.

Pickling steel plates used in lower parts of hull [to remove millscale]. Plates to be immersed in a bath of 19 parts water to 1 part hydrochloric acid for 12 hours, then washed and dried.

Welding of structural steel by metallic arc process with approved electrodes.

D and D.1 quality steel generally not to be heated before working [unlike mild steel]. Weldable quality. 37 to 44 tons per sq in ultimate tensile strength. Holes [for riveting] in D quality steel to be drilled not punched. Plate edges over 20lb [½in] to be planed; under may be sheared. [D quality steel was used in the more highly stressed regions of the ship: upper deck, side shell, main bulkheads, double bottom and gun supports.]

Mild steel to be from open hearth or electric furnace process. Rolling tolerance on plates 20lb thickness and above: 5% below, 0% above [also on steel sections]. Under 20lb 7½% under, 0% over.

A sample of every plate is to be subject to a bend test for ductility and to be bent double cold without cracking.

Test pieces for ultimate tensile strength between 26 and 30 tons per sq in. Elongation not less than 20% [both plates and sections].

Colour marking of steel to distinguish quality: Mild steel Yellow. D quality White. D.1 Red. Bar steel Blue.

Machinery

Efficiency in performance of the main and auxiliary machinery and boilers with due regard to economy of weight in this vessel is of the utmost importance.

The total weight of machinery not to exceed 2510 tons, otherwise liquidated damages [penalty] of £200 per ton in excess. Admiralty may reject if excess weight exceeds 3%.

Demarcation shipbuilder/machinery builder: engine and boiler bearers [seats], auxiliary machinery seats, shaft brackets, oil and water tanks if part of ship's structure, pipes and fittings in oil fuel tanks, ventilation trunks and fans to machinery spaces, boiler room airlocks, armoured gratings in decks [for uptakes and downtakes].

Oil fuel filling rate not to be less than 800 tons per hour.

Trials

Basin trial of a few hours to test machinery [with propeller shafts uncoupled].

Trials to be conducted over Talland [off Plymouth], Skelmorlie [Clyde], St Abbs [near Berwick] or Arran [measured mile] courses.

Trials to be at contractor's expense, with oil fuel to be purchased from Admiralty at 60s [£3] per ton.

Preliminary trial at rpm corresponding to full power.

Fuel consumption trials: 6 hours each at various powers up to 28000 shp [max on cruising turbines] with and without cruising turbines. 12 hours at 66000 shp plus 12 hours at 88000 shp. Steam consumption also measured.

Speed trials: 4 hours at 100000 shp plus 4 hours at 110000 shp [maximum].

Final trial: 2 hours at 50% power plus 1 hour at 110000 shp.

Measured mile runs: at 3000, 5600, 14000, 22000, 44000, 66000, 88000, 110000 shp. Both at 28ft design draft and at full load [about 33ft].

Further trials: astern [5 minutes at not less than 8000 shp], starting, stopping, turning, auxiliary machinery.

Circle trials at 12 knots and full speed to be carried out with rudder angle of 15 and 25 degrees.

Shipbuilder to carry out trials with own navigating party, with engine room staff from machinery contractor. Number of men in engine and boiler rooms not to exceed 60.

Naval Recording Staff to take measurements of horsepower, revolutions, steam pressures, vacuum etc on trial.

[In the event, wartime exigencies meant that few of these trials were actually carried out.]

DUKE OF YORK

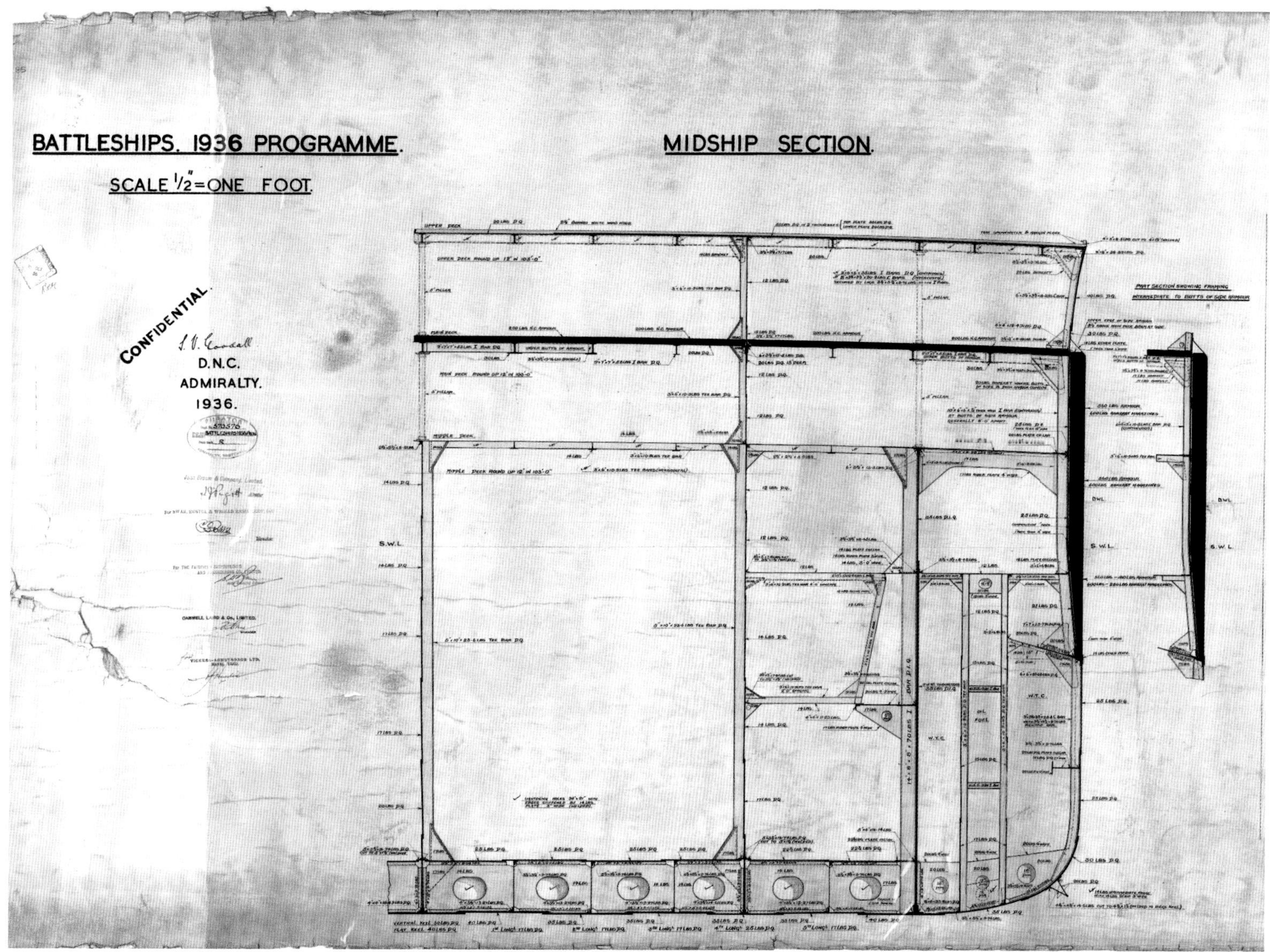
BATTLESHIPS. 1936 PROGRAMME.
MIDSHIP SECTION.
SCALE ½"=ONE FOOT.
CONFIDENTIAL
D.N.C.
ADMIRALTY.
1936.
S.W.L.

Midship Section

A midship section drawing shows the layout of a ship's structure at the middle of its length where the stresses are highest, indicating the scantlings (sizes of structural members). In the case of merchant ships, this drawing would be prepared by the shipbuilder for the approval of the shipowner and the classification society, e.g. Lloyd's Register, then as guidance for the draughtsmen preparing the production drawings, showing the plate thicknesses in inches. In the case of warships, the Admiralty prepared the midship section which had to be approved by the DNC, the newly-appointed Stanley Goodall, before submission along with the general arrangement plans to the Board of Admiralty. Admiralty practice was to show plating thicknesses in pounds per square foot, where 1in thickness weighed 40.8lb. It also showed which parts were high tensile D quality steel, the rest being mild steel. The overlap of the main riveted strakes was also shown. Stiffeners were shown with web and flange in inches but thickness in pounds per foot run, emphasising the Admiralty's concern to keep weight down. The drawing was made in black Indian ink on thick linen-backed cartridge paper, with a colour wash applied: blue for steel, black for armour, brown for timber. Only half the ship is shown, as most were symmetrical port and starboard.

This 1936 drawing was shown to the five shipbuilders invited to build, who could make notes and sketches for their guidance, each of whom then signed the drawing. The shipbuilder was expected to adhere to all the main scantlings but could change minor details such as brackets to suit production. The three layers of the torpedo protection system outboard of the forward boiler rooms are shown with an oil fuel tank sandwiched between watertight compartments. Inboard was the main protective bulkhead of two thicknesses of 35lb D.1 quality steel plates abreast the magazines, i.e. a total of 1.72in. The three 1937 battleships including *Duke of York* were built to the same plan. (©National Maritime Museum, London M2067A)

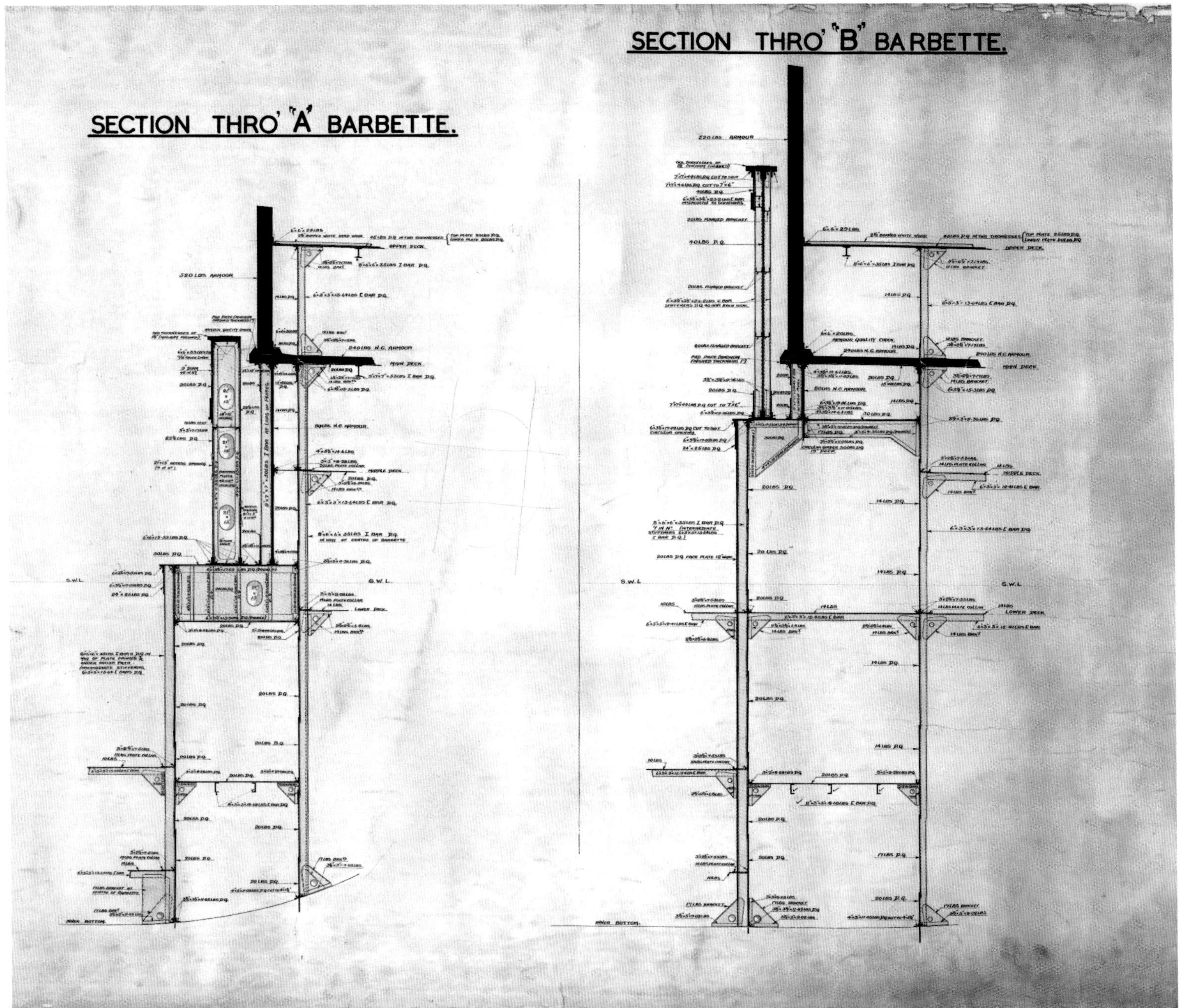
SECTION THRO' "A" BARBETTE.
SECTION THRO' "B" BARBETTE.

Barbette Sections

For the battleships, the drawing also detailed the structure in way of the 14in gun mountings – a double ring bulkhead to support the heavy quadruple 'A' but a single for the lighter twin 'B' – and the surrounding barbette armour and its supports.

(©National Maritime Museum, London M2067B)

Armament

THE ARMAMENT OF the *King George V*-class battleships made up about 30 per cent of their total cost, i.e. about £2.25 million, but this was paid to the armament suppliers so did not form part of the shipbuilder's contract. Contracts for guns and mountings were placed directly by the Admiralty with appropriate manufacturers, who then delivered them to the shipyard for installation. As a quadruple 14in mounting weighed 1200 tons excluding guns, it was delivered and erected in parts, the heaviest of which was the 200-ton rotating turntable supporting the gunhouse, below which were the working chamber and ammunition trunks (see drawing p39 right). The guns were supplied separately, made either by Vickers-Armstrongs at Elswick, Beardmore at Glasgow or the Royal Gun Factory at Woolwich.

As it took longer to construct the mountings than the ship, orders for the first two ships (two quadruple and one twin in each) were placed with Vickers-Armstrongs on 15 May 1936, and for the other three on 7 January 1937. A quadruple mounting plus four guns cost about £700,000 (see drawing on p43).

The 5.25in gun mountings were supplied complete with guns. All eight mountings were ordered from Harland & Wolff's Scotstoun works in 1937 at about £40,000 each excluding guns. But delays in manufacture plus the demand for similar mountings for *Dido*-class cruisers meant that H & W's first four were needed for *Prince of Wales*. *Duke of York*'s first four were for her starboard side, carried from the Scotstoun loading dock in Robertson's 638-ton coaster *Coral* in March 1941. Weighing with guns 80 tons, they could be lifted on board in one piece before connecting up to power supplies and ammunition handling systems. The ammunition routes for shell (80lb) and cartridge (38lb) were a combination of vertical hoists (one for anti-aircraft, one for surface shells and one for cordite cartridges) from the two main magazines (the after one between 'Y' 14in magazine and the after engine rooms, the forward one between 'B' 14in magazine and the forward boiler rooms) and horizontal conveyors to the working chamber beneath each gun mounting. Twelve of the sixteen guns were made by Woolwich, four by Elswick. (See drawing of 5.25in mountings on p37.)

The six eight-barrelled 2pdr pom-pom mountings each weighing 16 tons were supplied complete from Vickers-Armstrongs' Barrow works at about £9000 each. The last five arrived at the shipyard in August 1941, registered numbers 126–130. They were installed by the maker's staff, together with their main magazines; ready-use magazines by the shipbuilder. Similarly the two main 14in director control towers were supplied by Vickers-Armstrongs' Barrow works, and the four 5.25in directors from Vickers-Armstrongs' Crayford works. 20mm Oerlikon AA guns were in short supply, so while the ship left Clydebank with six positions fitted, the actual guns were only installed after she reached Rosyth.

The hull specification outlined the demarcation between the gun mounting manufacturer and the shipbuilder. The twenty pages are summarised:

14in gun mountings

Shipbuilder to provide, fit and machine: circular supports under lower roller path [ring bulkhead], training rack, structure for lateral guide rollers. Machine surfaces on the barbette armour for upper apron [for watertightness; see drawing p52 lower]. Cut access holes and passages for pipes. Fresh water supply for gun washout; drainage. Provide and fit voicepipes. Provide and fit seatings for training and depression cut-offs. Provide tanks for hydraulic fluid; steam heating; spare part stowage.

Seatings on fixed structure to accommodate gun mountings: machine surfaces of lower roller paths with ship waterborne, parallel to waterline. Max tilt 2½ minutes of arc in any direction. Supports strong enough to stand stresses when all guns fired.

Shipbuilder to allow erector [of gun mountings] all necessary facilities for erecting on board at a suitable berth. Erector to load and unload materials [from transport vessel] and lift on board. Shipbuilder to provide lifting power, steam, compressed air and electrical power. Gun mounting contractor to provide and fit gun mountings, shield, turntable, roller path, rollers, training rack, pipes and valves for power transmission outside revolving structure.

Guns and breech mechanisms will be supplied by Admiralty to contractor. Shipbuilder to transport guns to ship, hoist on board and secure in cradle. Provide sub-calibre guns and fit in stowage.

Transferable gun mountings (Multiple 2pdr, 0.5in machine guns, 3pdr saluting guns, Lewis guns)

Maker: erect 2pdr with clear working radius 10ft 9in. Shipbuilder: provide, fit and machine supports and packing rings (max tilt 2½ minutes). Fittings near blast of guns to be made sufficiently strong. Templates for holding down bolts will be supplied. Specially experienced men to be employed. [The 0.5in guns were not fitted.]

Gun directors (14in control tower forward, 14in armoured aft, four HA/LA 5.25in directors, 2pdr directors)

Shipbuilder to provide, fit and machine all necessary supports, voicepipes and protection trunks for cables.

Two 9ft tactical rangefinders and mountings supplied by Admiralty to be installed by shipbuilder. Rangefinders in turrets to be installed by erectors.

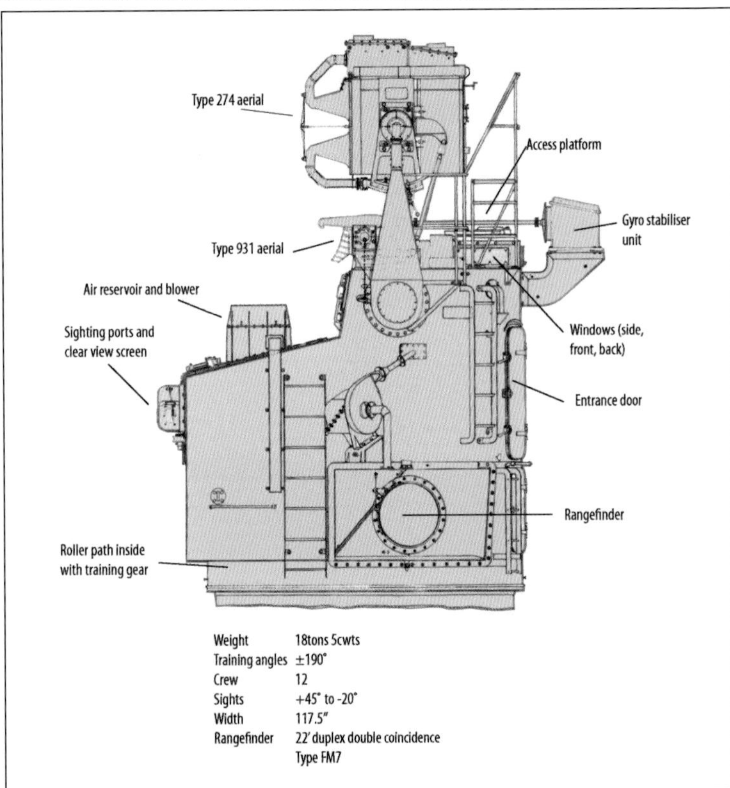
Type 274 aerial
Access platform
Gyro stabiliser unit
Type 931 aerial
Air reservoir and blower
Sighting ports and clear view screen
Windows (side, front, back)
Entrance door
Rangefinder
Roller path inside with training gear
Weight 18tons 5cwts
Training angles ±190°
Crew 12
Sights +45° to -20°
Width 117.5"
Rangefinder 22' duplex double coincidence Type FM7

The main director control tower of the *King George Vs* was similar to that in cruisers. This Vickers-Armstrongs general arrangement for *Mauritius* and *Kenya* has all the main features of *Duke of York's* forward DCT (the after one was armoured and had no radar). The Type 274 gunnery-control radar shown was not fitted in *Duke of York* until 1945, replacing the Type 284 she was completed with, which had separate transmitting and receiving aerials as seen in the photo on p150. Type 931 radar was for spotting shell splashes. The gunlayer and trainer sat in the lower front part, the control officers in the upper back part.

Ammunition Supply Arrangements

Shell and cordite hoists for 14in and lifting and transporting gear in shell rooms and magazines and handing rooms provided and fitted by makers of gun mountings. Hoists and conveyors for 5.25in provided by Admiralty and fitted by makers. Seatings by shipbuilders. Watertight ammunition lockers to be provided by shipbuilder: 5.25in 30 rounds per gun, 2pdr 2000 rounds per mounting.

Magazines and Shell Rooms

[See drawings of magazines and shell rooms on pp45 and 47.] To be built as watertight compartments. Arrangements for flooding magazines direct from the sea within 15 minutes. Cordite stowages, shell bins and fittings for 14in. Bottle racks for 5.25in. Transporter rails in shell rooms and flashtight scuttles by gun mounting contractor, supports by shipbuilder. Gun mounting contractor to provide lifts, rails and trolleys for striking down ammunition [from deck to magazines], shipbuilder the trunks and covers. Ship's derricks to be used for embarking [14in] ammunition [see drawing on p48 lower]. Davits for 5.25in and 2pdr ammunition. Air conditioning for magazines to be supplied by Admiralty.

While these systems were tested at the shipyard after installation, the gun firing trials were carried out at sea after leaving the shipyard by Vickers-Armstrongs and shipyard staff, an Admiralty trials party from the gunnery school at Portsmouth HMS *Excellent* and the ship's crew. The pom-poms and 5.25in were tested off the Mull of Kintyre on 9 September 1941 en route to Rosyth, with the 14in trials on 2 and 3 November on passage from Rosyth to Scapa. Four rounds were fired from each 14in gun at different bearings and elevations and measurements taken, with ten from each 5.25in gun.

Duke of York 14in Gun Mountings

Mounting Delivered	Type and Mark Total		Works to shipyard	weight tons incl guns
A	Quadruple Mark III	Elswick	Jun 1941 by *Sea Fisher*	1582
B	Twin Mark II	Elswick	May 1941 by *Empire Ness*	915
Y	Quadruple Mark III	Barrow	Apr 1941 by *Sea Fisher*	1582

5.25in Mark I Twin Gun Mountings

Mounting	Registered Number	Works	Delivered to shipyard
S3	24	Scotstoun	Feb 1941
S4	25	Scotstoun	Feb 1941
S1	23	Scotstoun	Mar 1941
S2	22	Scotstoun	Mar 1941
P3	27	Scotstoun	Apr 1941
P4	26	Scotstoun	Apr 1941
P1	28	Scotstoun	Jun 1941
P2	29	Scotstoun	Jun 1941

5·25 INCH H.A/L.A TWIN MARK I
WT. OF MOUNTING WITH
TONS CWTS. QRS.
WORKING CHAMBER COMPLETE 74 · 6 · 0
WT. OF COAMING PLATES 2 · 0 · 0
WT. OF BASE RING & ROLLERS 3 · 7 · 0
WT. OF CIRCULAR CHUTES 1 · 3 · 0
TOTAL WEIGHT 80 · 16 · 0
5·25 INCH HA/LA TWIN MARK I
VICKERS-ARMSTRONGS PATTERN
MADE BY HARLAND & WOLFF LTD. SCOTSTOUN, GLASGOW
TONS CWTS. QRS.
WT. OF CARRIAGE & TURNTABLE 18 · 5 · 0
WT. OF GUNHOUSE REAR 6 · 9 · 1
FRONT 9 · 18 · 3
WT. OF BASE RING & ROLLERS 3 · 7 · 0
WT. OF WORKING CHAMBER 7 · 2 · 0
WT. OF HOISTS 3 · 12 · 0
ADMY. REGD. NO. 23

Each Admiralty gun mounting had engraved plates showing its Mark, Maker, Weights and Registered Number – the latter in one series for each Mark of mounting and in a different series from the guns. These plates are from *Duke of York*'s S1 5.25in mounting No 23 made by Harland & Wolff at Scotstoun.

In conjunction with the manufacturer (usually Vickers-Armstrongs) the Admiralty prepared a handbook on each Mark of gun and associated Mark of gun mounting for operators and maintainers. In the case of the 5.25in, the handbook was confidential book C.B. 4108 Handbook for 5.25 inch, Q.F., Mark I Gun on HA/LA Twin, Marks I and II Mounting. The Mark I mounting was fitted in the *King George V*s, the Mark II in *Dido*-class cruisers. The foolscap-size handbook contained detailed coloured drawings of important parts of the mounting, often as fold out plates.

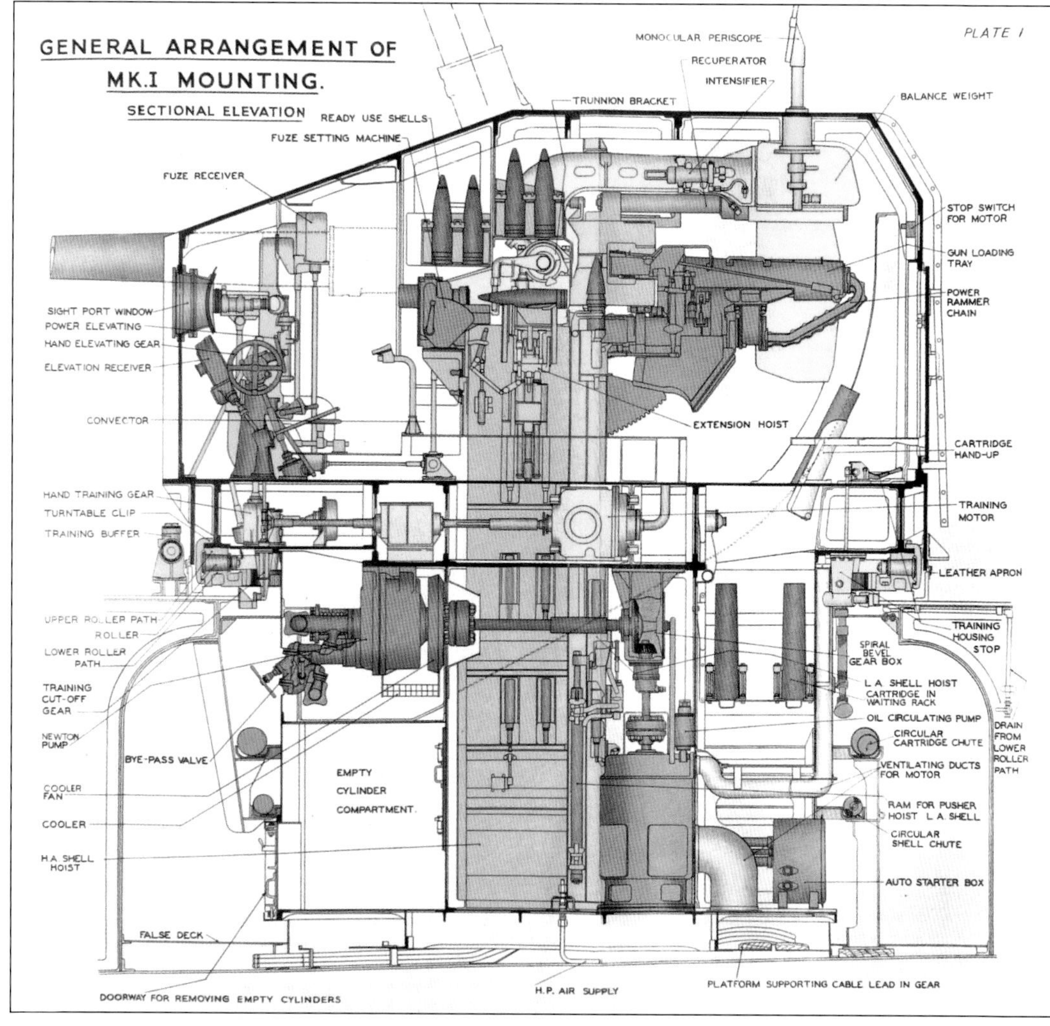
GENERAL ARRANGEMENT OF
MK.I MOUNTING.
SECTIONAL ELEVATION
PLATE I
MONOCULAR PERISCOPE
RECUPERATOR
INTENSIFIER
TRUNNION BRACKET
BALANCE WEIGHT
READY USE SHELLS
FUZE SETTING MACHINE
FUZE RECEIVER
STOP SWITCH FOR MOTOR
GUN LOADING TRAY
POWER RAMMER CHAIN
SIGHT PORT WINDOW
POWER ELEVATING
HAND ELEVATING GEAR
ELEVATION RECEIVER
CONVECTOR
EXTENSION HOIST
CARTRIDGE HAND-UP
HAND TRAINING GEAR
TURNTABLE CLIP
TRAINING BUFFER
TRAINING MOTOR
LEATHER APRON
UPPER ROLLER PATH
ROLLER
LOWER ROLLER PATH
TRAINING HOUSING STOP
SPIRAL BEVEL GEAR BOX
TRAINING CUT-OFF GEAR
L A SHELL HOIST
CARTRIDGE IN WAITING RACK
OIL CIRCULATING PUMP
NEWTON PUMP
BYE-PASS VALVE
CIRCULAR CARTRIDGE CHUTE
DRAIN FROM LOWER ROLLER PATH
VENTILATING DUCTS FOR MOTOR
EMPTY CYLINDER COMPARTMENT
COOLER FAN
COOLER
RAM FOR PUSHER HOIST L A SHELL
CIRCULAR SHELL CHUTE
H A SHELL HOIST
AUTO STARTER BOX
FALSE DECK
DOORWAY FOR REMOVING EMPTY CYLINDERS
H.P. AIR SUPPLY
PLATFORM SUPPORTING CABLE LEAD IN GEAR

Shows the general arrangement of the Mark I, apparently one of the superfiring ones as its base is on a cambered deck, probably the upper deck. The maximum elevation of 70° is indicated; depression was 5°. Unlike the 14in mountings, the primary power source was electric, with the (purple vertical at bottom) 80hp motor driving the Newton-Derby hydraulic pump through a bevel gear. Smooth hydraulic power then actuated training and elevating, hoists, rammers and breech. Key points include the cantilevered structure supporting roller path (blue) with its (yellow) tapered rollers for the 80-ton revolving mounting. The central ammunition hoist (also blue) takes the HA shells (brown) horizontally up to the (purple, left) fuze-setting machine (to set the time fuze for the enemy aircraft target predicted position), and the LA shells vertically, both 80lb. The price of this mounting was about £40,000.

PLATE 5

GUNHOUSE OF MARK II MOUNTING: PLAN

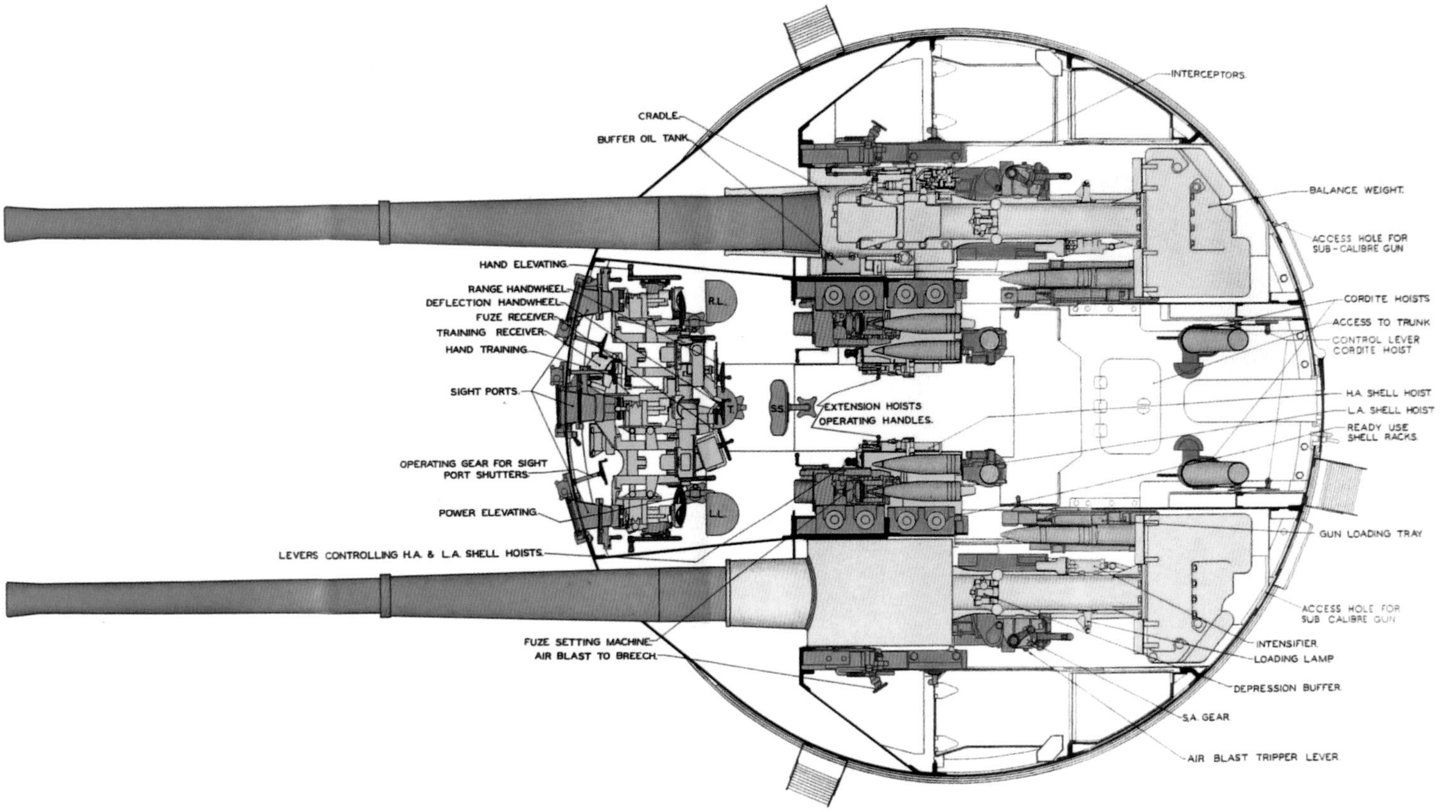

INTERCEPTORS.
CRADLE.
BUFFER OIL TANK.
BALANCE WEIGHT.
ACCESS HOLE FOR SUB-CALIBRE GUN
HAND ELEVATING.
RANGE HANDWHEEL.
DEFLECTION HANDWHEEL.
FUZE RECEIVER.
TRAINING RECEIVER.
HAND TRAINING.
R.L.
CORDITE HOISTS
ACCESS TO TRUNK
CONTROL LEVER CORDITE HOIST
SIGHT PORTS.
S.S.
EXTENSION HOISTS OPERATING HANDLES.
H.A. SHELL HOIST
L.A. SHELL HOIST
READY USE SHELL RACKS.
OPERATING GEAR FOR SIGHT PORT SHUTTERS.
POWER ELEVATING.
L.L.
GUN LOADING TRAY
LEVERS CONTROLLING H.A. & L.A. SHELL HOISTS.
ACCESS HOLE FOR SUB CALIBRE GUN
INTENSIFIER.
LOADING LAMP
FUZE SETTING MACHINE.
AIR BLAST TO BREECH.
DEPRESSION BUFFER.
S.A. GEAR.
AIR BLAST TRIPPER LEVER.

PLATE 2

WORKING CHAMBER OF MARK I MOUNTING SECTIONAL PLAN

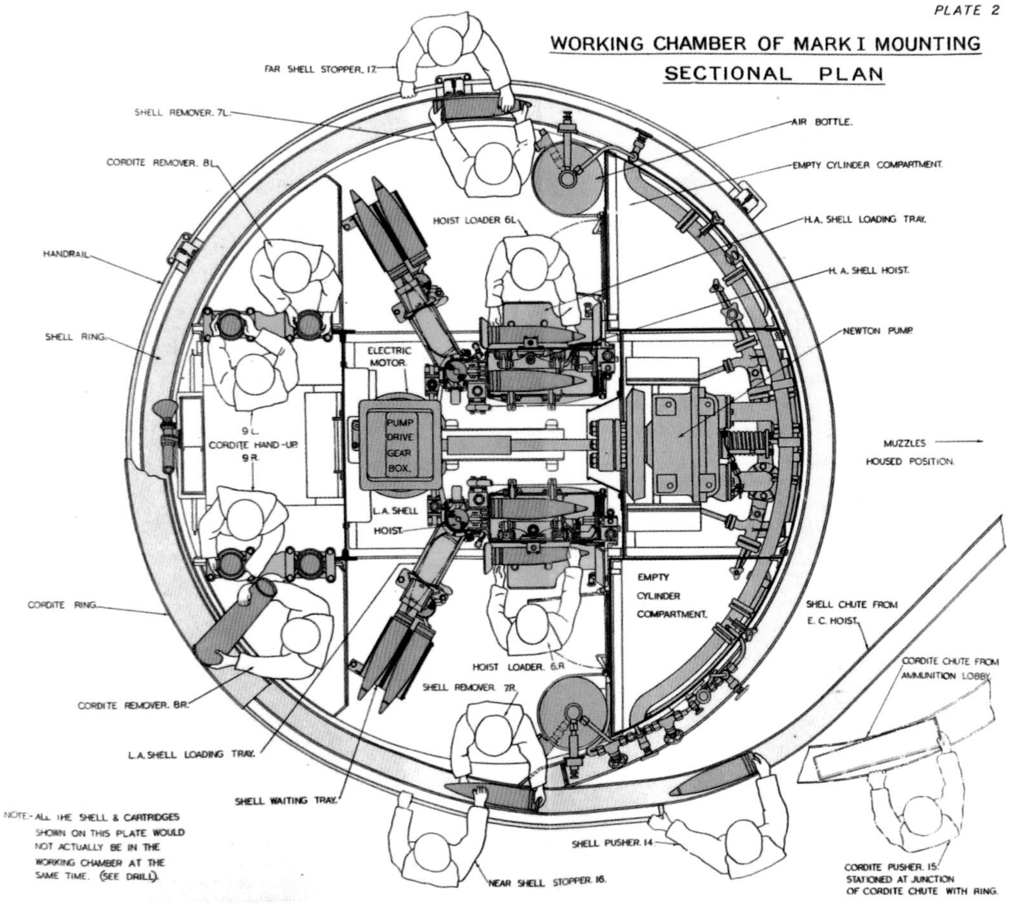

FAR SHELL STOPPER. 17.
SHELL REMOVER. 7L.
AIR BOTTLE.
CORDITE REMOVER. 8L.
EMPTY CYLINDER COMPARTMENT.
HOIST LOADER 6L.
H.A. SHELL LOADING TRAY.
HANDRAIL.
H. A. SHELL HOIST.
NEWTON PUMP.
SHELL RING.
ELECTRIC MOTOR.
9 L.
CORDITE HAND-UP.
9 R.
PUMP DRIVE GEAR BOX.
MUZZLES HOUSED POSITION.
L.A. SHELL HOIST.
EMPTY CYLINDER COMPARTMENT.
CORDITE RING.
SHELL CHUTE FROM E. C. HOIST.
HOIST LOADER. 6.R.
CORDITE CHUTE FROM AMMUNITION LOBBY.
SHELL REMOVER. 7R.
CORDITE REMOVER. 8R.
L.A. SHELL LOADING TRAY.
SHELL WAITING TRAY.
SHELL PUSHER. 14.
NEAR SHELL STOPPER. 16.
CORDITE PUSHER. 15. STATIONED AT JUNCTION OF CORDITE CHUTE WITH RING.

NOTE:- ALL THE SHELL & CARTRIDGES SHOWN ON THIS PLATE WOULD NOT ACTUALLY BE IN THE WORKING CHAMBER AT THE SAME TIME. (SEE DRILL).

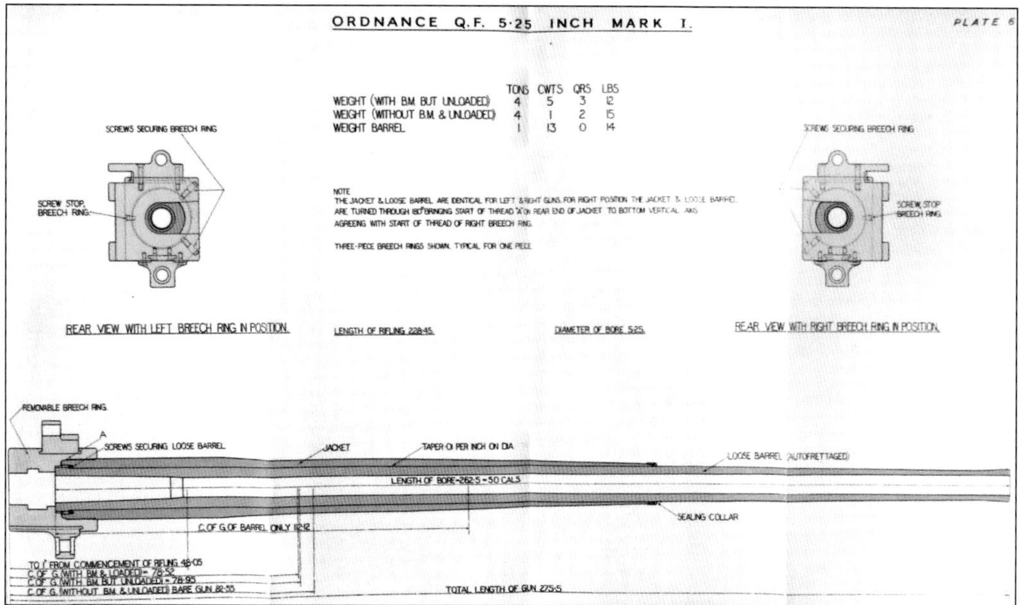

ORDNANCE Q.F. 5·25 INCH MARK I.
PLATE 6
TONS CWTS QRS LBS
WEIGHT (WITH B.M. BUT UNLOADED) 4 5 3 12
WEIGHT (WITHOUT B.M. & UNLOADED) 4 1 2 15
WEIGHT BARREL 1 13 0 14
SCREWS SECURING BREECH RING
SCREW STOP, BREECH RING
NOTE
THE JACKET & LOOSE BARREL ARE IDENTICAL FOR LEFT & RIGHT GUNS. FOR RIGHT POSITION THE JACKET & LOOSE BARREL ARE TURNED THROUGH 180° BRINGING START OF THREAD "A" ON REAR END OF JACKET TO BOTTOM VERTICAL AXIS AGREEING WITH START OF THREAD OF RIGHT BREECH RING.
THREE-PIECE BREECH RINGS SHOWN. TYPICAL FOR ONE PIECE
SCREWS SECURING BREECH RING
SCREW STOP BREECH RING
REAR VIEW WITH LEFT BREECH RING IN POSITION.
LENGTH OF RIFLING 228·45.
DIAMETER OF BORE 5·25.
REAR VIEW WITH RIGHT BREECH RING IN POSITION.
REMOVABLE BREECH RING.
A
SCREWS SECURING LOOSE BARREL
JACKET
TAPER ·01 PER INCH ON DIA
LOOSE BARREL (AUTOFRETTAGED)
LENGTH OF BORE-262·5 - 50 CALS
SEALING COLLAR
C. OF G. OF BARREL ONLY 112·2
TO 1" FROM COMMENCEMENT OF RIFLING 48·05
C. OF G. (WITH BM & LOADED) - 78·52
C. OF G. (WITH BM BUT UNLOADED) - 78·95
C. OF G. (WITHOUT BM & UNLOADED) BARE GUN 82·55
TOTAL LENGTH OF GUN 275·5

Opposite above. Shows the floor of the gunhouse (Mark II but similar to Mark I), with the HA and LA hoists in the centre. At the rear are the two (blue and orange) hoists for the 38lb cordite cartridges. At the rear of each gun is the (yellow) balance weight that keeps the centre of gravity of the elevating mass close to the trunnion. The (blue) semi-circular seats at the front are L.L. for left gunlayer (sets gun elevation), R.L. for right gunlayer and T for trainer, with their associated sights. The gunhouse is not armoured but protected by 40lb (1in) D quality steel.

Opposite below: Shows the working chamber beneath the gun turret, which is sited within the casemate. To the right (not shown) are the two shell hoists and cartridge hoist from the magazine, with shell and cartridge transferred manually to chutes (grey), then lifted onto the shell ring (lower) and cartridge ring (upper). Men inside the rings then carry the cartridges to the hand-ups (green left) to the turret, with the shells transferred to the hoists (blue). One twin mounting required a total crew of forty-eight men, in the magazines, transfer areas and turrets. Fully manning all eight mountings took nearly a quarter of the ship's crew.

Above: The 5.25in gun was designed in the mid-1930s as an HA/LA gun, 23ft long (50 calibres) and weighing 4.3 tons with its breech mechanism. It was capable of firing at attacking destroyers or at aircraft. With a muzzle velocity of 2690ft/sec, it could range to 24,000 yards or reach a height of 40,000ft. As a quick-firing gun with separate ammunition, its 18.6lb propellant charge was contained in a brass cartridge case. Its loose barrel (pink) with a life of 750 equivalent full charges could be relatively easily changed. Normally 400 rounds per gun were carried, fired at a maximum rate of 12 per minute. It cost about £2700 each.

The handbook for the 14in was C.B. 4169 Handbook for 14 inch BL Mark VII Gun on Twin, Mark II and Quadruple, Mark III Mounting.

Below right. The diagram shows the main parts of the twin 14in mounting divided into five flashtight zones – an important lesson learned from the losses at Jutland. The watertight seal (A) is shown in the lower drawing on p52.

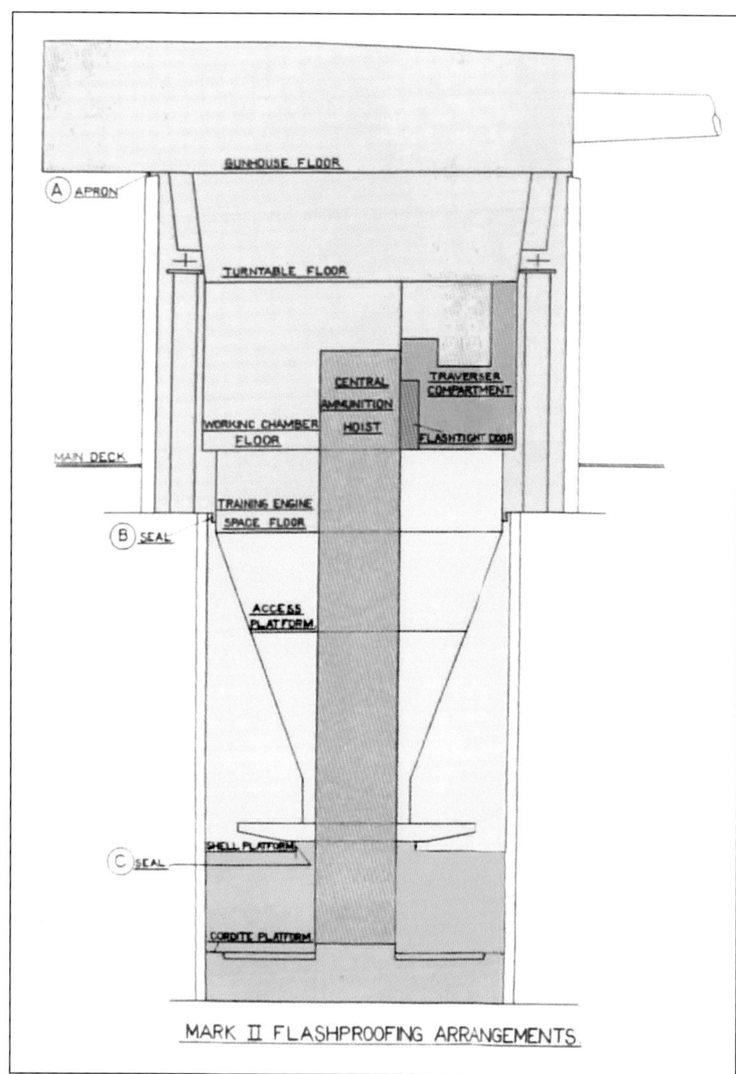

GUNHOUSE FLOOR
(A) APRON
TURNTABLE FLOOR
CENTRAL AMMUNITION HOIST
TRAVERSER COMPARTMENT
WORKING CHAMBER FLOOR
FLASHTIGHT DOOR
MAIN DECK
TRAINING ENGINE SPACE FLOOR
(B) SEAL
ACCESS PLATFORM
(C) SEAL
SHELL PLATFORM
CORDITE PLATFORM

MARK II FLASHPROOFING ARRANGEMENTS

The side elevation of the twin mounting shows all the rotating parts coloured. From top to bottom are: gunhouse; turntable; working chamber; training gear space; ammunition hoists. The entire 898-ton revolving weight rests on forty-eight tapered turntable rollers (green), with the lower roller path (purple) supported by the ring bulkhead (purple and white). Just beneath the roller path are the turntable holding-down clips (blue) which prevented the mounting lifting if the ship was pitching or rolling. Outside was the fixed barbette armour (white, see drawing p52 lower). The mounting was operated hydraulically, with water under 1100lb/in² pressure fed in at the very bottom (mauve centre pivot connection to hinged walking pipes from hydraulic engines in action machinery rooms). The entire gun cradle and gun (purple) was elevated by the angled hydraulic cylinder beneath (purple), allowing the gun to fire from 3° depression to 40° elevation (shown as dashed lines). The thick gunhouse armour and massive roof supports are shown in blue. The gun loading cage (yellow) is shown in line with the breech at the loading angle of 5° with the chain rammer (orange) behind. Its upper level held one 1590lb shell, its two lower levels two 84½lb cordite quarter charges each (338lb total). It was loaded at its lower level from the traverser (orange angled) in the working chamber before being lifted up rails by the vertical cage lifting cylinder (yellow at left). In the central hoist, the shell and cordite cages (yellow) are shown at the level they are fed from the magazines, similar for each gun.

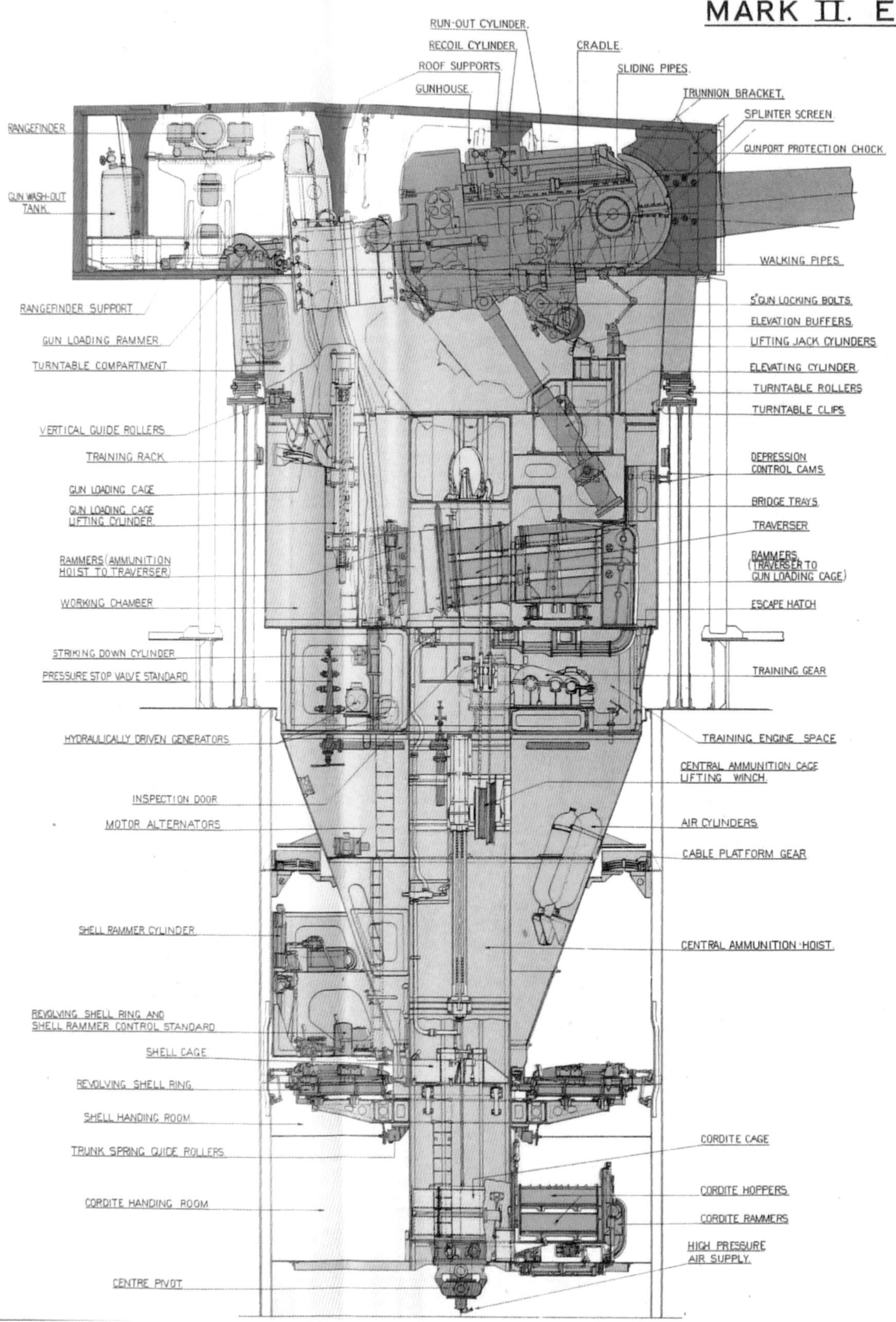
MARK II. E
RUN-OUT CYLINDER.
RECOIL CYLINDER.
ROOF SUPPORTS.
GUNHOUSE.
CRADLE.
SLIDING PIPES.
TRUNNION BRACKET.
SPLINTER SCREEN.
GUNPORT PROTECTION CHOCK.
RANGEFINDER
GUN WASH-OUT TANK.
WALKING PIPES.
RANGEFINDER SUPPORT
GUN LOADING RAMMER.
TURNTABLE COMPARTMENT
5°GUN LOCKING BOLTS.
ELEVATION BUFFERS.
LIFTING JACK CYLINDERS.
ELEVATING CYLINDER.
TURNTABLE ROLLERS
TURNTABLE CLIPS.
VERTICAL GUIDE ROLLERS
TRAINING RACK
GUN LOADING CAGE
GUN LOADING CAGE LIFTING CYLINDER.
DEPRESSION CONTROL CAMS.
BRIDGE TRAYS.
TRAVERSER
RAMMERS (AMMUNITION HOIST TO TRAVERSER)
RAMMERS. (TRAVERSER TO GUN LOADING CAGE)
WORKING CHAMBER
ESCAPE HATCH
STRIKING DOWN CYLINDER
PRESSURE STOP VALVE STANDARD
TRAINING GEAR
HYDRAULICALLY DRIVEN GENERATORS
TRAINING ENGINE SPACE
CENTRAL AMMUNITION CAGE LIFTING WINCH.
INSPECTION DOOR
MOTOR ALTERNATORS
AIR CYLINDERS.
CABLE PLATFORM GEAR
SHELL RAMMER CYLINDER.
CENTRAL AMMUNITION HOIST.
REVOLVING SHELL RING AND SHELL RAMMER CONTROL STANDARD
SHELL CAGE
REVOLVING SHELL RING
SHELL HANDING ROOM
TRUNK SPRING GUIDE ROLLERS
CORDITE CAGE
CORDITE HANDING ROOM
CORDITE HOPPERS.
CORDITE RAMMERS.
HIGH PRESSURE AIR SUPPLY.
CENTRE PIVOT

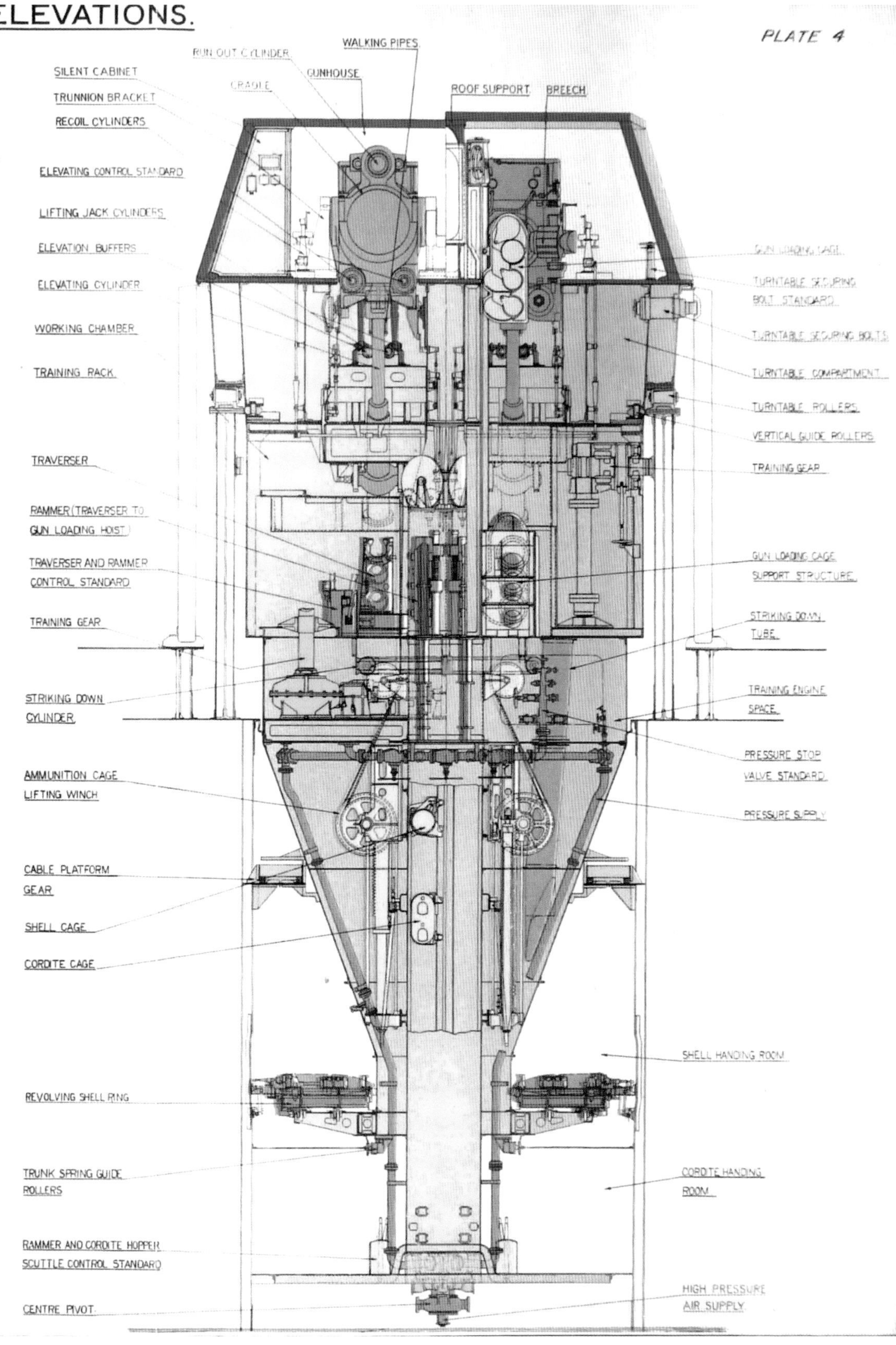
ELEVATIONS.
PLATE 4
WALKING PIPES.
RUN OUT CYLINDER.
SILENT CABINET
GUNHOUSE.
CRADLE
ROOF SUPPORT.
BREECH
TRUNNION BRACKET
RECOIL CYLINDERS
ELEVATING CONTROL STANDARD
LIFTING JACK CYLINDERS
ELEVATION BUFFERS
ELEVATING CYLINDER
WORKING CHAMBER
TRAINING RACK
TRAVERSER
RAMMER (TRAVERSER TO GUN LOADING HOIST)
TRAVERSER AND RAMMER CONTROL STANDARD
TRAINING GEAR
STRIKING DOWN CYLINDER
AMMUNITION CAGE LIFTING WINCH
CABLE PLATFORM GEAR
SHELL CAGE
CORDITE CAGE
REVOLVING SHELL RING
TRUNK SPRING GUIDE ROLLERS
RAMMER AND CORDITE HOPPER SCUTTLE CONTROL STANDARD
CENTRE PIVOT
GUN LOADING CAGE
TURNTABLE SECURING BOLT STANDARD
TURNTABLE SECURING BOLTS
TURNTABLE COMPARTMENT
TURNTABLE ROLLERS
VERTICAL GUIDE ROLLERS
TRAINING GEAR
GUN LOADING CAGE SUPPORT STRUCTURE
STRIKING DOWN TUBE
TRAINING ENGINE SPACE
PRESSURE STOP VALVE STANDARD
PRESSURE SUPPLY
SHELL HANDING ROOM
CORDITE HANDING ROOM
HIGH PRESSURE AIR SUPPLY

The mounting hydraulic training gear (green) is divided into two to give an even torque, engaging with the training rack (purple). The gun loading cage (yellow) is shown both at its upper and lower position (dotted). The twin recoil cylinders are shown beneath the left-hand gun (purple). The run-out cylinder on top of the gun (purple) was used to push the recoiled gun back into the loading position in 2 seconds.

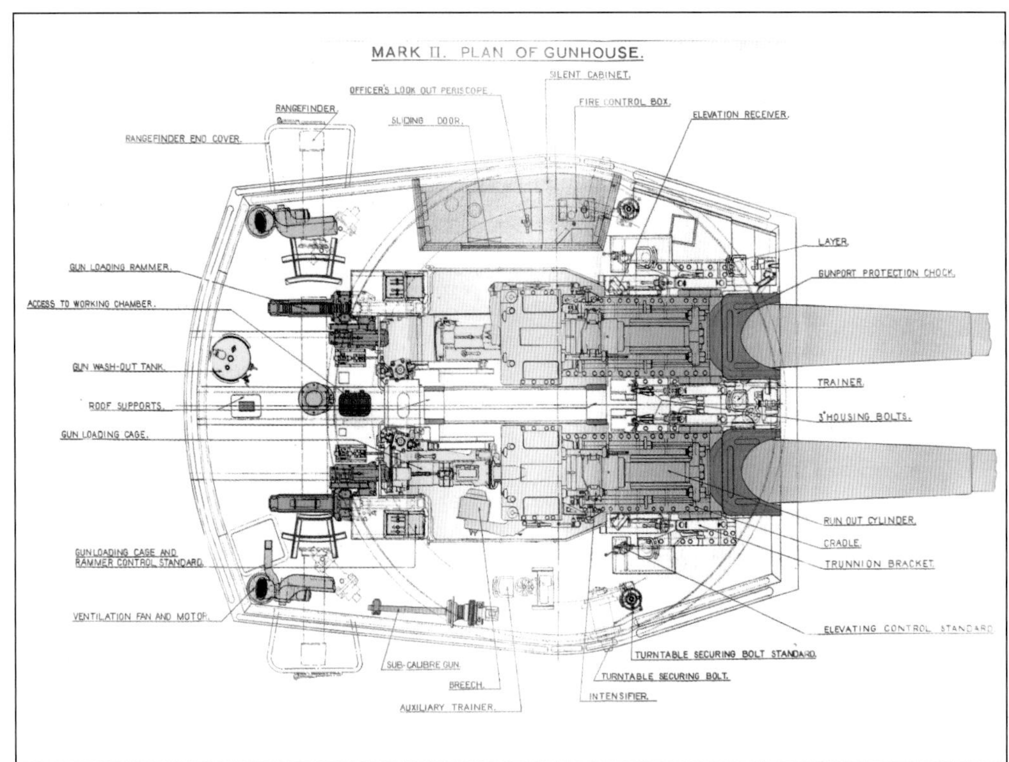
MARK II. PLAN OF GUNHOUSE.
SILENT CABINET.
OFFICER'S LOOK OUT PERISCOPE.
FIRE CONTROL BOX.
RANGEFINDER.
SLIDING DOOR.
ELEVATION RECEIVER.
RANGEFINDER END COVER.
LAYER.
GUN LOADING RAMMER.
GUNPORT PROTECTION CHOCK.
ACCESS TO WORKING CHAMBER.
GUN WASH-OUT TANK.
TRAINER.
ROOF SUPPORTS.
3" HOUSING BOLTS.
GUN LOADING CAGE.
RUN OUT CYLINDER.
CRADLE.
GUNLOADING CAGE AND
RAMMER CONTROL STANDARD.
TRUNNION BRACKET.
VENTILATION FAN AND MOTOR.
ELEVATING CONTROL STANDARD.
TURNTABLE SECURING BOLT STANDARD.
SUB-CALIBRE GUN.
TURNTABLE SECURING BOLT.
BREECH.
INTENSIFIER.
AUXILIARY TRAINER.

This plan of the Mark II gunhouse floor shows clearly the gun loading cage (yellow) and rammer (orange) for the right-hand gun. The breech (purple) is shown open for this gun. The two gunlayers (each gun could elevate independent of the other) at each front corner normally followed their indicator from the director control tower and transmitting station, but in an emergency could use the sight through a port in the face of the gunhouse. The trainer in the centre also followed the indicator from the transmitting station. At the right side is a 6pdr sub-calibre gun (purple) which fitted into the breech for drill purposes. At the rear of the gunhouse is shown dotted the 30ft Barr & Stroud rangefinder, which could slew ±5° independent of the gunhouse bearing itself. The silent cabinet (blue left side) housed basic fire-control instruments which could control all the 14in guns in an emergency.

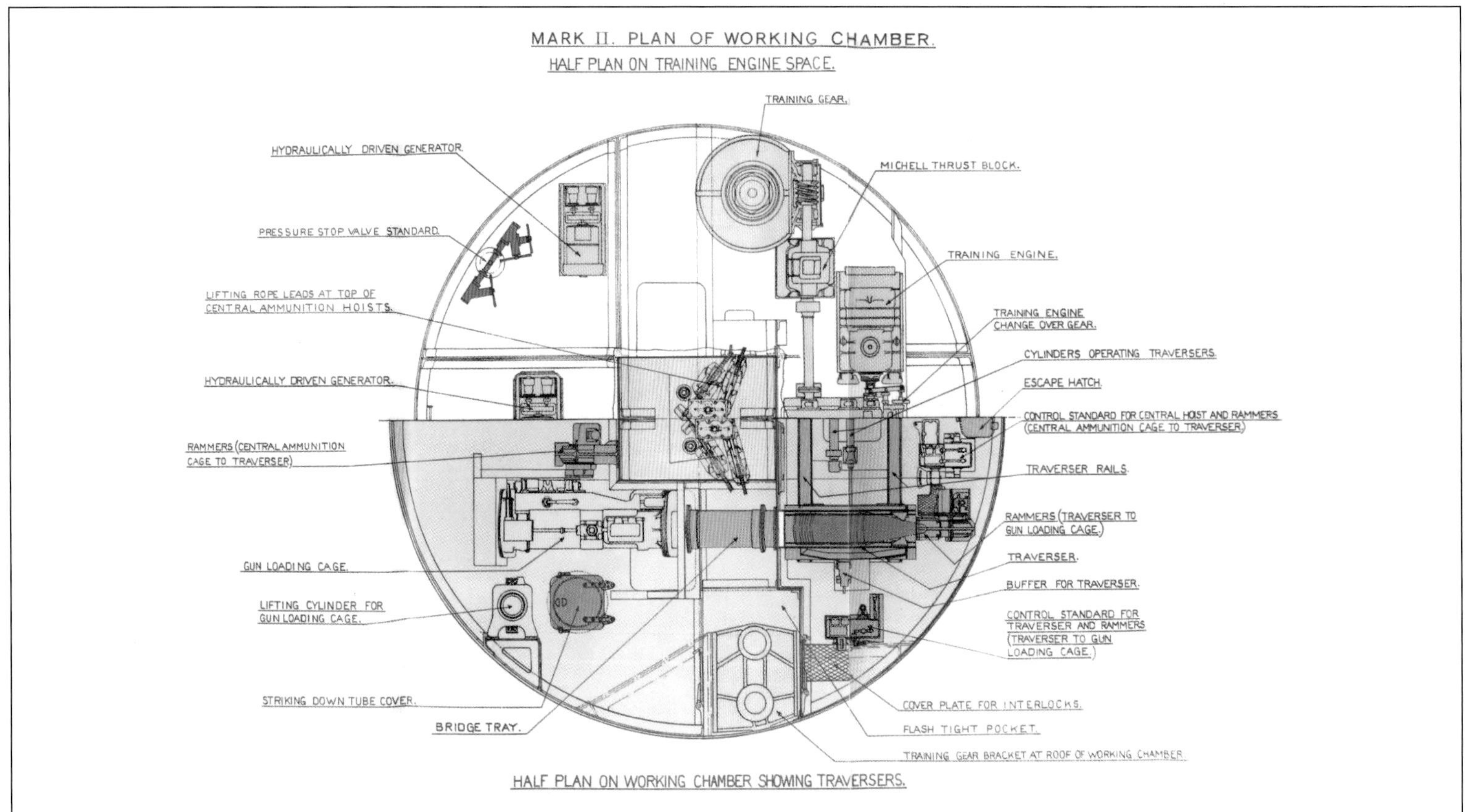
MARK II. PLAN OF WORKING CHAMBER.
HALF PLAN ON TRAINING ENGINE SPACE.
TRAINING GEAR.
HYDRAULICALLY DRIVEN GENERATOR.
MICHELL THRUST BLOCK.
PRESSURE STOP VALVE STANDARD.
TRAINING ENGINE.
LIFTING ROPE LEADS AT TOP OF
CENTRAL AMMUNITION HOISTS.
TRAINING ENGINE
CHANGE OVER GEAR.
CYLINDERS OPERATING TRAVERSERS.
HYDRAULICALLY DRIVEN GENERATOR.
ESCAPE HATCH.
CONTROL STANDARD FOR CENTRAL HOIST AND RAMMERS
(CENTRAL AMMUNITION CAGE TO TRAVERSER.)
RAMMERS (CENTRAL AMMUNITION
CAGE TO TRAVERSER)
TRAVERSER RAILS.
RAMMERS (TRAVERSER TO
GUN LOADING CAGE.)
GUN LOADING CAGE.
TRAVERSER.
BUFFER FOR TRAVERSER.
LIFTING CYLINDER FOR
GUN LOADING CAGE.
CONTROL STANDARD FOR
TRAVERSER AND RAMMERS
(TRAVERSER TO GUN
LOADING CAGE.)
STRIKING DOWN TUBE COVER.
COVER PLATE FOR INTERLOCKS.
BRIDGE TRAY.
FLASH TIGHT POCKET.
TRAINING GEAR BRACKET AT ROOF OF WORKING CHAMBER.
HALF PLAN ON WORKING CHAMBER SHOWING TRAVERSERS.

The top half of the drawing shows the lower level which housed the two hydraulic training engines and gear (green). Ammunition arrived up the central trunk hoist (grey) from the magazine levels. The bottom half shows the traverser space of the working chamber. The chain rammer (brown centre left) pushed a shell (purple) from the central hoist forward on to the traverser tray and rails (brown), which moved it outwards to be in line for ramming into the gun loading cage (yellow). One twin mounting required a total crew of sizty men, in the magazines, transfer areas and turrets.

The key components of the Mark III quadruple mounting at the gunhouse floor are similar to the twin mounting shown opposite, but in this plan the gunhouse roof is shown. It is made up of four 240lb NC plates. The securing bolts shown enable the gunhouse to be opened up to replace worn-out guns or other equipment. The access hatch (brown) in the roof is thinner, while also shown in brown are an escape manhole through the overhanging rear of the turret and one down to the working chamber (centre). The gun wash-out tank (yellow left) is used to clear a gun of any burning propellant residue after it has been fired.

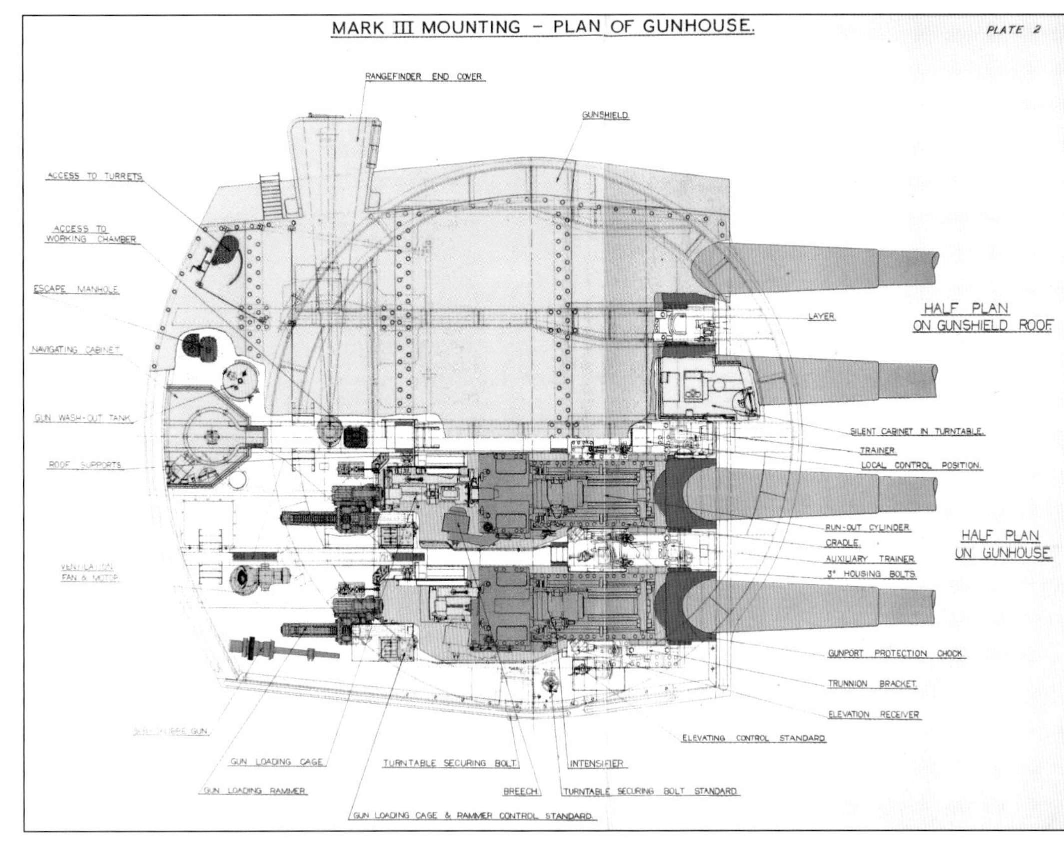
MARK III MOUNTING - PLAN OF GUNHOUSE.
PLATE 2
RANGEFINDER END COVER
GUNSHIELD
ACCESS TO TURRETS
ACCESS TO WORKING CHAMBER
ESCAPE MANHOLE
NAVIGATING CABINET
GUN WASH-OUT TANK
ROOF SUPPORTS
VENTILATION FAN & MOTOR
LAYER
HALF PLAN ON GUNSHIELD ROOF
SILENT CABINET IN TURNTABLE.
TRAINER
LOCAL CONTROL POSITION.
RUN-OUT CYLINDER
CRADLE.
AUXILIARY TRAINER
3" HOUSING BOLTS.
HALF PLAN ON GUNHOUSE
GUNPORT PROTECTION CHOCK
TRUNNION BRACKET.
ELEVATION RECEIVER
ELEVATING CONTROL STANDARD
GUN LOADING CAGE
TURNTABLE SECURING BOLT
INTENSIFIER
GUN LOADING RAMMER
BREECH
TURNTABLE SECURING BOLT STANDARD
GUN LOADING CAGE & RAMMER CONTROL STANDARD.

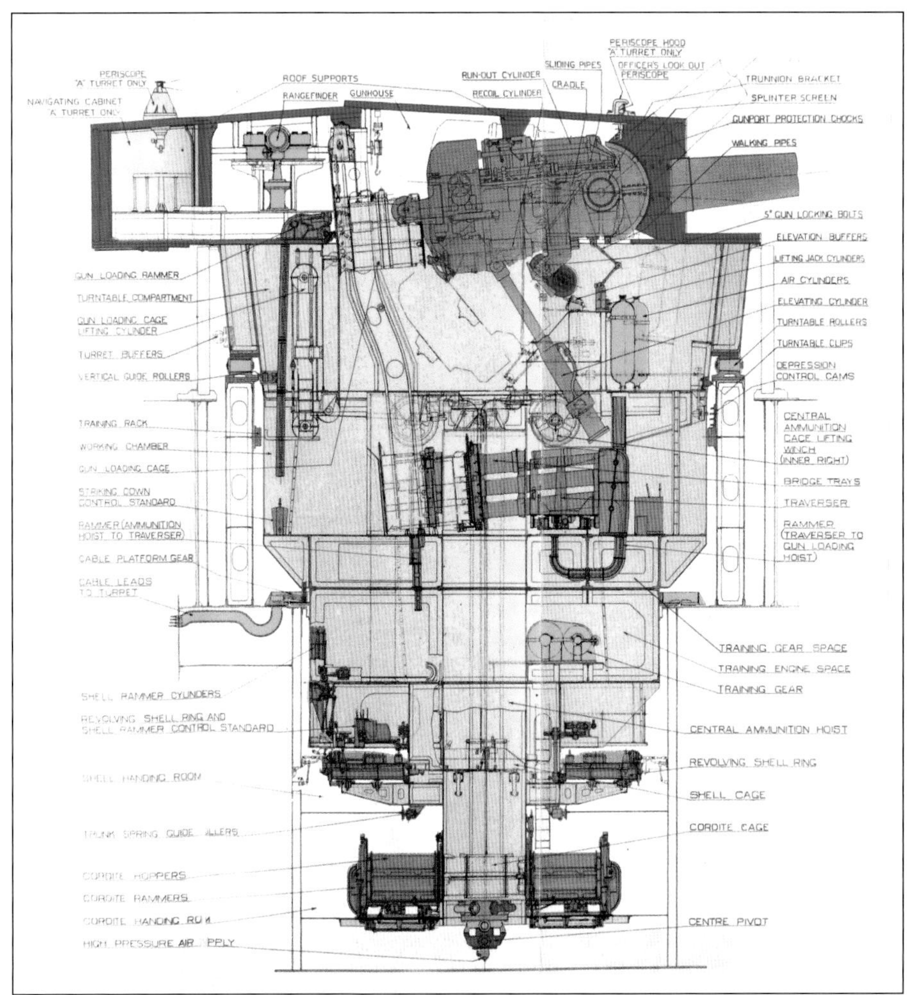
PERISCOPE "A" TURRET ONLY
NAVIGATING CABINET "A" TURRET ONLY
ROOF SUPPORTS
RANGEFINDER
GUNHOUSE
RUN-OUT CYLINDER
RECOIL CYLINDER
SLIDING PIPES
CRADLE
PERISCOPE HOOD "A" TURRET ONLY
OFFICER'S LOOK OUT PERISCOPE
TRUNNION BRACKET
SPLINTER SCREEN
GUNPORT PROTECTION CHOCKS
WALKING PIPES
5" GUN LOCKING BOLTS
ELEVATION BUFFERS
LIFTING JACK CYLINDERS
AIR CYLINDERS
ELEVATING CYLINDER
TURNTABLE ROLLERS
TURNTABLE CLIPS
DEPRESSION CONTROL CAMS
GUN LOADING RAMMER
TURNTABLE COMPARTMENT
GUN LOADING CAGE LIFTING CYLINDER
TURRET BUFFERS
VERTICAL GUIDE ROLLERS
TRAINING RACK
WORKING CHAMBER
GUN LOADING CAGE
STRIKING DOWN CONTROL STANDARD
RAMMER (AMMUNITION HOIST TO TRAVERSER)
CABLE PLATFORM GEAR
CABLE LEADS TO TURRET
CENTRAL AMMUNITION CAGE LIFTING WINCH (INNER RIGHT)
BRIDGE TRAYS
TRAVERSER
RAMMER (TRAVERSER TO GUN LOADING HOIST)
TRAINING GEAR SPACE
TRAINING ENGINE SPACE
TRAINING GEAR
SHELL RAMMER CYLINDERS
REVOLVING SHELL RING AND SHELL RAMMER CONTROL STANDARD
SHELL HANDING ROOM
CENTRAL AMMUNITION HOIST
REVOLVING SHELL RING
SHELL CAGE
CORDITE CAGE
CORDITE HOPPERS
CORDITE RAMMERS
CENTRE PIVOT

The key components of the quadruple mounting are similar to the twin mounting shown on p40. At the bottom in the cordite handing room are the paired hoppers (brown) fed via flashtight scuttles from the magazine, which feed into the cordite cage (yellow) in the central ammunition hoists. Above in the shell handing room is the shell revolving ring with four waiting trays on the four quadrants, better seen in the photo on p130 right. The ring enabled the shell waiting trays to be lined up with scuttles in the shell room, before being revolved to line up with the central hoists. In the gunhouse is the 42ft rangefinder (green). The apparent double thickness of rear armour (blue) is due to fitting a 10in-thick balance plate to bring the centre of gravity of the whole (A) mounting in line with its axis. The price of such a mounting including guns was about £700,000, nearly 10 per cent of the whole ship.

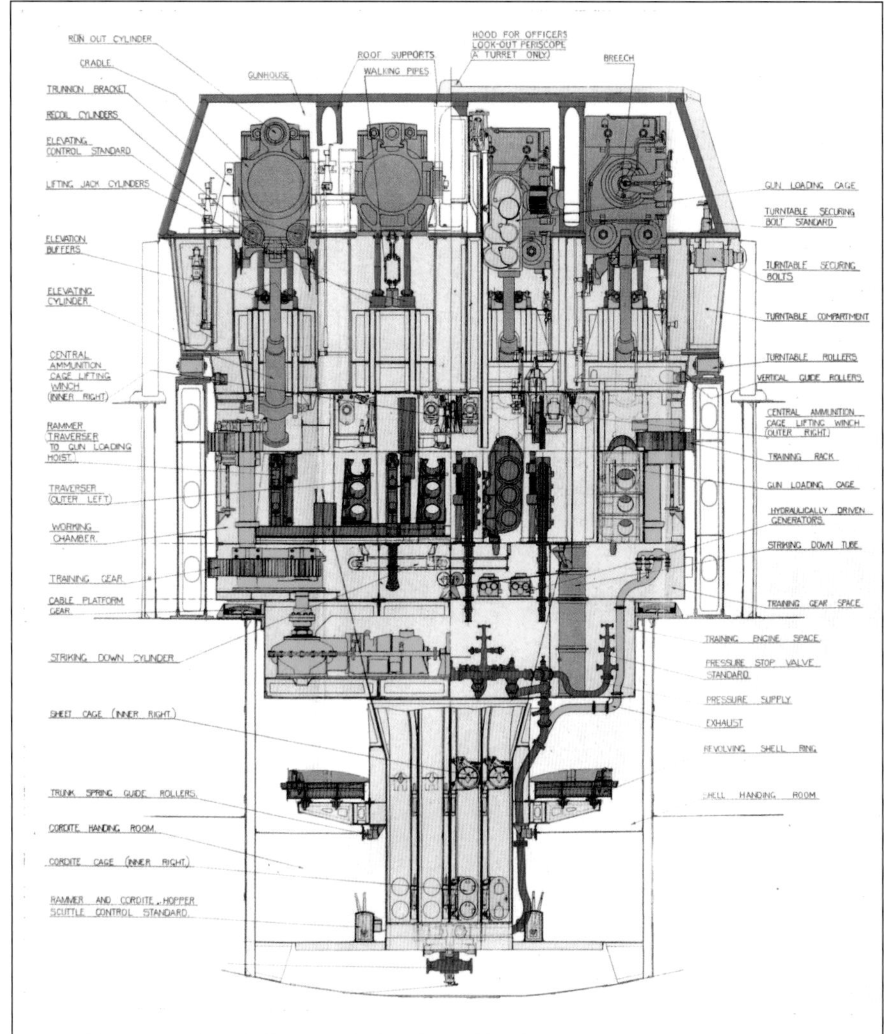
RUN OUT CYLINDER
CRADLE
TRUNNION BRACKET
RECOIL CYLINDERS
ELEVATING CONTROL STANDARD
LIFTING JACK CYLINDERS
ELEVATION BUFFERS
ELEVATING CYLINDER
CENTRAL AMMUNITION CAGE LIFTING WINCH (INNER RIGHT)
RAMMER TRAVERSER TO GUN LOADING HOIST
TRAVERSER (OUTER LEFT)
WORKING CHAMBER
TRAINING GEAR
CABLE PLATFORM GEAR
STRIKING DOWN CYLINDER
SHELL CAGE (INNER RIGHT)
TRUNK SPRING GUIDE ROLLERS
CORDITE HANDING ROOM
CORDITE CAGE (INNER RIGHT)
RAMMER AND CORDITE HOPPER SCUTTLE CONTROL STANDARD
GUNHOUSE
ROOF SUPPORTS
WALKING PIPES
HOOD FOR OFFICERS LOOK-OUT PERISCOPE A TURRET ONLY
BREECH
GUN LOADING CAGE
TURNTABLE SECURING BOLT STANDARD
TURNTABLE SECURING BOLTS
TURNTABLE COMPARTMENT
TURNTABLE ROLLERS
VERTICAL GUIDE ROLLERS
CENTRAL AMMUNITION CAGE LIFTING WINCH (OUTER RIGHT)
TRAINING RACK
GUN LOADING CAGE
HYDRAULICALLY DRIVEN GENERATORS
STRIKING DOWN TUBE
TRAINING GEAR SPACE
TRAINING ENGINE SPACE
PRESSURE STOP VALVE STANDARD
PRESSURE SUPPLY
EXHAUST
REVOLVING SHELL RING
SHELL HANDING ROOM

The key components of the quadruple mounting are similar to the twin mounting shown on p41. The traverser (brown) which moves the shell and cordite from the central hoists to the gun loading cages (yellow) is better seen in this view. The securing bolts (green) just below the gunhouse floor secure the mounting to the barbette armour, preventing it from rotating when not in operation, without stressing the training gear. One quadruple mounting required a total crew of 107 men, in the magazines, transfer areas and turrets.

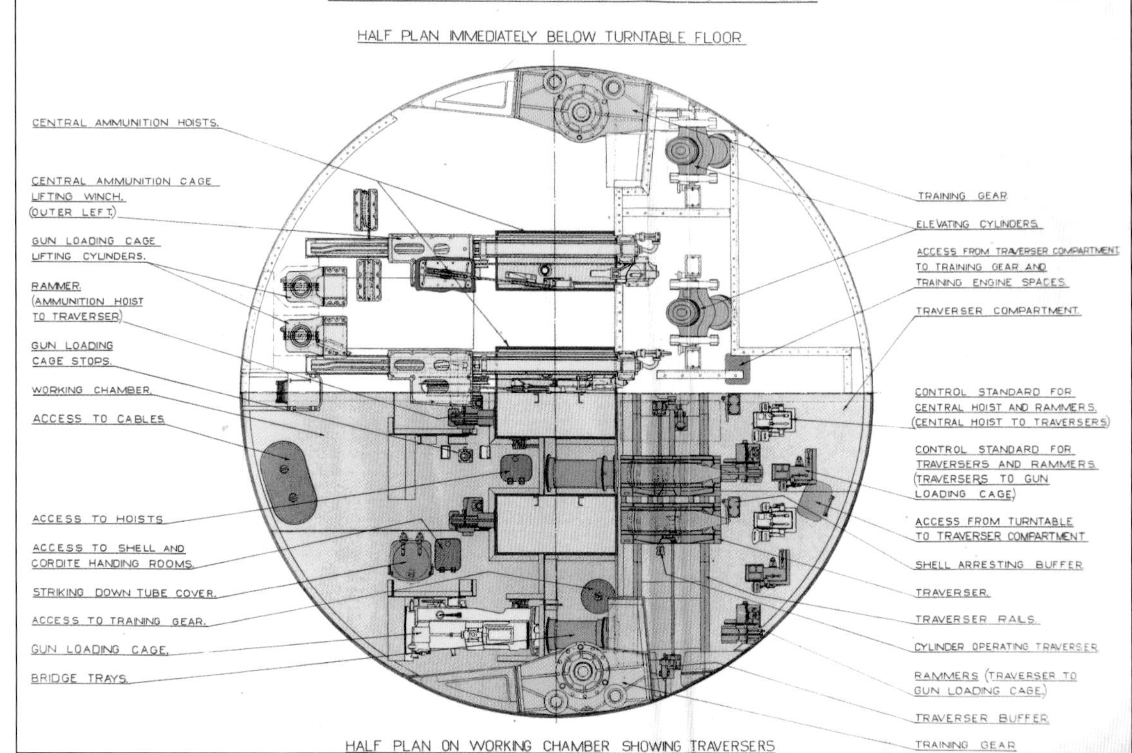
MARK III MOUNTING – PLAN OF WORKING CHAMBER.
HALF PLAN IMMEDIATELY BELOW TURNTABLE FLOOR
CENTRAL AMMUNITION HOISTS.
CENTRAL AMMUNITION CAGE LIFTING WINCH. (OUTER LEFT)
GUN LOADING CAGE LIFTING CYLINDERS.
RAMMER. (AMMUNITION HOIST TO TRAVERSER)
GUN LOADING CAGE STOPS.
WORKING CHAMBER.
ACCESS TO CABLES.
ACCESS TO HOISTS.
ACCESS TO SHELL AND CORDITE HANDING ROOMS.
STRIKING DOWN TUBE COVER.
ACCESS TO TRAINING GEAR.
GUN LOADING CAGE.
BRIDGE TRAYS.
TRAINING GEAR
ELEVATING CYLINDERS.
ACCESS FROM TRAVERSER COMPARTMENT TO TRAINING GEAR AND TRAINING ENGINE SPACES.
TRAVERSER COMPARTMENT.
CONTROL STANDARD FOR CENTRAL HOIST AND RAMMERS. (CENTRAL HOIST TO TRAVERSERS)
CONTROL STANDARD FOR TRAVERSERS AND RAMMERS. (TRAVERSERS TO GUN LOADING CAGE)
ACCESS FROM TURNTABLE TO TRAVERSER COMPARTMENT
SHELL ARRESTING BUFFER
TRAVERSER.
TRAVERSER RAILS.
CYLINDER OPERATING TRAVERSER
RAMMERS (TRAVERSER TO GUN LOADING CAGE)
TRAVERSER BUFFER
TRAINING GEAR
HALF PLAN ON WORKING CHAMBER SHOWING TRAVERSERS

The key components are similar to the twin mounting shown on p42 lower, but with more ammunition hoists (grey centre) and showing (in the top half) their lifting winches (yellow). The bottom of the gun elevation cylinders (purple upper) are fixed below the turntable floor.

This diagram shows how the leather cordite cases (brown, each containing two quarter charges) were embarked from upper deck level using a perambulator (blue) via a hatch, davit and sling (left). The case was lowered to magazine level (right) powered by the hydraulic press (top green), whence it was moved horizontally to stowage in the magazine by overhead rails (see diagram below).

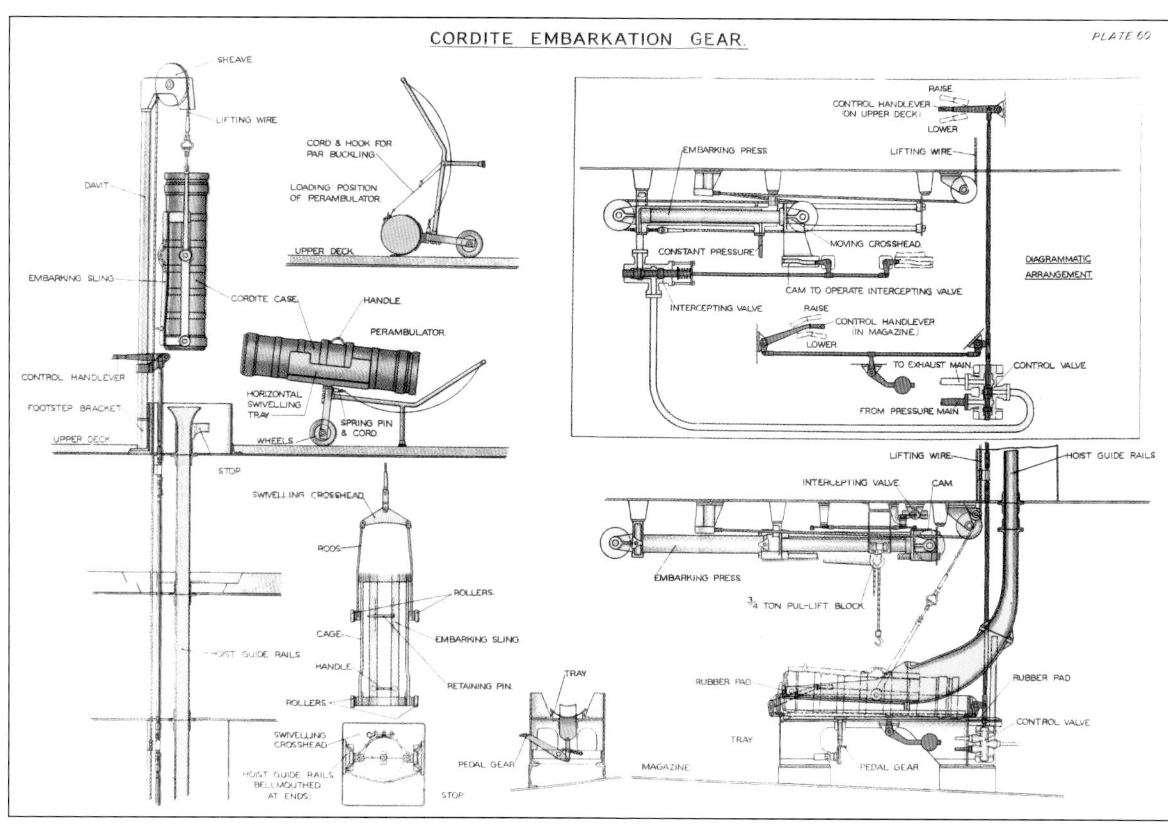
CORDITE EMBARKATION GEAR.
SHEAVE
LIFTING WIRE
DAVIT
CORD & HOOK FOR PAR BUCKLING
LOADING POSITION OF PERAMBULATOR
UPPER DECK
EMBARKING SLING
CORDITE CASE
HANDLE
PERAMBULATOR
CONTROL HANDLEVER
FOOTSTEP BRACKET
UPPER DECK
HORIZONTAL SWIVELLING TRAY
WHEELS
SPRING PIN & CORD
STOP
SWIVELLING CROSSHEAD
RODS
ROLLERS
CAGE
EMBARKING SLING
HANDLE
RETAINING PIN
ROLLERS
SWIVELLING CROSSHEAD
TRAY
PEDAL GEAR
STOP
RAISE
CONTROL HANDLEVER (ON UPPER DECK)
LOWER
EMBARKING PRESS
LIFTING WIRE
CONSTANT PRESSURE
MOVING CROSSHEAD
DIAGRAMMATIC ARRANGEMENT
CAM TO OPERATE INTERCEPTING VALVE
INTERCEPTING VALVE
RAISE
CONTROL HANDLEVER (IN MAGAZINE)
LOWER
TO EXHAUST MAIN
CONTROL VALVE
FROM PRESSURE MAIN
LIFTING WIRE
HOIST GUIDE RAILS
INTERCEPTING VALVE
CAM
EMBARKING PRESS
¾ TON PUL-LIFT BLOCK
RUBBER PAD
RUBBER PAD
CONTROL VALVE
TRAY
MAGAZINE
PEDAL GEAR

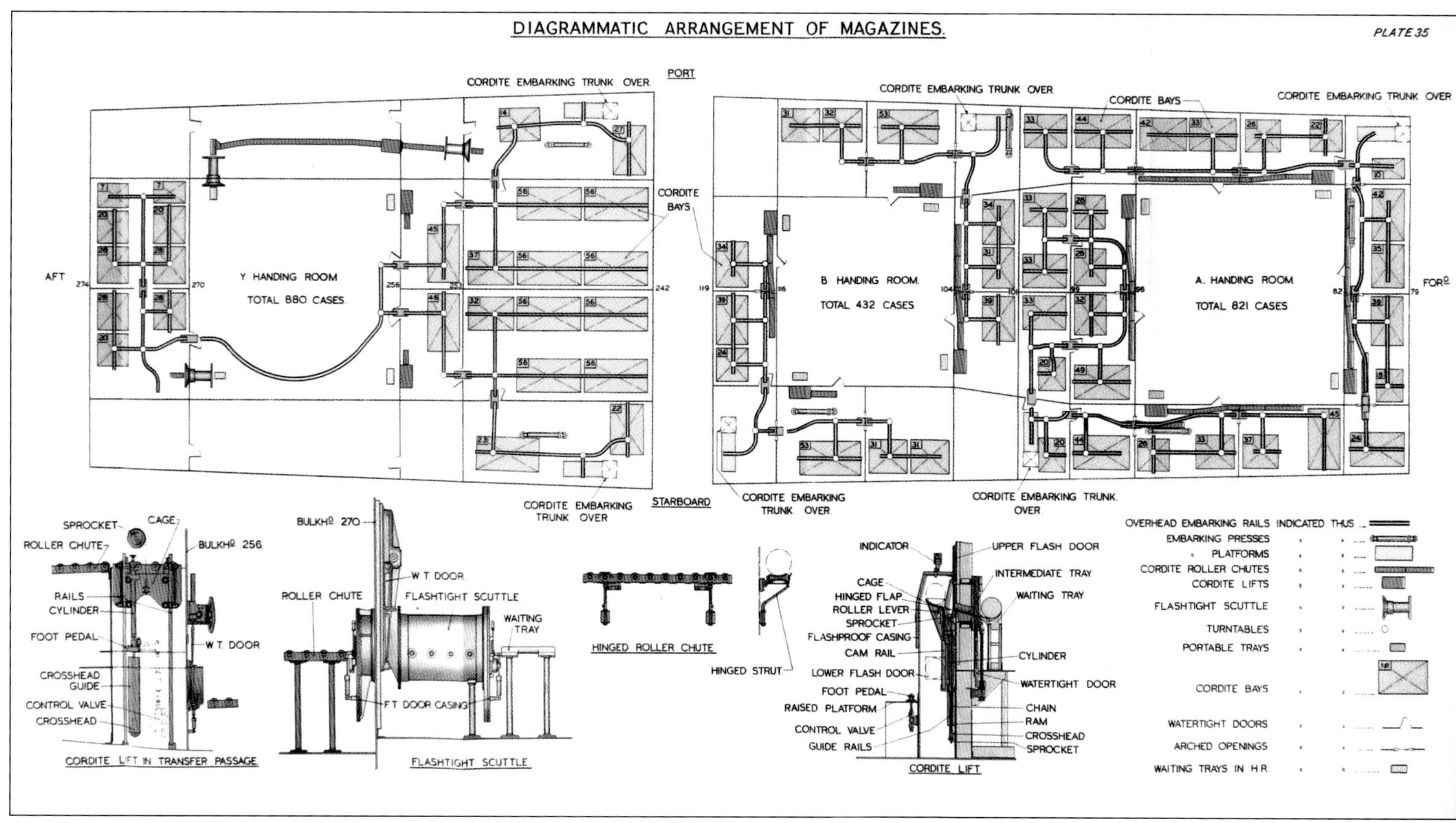
DIAGRAMMATIC ARRANGEMENT OF MAGAZINES.
PLATE 35
PORT
CORDITE EMBARKING TRUNK OVER
CORDITE BAYS
AFT
Y HANDING ROOM
TOTAL 880 CASES
B HANDING ROOM
TOTAL 432 CASES
A. HANDING ROOM
TOTAL 821 CASES
FORD
STARBOARD
CORDITE EMBARKING TRUNK OVER
SPROCKET
CAGE
ROLLER CHUTE
BULKHD 256
RAILS
CYLINDER
FOOT PEDAL
W.T. DOOR
CROSSHEAD GUIDE
CONTROL VALVE
CROSSHEAD
CORDITE LIFT IN TRANSFER PASSAGE
BULKHD 270
ROLLER CHUTE
W.T. DOOR
FLASHTIGHT SCUTTLE
WAITING TRAY
F.T. DOOR CASING
FLASHTIGHT SCUTTLE
HINGED ROLLER CHUTE
HINGED STRUT
INDICATOR
UPPER FLASH DOOR
INTERMEDIATE TRAY
WAITING TRAY
CAGE
HINGED FLAP
ROLLER LEVER
SPROCKET
FLASHPROOF CASING
CAM RAIL
CYLINDER
LOWER FLASH DOOR
WATERTIGHT DOOR
FOOT PEDAL
RAISED PLATFORM
CHAIN
RAM
CONTROL VALVE
CROSSHEAD
GUIDE RAILS
SPROCKET
CORDITE LIFT
OVERHEAD EMBARKING RAILS INDICATED THUS
EMBARKING PRESSES
PLATFORMS
CORDITE ROLLER CHUTES
CORDITE LIFTS
FLASHTIGHT SCUTTLE
TURNTABLES
PORTABLE TRAYS
CORDITE BAYS
WATERTIGHT DOORS
ARCHED OPENINGS
WAITING TRAYS IN H.R.

This diagram shows cordite stowage in all three 14in magazines. The cases were embarked down the trunks next to the yellow platforms (see drawing above) then transferred via overhead rails (double grey lines) to the stowages (blue). When needed by the guns, the charges were removed from the cases and transferred via the roller chutes (mauve) and flashtight doors and scuttles to the four lifts (small grey rectangles in corners) to the handing room and hoists. All such equipment was supplied and fitted by Vickers-Armstrongs.

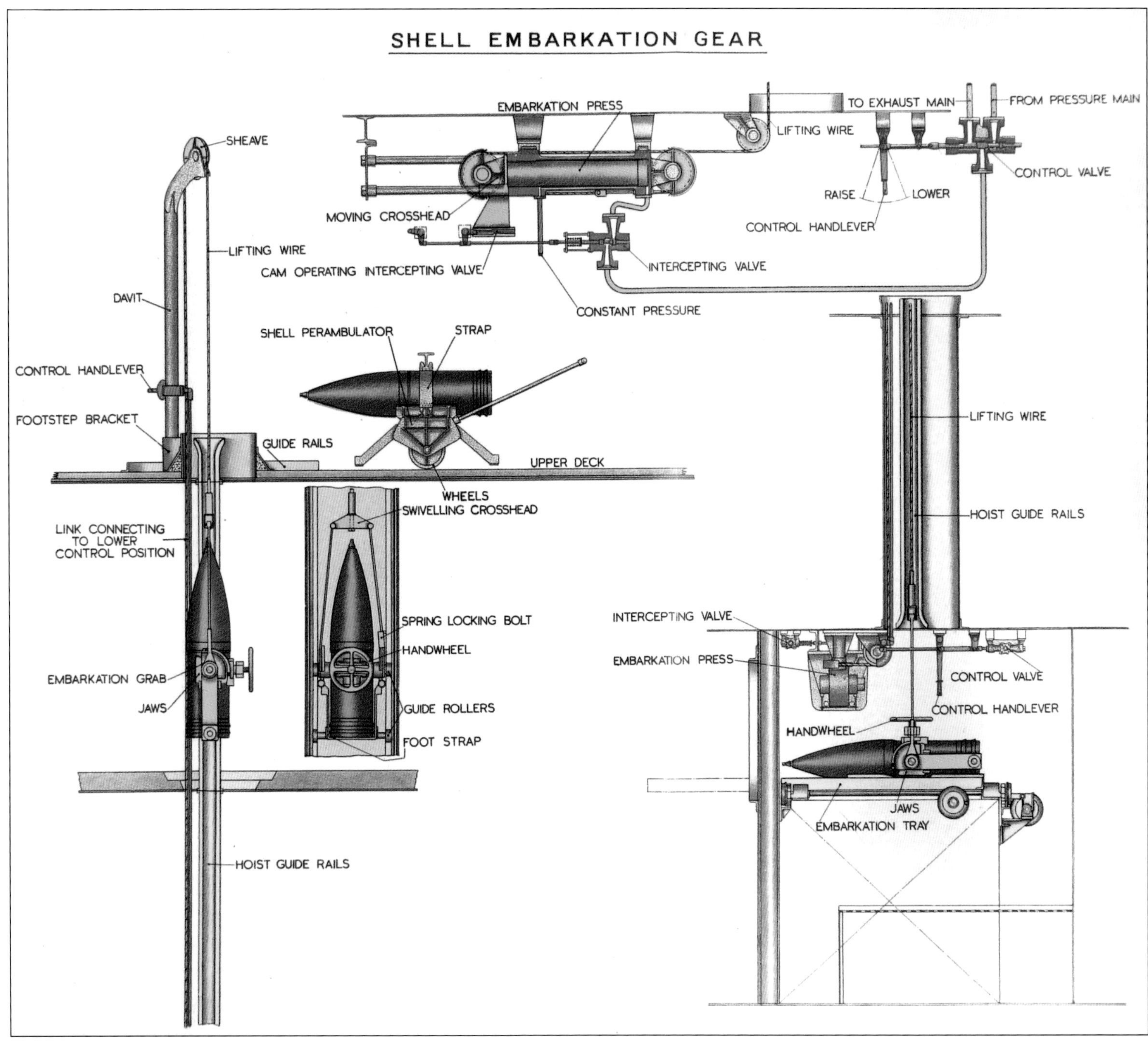
SHELL EMBARKATION GEAR
EMBARKATION PRESS
TO EXHAUST MAIN
FROM PRESSURE MAIN
LIFTING WIRE
CONTROL VALVE
RAISE
LOWER
CONTROL HANDLEVER
SHEAVE
MOVING CROSSHEAD
LIFTING WIRE
CAM OPERATING INTERCEPTING VALVE
INTERCEPTING VALVE
DAVIT
CONSTANT PRESSURE
SHELL PERAMBULATOR
STRAP
CONTROL HANDLEVER
FOOTSTEP BRACKET
GUIDE RAILS
UPPER DECK
LIFTING WIRE
WHEELS
SWIVELLING CROSSHEAD
HOIST GUIDE RAILS
LINK CONNECTING TO LOWER CONTROL POSITION
SPRING LOCKING BOLT
INTERCEPTING VALVE
HANDWHEEL
EMBARKATION PRESS
EMBARKATION GRAB
CONTROL VALVE
JAWS
GUIDE ROLLERS
CONTROL HANDLEVER
HANDWHEEL
FOOT STRAP
JAWS
EMBARKATION TRAY
HOIST GUIDE RAILS

This diagram shows how each 1590lb shell (brown) was embarked from upper deck level using a perambulator via a hatch, davit and grab (left). It was lowered vertically to shell room level (right) powered by the hydraulic press (top green), whence it was moved horizontally to stowage in the shell room by overhead rails (see illustrations on p48).

Opposite below. The breech mechanism, shown open and closed, could be operated by hydraulic pressure or by hand. It was manufactured separately from the gun barrel itself. The breech screw (blue) has an interrupted thread allowing it to be closed with just one twelfth of a turn. The firing lock (pink) which initiated detonation of the cordite was fired electrically either from the turret or the director (see also the photo on p140).

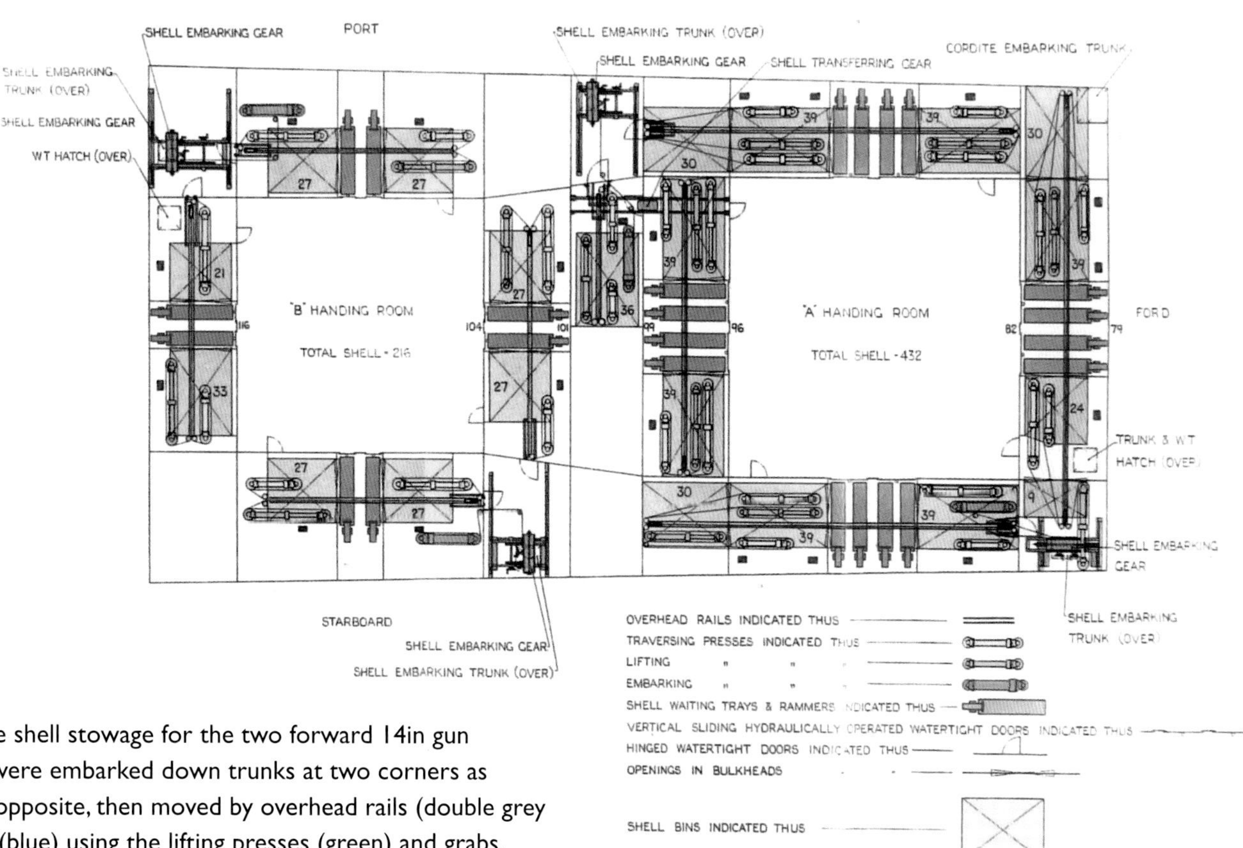
DIAGRAMMATIC ARRANGEMENT OF SHELL ROOMS
SHELL EMBARKING GEAR
PORT
SHELL EMBARKING TRUNK (OVER)
SHELL EMBARKING GEAR
SHELL TRANSFERRING GEAR
CORDITE EMBARKING TRUNK
SHELL EMBARKING TRUNK (OVER)
SHELL EMBARKING GEAR
WT HATCH (OVER)
'B' HANDING ROOM
TOTAL SHELL - 216
'A' HANDING ROOM
TOTAL SHELL - 432
FORD
TRUNK & W.T HATCH (OVER)
SHELL EMBARKING GEAR
STARBOARD
SHELL EMBARKING GEAR
SHELL EMBARKING TRUNK (OVER)
SHELL EMBARKING TRUNK (OVER)
OVERHEAD RAILS INDICATED THUS
TRAVERSING PRESSES INDICATED THUS
LIFTING " "
EMBARKING " "
SHELL WAITING TRAYS & RAMMERS INDICATED THUS
VERTICAL SLIDING HYDRAULICALLY OPERATED WATERTIGHT DOORS INDICATED THUS
HINGED WATERTIGHT DOORS INDICATED THUS
OPENINGS IN BULKHEADS
SHELL BINS INDICATED THUS
CONTROL STANDARDS INDICATED THUS

The diagram shows the shell stowage for the two forward 14in gun mountings. The shells were embarked down trunks at two corners as shown in the drawing opposite, then moved by overhead rails (double grey lines) to the shell bins (blue) using the lifting presses (green) and grabs. When needed for the guns, the shells were moved to the waiting trays (purple) to be rammed through watertight doors to the handing room and hoists (white centre square). 'A' shell room had stowage for 432 shells, i.e. 108 per gun, with 10 practice and the rest armour piercing, capped, unless on shore bombardment duties when high explosive would be shipped. The photo on p250 shows the compartment during demolition.

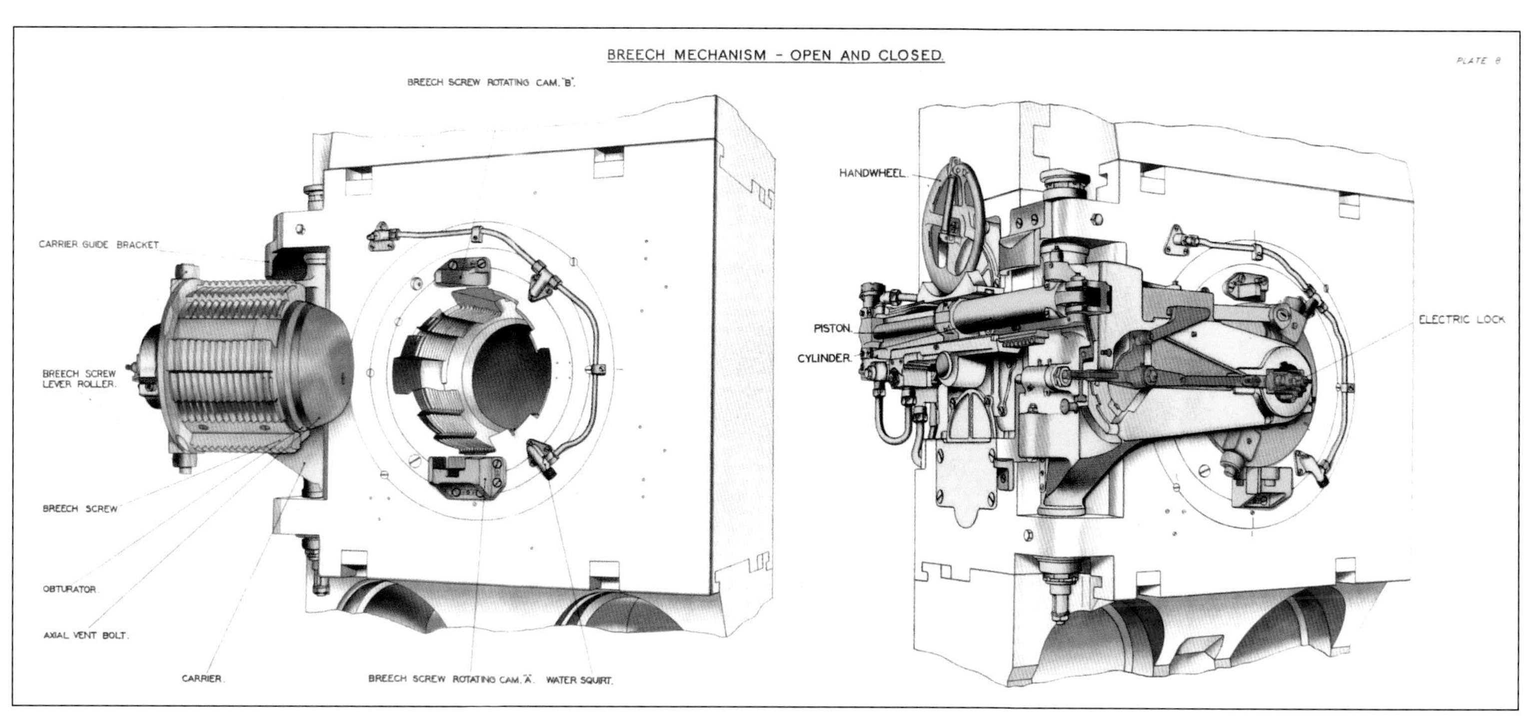
BREECH MECHANISM - OPEN AND CLOSED.
PLATE 8
BREECH SCREW ROTATING CAM "B".
CARRIER GUIDE BRACKET
BREECH SCREW LEVER ROLLER.
BREECH SCREW
OBTURATOR
AXIAL VENT BOLT.
CARRIER
BREECH SCREW ROTATING CAM "A".
WATER SQUIRT.
HANDWHEEL
PISTON
CYLINDER
ELECTRIC LOCK

Transferring a 14in shell from derrick to embarkation hatch. (Imperial War Museum)

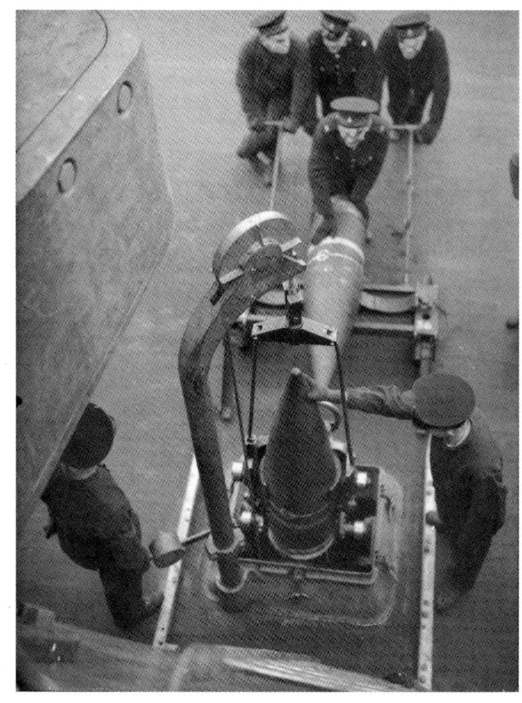

GUIDE TO COLOURS

14" CORDITE SHOWN IN BLACK.
14" SHELL SHOWN IN BLACK DOTTED
5·25" CORDITE SHOWN IN RED
5·25" SHELL SHOWN IN RED DOTTED
BOMBS SHOWN IN BROWN DOTTED
POM-POM AMMUNITION SHOWN GREEN
3 PDR BLANK & SAL^G & SUB CALIBRE AMM^N SHEWN BLUE
FIREWORKS & SMALL ARMS AMMUNITION SHOWN YELLOW

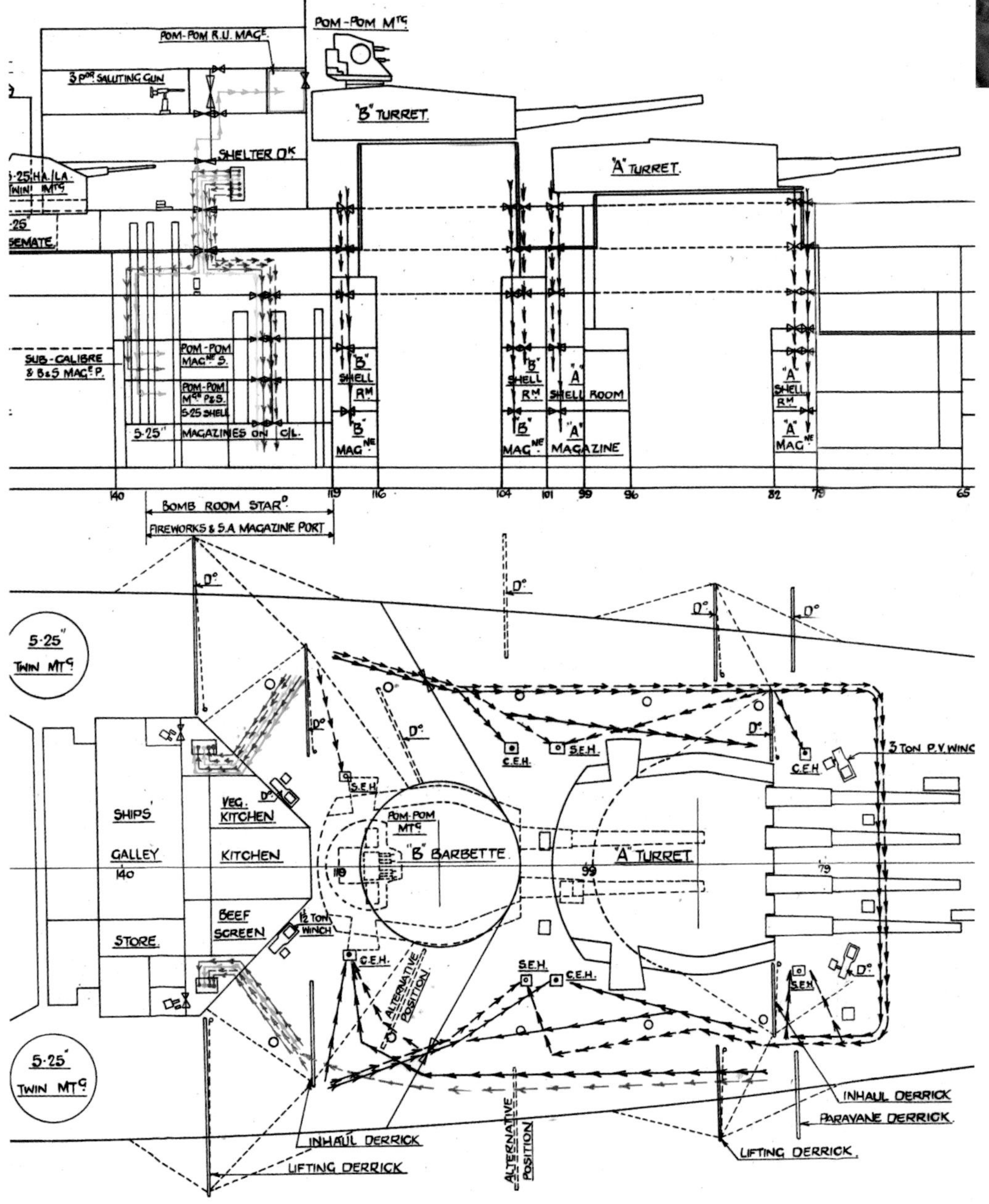
POM-POM R.U. MAG^E
POM-POM MT^G
3 PDR SALUTING GUN
'B' TURRET
'A' TURRET
SHELTER D^K
5·25 H.A./L.A. TWIN MT^G
SUB-CALIBRE & S.&S. MAG^E P.
POM-POM MAG^NE S.
POM-POM M^GS P.&S.
5·25 SHELL
5·25" MAGAZINES ON C/L.
'B' SHELL RM
'B' MAG^NE
'B' SHELL R^M
'A' SHELL ROOM
'A' MAGAZINE
'A' SHELL R^M
'A' MAG^NE
140
119
116
104
101
99
96
82
78
65
BOMB ROOM STAR^D
FIREWORKS & S.A MAGAZINE PORT
5·25" TWIN MT^G
SHIPS' GALLEY
VEG. KITCHEN
KITCHEN
BEEF SCREEN
STORE
POM-POM MT^G
'B' BARBETTE
'A' TURRET
S.E.H.
C.E.H.
3 TON P.V. WINC
1½ TON WINCH
ALTERNATIVE POSITION
INHAUL DERRICK
LIFTING DERRICK
PARAVANE DERRICK

Left. This shows part of the As Fitted plan for embarking and striking down ammunition, covering the forward magazines. The black arrows show the route of 14in shells (full lines) and cordite (dashed); red 5.25in shells (full lines) and cartridges (dashed); green 2pdr ammunition; blue 3pdr saluting and 6pdr sub-calibre gun rounds; yellow small arms ammunition and fireworks; brown aircraft bombs. S.E.H. = shell embarking hatch, C.E.H. = cordite embarking hatch. Plans on p45 and p46 show detail for handling 14in ammunition. (© National Maritime Museum, London M2061)

Armour

THE *KING GEORGE V* class were given very good armour protection. Their sides had cemented armour 15in thick over magazines, 14in over machinery spaces, and their main deck non-cemented (against bombs and plunging shells) 6in over magazines and 5in over machinery spaces (nominal thicknesses, actual 2 per cent less). Cemented armour had a hard face to resist armour-piercing projectiles, while non-cemented was more ductile to resist oblique attack from shells and bombs. The composition of armour, its manufacture and pricing are discussed in *The Battleship Builders*, Chapter 9. As armour-making capacity had been greatly reduced after the First World War, the Admiralty financed new plant at the three remaining makers: English Steel Corporation at Sheffield, Firth-Brown at Sheffield and Beardmore at Glasgow to meet the expected demand of about 40,000 tons a year.

Armour plates were to be supplied to the shipbuilder by the Admiralty, machined to size, bent to shape, edges rounded, tongues and grooves cut, securing holes drilled and tapped, hatches and other openings cut and machined, in accordance with sketches, patterns and moulds prepared by the shipbuilder.

Side armour plates to have horizontal joints tongued and grooved, vertical joints keyed [diamond section]. Supported by I frames 10 x 6 x 6 x ½in web D quality steel spaced 8ft apart and at butts. [See midship section M2067A on p33.] Backing of teak strips 6 x 1in and spaces between filled with approved plastic composition (cork dust, oxide in oil, whiting, solution). Side to be coated before armour plates fitted. Each plate was about 16 x 8ft weighing about 25–40 tons.

Main deck armour to have plain butts [ends], edges tongued and grooved. Rabbeted [stepped] edges where removable [to ship machinery]. Armour bolts along edges plus one intermediate bolt every 10 sqft. The deck under to be 20lb D quality, flush with treble riveted butt straps [to join ends of adjacent plates] edges joggled [to nest flush with adjoining plate] and double lap riveted. Each plate supported along its edges and butts by I beams 9 x 7 x 7in x 53lb/ft D quality steel. Curved to the camber of the decks [about 12in rise at centre in ship breadth]. Each plate was about 20 x 12ft weighing about 20–35 tons.

Armour gratings to be fitted at boiler uptakes and vent openings where fans 17½in or over.

Anson's actual armour weights were carefully recorded (and used by Shipbreaking Industries in her demolition). *Duke of York* would have been similar.

1in thickness = 40.8lb/ft^2 (600 = 14.7in)
C = cemented armour. NC = Non-cemented

Side	Port	Stbd	Thickness lb/ft^2
Lower tier	722	725	560–600C tapered to 180–220C at bottom
Middle tier	755	756	560C machinery, 600C magazines
Upper tier	812	819	560C machinery, 600C magazines
Total tons	2289	2300	Total 4589 tons
Manufacturer	Beardmore		

Deck	Tons	Thickness lb/ft^2
Main	3138	200NC machinery, 240NC magazines
Lower fwd	312	100–200NC
Lower aft	436	180–200NC
Total	3884	
Manufacturer	Firth-Brown	

Bulkheads	Tons	Thickness lb/ft^2
Frame 79	223	400–480C
Frame 274 + 289, 319	233	400–480C
Total	456	289+319: 160–240NC
Manufacturer	Firth-Brown	

Barbettes and rings	Tons	Thickness lb/ft^2
'A'	358	440–520C
'B'	434	440–520C
'Y'	359	480–520C
Total	1151	Rings 80NC 145 tons
Manufacturer	A ESC, B & Y Firth-Brown	

Total armour weight 10,082 tons excluding gunhouse armour, keys and bolts, conning tower and D quality protective plating. Rolling tolerance for deck: 0 over, 2.5lb/ft^2 under (i.e. actual weight not to exceed designed), 0/10lb side & barbette armour.

14in gunhouses: Front 520C, side front 360C, side rear and back 280NC, roof 240NC. Armour for 'A' by English Steel Corporation, 'Y' by Beardmore, 'B' by ESC. For quadruple mounting approximately 87 tons C, 340 NC [included in turret weight].

Ship supplied with armour lifting bolts. Side: 3 sets of 2 bolts, deck 2 sets of 4 bolts, bulkheads and barbettes 1 set of 2 bolts.

Barbette armour

armour was specified by weight (pounds per square foot) and not thickness. These diagrams show plate number with associated poundage. The table at right shows the inch equivalent.

Lb	Inch
520	12.74
480	11.76
440	10.78

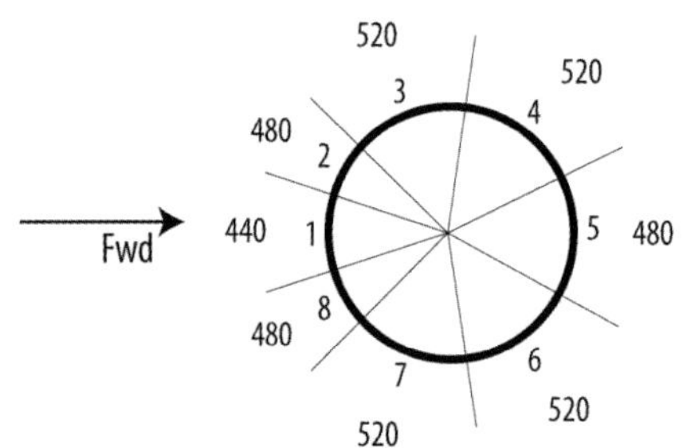
Fwd
520
3
520
4
480
2
440
1
5
480
8
480
7
6
520
520

A Barbette **Total 295 tons** heaviest plate 46.75 tons

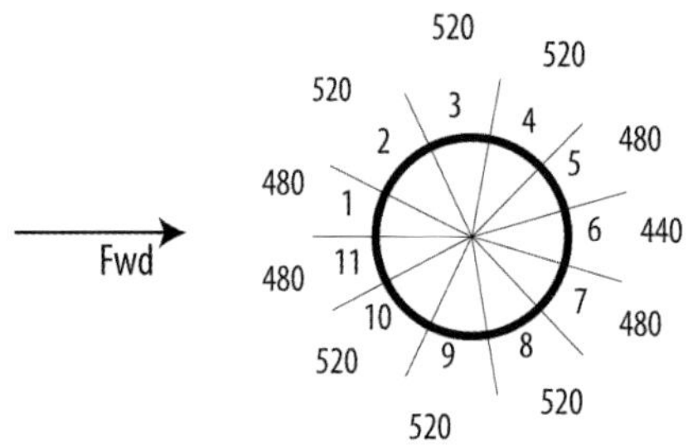
Fwd
520
520
3
4
520
2
5
480
480
1
6
440
11
480
7
10
480
9
8
520
520
520

B Barbette **Total 430 tons** heaviest plate 44.25 tons

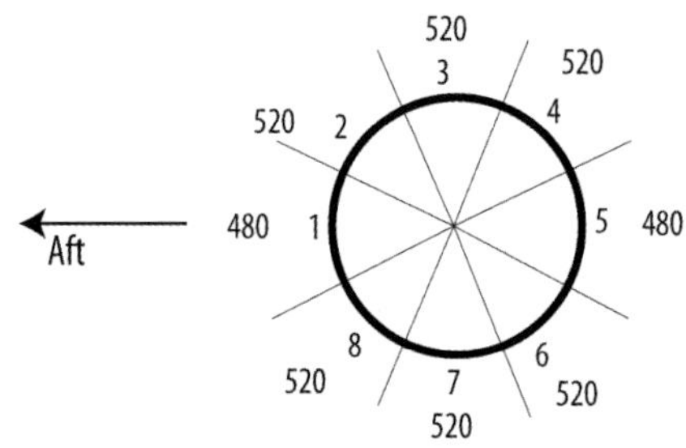
Aft
520
3
520
4
520
2
480
1
5
480
8
7
6
520
520
520

Y Barbette **Total 295 tons** heaviest plate 45.75 tons

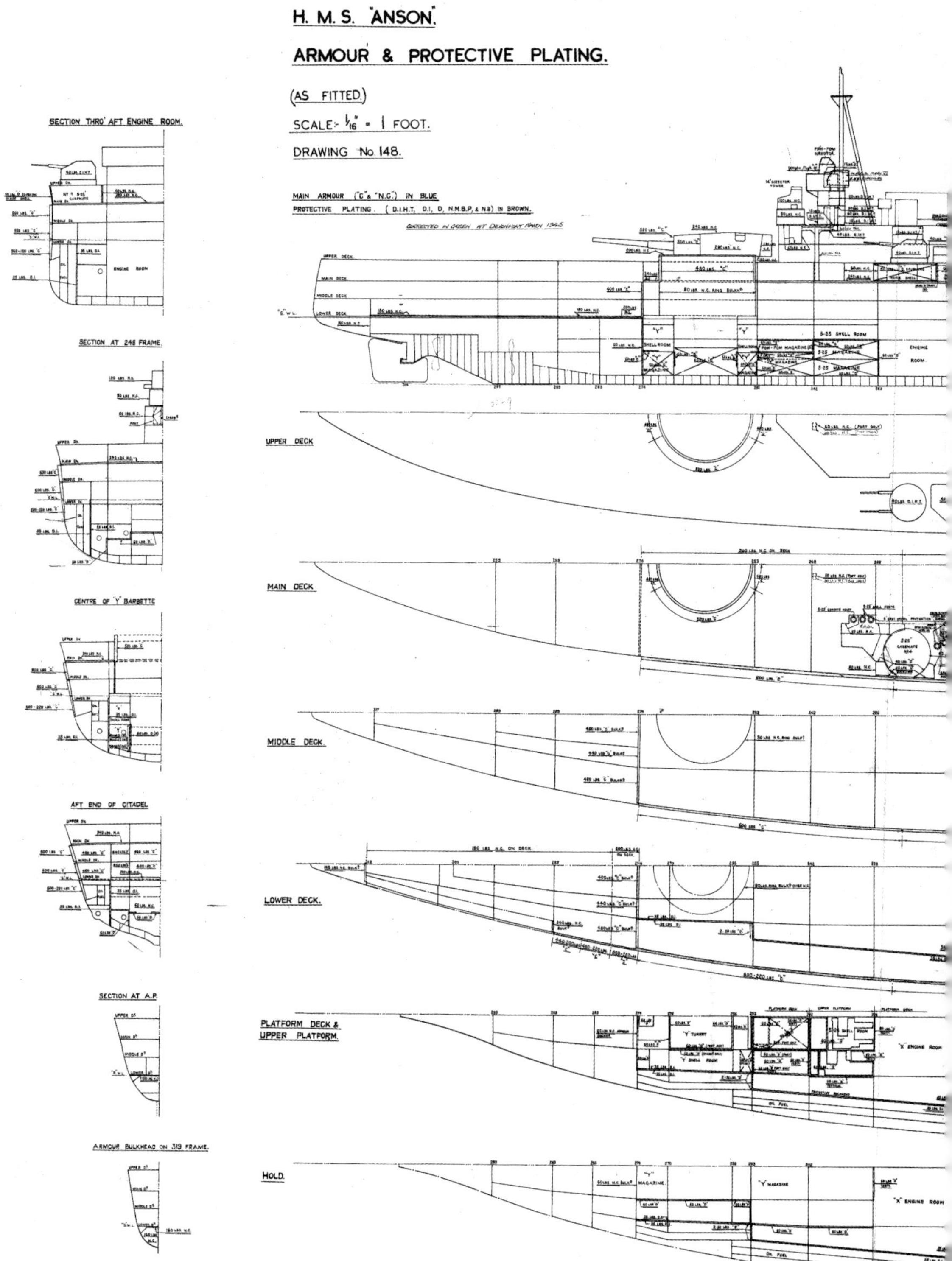

H. M. S. 'ANSON.'

ARMOUR & PROTECTIVE PLATING.

(AS FITTED)

SCALE:- 1/16" = 1 FOOT.

DRAWING No. 148.

MAIN ARMOUR ('C' & 'N.C.') IN BLUE

PROTECTIVE PLATING. (D.I.H.T., D.I., D., N.M.S.P. & N.S.) IN BROWN.

SECTION THRO' AFT ENGINE ROOM.

SECTION AT 248 FRAME.

CENTRE OF 'Y' BARBETTE

AFT END OF CITADEL.

SECTION AT A.P.

ARMOUR BULKHEAD ON 319 FRAME.

UPPER DECK

MAIN DECK

MIDDLE DECK.

LOWER DECK.

PLATFORM DECK & UPPER PLATFORM.

HOLD.

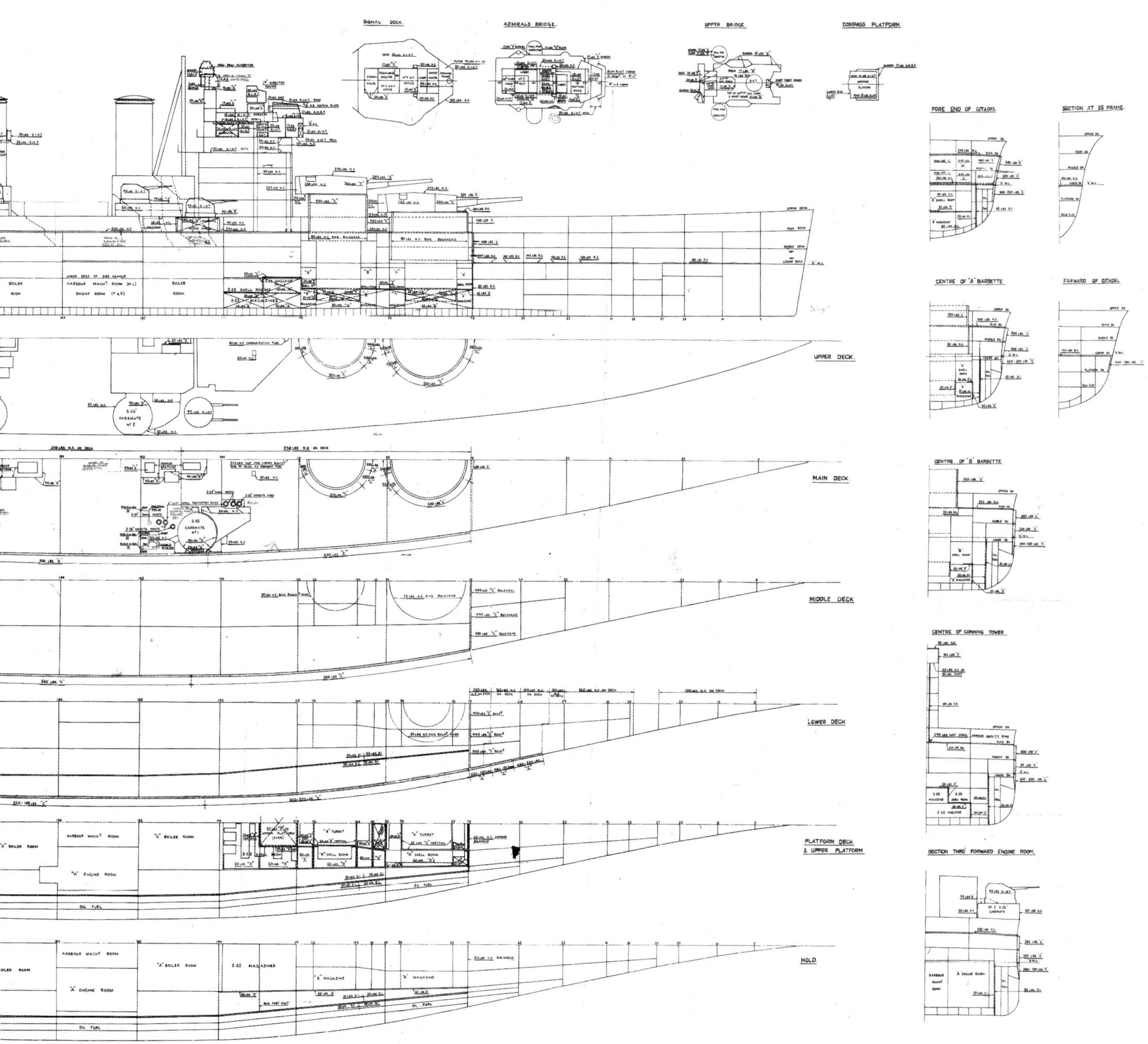
SIGNAL DECK
ADMIRALS BRIDGE
UPPER BRIDGE
COMPASS PLATFORM
FORE END OF CITADEL
SECTION AT 25 FRAME
CENTRE OF 'A' BARBETTE
FORWARD OF CITADEL
CENTRE OF 'B' BARBETTE
CENTRE OF CONNING TOWER
SECTION THRO' FORWARD ENGINE ROOM
UPPER DECK
MAIN DECK
MIDDLE DECK
LOWER DECK
PLATFORM DECK & UPPER PLATFORM
HOLD

Among the guidance drawings that DNC provided for potential shipbuilders was one of Armour and Protection, at a scale of 1/16in to the foot, showing the profile, the decks and typical sections. As the ship neared completion, the shipyard prepared a similar plan but As Fitted. The principal difference was the addition of 60lb D quality protective plating around the 14in and 5.25in magazines, but not shell rooms. The drawing for *Duke of York* is folded and not as clear as the rolled linen print provided for use on board *Anson*, so the latter is reproduced here.

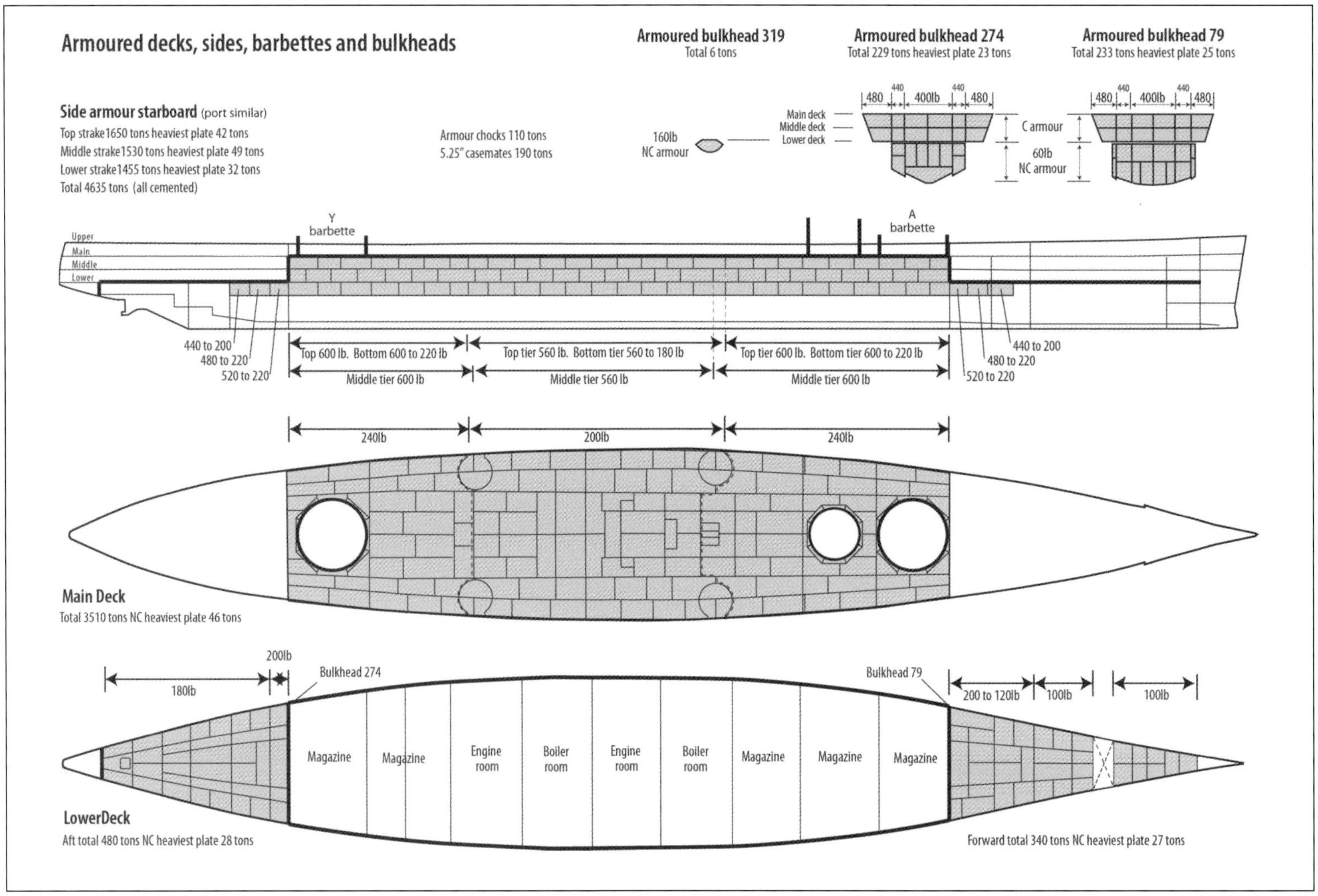

Armoured decks, sides, barbettes and bulkheads

Side armour starboard (port similar)
Top strake1650 tons heaviest plate 42 tons
Middle strake1530 tons heaviest plate 49 tons
Lower strake1455 tons heaviest plate 32 tons
Total 4635 tons (all cemented)

Armour chocks 110 tons
5.25" casemates 190 tons

Armoured bulkhead 319
Total 6 tons

160lb
NC armour

Armoured bulkhead 274
Total 229 tons heaviest plate 23 tons

Main deck
Middle deck
Lower deck
480 440 400lb 440 480
C armour
60lb
NC armour

Armoured bulkhead 79
Total 233 tons heaviest plate 25 tons

480 440 400lb 440 480

Upper
Main
Middle
Lower
Y barbette
A barbette
440 to 200
480 to 220
520 to 220
Top 600 lb. Bottom 600 to 220 lb
Middle tier 600 lb
Top tier 560 lb. Bottom tier 560 to 180 lb
Middle tier 560 lb
Top tier 600 lb. Bottom tier 600 to 220 lb
Middle tier 600 lb
440 to 200
480 to 220
520 to 220

240lb
200lb
240lb

Main Deck
Total 3510 tons NC heaviest plate 46 tons

180lb
200lb
Bulkhead 274
Bulkhead 79
200 to 120lb
100lb
100lb
Magazine
Magazine
Engine room
Boiler room
Engine room
Boiler room
Magazine
Magazine
Magazine

LowerDeck
Aft total 480 tons NC heaviest plate 28 tons

Forward total 340 tons NC heaviest plate 27 tons

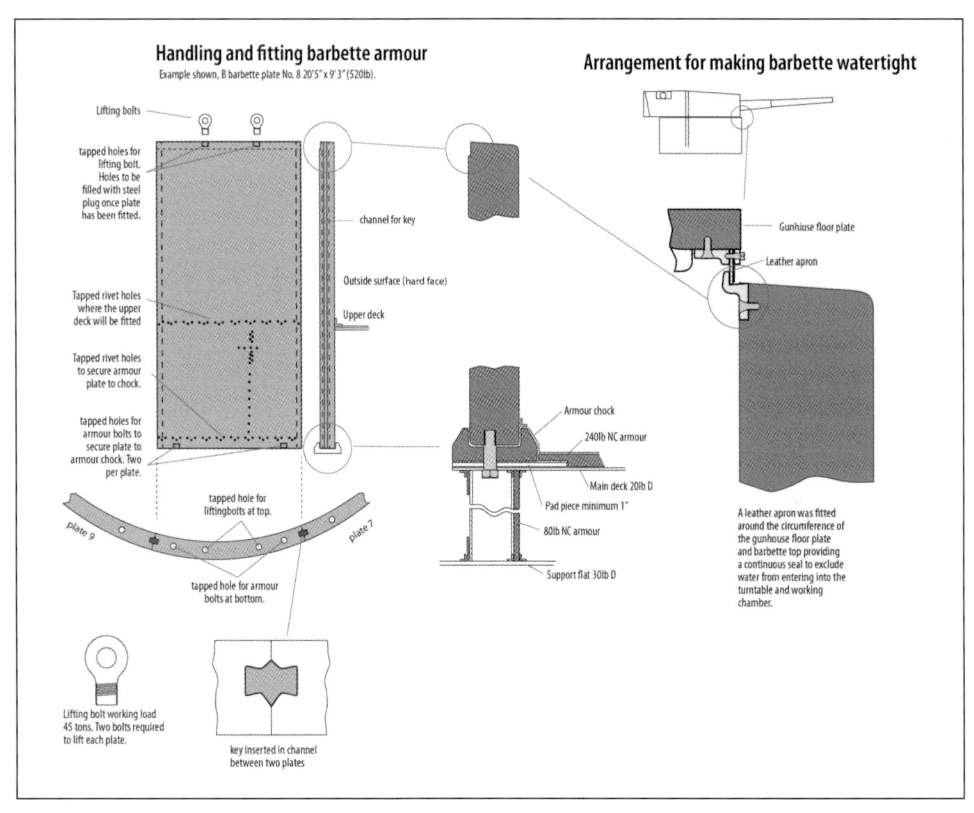
Handling and fitting barbette armour
Example shown, B barbette plate No. 8 20'5" x 9'3" (520lb).
Lifting bolts
tapped holes for lifting bolt. Holes to be filled with steel plug once plate has been fitted.
Tapped rivet holes where the upper deck will be fitted
Tapped rivet holes to secure armour plate to chock.
tapped holes for armour bolts to secure plate to armour chock. Two per plate.
channel for key
Outside surface (hard face)
Upper deck
tapped hole for liftingbolts at top.
plate 9
plate 7
tapped hole for armour bolts at bottom.
Lifting bolt working load 45 tons. Two bolts required to lift each plate.
key inserted in channel between two plates
Armour chock
240lb NC armour
Main deck 20lb D
Pad piece minimum 1"
80lb NC armour
Support flat 30lb D
Arrangement for making barbette watertight
Gunhiuse floor plate
Leather apron
A leather apron was fitted around the circumference of the gunhouse floor plate and barbette top providing a continuous seal to exclude water from entering into the turntable and working chamber.

Construction

Shipyard Reports January 1937 – December 1941 integrated with dated photographs

Ship No 554, HMS *Duke of York*
(originally to be named *Anson*)

WHAT FOLLOWS ARE monthly reports made describing progress on the ship. Many reports are missing and what is presented here is all that have survived in the archive of John Brown & Company at the University of Glasgow.

While these reports record construction in general, what makes them of particular interest are the comments concerned with the broader context of this ship's construction before and during the Second World War, such as feedback from other ships in class, delays in delivery of armour and gun mountings, the loss of *Hood*, the bombing of Clydebank and the occasional reference to the Admiralty. The reports have been edited to remove repetition but are otherwise verbatim. Where frame numbers are mentioned, their location is shown on the drawing below and on pp203–06.

The minutes of these meetings from which these reports are drawn discussed every contract going through the Works. They are presented here in chronological order and where the reports have the same date, the order is *SDO*, *Shipyard*, *Engine Works*, *Committee* and *Board*. Where words have been inserted for clarity, square brackets are used.

Altogether there were five meetings each month held routinely to discuss and record progress.

1. *Shipyard Reports*: The principal source of information about progress on building the hull.
2. *Engine Works Reports*: Recording progress on manufacturing machinery (turbines, gearing, shafting, boilers, condensers, funnels and auxiliary machinery).
3. *Shipyard Drawing Office (SDO) Reports*: Generally working several months ahead of steelwork on the ship, the SDO received guidance drawings from the Admiralty and developed these into detailed production drawings for the Shipyard Department. Equally, where the shipyard was to develop plans of details, these were submitted to the

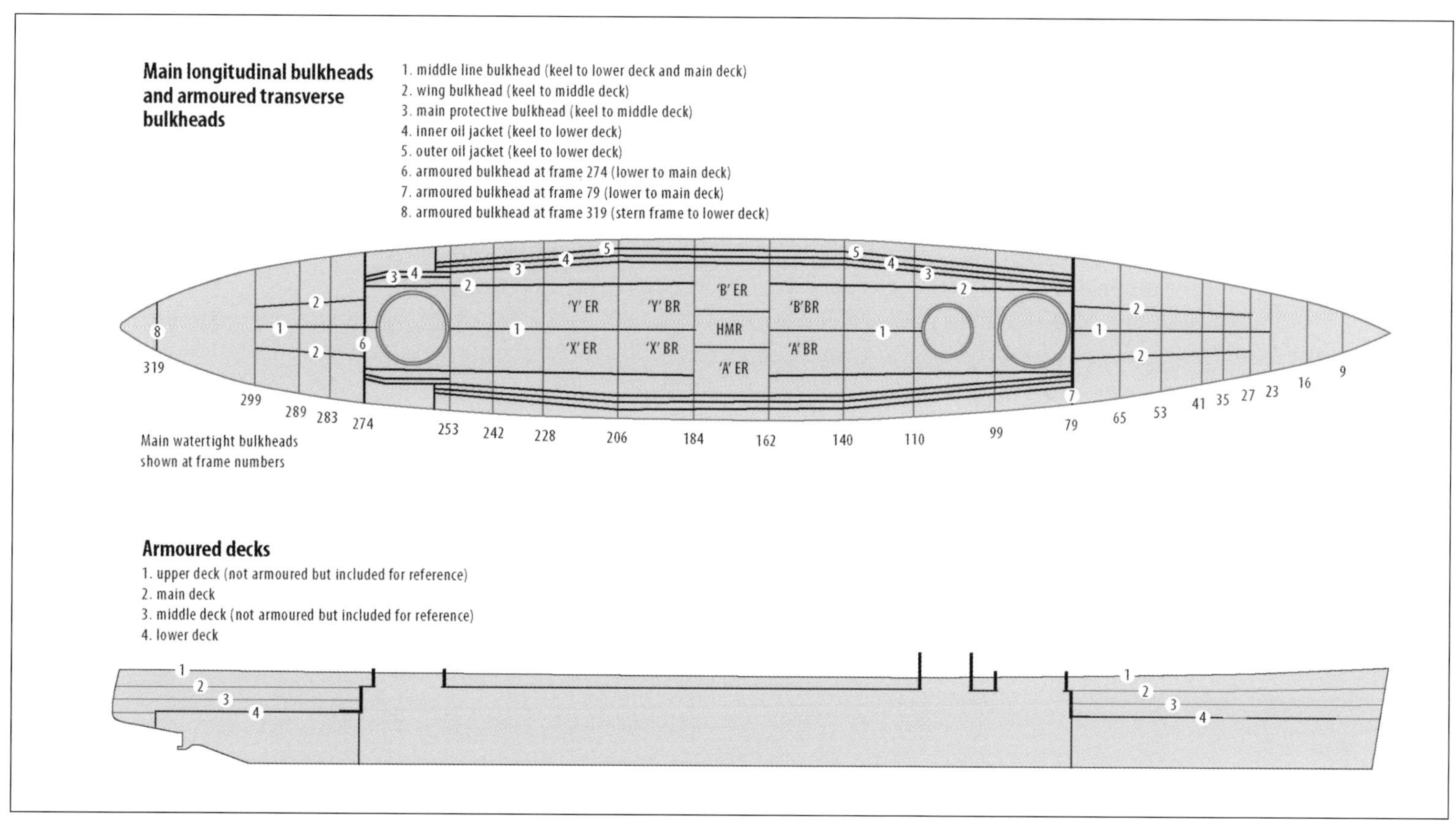

Main longitudinal bulkheads and armoured transverse bulkheads
1. middle line bulkhead (keel to lower deck and main deck)
2. wing bulkhead (keel to middle deck)
3. main protective bulkhead (keel to middle deck)
4. inner oil jacket (keel to lower deck)
5. outer oil jacket (keel to lower deck)
6. armoured bulkhead at frame 274 (lower to main deck)
7. armoured bulkhead at frame 79 (lower to main deck)
8. armoured bulkhead at frame 319 (stern frame to lower deck)
'Y' ER
'Y' BR
'B' ER
HMR
'A' ER
'B'BR
'X' ER
'X' BR
'A' BR
319 299 289 283 274 253 242 228 206 184 162 140 110 99 79 65 53 41 35 27 23 16 9
Main watertight bulkheads shown at frame numbers
Armoured decks
1. upper deck (not armoured but included for reference)
2. main deck
3. middle deck (not armoured but included for reference)
4. lower deck

Admiralty for approval. A similar function was carried out by the Engine Drawing Office although it did not make monthly reports.

The other two meetings were high-level summaries which brought forward the above minutes together with other administrative information:

1. *Committee*: summary progress report by senior management at Clydebank.
2. *Board*: high-level meeting of the John Brown Board of Directors in London.

Reports Prior to Laying Down

1937

January *Board*
Approximately 1300 tons of structural steel for keel and double bottom have been ordered from Messrs Colville [major Scottish steelmaker]. Before the end of December, Admiralty approval was obtained in our choice of suppliers of various materials and orders were placed to avoid rises in market prices. Recently, authority was given to other firms to proceed with work on the 4th and 5th vessels. Official tenders are now in preparation for submission to the Admiralty on 16 February by all five builders [tenders had not been submitted for the first two before their contracts were awarded].

25 January *SDO*
Steel material is being ordered as soon as the necessary information comes to hand. This mainly comprises the structure in way of the double bottoms and main protective bulkheads. As a result of a conference held in Newcastle with the other contractors concerned, a schedule for the preparation of drawings split up among the various firms has been put forward to the Admiralty. Arrangements have also been concluded for the circulation of plans before submission and after approval for the guidance of the different builders.

13 February *SDO*
Sundry plans and particulars are being received in circulation and the plan of oil jacket bulkheads has been issued to the yard. Approved plan of protective bulkheads has been received and is now being modified for issue. About 2600 tons of steel material has been ordered to date.

15 February *Shipyard*
A commencement has been made to adjust the levels and declivities for the purpose of laying keel blocks [on building berth No 3].

17 February *Committee*
Approximately 400 tons of hull material for this battleship is now in our yard. The delivery of plates and sections for the hulls now under construction is giving rise to concern and we are daily in touch with Messrs Colvilles in this connection.

19 February *Board*
The design with the Admiralty is progressing very slowly, and we are only now in a position to commence work in our shipyard shops on the keel and double bottom structure. For both hull and machinery we have covered early for material and equipment so far as this is possible of detailed drawings being available. On 15th instant [i.e. February] we forwarded to the Admiralty our formal tender for this vessel [see Appendix p256]. Unless unforeseen conditions arise during the construction period, the outcome of this contract should be quite satisfactory. The tender calls for completion in January 1941.

20 March *Shipyard*
Loft department is engaged on scrieving [scribing the ships' lines on the mould loft floor] and a commencement has been made by ironworker on framing between keel and first longitudinal [fore and aft stiffening in double bottom]. The welding of this work is now in hand.

23 March *Committee*
For the battleship, a detailed order of particulars has been supplied for about 3000 tons [of steel] and about 1000 tons of plates and sections have been delivered. Progress with the work in our shops is proceeding very slowly due to the very slow progress with this design and then obtaining Admiralty approval. Excepting that we have laid no part of the keel, it would seem that work on our contract is as far advanced as with the vessels building by Messrs Vickers[-Armstrongs] and Messrs Cammell Laird [both keels were laid on 1 January]. In order to provide work for our framing squads until such times as more rapid progress is possible with the battleship, we have arranged with the Admiralty to proceed with the repeat *Maidstone* although official acceptance of our tender has not yet reached us. Excepting that parts of the structure which were welded in [ship] number 549 [*Maidstone*] will be riveted on the similar vessel, our number 555 [*Forth*], this ship and machinery will be a full repeat of the *Maidstone*. The delivery in 24 months will be assisted by reverting to riveting.

27 March *SDO*
Plans of the main steel structure are now being circulated from the DNC's Department including transverse bulkheads and double bottom framing. Prints of the keel plans have now been issued to the yard. All the plans received to date have

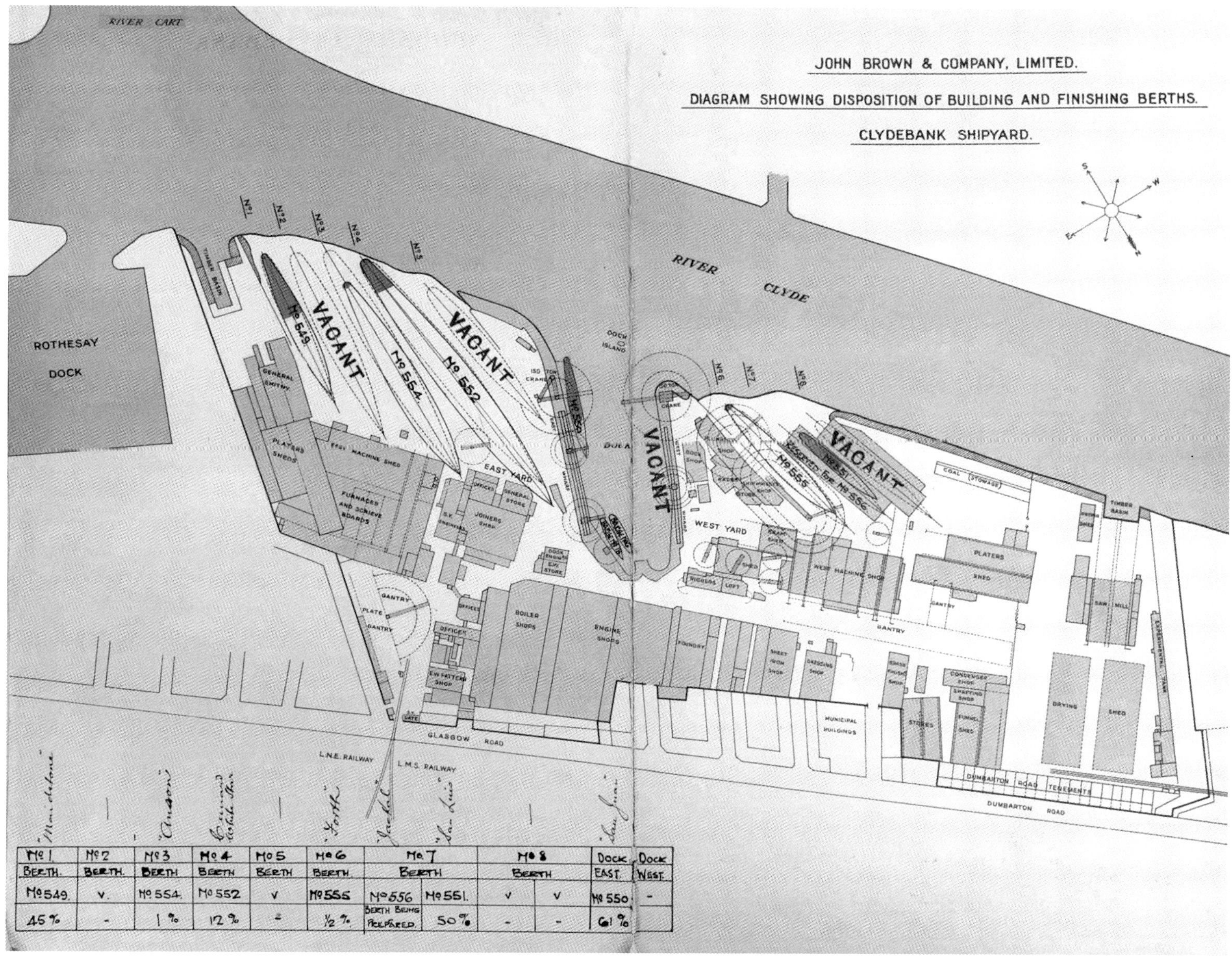
JOHN BROWN & COMPANY, LIMITED.
DIAGRAM SHOWING DISPOSITION OF BUILDING AND FINISHING BERTHS.
CLYDEBANK SHIPYARD.
RIVER CART
ROTHESAY
DOCK
RIVER
CLYDE
VACANT
Nº 549
Nº 554
Nº 552
Nº 550
Nº 555
Nº 551
EAST YARD
WEST YARD
BOILER SHOPS
ENGINE SHOPS
FOUNDRY
WEST MACHINE SHOP
PLATERS SHED
SAW MILL
DRYING SHED
MUNICIPAL BUILDINGS
GLASGOW ROAD
L.N.E. RAILWAY
L.M.S. RAILWAY
DUMBARTON ROAD
Nº 1 BERTH. Nº 549. 45 %
Nº 2 BERTH. V. -
Nº 3 BERTH Nº 554. 1 %
Nº 4 BERTH Nº 552 12 %
Nº 5 BERTH V
Nº 6 BERTH Nº 555 ½ %
Nº 7 BERTH Nº 556 BERTH BEING PREPARED. Nº 551. 50 %
Nº 8 BERTH V V - -
DOCK EAST. Nº 550 61 %
DOCK WEST. -

necessitated considerable checking and revision. About 3100 tons of steel material is on order.

March *Engine Works*

Drawing office work is proceeding and the principal turbine and gearing forgings are in hand.

2 April *Board*

As this vessel is part of the 1937–38 programme, official confirmation of the order to build cannot yet be given by the Admiralty. The progress with the design by Vickers and Cammell Laird and approving by the Admiralty has been very slow. By agreement with the Controller [Third Sea Lord, Vice Admiral Sir R Henderson], we cannot lay the keel of this vessel until about the end of April, but good progress is being made in our shipyard shops with the keel, and with floors and longitudinals.

July 1937. The monthly reports which are reproduced here were contained within a folder on which was printed a plan of the shipyard showing the position of each vessel under construction together with a percentage completion estimate. In the plan shown here for July 1937, the following vessels are shown from left to right: No 1 berth, the depot ship *Maidstone* 45 per cent complete; No 2 berth vacant; No 3 berth *Anson* (*Duke of York*) 1 per cent complete; No 4 berth the Cunard liner *Queen Elizabeth* 12 per cent complete; No 5 berth vacant; No 6 berth the depot ship *Forth* 5 per cent complete; No 7 berth is shared by the destroyers *Jackal* which has yet to be laid down and Argentine *San Luis* which is 50 per cent complete; No 8 berth is vacant. The destroyer *San Juan* was in the fitting-out basin at 61 per cent complete. Further contracts had been booked and were either yet to reach production departments or in the early stages of production.

19 April *SDO*

The principal structural plans up to the lower deck have been received in circulation from the Admiralty and these are being issued as the modifications required are completed. Advance information on the shell expansion has resulted in the ordering of the main shell plating amidships up to the lower armour shelf and it is hoped to obtain similar approval for the inner bottom plating before the end of this month. The principal particulars for launching declivities etc., and the re-inforcement of the building berth foundations have been issued to the yard. The following plans have been issued: main protective longitudinal bulkhead, oil jacket bulkheads, double bottom framing, longitudinals in double bottom, and transverse bulkhead number 35; also, preliminary prints of inner and outer bottom plating as submitted to Admiralty. About 3500 tons of steel material have now been ordered.

19 April *Shipyard*

Good progress is being made in shops on keel and on main framing in way of double bottoms. Shipwright is engaged on completing keel blocks upon which it is expected to lay keel early in May.

20 April *Committee*

On the 8th instant the Controller, Sir Reginald Henderson, stated that work on the Clydebank battleship could proceed openly as the government had on the previous day authorised the building of the further three vessels provisionally allocated with Fairfield, Swan Hunter and John Brown & Co. Accordingly, work was at once commenced on our building berth in preparation for beginning the laying of the keel early in May. Also, arrangement was then made with Messrs Arrol for the necessary piling at the lower end of the building berth. The driving of the piling will commence before the end of April.

30 April *Board*

Of approximately 4000 tons of hull structure material ordered from Messrs. Colville, somewhat more than one half has been delivered to our yard. Good progress is being made with the keel and bottom.

Reports from Laying Down to Launch

24 May *SDO*

Plans of middle line bulkhead and wing bulkhead in forward engine room have been issued to the yard and the following plans are approaching completion: framing between armour shelf and main protective bulkhead: side longitudinal girder between armour shelf and oil jacket bulkhead: transverse bulkheads forward and fore end framing.

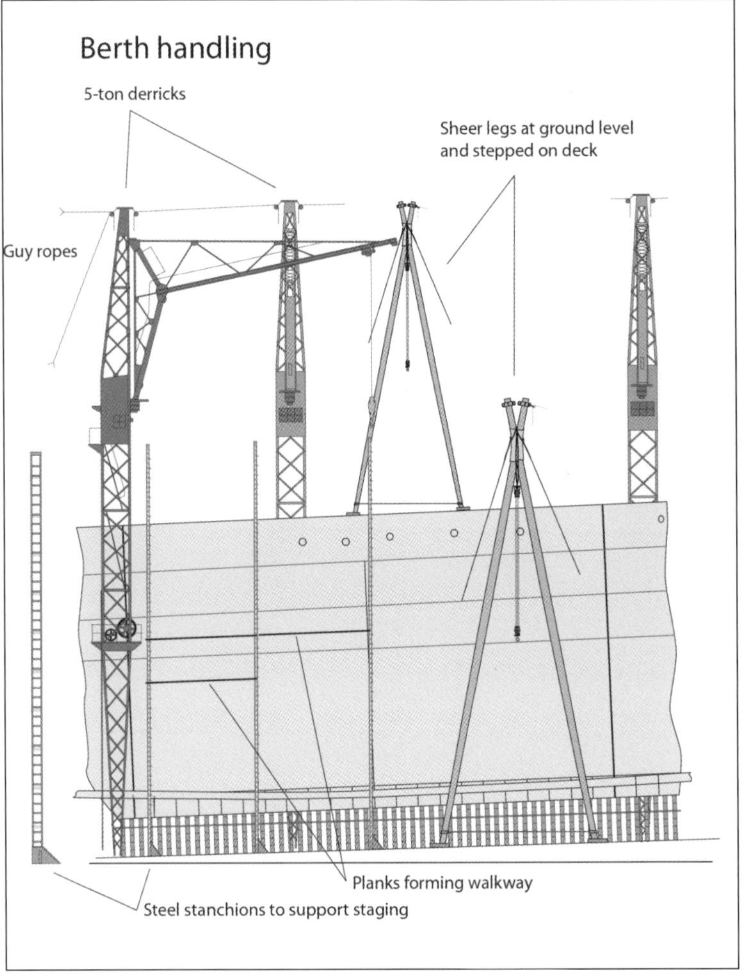
Berth handling
5-ton derricks
Sheer legs at ground level and stepped on deck
Guy ropes
Planks forming walkway
Steel stanchions to support staging

This shows the principal means of handling plates, frames and beams at the berth against a section of the hull. Twelve to fourteen derricks were placed around the berth, each capable of a maximum lift of 5 tons. Heavier lifts, boilers, castings etc., required sheer legs either on the ground or stepped on the hull. The drawing also shows the steel stanchions used to support staging, usually two or three planks to form a walkway around the hull at various heights. Shipwrights and riggers assembled all of the foregoing, not made easy by the declivity of the berth on which the hull sat.

24 May *Shipyard*

Keel was laid on 5th May. Sighting and fairing [the process of aligning plates and stiffeners smoothly with adjoining material, often using timber baulks] is now completed and a commencement has been made on riveting same. Good progress has been made in shop on double bottom framing on which work about 50% is now completed. Work has commenced on first and second longitudinals, middle line bulkhead aft and main protective longitudinal bulkhead. Piling at after end of berth is now in hand. General progress satisfactory.

5 May 1937. A view across berths Nos 1, 2 and 3 with the first keel plates on No 3 for *Duke of York* laid that day on prepared keel blocks. These blocks of heavy section timber, most likely pitch-pine, have been set-up at the declivity of 17/32in per foot (4.4 per cent or 1 in 22.5) by shipwrights some weeks before the first keel plates were laid. Note that the keel plates are joined by riveted butt straps so are flush on their outer side, rather than overlapped. The depot ship *Maidstone* is well advanced in No 1 berth. This view shows the typical arrangement of berth cranes that will construct No 554 *Duke of York*. They are predominantly 5-ton capacity steel derrick type which although fixed in position with a series of guy ropes, can, with some effort, be repositioned as required. No 1 berth has been equipped with fixed 12-ton tower cranes which had been acquired from McMillan's Dumbarton shipyard in 1932 when its plant was auctioned off. Also visible is the moveable tower, one of two, fitted with an elevator as well as stairs to enable men and materials to be delivered at various deck levels on hulls under construction. On either side of No 3 berth, a large number of parts for the *Duke of York*'s double bottom, plates with lightening holes and steel angles already riveted in place, have been delivered from the steelworking sheds ready for erection in due course. Note the steam-driven crane on temporary rails in use for handling steelwork in the very early stages of construction. Note also the large amount of timber props and shores that will be used to support the steelwork as it expands over the berth.

24 May *Engine Works*

Patterns are in hand for HP, LP [High Pressure and Low Pressure] and cruising turbine casings, the principal auxiliaries have been ordered and the turbine and gearing forgings are in hand. Drawing office work is proceeding.

26 May *Board*

Of about 5000 tons of material on order, some 3000 tons have been delivered.

26 May *Committee*

Although the official acceptance of our tender for the battleship was received on 28 April and we are advised of the name, HMS *Anson*, the basis of insurance is yet unsettled and the completion of the contract is thereby delayed. We have pressed for decision and emphasised that we are in a position to claim at least two instalments amounting to fully £50,000. Early action is now promised.

22 June *SDO*

A number of important structural plans have been received and these are now issued to the yard as undernoted: Cable lockers: six transverse bulkheads: framing between armour shelf and protective bulkhead: longitudinal girder between oil jacket bulkhead and armour shelf: lower deck armour forward; and rolling sizes of bulkheads and barbette armour: cast steel shaft tubes: inner and outer shaft brackets and rudder gland and stuffing boxes. The plan of uprights and also plan of structure on the fore end of the vessel has been issued to the yard. The plans on hand include the following: framing above armour: upper deck plating: pillaring arrangements: fore and aft end framing: ventilation arrangements. The plate line model is approaching completion. Total steel ordered to date is about 5850 tons.

22 June *Shipyard*

Keel is now in position faired and riveted. Work continues in shop on floors, longitudinals, centreline bulkheading and on main protective bulkheads. A and B strakes [the fore and aft line of plates adjacent to the keel] of bottom shell [external] plating for two thirds length erected and riveted on which shipwright is engaged on erecting longitudinals and main framing.

25 June *Board*

Approximately one-half of the materials required for the hull of this vessel are on order and about one-quarter of the total quantity required has been delivered by Messrs Colville. We are following up very closely all possibility of increasing supplies and are assured that deliveries will be improved. The structure of double bottom, main longitudinal bulkhead and the lower side structure is becoming very evident.

21 June 1937. Looking towards the River Clyde and the mouth of the River Cart, this view shows work proceeding on double bottom steelwork. A crane is holding a 17lb (0.42in) vertical longitudinal girder in place which is being 'faired' (pulled into the correct alignment with surrounding steelwork) then 'screwed-up' (bolted in place) and will finally be riveted and bolts removed. Numerous other plates with steel angles pre-assembled await similar treatment. The centre girder which forms the base of the middle line bulkhead is prominent. The outermost longitudinal girders are watertight, the inner ones not. The transverse structures are called floors despite their being vertical. The outer bottom shell plating has overlapped seams with a double row of rivets. The whole structure is being supported by timber props. The massive hull of *Queen Elizabeth* is taking shape at right where inner strakes of plating have been screwed-up prior to erection of outer strakes.

June *Engine Works*

Patterns for HP and cruising turbine casings have been sent to foundry and patterns for LP turbine and gearcase are in hand. Boiler, steam and water drum ends are being flanged. Drawing office work is proceeding.

July *Engine Works*

Castings for HP and cruising turbine casings are in hand and LP and gearcase patterns are being completed. Work on boiler drum ends is proceeding. Drawing office work is proceeding.

July *Board*

Good progress has been made with the building of the keel and double bottom structure out to the second longitudinal on either side of the keel. In the shipyard shops work is in progress on framing, longitudinals and bulkheads. The delivery of steel has not been as rapid as originally promised, but improvement is promised by Messrs Colvilles. The patterns for the main machinery parts are completed and have

This photograph shows four strakes of bottom shell plates laid out in the east plater's shed at Clydebank. They are for the Cunard liner *Queen Mary* as no equivalent picture exists for *Duke of York*. The strakes have been overlapped as they will be on the ship allowing the alignment of rivet holes to be checked and corrected with far greater ease than during erection on the ship. The inner flat plate keel is second from the left. Each plate, typically over 30ft long, was lifted into position by overhead crane. Angle iron is being riveted to the vertical keel plate at right. The plater's shed, sometimes referred to as the ironworkers' machine shop, would latterly and more accurately be referred to as the steelworking sheds. The punching and shearing machines in which rivet holes were punched and edges cut are barely visible at right. The building berths are immediately beyond the shed.

been sent to foundry where moulding is in progress. There has much delay in dealing with the Contract with the Admiralty but this document was received on 10 July and duly signed and sealed and returned to the Admiralty on that day [see final page of Contract p29].

9 July *SDO*

The preparation and circulation of the main structural plans is proceeding in collaboration with other shipbuilders. The total steel order to date is about 6200 tons.

15 July 1937. Looking forward from the after engine room area, this view shows the amount of steelwork that has been erected in just over three weeks since the preceding photograph. Pneumatic riveting is in progress for which two compressed-air lines have been fitted running down the length of the steelwork. Two rivet-heating braziers stand on wooden planks at left centre. In the background plates are being lifted off the railway wagon. The buildings at the head of the berth are offices and the general store.

9 July *Shipyard*

Shell in way of flat of bottom is now erected and fairing and riveting is proceeding. Erecting and fairing of second longitudinal and floors is in hand. Work continues in ironworkers' shops on framing, longitudinals, centre line and main protective bulkheads.

24 September *SDO*

The structural plans recently issued included several main transverse bulkheads, outer bottom plating aft, lower deck plating aft, longitudinal wing bulkhead and magazine bulkhead, after end framing, main circulating inlets and discharges, Docking and bilge keels also armour plans for bulkheads 79, 274 and 319 and for lower deck forward and aft. Details of all the above mentioned armour have been sent to the armour makers. Steps are being taken to hasten the receipt of information for the remaining armour. The eighth-scale rigging model is now in hand and the plans submitted to the Admiralty include: deck coverings, middle deck plating, upper deck plating and girders, pillaring arrangements and plan of water and air testing. The total steel ordered to date is about 9600 tons.

19 August 1937. Looking forward at the double bottom framing where plating of the inner bottom has just begun. The middle line bulkhead is now paralleled on either side by the innermost longitudinal bulkheads bounding the machinery spaces, one of whose plates is being lifted into place centre right. Various pre-assembled sections of steelwork are lying to the side delivered in a constant stream as required from the steelworking sheds which lie to the right of shot, with a horse-drawn cart outside. The original negative is sharp enough to see individual rivets, a bowler-hatted foreman at the forward end and the spark of a welder in line with the crane hook.

24 September *Shipyard*

Erecting, riveting and/or welding of double bottom framing continues. Good progress has been made on erecting of longitudinal protective bulkhead of which about 50% is erected. Same is faired and riveting is in progress. Erecting of middle line bulkhead is proceeding: fairing and welding of same is in hand. Work is proceeding on plating of inner bottom. Good progress has been made in Ironworkers' shops on the remainder of the main protective bulkhead and on main transverse bulkheads.

September *Engine Works*

One cruising turbine casing has been delivered and the three other cruising and two LP astern casings have been cast. The 1st HP top half casing and 3rd LP astern casing are moulded and 1st LP ahead casing and 1st gearcase are being moulded. Work on principal forgings is progressing. The first boiler drum has been delivered, all boiler drum ends are being pickled and jigs are in hand for drilling.

20 September 1937. In this view looking towards the stern, the most obvious development is the erection of major sections of the middle line bulkhead and the port and starboard protective bulkheads, formed of a double thickness of 30lb (¾in) D.1 quality steel abreast the machinery spaces, all extending the full height of the boiler rooms. See midship section drawing (M2067A) on p33. Pneumatic riveting of inner bottom plates is underway with a riveter completing the joint between two inner bottom plates. Although mostly riveted, there was a significant amount of welding in non-critical areas of the structure. A welder is poised at work on the forward section of the middle line bulkhead where the stiffeners were welded T bars but the plating was riveted. While this shot gives some indication of the size of the ship, its true beam has yet to be established.

29 October *Board*

[Ship No 554] is becoming a very noticeable structure on our No.3 berth. The supply of armour will become a pressing matter early next year, and all that can be stated now is that the supply of the details of the design requirement is well in advance of the work on armour plate production. The work on the machinery is proceeding in keeping with schedule, and the supply of forgings and main castings is satisfactory.

October *Engine Works*

The first LP top half casing has been delivered, the 1st HP ahead and 3rd LP astern casings are cast and moulding of the other turbine casing parts and 1st gearcase is well in hand. Work on principal forgings is progressing and two gearwheel rims have been delivered. One boiler steam drum, three water drums and one superheater header have been delivered.

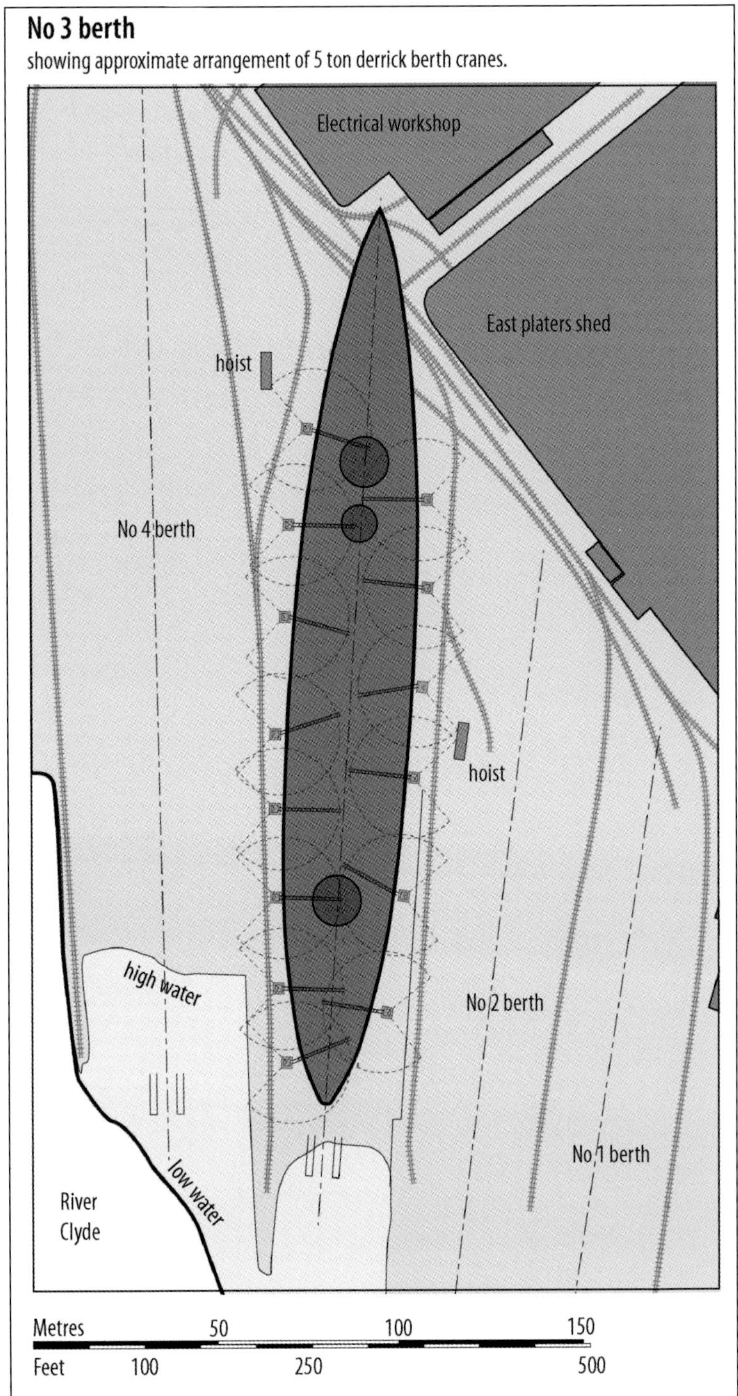
No 3 berth
showing approximate arrangement of 5 ton derrick berth cranes.
Electrical workshop
East platers shed
hoist
No 4 berth
hoist
high water
No 2 berth
No 1 berth
low water
River
Clyde
Metres 50 100 150
Feet 100 250 500

20 October 1937. Another view looking aft showing good progress on the middle line and protective bulkheads. Note that for simplicity of construction, these bulkheads run in a series of straight lines and do not follow the curved lines of the hull. The lower section of watertight bulkhead at Frame 162, which separates the forward boiler rooms from the engine rooms, has been erected. It was the first of the transverse bulkheads to be erected, with temporary fairing baulks of timber. Further aft, a start has been made to the bulkhead at Frame 184. The original negative is sharp enough to read the painted frame numbers showing their location in the ship. Staging, usually two or three planks wide (without handrails), has been arranged using timber, brackets and ropes by riggers throughout vertical surfaces. The depot ship *Maidstone* at left has been painted and is being made ready for launching which took place on the day after this photograph was taken.

24 November *SDO*

The principal structural plans issued to the yard include the following: middle deck plating, boiler seats, oil fuel tank depth indicators. A revised plan of the upper deck plating is on hand to meet Admiralty modifications. The after section of the ventilation arrangements together with the arrangement of sidelights have been submitted and details of petrol tanks have been forwarded to the makers to enable them to proceed with the manufacture. The total steel order to date is about 10,800 tons. A revised schedule giving detailed requirements of delivery dates for the various sections of armour has been forwarded to the Admiralty to enable them to assess their armour production requirements.

24 November *Shipyard*

Main protective bulkhead is 95% erected: riveting and welding proceeding. Inner oil jacket bulkhead 50% erected together with framing between jacket bulkheads: welding in progress: erecting of outer oil jacket bulkhead commenced. With additional manholes now cut, riveting of inner bottom plating is proceeding, erection of bulkhead on fourth longitudinal is

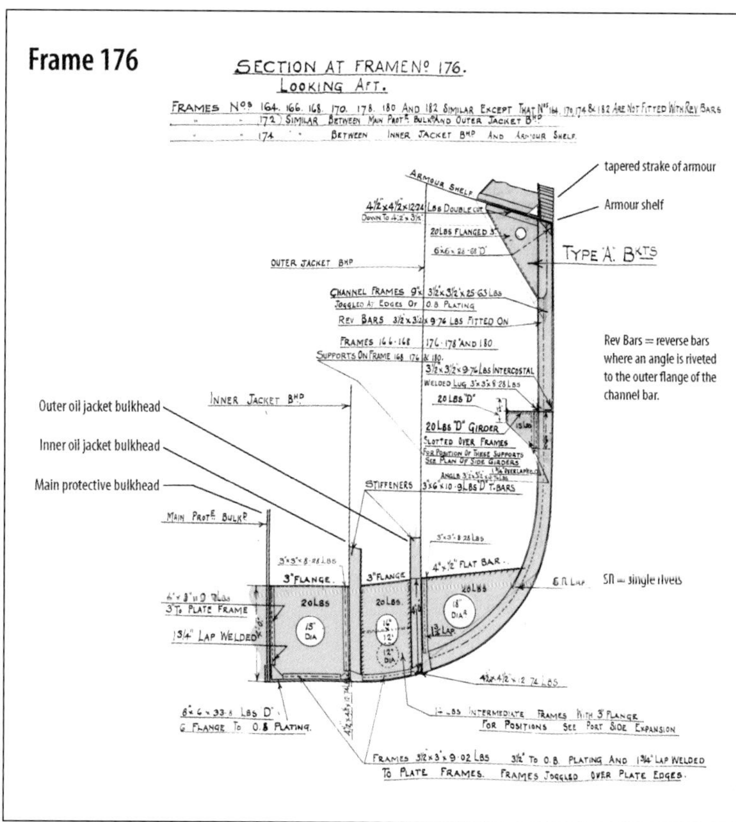
Frame 176
SECTION AT FRAME No 176.
LOOKING AFT.
tapered strake of armour
Armour shelf
TYPE 'A' BKTS
Rev Bars = reverse bars where an angle is riveted to the outer flange of the channel bar.
Outer oil jacket bulkhead
Inner oil jacket bulkhead
Main protective bulkhead
SR = single rivets

Another example of an original steelwork drawing showing construction details at Frame 176 on the port side midships looking aft. Importantly it shows elements of the ship's side protective system from the main protective bulkhead comprising two plates of 30lb D.I quality at left, to the inner and outer oil jacket bulkheads each of 15lb D quality. Note that the other longitudinal bulkheads to the left of the main protective bulkhead are not shown on this drawing. Although substantially riveted, there was significant welding in non-critical areas as this drawing shows with hatching. The vertical floors are also seen in the photo on p59 right. The drawing has not been altered apart from applying a grey mask to define steelwork.

in hand and the portion which is erected is faired to allow welding to proceed. Main transverse bulkheads in machinery spaces about 50% erected, fairing and welding in progress. Work continues in ironworkers' shops on outer jacket bulkheads, transverse bulkheads and main framing.

26 November *Board*

The construction of the hull is progressing well although better progress would be possible if more steel was available. We have ordered about 11,000 tons and have received delivery of approximately 7000 tons. The erection of the mid-line bulkhead and other fore and aft bulkheads, viz: main protective, intermediate, inner and outer oil compartment, etc., are all proceeding to schedule. Also, several of the transverse bulkheads are partially erected. Much welding is required by the design of these parts. We have indicated to the Admiralty our schedule requirement for the delivery of armour.

Probably December 1937. A general view of the after part of the ship showing the after boiler and engine spaces. The outermost longitudinal bulkhead is that of the outer oil jacket. The last bulkhead visible towards the stern is bulkhead 274 which will be armoured above this level between the lower and main decks, ahead of which will be 'Y' gun mounting. Note the rail track at left for delivering material to be lifted by the berth cranes. What appears to be a Brocklebank cargo ship in ballast is passing the end of the berth going upstream to Glasgow.

17 December *Engine Works*

All cruising turbine casings have been delivered and machining is in progress. Delivery of the other turbine casings and forgings has commenced. Four boiler steam drums, five water drums and six superheater headers have been delivered. Drawing office work is proceeding. One turbine casing is being finally bored, two have been rough bored and one is being prepared for rough boring.

1938

14 February *Shipyard*

Inner and outer oil jacket bulkheads are now welded and riveted and main framing outside same in way of armour shelf 90% erected. Progress is being made on plating of shell in way of these parts, structure in way of the shelf is 90% erected, being faired and riveting in progress. Framing at forward and after ends is in progress of erecting, fairing and riveting. Erection of main longitudinal bulkheads is continued: welding of seams and stiffening in progress. Transverse bulkheads between [Frames] 9 and 289 are about 90% erected to lower deck; welding and riveting in progress. Side stringers below armour shelf are erected, faired and being welded. A commencement has been made on the erecting of lower platform deck where fairing and welding is in progress. Work is proceeding in ironworkers' shops on main transverse bulkheads main framing and framing behind side armour.

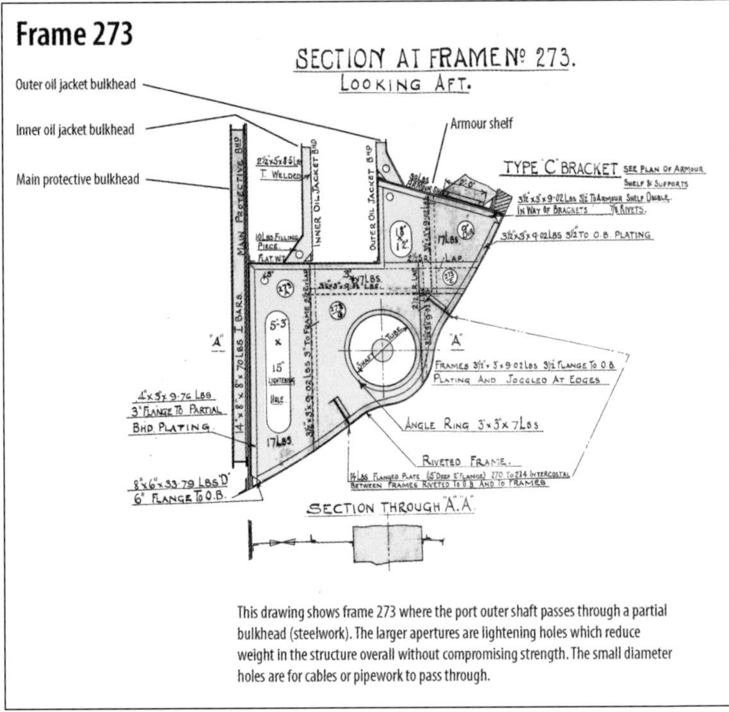
Frame 273
SECTION AT FRAME Nº 273.
LOOKING AFT.
Outer oil jacket bulkhead
Inner oil jacket bulkhead
Main protective bulkhead
Armour shelf
TYPE 'C' BRACKET
ANGLE RING 3×3×7LBS
RIVETED FRAME
SECTION THROUGH 'A.A'

This drawing shows frame 273 where the port outer shaft passes through a partial bulkhead (steelwork). The larger apertures are lightening holes which reduce weight in the structure overall without compromising strength. The small diameter holes are for cables or pipework to pass through.

This original shipyard drawing shows Frame 273 where the port outer shaft passes through a partial bulkhead (steelwork). The larger apertures are lightening holes which reduce weight in the structure overall without compromising strength. The small-diameter holes are for cables or pipework to pass through. The stiffener sizes are given in pounds per foot run. Note that the propeller shaft is hollow and not solid as shown here (17.5in outside diameter, 11.5in inside).

17 February *Committee*

HMS *Anson* armour. Reported that we were keeping in touch with Sheffield regarding the armour position, but it now looks as if the launch would be about September 1939, and completion about June 1941, which is some five months after the contract date.

28 March *SDO*

The plans issued to the yard include the following: upper deck plating (revised), upper deck deep beams, A barbette supports, main deck armour, watertight bulkheads main to upper deck, oil fuel settling tanks, list of standard furniture, and various piping plans. The pillaring arrangements and details of minor bulkheads on lower deck forward have been

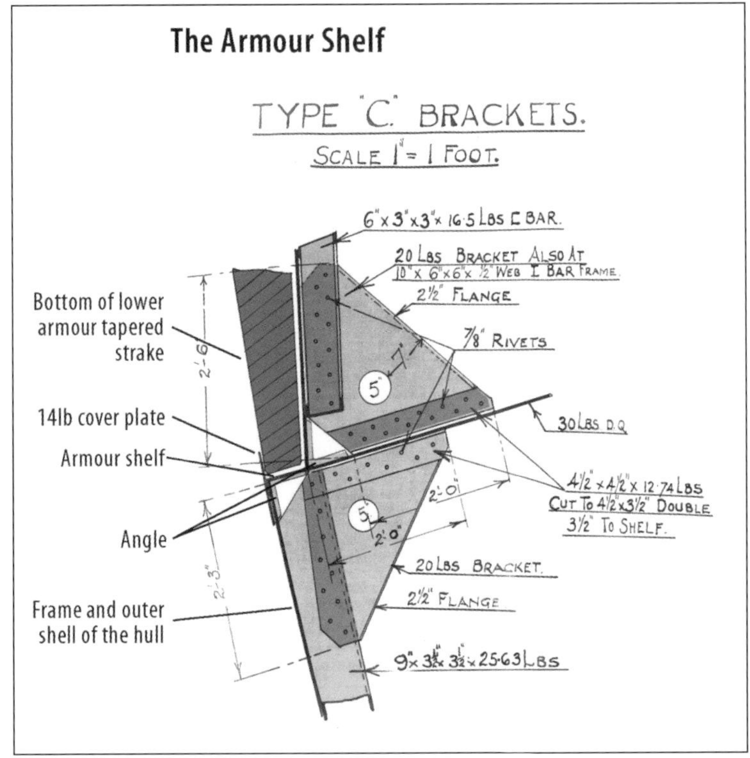
The Armour Shelf
TYPE 'C' BRACKETS.
SCALE 1" = 1 FOOT.
6"x3"x3"x 16.5 LBS [BAR.
20 LBS BRACKET ALSO AT
2½" FLANGE
⅞" RIVETS
30 LBS D.Q.
4½"x4½"x 12.74 LBS
CUT TO 4½x3½" DOUBLE
3½" TO SHELF.
20 LBS BRACKET
2½" FLANGE
9"x 3½" 3½"x 25.63 LBS
Bottom of lower armour tapered strake
14lb cover plate
Armour shelf
Angle
Frame and outer shell of the hull

An original detailed shipbuilder's structural steelwork drawing, one of very few surviving, which shows the armour shelf, the brackets above and below and location of the tapered lower strake of the side armour. For clarity the steelwork has been shaded.

approved and will be issued shortly. Plans of minor bulkheads on middle and main decks have been submitted. Arrangements are being made to provide the additional 60lb. D quality splinter protection over all magazines, and to modify the protection arrangements in way of the 5.25-inch casements [casemates] as required by the Admiralty, this latter involving about 150 tons of NC [non-cemented] armour. The rigging model is almost complete. Total steel ordered to date is about 12,100 tons.

28 March *Shipyard*

Contour plates connecting stern castings are in position, faired and being riveted and a commencement made to erect main framing in way of same. Ironworker is engaged on erecting, fairing and welding platform deck and lower deck plating; also, a commencement has been made on main turbine and on boiler seatings. Good progress has been made on shell plating. In ironworkers' shops work is proceeding on remainder of lower deck plating and on middle deck beams and girders.

30 March *Committee*

The armour supply will dictate the launching date of both *Anson* and *Fiji* and the supply of guns and turrets will dictate the date of completion of *Anson*. In keeping with the latest

1⅜ HOLES

Admiralty schedule, the deck armour for *Anson* will be supplied by Firth-Brown and side armour by Beardmore.

March *Engine Works*

One HP turbine casing, one cruising casing and one astern LP casing have been water tested and two further cruising casings have been rough bored. Delivery of forgings, castings and boiler drums are proceeding and machining is in hand. One boiler steam drum has been drilled.

March 1938. Another view dominated by the great bulk of the *Queen Elizabeth*, this one shows watertight bulkhead 299 at the after end of the hull at the point where the keel angles upwards to connect with the cast steel stern frame that will support the rudder. The stern frame is lying on the ground, showing the hole for the rudder stock, with a broad white-painted centreline stripe, waiting to be lifted into position by the waiting sheers and riveted. The steel casting weighed 24.3 tons and was manufactured by William Beardmore & Co at the Parkhead Forge in Glasgow at a cost of £3165.

April 1938. A starboard view in the vicinity of 'X' engine room, about Frames 220–236, looking forward. The shell plating (generally 25lb or ⅝in) now extends to just above main deck level. Just above the lowest level of staging is the armour shelf, supporting the lowest strake of (tapered) armour. The great amount of numbers, symbols and instructions painted on the steelwork gives some indication of how this system of iconography enabled such a maze of steelwork to be erected. Every item of steelwork, plate, frame, angle etc., had numbers which enabled it to be fitted in the right place. The lines painted around runs of rivets seen here denotes that these rivets have been counted (and can not be counted twice) and that the rivet squads on piecework who drove them will be paid accordingly.

May 1938. The internal layout can be seen before the deck plating is added. The compartment at bottom left where the men are rigging the staging is 'A' boiler room. On the other side of bulkhead 140 will be the fire-control rooms. The light-coloured double angle bar running forward centre right is the top of the protective bulkhead at middle deck level. The far side is the outer shell and its framing.

1 April *Board*

Of a total of about 15,000 tons of materials approximately 13,000 tons are on order and 10,000 delivered. The consignments have not, however, been in keeping with the requirements of best progress. The supply of armour for decks and side of the vessel will prove the measure of progress and it would now appear that the launch cannot be earlier than September 1939, and about six months later than would otherwise obtain. Also the supply of guns and turrets will determine the date of completion and the forecast is fully five months later than called for by Contract.

27 April *Shipyard*

All longitudinal bulkheads below middle and lower decks are erected, welded and riveted between frames 35 and 283. All transverse bulkheads below middle and lower decks are erected between frames 9 and 299. Transverse framing below armour shelf together with shelf is now completely erected faired and riveted and framing behind side armour is being erected. Ironworker is making good progress in erecting and riveting of shell plating. Supports under A and Y barbettes are erected, faired and being riveted and good progress has been made on main turbine and on boiler seatings. Erecting of framing at forward and aft end continues. Shipwright is engaged on erecting lower deck aft together with lower deck plating and ironworker has commenced work on ring bulkhead in the way of Y barbette.

31 May *SDO*

Plans issued to the yard include: side armour upper tier, supports to B barbette, auxiliary engine seats in boiler rooms, sidelight arrangements and key plan of pillaring, together with detail of pillar heads and heels. The ventilation arrangements, shelter deck plating, messing and sleeping arrangements, skylights and ladder ways and piping plans generally are in hand. The total steel ordered to date is about 12,700 tons.

31 May *Shipyard*

Port and starboard inner shaft brackets together with the inner and outer stern tube castings are erected; fairing proceeding.

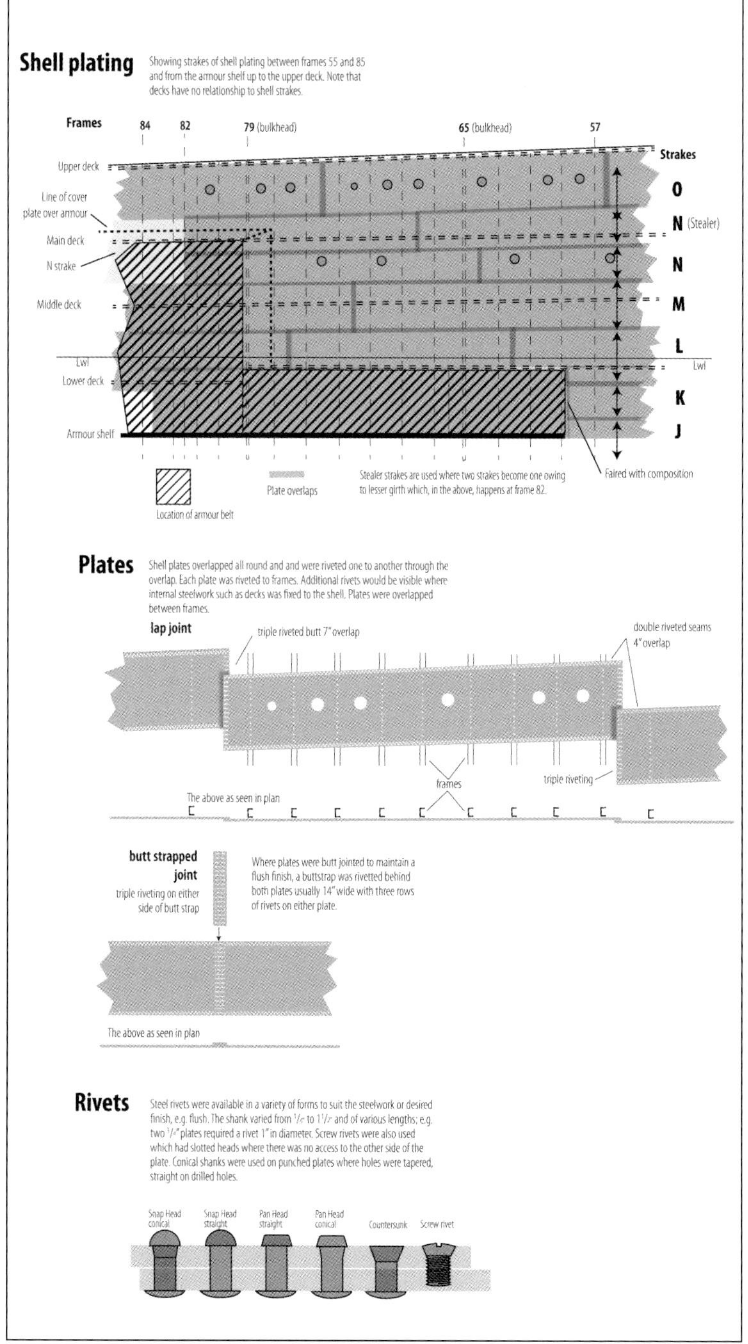
Shell plating
Showing strakes of shell plating between frames 55 and 85 and from the armour shelf up to the upper deck. Note that decks have no relationship to shell strakes.
Frames
84
82
79 (bulkhead)
65 (bulkhead)
57
Strakes
Upper deck
Line of cover plate over armour
Main deck
N strake
Middle deck
Lwl
Lower deck
Armour shelf
O
N (Stealer)
N
M
L
K
J
Lwl
Location of armour belt
Plate overlaps
Stealer strakes are used where two strakes become one owing to lesser girth which, in the above, happens at frame 82.
Faired with composition
Plates
Shell plates overlapped all round and and were riveted one to another through the overlap. Each plate was riveted to frames. Additional rivets would be visible where internal steelwork such as decks was fixed to the shell. Plates were overlapped between frames.
lap joint
triple riveted butt 7" overlap
double riveted seams 4" overlap
frames
triple riveting
The above as seen in plan
butt strapped joint
triple riveting on either side of butt strap
Where plates were butt jointed to maintain a flush finish, a buttstrap was rivetted behind both plates usually 14" wide with three rows of rivets on either plate.
The above as seen in plan
Rivets
Steel rivets were available in a variety of forms to suit the steelwork or desired finish, e.g. flush. The shank varied from 1/4" to 1 1/2" and of various lengths; e.g. two 1/4" plates required a rivet 1" in diameter. Screw rivets were also used which had slotted heads where there was no access to the other side of the plate. Conical shanks were used on punched plates where holes were tapered, straight on drilled holes.
Snap Head conical
Snap Head straight
Pan Head straight
Pan Head conical
Countersunk
Screw rivet

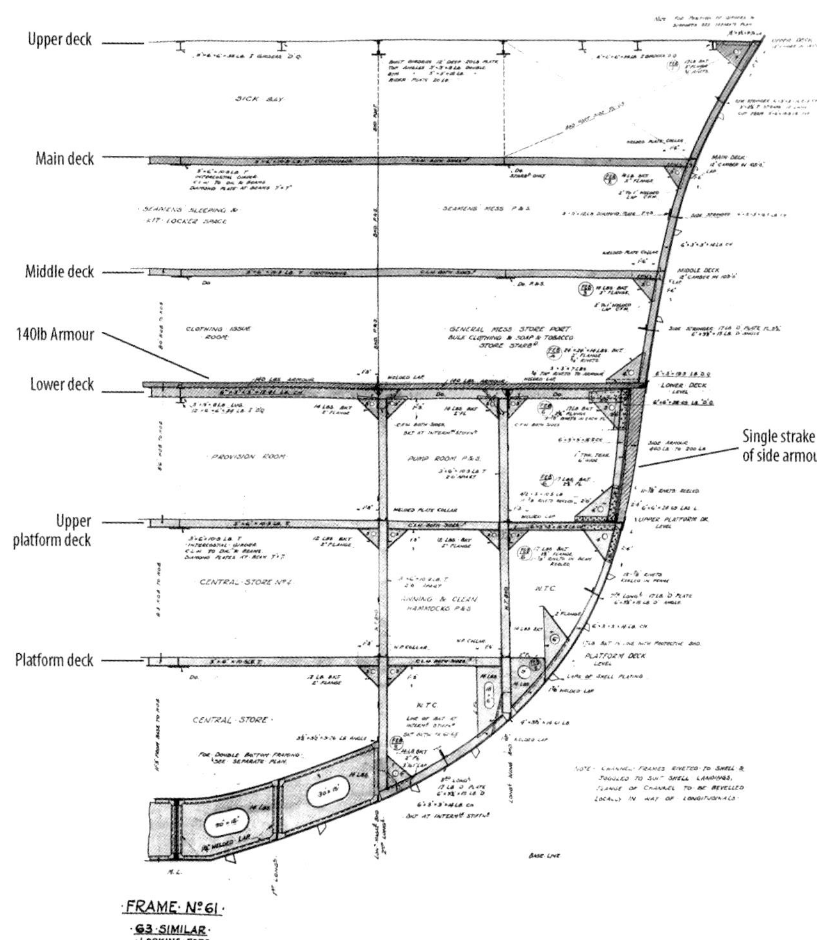
Upper deck
Main deck
Middle deck
140lb Armour
Lower deck
Upper platform deck
Platform deck
Single strake of side armour
FRAME Nº 61
63 SIMILAR
LOOKING FORD

Shipyard steelwork drawing of Frame 61 starboard side looking forward. The main three-strake armoured belt has ended and just the lower strake continues as a single strake tapered from 440lb down to 200lb. The armoured deck has reduced in thickness to 140lb. W.T.C. = water tight compartment.

Welding and riveting of remaining portions of main longitudinal and transverse bulkheads continues. Framing behind the side armour is erected and good progress is being made on plating of same. Erecting of outer bottom plating is proceeding, and good progress is being made on fitting of platform deck and upper platform deck, and lower deck beams, girders and plating, where welding and riveting is well forward. A proportion of middle deck beams and girders is now erected and a commencement to erect middle deck stringer plates has been made. Work is proceeding in ironworkers' shops on middle deck plating, A and Y barbette supports and on barbette ring bulkheads. Water testing of compartments is commenced.

May *Engine Works*

One cruising casing has been finally bored, one is being bored and the remaining two are being prepared for final boring. One HP casing is being prepared for final boring and the others are being machined. All LP casings have been rough bored and are being put together for water testing. One cruising, two HP and two LP rotors have been finally turned and grooved. Machining is proceeding on two gearcases and on gearwheels. Six boiler steam drums and eight water drums have been drilled. Work on oil fuel suction and heating connections is progressing on-board ship.

2 June *Committee*

On 30 May the Director of Naval Construction spent some hours at Clydebank, his chief interest being the progress with

No. 554. Regarding armour and armament for Admiralty vessels, we are concerned over the late delivery of lower deck and main deck armour required for *Anson* before launching, and concerning the guns for destroyers, which we are advised that delivery may delay the completion of the *Jackal* by possibly three months and the *Kashmir* by possibly nine months.

3 June *Board*

Construction is proceeding satisfactorily with framing, plating and bulkheads. Both port and starboard inner shaft brackets are erected in position and some of the armour for the bulkheads below the lower deck is now in our yard and being prepared for erection. Considerable concern is felt regarding the delivery of the armour for the lower deck forward and aft and for the side portions of the main deck. In the engine and boiler shops the progress is in keeping with schedule.

20 June *SDO*

Plans issued to the yard include: minor bulkheads main deck, forward engine room auxiliary seats, longitudinal wing bulkhead aft, arrangements and detail of watertight doors, lower deck armoured hatches, key plan of side armour backing, arrangement of oil fuel suctions in engine rooms. The third section of the ventilation arrangements has been submitted together with furniture plan. Work is proceeding on the remaining sections of the ventilation, including engine room ventilation and also messing and sleeping arrangements, skylights and ladderways, shelter deck plating, deck planking arrangement and armour arrangements and details. The total steel ordered to date is about 12,800 tons.

20 June *Shipyard*

Welding and riveting of remaining portion of main transverse bulkheads is continuing. Beams, girders and plating of upper platform and lower deck flats are being erected, faired and welded. Good progress has been made on middle deck where plating and riveting is proceeding. Supports under A and Y barbettes are erected, faired and being riveted. Dry surveying and water-testing of double bottom compartments continues. Work of plumbing and engineering departments in connection with double bottom piping has commenced. Good progress has been made by ironworker on plating behind side armour.

24 June *Board*

The third shaft bracket [starboard outer] is now in position. Approximately ⅘ of the plates and sections required for the whole structure are now delivered and work generally is making satisfactory progress. In the machine shops the machining of turbines, gearing and boiler drums is proceeding to schedule.

June 1938. The cast steel starboard outer shaft bracket being lifted into position with a tubular steel A frame rigged for the purpose. The number of rivet holes (eighty-eight) in the palm indicate how securely attached shaft brackets had to be. Note the legs of the A frame on the port side indicating that a similar operation is in progress with the port outer shaft bracket. Although the lower deck has been plated, it has yet to receive its armour.

Opposite, June 1938. The starboard outer shaft bracket being fitted viewed from the ground. Note the lower palm in shadow slightly inboard with a similar set of holes. [See diagram Shoring 03 p101.] Many of the steel castings for the ship came from John Brown's Atlas Works in Sheffield but this casting which weighed 23.5 tons came from Beardmore's Parkhead Forge in Glasgow.

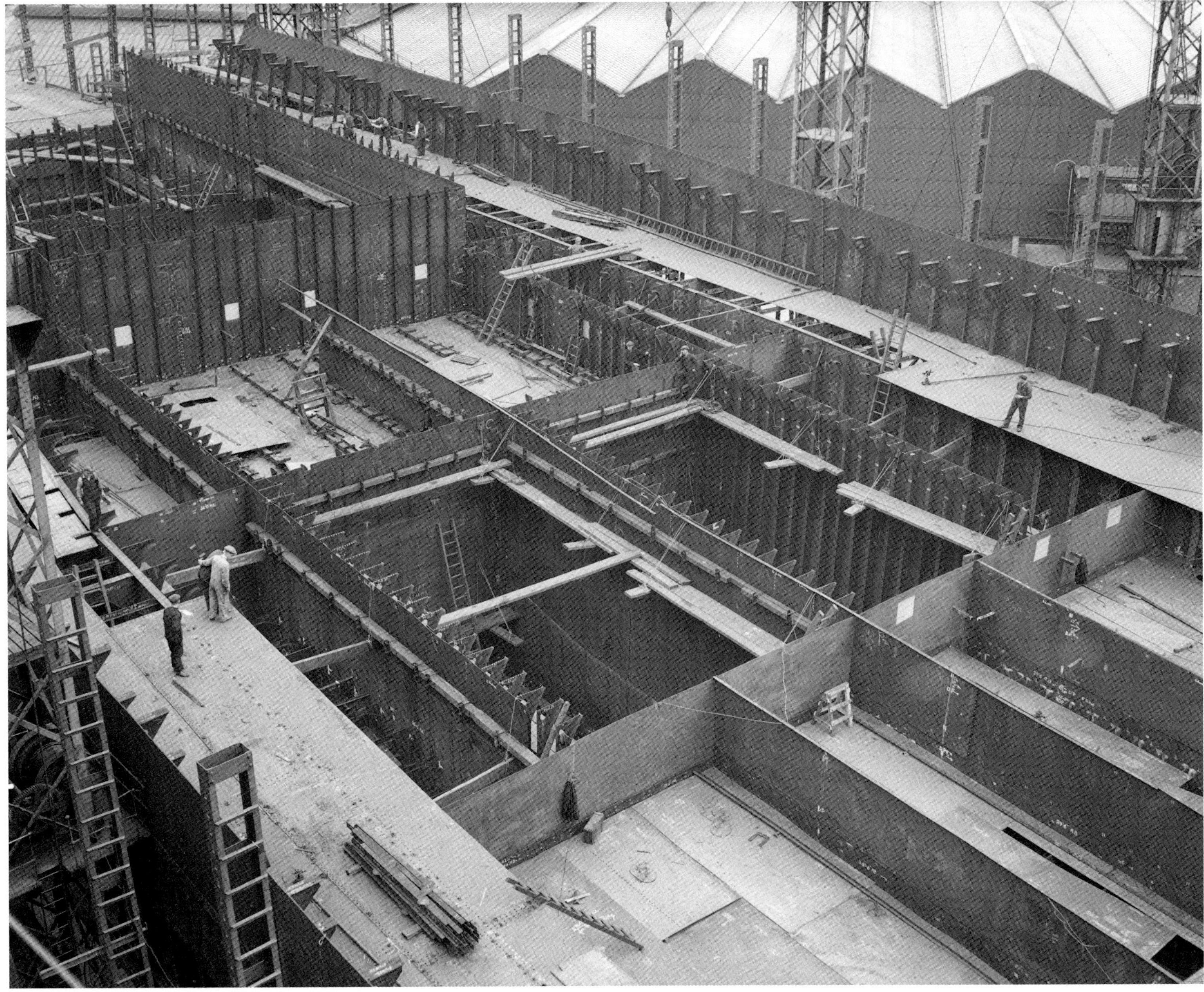

June 1938. Looking forward at the midships area with bulkhead 162 nearest the camera. The spaces immediately forward of that are where 'B' (port) and 'A' (starboard) boiler rooms will be with bulkhead 140 at the far end. The spaces on the other side of bulkhead 140 will be for wireless transmitting stations, fire-control rooms and at the lowest level 5.25in shell rooms and magazines. The deck on which the men are standing is the middle deck which is the upper level of the boiler rooms. The narrow compartments at bottom right are for electrical equipment.

June *Engine Works*

The first HP casing and the third cruising casing are being finally bored, the first LP casing is being prepared for water-test and final turning and grooving of rotors is proceeding. Machining of gearcases and gearwheels is in hand. All boiler drums have been delivered and drilling is progressing [drilling holes for boiler tubes]. Work on oil fuel suctions, heating connections and sea valves is proceeding.

8 July *SDO*

Plans issued to the yard include: auxiliary engine seats in aft engine rooms, sea tubes outside machinery spaces, rapid flooding arrangements (preliminary), arrangement of O.F. [oil fuel] suctions outside machinery spaces, list of heavy watertight doors. Plans of the messing and sleeping arrangements, and also upper deck planking have been submitted. Work is proceeding on the remainder of the ventilation trunking plans, together with ladderway arrangements, skylight details, rearrangement of cabins, auxiliary seats in forward engine rooms, armour arrangement and details, list of valves, pumping etc. The contract for the deck cranes has been placed. Total steel ordered to date about 12,880 tons.

Compartments at Lower and Middle Deck level

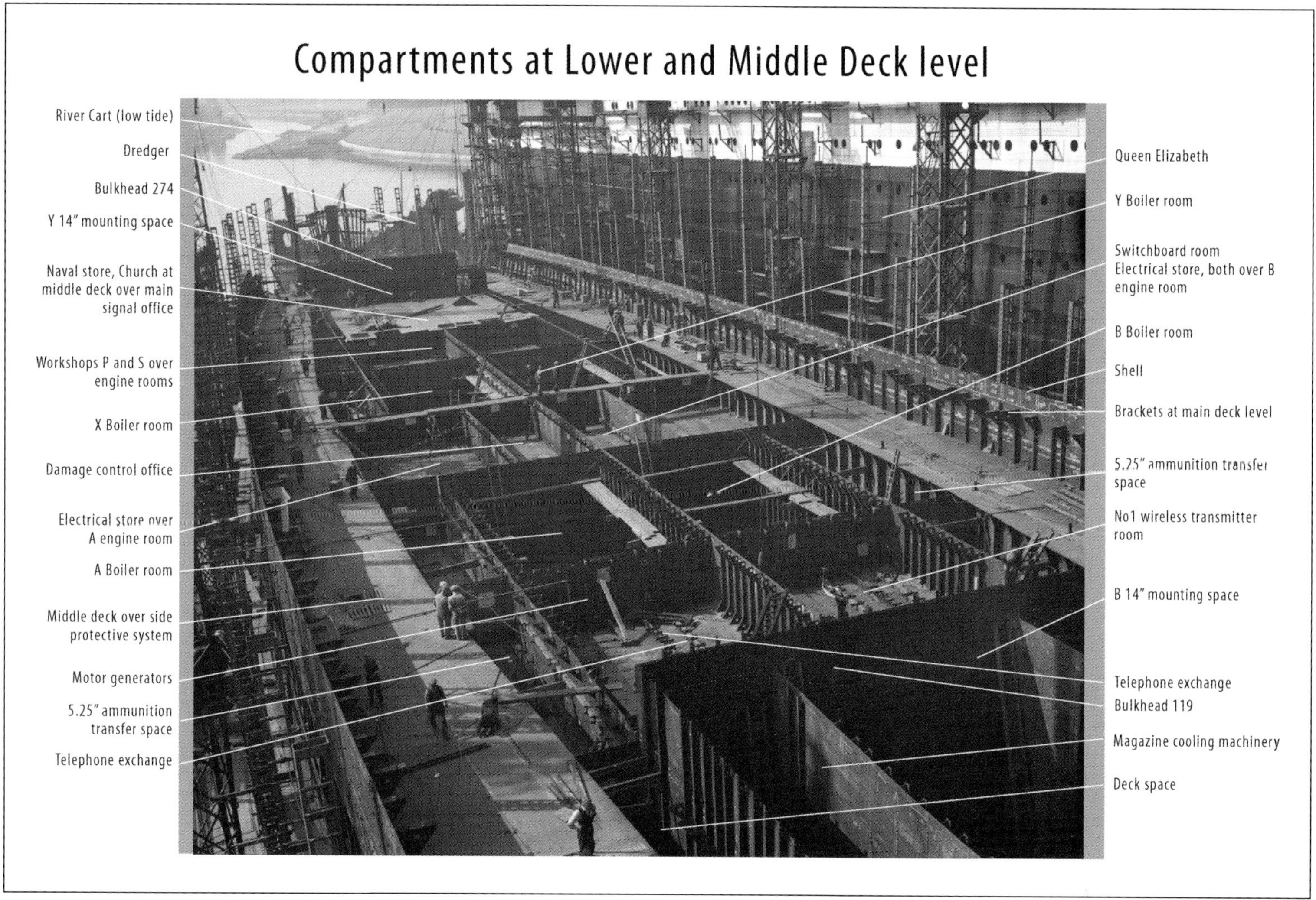
River Cart (low tide)
Dredger
Bulkhead 274
Y 14" mounting space
Naval store, Church at middle deck over main signal office
Workshops P and S over engine rooms
X Boiler room
Damage control office
Electrical store over A engine room
A Boiler room
Middle deck over side protective system
Motor generators
5.25" ammunition transfer space
Telephone exchange
Queen Elizabeth
Y Boiler room
Switchboard room
Electrical store, both over B engine room
B Boiler room
Shell
Brackets at main deck level
5.25" ammunition transfer space
No1 wireless transmitter room
B 14" mounting space
Telephone exchange
Bulkhead 119
Magazine cooling machinery
Deck space

30 July 1938. One month later, this view is looking aft along the middle deck. The plated section running down either side of the hull that men are standing on is approximately the width of the ship's side protective system and gives some idea of its overall width in relation to the beam of the ship. Although not visible under the deck, it comprises the armoured belt (not yet fitted), an outer watertight compartment (air), the outer and inner oil jacket bulkheads with fuel oil between, an inner watertight compartment (air) and the main protective bulkhead. The large compartment at bottom right is for 'B' gun mounting. Note the bucket ladder dredger off the end of the ways deepening the river for *Queen Elizabeth*'s forthcoming launch.

8 July *Shipyard*

Erecting, fairing and welding of flats on platform and upper platform decks and lower decks continuing. Middle deck beams at sides together with stringer plates and deck plates are erected from frame 79 to frame 274; fairing and riveting proceeding. Beams, girders and plating at centre of middle deck are being erected between frames 228 and 253. Lower deck plating from stem to 79 and 274 to stern is erected faired and being riveted. All armour on bulkheads 79 and 274 below lower deck is shipped and secured. Barbette supports below A and Y barbettes are erected and being riveted. The fourth shaft bracket [port outer] has now been received and arrangements for erecting are in hand.

22 July *Board*

The general hull construction is proceeding satisfactorily especially between frames 79 and 274 at which positions the cross bulkheads are now armoured. The erection of the barbette supports and of the barbette under each of the three gun turret positions A, B and Y is in progress. The fourth shafting A bracket has been delivered and arrangement is being made for placing in position. In the engine shops machining is in progress on turbine parts, gearing parts and the drilling of boiler drums.

8 August *SDO*

Plans issued to the yard and include: minor bulkheads main deck, turbo generator seats, key plan of watertight doors, 350 t and 50 t pumping arrangements, list of seacocks, details of storm valves, sea tubes outside machinery space, guard rail stanchions and oil fuel suctions aft. The steam heating arrangements, ventilation arrangements fore end and aft end,

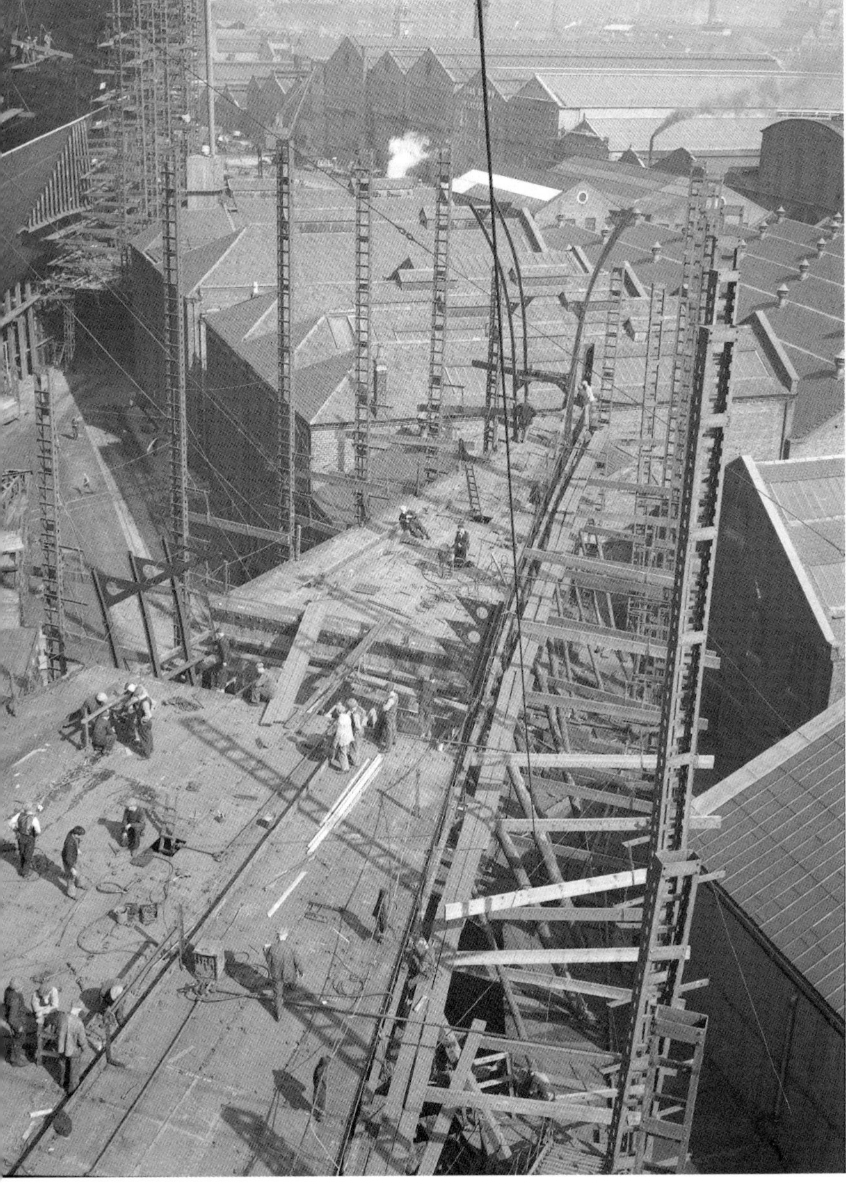

August 1938. Looking forward and down on to the lower deck. The opening on the lower deck bridged by planks is for the anchor cable locker between Frames 27 and 35. The upper platform deck lies below this. On either side, three frames (6in x 3in x 3in channel bars) have been erected, numbers 29, 31 and 33 with brackets in place, which will support the middle deck. At the bow four frames have been erected which show the final height of the hull at upper deck level. The precarious nature of the staging system is well illustrated. There were sixty-three deaths reported in UK shipyards in 1938, many due to falls. Note the symmetry of construction, steelwork prepared for the starboard side was always done in conjunction with the port side equivalent. The four-man squad at centre left are drilling rivet holes, more accurate than punching. Bottom left can be seen rivet guns, compressed-air piping and a welding transformer. Note the roadway between the bow of *Queen Elizabeth* and *Duke of York* which gives a clear indication of the scale of operations in the shipyard. In the background are the shops of the engine works with pitched roofs.

breakwaters and key plan of ladders and hatches have been approved, and advance approved prints of the cabin arrangements have been received. Work is proceeding on the remaining ventilation arrangements and also main deck armour, side armour upper tier, splinter proof plating, boat and shelter deck plating, auxiliary machinery seats and details of valves. The total steel ordered to date is about 13,000 tons.

11 August *Engine Works*

All forgings and castings have been delivered with the exception of one gearcase casting. The first HP casing has been finally bored, the last cruising casing is being finally bored, and grids are being fitted in the second LP casing.

7 September 1938. Looking aft onto the middle deck in the vicinity of Frame 190 and above 'X' and 'Y' boiler rooms. The deck is being plated with 14lb (0.34in) steel plates about 7ft wide. Note how flimsy the steel deck plate appears to be as it is manipulated into position. Note also the template at top right which is for 160lb armoured bulkhead 319.

Three HP, two cruising and two LP rotors have been finally turned and grooved. The second gearcase is being machined and the first gearwheel is ready for turning of rims. All boiler drums have been delivered and drilling is well advanced. Work on boiler casings and condensers is in hand.

7 September 1938. The lower deck aft with one of the first 180lb armour plates being lowered into position by the sheers. The photograph also shows a rivet squad in a confined space riveting the upper palm of the port outer shaft bracket to the structure of the ship.

28 September *SDO*

The plans of the 60lb splinter proof plating have been issued to the yard, also details of breakwaters, sea tubes, auxiliary seatings in harbour machinery room, accommodation ladders, anchor and cable arrangements, scheme of painting and list of details of watertight hatches. The shelter and boat deck steel plans have been submitted to the Admiralty, also sections of the ventilation arrangements. Work is proceeding on the remaining ventilation and air filtration arrangements, also details of magazines, cabin lining, upper tier side armour and various storerooms. Orders have been placed for the capstan gear, cranes, cooling machinery and HP air compressors.

30 September *Board*

The erection of the structure to the lower deck forward and aft of the midship section is well advanced and armour plating on these lower deck portions is in progress of fitting. The erection of the midships structure above the lower deck level is well in progress and the main deck will soon be ready to receive armour plating. Good progress is being maintained with the construction of the main propelling machinery and boilers.

September *Engine Works*

All forgings and castings have now been delivered. Two HP casings and all cruising casings have been finally bored and grooved. Two HP and all LP casings have been rough bored

September 1938. A general view of No 3 berth looking forward with *Duke of York* at middle deck level, lower deck aft. Big as the battleship is, it is dwarfed by the *Queen Elizabeth* painted nearly ready for launching on 27 September. On completion she was the largest ship in the world at 83,600 gross tons or well over three times *Duke of York*'s 24,500 gross tons, i.e. in volume terms.

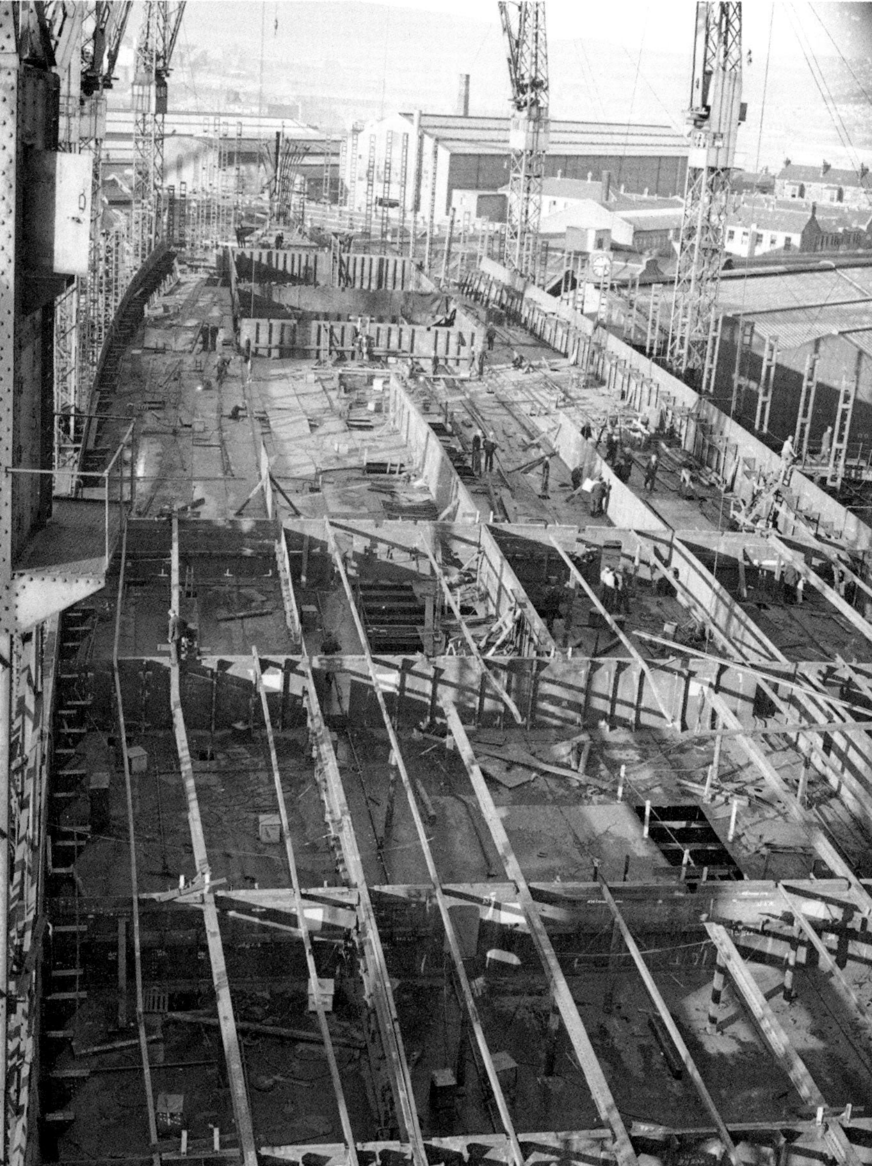

7 October 1938. Looking forward from Frame 240 (just aft of P4 5.25in mounting) across the middle deck with longitudinal girders to support the armoured main deck in place amidships. The two 'box' areas forward are for 'A' and 'B' 14in mountings.

and one of each water-tested. All HP, two LP and all cruising rotors have been finally turned and grooved, and two LP rotors roughly turned. The first gearwheel and all pinions are ready for cutting of teeth. Tube holes have been drilled in all boiler drums and ends are being fitted. Work is in hand at ship on sea valves, oil fuel suctions and heating etc.

24 October *SDO*

The plans issued to the yard include: ventilation arrangements, Section No. 1 [the forward part of ship], list of sanitary fittings, officers' bathrooms, side armour upper tier, key plan of hatches, course of ammunition, also various storerooms. Plans of the upper deck planking and minor bulkheads on main deck forward have been approved by the Admiralty.

24 October *Shipyard*

Work on middle deck beams, plating and girders is now 95% completed between frames 79 and 274. All transverse and fore and aft bulkheading between middle and main decks is in position; fairing and riveting proceeding. Ironworker is engaged on erecting minor bulkheads between lower and middle decks. Piping work, plumbing, and engineering departments, are proceeding on double bottom tanks, and in watertight compartments outside protective bulkheads.

Circa October 1938. Looking aft from armoured bulkhead at Frame 274 (bottom of image) down onto the lower deck which is being fitted with 200lb and 180lb armour plates. The thickness can be gauged from the hatchway with the ladder bottom left. The heaviest plate will weigh 28 tons. Right aft at the stern, six frames have been erected each side. The brackets at the top of the frames mark the position of the upper deck, the final height of the hull. At extreme bottom left an armoured plate, probably 440lb and weighing in the region of 12 tons, is being manoeuvred into position to form part of the armoured bulkhead at Frame 274. Note the lifting eyes on the plate edge. Lifting heavy loads such as armoured plates which could weigh up to 40 tons or more was accomplished by using sheers, steel frames or heavy baulks of timber securely rigged in place. Both lifting methods can be seen in this photograph.

Circa October 1938. In a forest of staging, shores, cranes and guy ropes, this is the same area of the ship as in the previous photograph and taken on the same day but this time looking from the stern forward. The starboard inner and outer shaft brackets are just visible among the clutter. *Queen Elizabeth* is now in the fitting-out basin.

28 October *Board*

The fitting in place of the armour on the lower deck aft and on bulkhead 274 is completing, and start is being made with the laying of the armour on the lower deck forward. The delivery of the forward lower deck armour is practically complete. The midsection of the vessel between bulkheads 79 and 274 is progressing well and the main deck will soon be ready for armour plates. The work of the surveying and testing of the double bottom compartments is proceeding. In the engine shops, machining and testing of turbine casings is proceeding. The hobbing [cutting teeth on a gear wheel on a hobbing machine] of the first of the four main gearwheels has been started and the ends are being riveted to the boiler drums.

October *Engine Works*

The third HP turbine casing and the first LP casing are being finally bored and grooved. The last HP and the second LP casings have been water-tested. Blading of rotors has commenced and also cutting of teeth on first gearwheel and pinions. Riveting of boiler drum ends has commenced.

7 October 1938. The lower deck aft with 180lb armour already fitted, as indicated by the absence of rivets. This photograph shows three armour plates: 400lb (the two rectangular ones) and 440lb (the square one) waiting to be lifted and bolted onto the after side of armoured bulkhead 274 which is immediately to the left but out of view. Note the template showing the position of armour bolt holes for the nearby plate, which would have been prepared in the shipyard and sent to the steelworks, in this case Firth-Brown of Sheffield, where the plate was rolled and machined. The holes in the plates are threaded and will be attached to the steelwork of the bulkhead with armour-quality bolts.

5 November *Shipyard*

Middle deck beams, girders and plating are now erected, and good progress has been made on erecting longitudinal and cross bulkheading on main deck, together with beams and girders; plating is now in position from midship to aft end. Erecting, fairing and riveting of A, B and Y barbette supports continues. In platers' shop good progress has been made on preparing and erecting Y barbette ring bulkhead. Plumbing and engineering departments are engaged on various piping installations throughout double bottoms and oil tanks. Surveying and water testing of the above tanks continues.

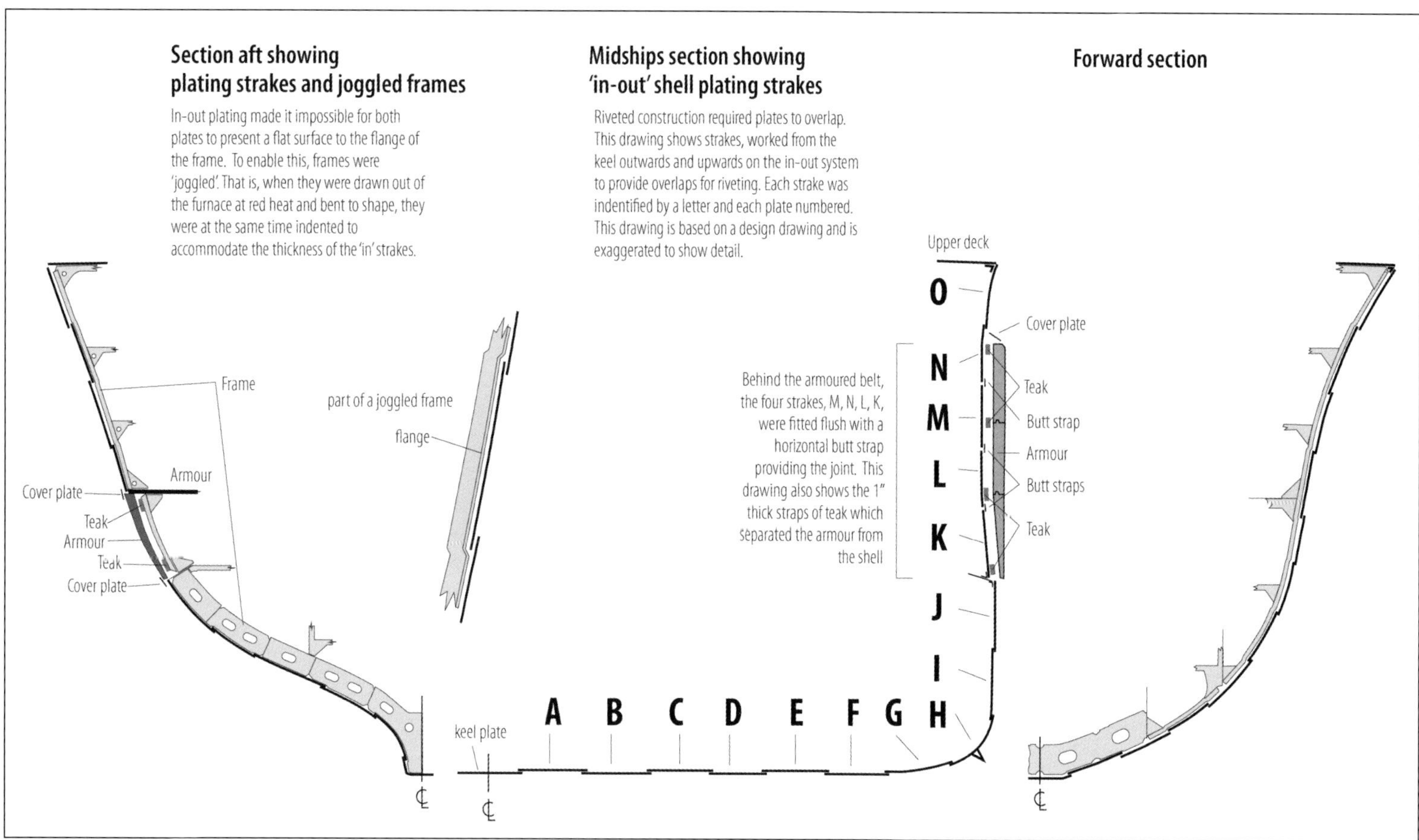
Section aft showing
plating strakes and joggled frames
In-out plating made it impossible for both plates to present a flat surface to the flange of the frame. To enable this, frames were 'joggled'. That is, when they were drawn out of the furnace at red heat and bent to shape, they were at the same time indented to accommodate the thickness of the 'in' strakes.
Frame
part of a joggled frame
flange
Armour
Cover plate
Teak
Armour
Teak
Cover plate
Midships section showing
'in-out' shell plating strakes
Riveted construction required plates to overlap. This drawing shows strakes, worked from the keel outwards and upwards on the in-out system to provide overlaps for riveting. Each strake was indentified by a letter and each plate numbered. This drawing is based on a design drawing and is exaggerated to show detail.
Behind the armoured belt, the four strakes, M, N, L, K, were fitted flush with a horizontal butt strap providing the joint. This drawing also shows the 1" thick straps of teak which separated the armour from the shell
Upper deck
O
N
M
L
K
J
I
H
A B C D E F G
keel plate
Cover plate
Teak
Butt strap
Armour
Butt straps
Teak
Forward section

Armour on lower deck aft is completely erected and erecting of framing superimposed on same is in progress.

8 November *SDO*

The steelwork plans issued to the yard include: funnel bearers and supports, steelwork in forward and after shell rooms and minor bulkheads on middle deck. Plan of shelter and boat deck plating has been approved by the Admiralty, and work is proceeding on the ventilation arrangements and steam heating plans etc. About 13,370 tons of steel material have been ordered.

10 November *Engine Works*

One half of the third HP turbine casing is finally bored and grooved and the first LP turbine casing is being finally bored and grooved. The last HP casing and the second LP casing are being prepared for final boring. Blading of rotors and cutting of teeth in first gearwheel and pinions is in hand. Riveting of boiler drum ends is proceeding and also the work at ship on the sea valves, oil fuel suctions and heating etc.

25 November *Board*

Progress generally on this vessel is satisfactory in keeping with the deferred launching in September 1939. At the aft end of the vessel the fitting of armour plates on the lower deck is completed and also the lower tier of heavy armour on bulkhead number 274. The erection of the ship's structure above the lower deck is in progress at the forward end. The laying of armour on the lower deck is completed and the first tier of heavy armour on bulkhead number 79 is being shipped into position. The armour for the upper tier on both bulkheads 79 and 274 is available for shipping when the structure is suitably advanced and eight out of a total of 166 plates of main deck armour are now delivered in our yard. Of the side armour lowest tier, which is all that can be erected prior to launching, Messrs Beardmore promise to commence delivery in December and to complete by the end of February. The detailing of the hull design is well advanced and approximately 14,000 tons of materials have been delivered of an expected total of about 15,000 tons. In the engine shops the machining of machinery and boiler parts is proceeding.

19 December *SDO*

Steelwork plans issued to the yard include Y barbette armour, supports to No. 4 5.25-inch gun mounting and upper deck in way of funnel casing. The 5.25-inch magazine arrangements and the upper deck planking plans forward and aft, also details of seamen's and boys' wash-places and various plans of store rooms have been issued. Work is proceeding on the ventilation arrangements No. 4 Section [aft], mast arrangements and details, steam heating details, A barbette armour and new plan of houses on upper deck aft and boat deck. The plans of auxiliary seats for X and Y action machinery rooms have been submitted to the Admiralty. Technical particulars for launching have been investigated and plan of internal shoring inside structure has been issued to yard.

19 December *Shipyard*
Middle deck aft portion is now erected and welded and a commencement made to erect main bulkheads in way of same. Shipwright and ironworker are engaged on the erecting of middle deck beams and plating, forward section, which work is now in process of being faired and welded. Ring bulkhead in way of Y barbette is now in position at ship with a view to fairing and riveting, and in ironworkers' shop, work is proceeding on ring bulkhead for A barbette. Water testing of compartments is proceeding satisfactorily.

21 December *Engine Works*
Three HP, two LP and four cruising turbine casings are been finally bored and grooved. Blading of rotors is proceeding and teeth have been cut in one gearwheel and two pinions. Two boilers are being tubed and work is in hand on casings, air heaters and condensers. Fitting of oil fuel suctions, heating connections etc. is progressing.

21 December *Committee*
After considerable delay, the delivery of deck armour for *Anson* has in recent weeks been quite satisfactory.

21 December *Board*
Agreement in duplicate with Admiralty for insurance of HMS *Duke of York* up to £2 million, Admiralty indemnifying the company for any balance.

28 January 1939. This view looking aft shows the ring bulkhead for 'A' barbette in place with armoured bulkhead 79 immediately forward of it. This bulkhead is armoured between the lower and main decks only and the section visible has yet to have its plates fitted on its forward side by the A frame, resting on the middle deck. The deck plating at right is the main deck before its armour has been fitted, which will support the actual barbette armour. A compass trammel-like device has been placed at the centre of the barbette to ensure the accuracy of steelwork. The ring bulkhead has only had its inner cylinder fitted. It will support the whole weight of the revolving gun mounting. 'B' barbette, immediately aft of 'A', is being prepared for its ring bulkhead.

(554) Port. 71
UPPER

23 December *Board*

The laying of armour on the lower deck forward and aft is now completed. The armouring of the bulkhead aft is completed and one half completed on the bulkhead forward. The laying of armour on the main deck will commence on 26 December. Generally the position with the armouring of these decks is satisfactory. The delivery of side armour lowest tier will commence in January and complete in March. The ring bulkhead of the aftermost barbette is now in position and similar work is in progress for the foremost barbette. In the engine works the progress of main machinery and boilers is satisfactory.

Name formally changed from *Anson* to *Duke of York* on 28 December 1938.

1939

14 January *SDO*

Steel plans of the minor bulkheads on lower deck and stiffening under after capstan have been issued, together with B barbette armour [see drawing p52 lower], ventilation arrangements after end, details of ventilation valves and stowage of 2 pounder magazine. Work is proceeding on the sketch of rig, including mast arrangement and details, ventilation arrangements, steam heating, deckhouse on upper deck and minor bulkheads on shelter deck aft. The arrangements of ladderways, auxiliary engine seats in action machinery rooms and arrangement of vent trunks and engine rooms have been submitted to the Admiralty.

19 January *Engine Works*

Blading is completed on the first HP turbine casing and is in hand on the second casing. The last turbine casing, an LP, is being finally bored and grooved. Blading of rotors is proceeding and the first gearcase is being prepared for boring out. The first boiler has been water tested, the third is being tubed, and work is in hand on casings, air heaters and condensers. Fitting of oil fuel suctions, heating connections, sea valves, etc is progressing.

28 January 1939. Looking down at the main deck, the ring bulkhead with both inner and outer cylinders in place for 'Y' gun mounting is in place and the 40lb D quality casemates for P4 and S4 5.25in mountings have been erected. The 240lb main armoured deck is being laid forward and abreast of 'Y' barbette, which will support the heavy barbette armour outside of the ring bulkhead to be fitted after the ship has been launched.

PLUMBER

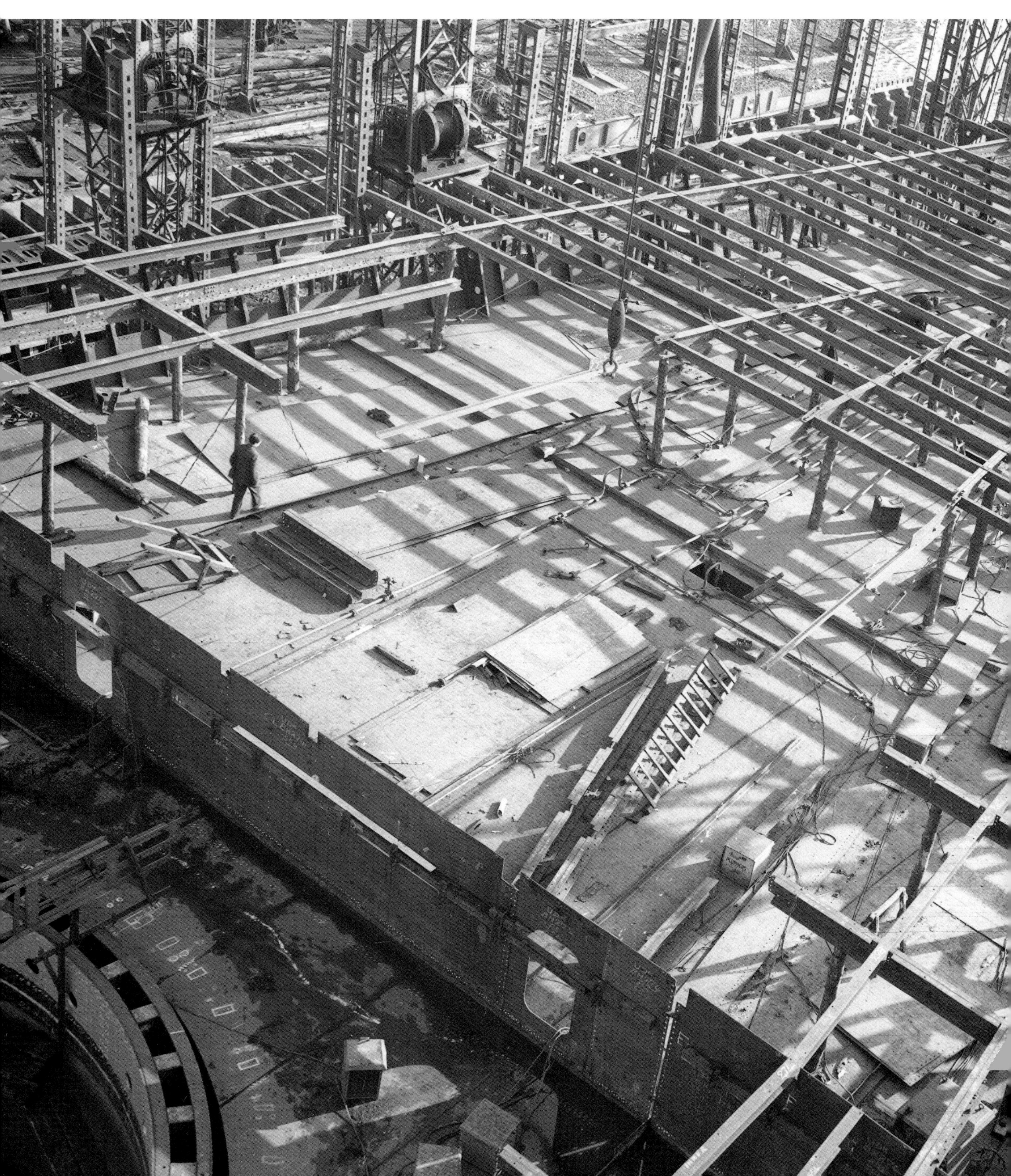

27 January *Board*

The armour plating of the lower deck aft and forward is now completed and the middle deck is erected above this armour. The armouring of the main deck is in progress just aft of midship and the turret supporting ring structure is erecting at both aft and forward end to take Y and A turrets. Generally, the progress is to schedule for a launching of this vessel in September. The progress with boilers and main machinery parts is satisfactory.

18 February *SDO*

Steel plans of deckhouse on upper deck aft, minor bulkheads main deck aft, supports to No. 1 5.25-inch mounting, funnel casings and boiler room vent aft have been issued, also list of watertight doors, detail of chain pipes, upper deck planking and 350 ton [per hour] pump suctions. Plans are submitted to the Admiralty include: ventilation of A, B, X and Y action machinery rooms, mast details and details of holes in armour for vent trunks. The plans of the messing and sleeping arrangements have been approved.

18 February *Shipyard*

Main deck beams, girders and plating are completed from frame 274 to stern, and a commencement has been made by shipwright on erecting of upper deck beams, girders and transverse bulkheading. Good progress has been made on erecting of minor bulkheads on lower and on middle decks, which work is being faired, welded and completed. Y barbette ring bulkhead is now erected, faired and riveted, and work is proceeding on erecting of A barbette, which is now in place, faired and being riveted. Armour supports Nos 1 and 4 by way of 5.25-inch guns, are erected on main deck, faired and being riveted. Finishing trades have commenced work in certain of the ship's storerooms, and good progress is being made by plumbing and engineering departments with rapid flooding installation. A further consignment of eight main deck armour plates are to hand, and arrangements to erect same have been made. There are now 41 armour plates erected on main deck.

22 February 1939. The 8in x 3½in x 3½in channel beams in place at the after end of the hull will support the upper deck. The already plated main deck is immediately below. Bulkhead 274 is at lower left forward of which is 'Y' gun mounting space. The top of the ring bulkhead is just visible, before the roller path is fitted. 'Y' barbette armour will sit on armoured chocks to be placed where marked in white rectangles on the main deck. (See 'B' barbette armour drawing p52 lower for detail.)

22 February 1939. Looking forward over the main deck and the casemates for P1, P4, S1 and S4 5.25in mountings. Abaft 'A' barbette a set of sheers is waiting to be lifted into position. Towards the bow the framing is in position to take the shell plating up to upper deck level.

22 February 1939. A general view of the East Yard showing *Duke of York* on No 3 berth. Reserved by the Admiralty for construction of an aircraft carrier, the 1000-foot long No 4 berth, nearest the camera, lay vacant for over a year after the launch of the Cunard liner RMS *Queen Elizabeth* and it was not until 3 November 1940 that *Indefatigable* was laid down. The joiners' shop is in the block of buildings to the left.

22 February 1939. The port side amidships showing derricks and staging columns. The hull has reached the level of the main deck with frames in place to take shell plating to the upper (and final continuous) deck. Work on the V-shaped bilge keel is underway with the underside 20lb plating already in place. Side armour plates will be fitted outside the grey plated area at right. Note the elevator at left.

22 February *Engine Works*

Blading of the fourth HP casing has commenced and the fourth LP casing is being finally bored and grooved. Blading of rotors is proceeding. The third boiler has been water tested, the fourth is being tubed and work on casings, air heaters etc. is in hand.

18 March *SDO*

The plans issued to the yard include – steel plans of minor bulkheads on middle and shelter decks and shelter deck plating, also details of catapult seats, copper pipe fittings together with cabin arrangements, deck covering plans and arrangement of scupper and discharges. The details of ventilation fittings and arrangement of air-filtration, also support to pom-poms, have been submitted to the Admiralty. Sections 1 and 2 [the forward parts of ship] of the general ventilation scheme have been approved by the Admiralty, and work is proceeding on the remaining sections, also the steam heating arrangements and details.

18 March *Shipyard*

Main deck plating is erected and faired; riveting and welding proceeding. Upper deck beams and girders are erected from stern to midship. Plating of same in hand. Good progress has been made on erecting of minor bulkheads on lower, middle and main decks. A barbette ring bulkhead is in position, faired, and being riveted. B barbette ring bulkhead is in course of erection at ship. 80lb [2in] protective bulkhead at Y barbette is in position and being riveted. The first consignment of ship's side armour has been received, and erection of same has commenced. Surveying and water-testing of oiltight and watertight compartments is proceeding satisfactorily.

22 March *Engine Works*

Blading of the fourth HP casing, the second LP casing and of rotors is proceeding. The fourth boiler has been water tested, the fifth is being prepared for erection, and work is in hand on casings, condensers etc. Fitting of oil fuel suctions, heating connections, sea valves, etc is progressing.

31 March *Board*

We have advised the Admiralty that our schedule provides for the launching of this vessel on 16 September 1939, and await reply. Work on hull construction and the fitting of armour in position is satisfactory. In our engine shops the progress is to schedule.

24 April *SDO*

Plans issued to the yard include the piping for fresh and salt water services, steel plans of minor bulkheads, main deck, and arrangement of various storerooms. The sketch of rig and the ventilation arrangements, Section 3, have been submitted to the Admiralty. Work is now proceeding on the new plans of the messing arrangements, also rigging warrant, ventilation details and specification of upholstery. The details of the forward poppet structure for launching have now been issued to yard. [Poppets were temporary wooden structures which transmitted the weight of a ship's narrow section fore and aft to the launchways – see photo on p103 bottom.]

24 April *Shipyard*

Upper deck beams, girders and plating from stem to B barbette are now in position: fairing, adjusting and riveting is proceeding. Work is also proceeding in completing all 'tween deck minor bulkheads and on lower middle and main decks. All 80lb protective bulkheads are in position and riveted. Main deck armour with the exception of one plate, is delivered, erected and secured. [Excluding those over machinery spaces to allow for shipping.] Satisfactory supplies of ship's side armour are to hand, and work is proceeding on erecting same. A commencement has been made to erect the large planing machine on Y barbette.

23 March 1939. A view looking aft from the position of 'A' barbette. The upper deck is in place from the stern to midships and about to cover the casemates for the foremost 5.25in mountings. A set of sheers has been stepped immediately aft of 'B' barbette, probably to lift main deck armour plates. On the port side between 'A' and 'B' barbettes, a small rectangular section of the main deck is being water tested to check for leaking rivets.

24 April *Board*

Work on the main gun barbettes is well advanced and the armour plating of the main deck is nearing completion. Also the protective armour surrounding the smaller main deck gun[bay]s is well advanced. The structural work on the deck just above the main armoured deck is now well in progress. The supply of the lower strake of side armour is satisfactory and the plates are being fitted in position. In the engine and boiler shops the progress of work is satisfactory on turbines, gearing and boilers.

28 April *Engine Works*

Blading of all HP casings is almost completed, and blading of LP and cruising casings and of rotors is proceeding. The second gearwheel is being set up for cutting of teeth. Casings are being fitted on the fourth boiler and eight superheaters have been choked, water tested and put in position.

24 May *SDO*

The following plans have been issued to the yard: boat deck plating, forward superstructure and bridge, hangar roof, ventilation arrangements – Section 4, messing and sleeping arrangements, protection rings to shell hoists and various storerooms. Sketch of rig and ventilation arrangements, Section 3, have been issued to the yard.

24 May *Shipyard*

Upper deck plating is now in position from stem to stern; riveting and welding proceeding. All transverse and longitudinal bulkheading between main and upper decks is erected; riveting proceeding. In ironworkers' shops, work is proceeding on superstructure bulkheading, and a commencement to erect same has been made at ship. Good progress is being made on structure in way of Nos. 2 and 3 5.25-inch gun supports. Erecting of ship's side armour continues, and deliveries of same are keeping step with our ability to erect this armour. A commencement has been made on the lining-off and fitting-out of storerooms, magazines and shell rooms. Surveying and water testing of underwater compartments making good progress.

26 May *Board*

The upper deck plating is now in position from stem to stern and welding and riveting is now proceeding; the transverse and longitudinal bulkheading between the main and upper decks is in a position. Good progress is being made with the fitting in position of the lower tier of deck side armour. In the engine shops the blading of turbines and the hobbing of gearing parts are in progress.

31 May *Engine Works*

The blading of the 2nd HP casing and the 1st LP casing is completed and being tipped, and blading of the other casings and rotors is progressing. Teeth are being cut in the 2nd gearwheel and have been cut in two sets of pinions. Work is in hand on boiler casing etc., the 5th boiler is being tubed and the 6th prepared for erection, and condensers are being machined. Fitting of oil fuel suctions, heating connections and sea valves on board the vessel is in hand.

31 May *Committee*

Minutes of meeting held on Thursday, 4th of May, were read, approved and signed. Sir Stephen Pigott's report, dated 30th of May, was read, special mention being made regarding the weight of the turrets for the *Duke of York* and the lifting capacity of the West Crane. [Uprated in April 1938 from 150 tons to 200 tons.] Also, we are concerned by the recent report that the mid and heaviest section of the turrets for the *Duke of York* has worked out in designing considerably in excess of the early estimated weight. It now appears that the bare weight will be about 205 tons, whereas our West Crane which must take these lifts, is designed for 200 tons. The crane, after overhaul, was tested with a weight of 225 tons and we are confident that with the exercise of great care these turret parts can be satisfactorily handled.

24 June *SDO*

Plans issued to the yard include cabin arrangements, sundry storerooms, list of doors, details of fresh water arrangements, skylights, platforms in shell rooms and sea tubes for magazine cooling. The upholstery specification has been submitted to the Admiralty.

24 June *Shipyard*

A commencement has been made to erect superstructure at ship, where the after portion is in position, and being faired and riveted. Work is also proceeding in our ironworkers' shops on bridges and a commencement to fit foundation work at ship has been made. Pads for armour chocks in way of A, B and Y barbettes are fitted at ship. Shipwright is engaged on fitting weather deck fittings, including bollards and fairleads, and a commencement to fit deck planking on upper deck has also been made. Final delivery of main deck armour outside fore and aft bulkhead has been made, and the last plate has been placed in position on ship, enabling upper deck to be closed over. Erecting of ship's side armour continues satisfactorily [lowest strake]. Shipwright is engaged on preparations for launch.

28 June *Engine Works*

Blading of all the casings and rotors for the first and second sets has been completed and is proceeding on the remainder. Teeth are being cut in the third gearwheel and last set of pinions, and last gearcase is being bored out. The sixth boiler is being prepared for a water test, the seventh is being erected for tubing, and diaphragms are being fitted into condensers. Boring out of stern tubes has been completed for port inner and outer shafts and the boring gear is being shipped on the starboard side.

30 June *Board*

The fitting of the lower tier of side armour is progressing satisfactorily with nine plates yet to fit out of a total of 64 plates which must be in place before launching. This work will be

completed by the end of August. The launching of this vessel is provisionally fixed for 16th September, but this date cannot be confirmed until about the end of July. I have submitted to the Controller that if this launch is not to be a special feature, it is possible that we may desire to consider a later launching to remove the anxiety caused by certain uncertainties of progress with the work on other contracts.

11 July *Shipyard*

Commencement has been made to erect forward superstructure in way of bridges at ship. Good progress has been made on barbette ring bulkheads. Rough machining is completed on Y and machining work is proceeding on A whereas machining on B armour chock pad is in hand. Hawse pipes are fitted, enabling hull to be completely plated which work is in hand. Electrical department is engaged on fitting boxes etc., for ring mains. Piping installations by plumbing department and engineering departments continues satisfactorily. Fitting of ventilation trunking is proceeding.

27 June 1939. Both starboard anchor hawse pipes in position, fixed at the upper deck but awaiting the shell plating to be cut to shape in the steelworking shops and fitted. The hawse pipes have been cast in steel with holes showing where they will be riveted to the shell. Note the painted rivet heads on shell plating indicating that they have been counted off and can't be counted again. Most riveters worked on piecework rather than time work, meaning they were not paid a fixed hourly wage but paid by the amount of work done, i.e. by the number and size of rivets driven.

27 June 1939. Looking forward across the upper deck from the position of S4 5.25in mounting, the boiler room vent for the aft funnel is to the left. The two cylindrical objects in the centre are oil fuel heaters for the boiler rooms. A start has been made on the forward and after superstructures while the barbette planing machine is on deck in pieces being prepared for lifting into 'A' barbette. Note the sheers stepped on the port side deck edge, probably for lifting the lower strake of side armour plates, and heavy posts rigged to lift heavy items onboard. The elevator beside the sheers has a narrow gangway leading to the deck edge. This gangway does have handrails. *Queen Elizabeth* in Cunard colours is in the fitting-out basin.

29 July *Board*

By letter of the 10th instant the Board of Admiralty approve of the launching of HMS *Duke of York* on 16th September and intimate that Her Majesty the Queen will perform the launching ceremony. We had hoped that it would be possible to limit our guests on the occasion of this launching to a number which could be accommodated for refreshments in our shipyard tracing office but, under conditions which must now obtain, it seems that the use of the mould loft is essential, and arrangements made to protect, by covering, any work there now in progress. The progress with the work which must be accomplished before the launching is satisfactory. Our schedule provides for all plates of the lower strake of side armour being secured in position by the end of August and commencement has been made with the fitting of stern tube bushes in position preparatory to the shipping of propeller shafts. Also, the work of fitting all underwater valves and other connections is well advanced.

11 September *SDO*

Plans issued to the yard include: lower bridge plating, upper bridge plating, lagging and lining, list of watertight doors, also various offices, storerooms and workshops throughout the ship. The ventilation arrangements of hangars and magazines and also air filtration system have been submitted to the Admiralty.

11 September *Shipyard*

Riveting and welding of longitudinal and transverse bulkheads between main and upper decks is well advanced. Forward and after superstructure bulkhead is in course of erection; riveting and welding proceeding. Deck pads in way of armour chocks of A and B barbettes are now machined, preparatory to receiving circular armour protection. Good progress is being made by finishing trades on magazine and shell rooms and store rooms. Lower tier of side armour is in position and secured. All water testing below main deck is completed. Launch arrangements are well advanced.

14 September *Engine Works*

The first and second sets of turbines have been shop steamed [at low pressure not working pressure], clearances are being taken in the third set and blading of the fourth set has been completed. Teeth are being cut in the fourth gearwheel. All boilers have been water-tested, work on casings is proceeding and the last condenser is being tubed. All propeller shafts, propellers and sea valves have been shipped ready for launching. [The photo on p104 shows the propellers.] Fitting of oil fuel suctions, heating connections and the shipping of auxiliary machinery is in hand.

14 September *Committee*

On 4th September we were advised by telegram from the Controller that the launching arranged for 16th September must be postponed and that the Admiralty had advised Buckingham Palace. In his confirming letter the Controller asked that we would, in due course, propose a suitable later

date. We are now advised that the delay in supply of armaments will defer the handing over from the contract date of January 1941 to the now proposed date of August 1941. We consider that the *Duke of York* can usefully be retained upon the building berth for several months during which time work will proceed on magazines, store rooms, officers' accommodation, crew's quarters, auxiliaries, electrical equipment etc. And in fact, it would now seem desirable that the launching be deferred until the *Fiji* leaves our basin for drydocking trials and handing-over. We are hopeful that this may be accomplished by early January at latest. It is even possible that the launching could be delayed until the *Queen Elizabeth* is removed from our basin, provided that this removal is accomplished in February. With Board concur-

27 September 1939. In this view the massive planing machine sitting in what will become 'A' barbette is making the preliminary machining of the surface for the rollers supporting its 40ft-diameter turntable. After launching, the planing machine will be used again to plane the top surface of the roller path on top of the circular ring bulkhead parallel to the other mountings and directors. Originally intended to be launched on 16 September 1939, for which the hull had been painted and the launch poppet structure (just visible towards the bow) fitted to the hull, launching was delayed until February 1940. This brought the ship into line with the reworked timetable for delivery of the main armament and also enabled the Cunard liner *Queen Elizabeth*, seen in the background, to be completed and removed from the fitting-out basin, thus making way for the battleship.

rence, we would prefer to allow conditions to develop more fully before proposing a new date for launching.

29 September *Board*

With the 14-inch gun mountings more than a year late as now promised, the launching of this vessel is not urgent, especially as work on such parts as magazines, officers' and crew accommodation and electric wiring, also the fitting of deck armour can be carried out equally well with the vessel on the building berth. Accordingly, it is now our intention to defer the launching of the *Duke of York* until the *Queen Elizabeth* is removed from our basin. The arrangements for the expected launching on 16th September were necessarily virtually completed when we were advised of cancellation. It has been found necessary to dismantle all stands and the bow end of the launching ways in order that work on other contracts will not be impeded. In both Shipyard and Engine Works the progress with the work on this contract is being scheduled in keeping with the deferred completion dictated by delivery of armaments.

10 October *SDO*

The plans of the hull structure and the superstructure are generally complete, and the various detail prints such as the magazine and shell room arrangements, store rooms, and various fittings are now being issued.

10 October *Shipyard*

Riveting and welding of minor bulkheads on main deck forward is well in hand. The remainder throughout the ship, except in way of loose work, is completed. [Loose work is structure only temporarily secured which will be finally fixed once items below have been installed.] Watertight doors are being fitted on middle and main decks. Splinter protection plating is being fitted to Y barbette. Shipwright is engaged on laying deck planking on upper deck aft. Good progress has been made by finishing trades in store rooms, magazines and shell rooms. Flooding and hosing of compartments continues satisfactorily.

27 September 1939. The after superstructure is well advanced. The sheers at extreme right have been stepped to lower equipment into 'X' engine room. The opening for S4 5.25in gun mounting is being worked to ensure circularity while the circular angle bar for S3 mounting is being riveted to the deck and to which the casemate will subsequently be riveted. Note the ladder being lowered into the hatch right aft The top of the lower strake of the armoured belt shows its true thickness of 14.75in (600lb); the teak backing strips to support the upper strakes are already in place.

Their Majesties The King and Queen
having graciously consented to attend
the naming and launching of
His Majesty's Battleship "Duke of York"
by
Her Majesty The Queen
at Clydebank Shipyard
on Saturday, the 16th September 1939, at 3.15 p.m.
The Chairman and Directors of John Brown and Company Limited
request the honour of the Company of
Mr. John Brown and Lady.
to witness the Ceremony.

Clydebank
August 1939

RSVP to The Secretary
John Brown & Co. Ltd.
Clydebank, Dumbartonshire

With reference to your kind acceptance of invitation
to witness the launching of
His Majesty's Battleship, "Duke of York,"
at Clydebank, on the 16th September,
The Chairman & Directors of John Brown & Company,
regret to advise you that arrangements for this
launching are necessarily cancelled.

September 1939. The invitation, and subsequent cancellation notice, to the launch of the ship on 16 September 1939 showing just how far advanced preparations were when the launch was postponed. John Brown was a naval architect with the company, though no relation to the founder. It would be another five months before the event took place.

13 October *Engine Works*

The two lower tiers of the aft funnel have been shipped. The third set of turbines has been shop steamed and the fourth set is being prepared for steaming. Boilers and condensers have been completed and put out to storage. [See photo opposite, bottom.] The fitting of oil fuel suctions and heating connections and the shipping of auxiliary machinery is in hand.

13 October *Committee*

As reported at our committee meeting on 14th September, the progress of work on the *Queen Elizabeth* had been curtailed through the necessity of more fully manning the cruiser *Fiji*, the destroyer depot vessel *Hecla*, the escort destroyers *Fernie* and *Garth* and the battleship *Duke of York*. It was not, however, until the receipt of a letter from the [new] Controller, [Vice] Admiral Fraser, on 20th September, that question was definitely raised concerning the policy to be adopted with this vessel. By letter of 21st September we made submissions to Admiral Fraser that we be authorised to fully complete the *Queen Elizabeth* without further delay. In reply, Admiral Fraser could then only authorise that the work proceed with the reduced numbers of tradesmen then employed.

25 October *SDO*

The plans of the hull structure and the superstructure are generally complete, and the various detail prints such as the magazine and shell room arrangements, store rooms, and various fittings are now being issued. Consideration is being given to elimination of copper and aluminium as far as possible.

25 October *Shipyard*

'Tween deck structural work including minor 'tween deck bulkheads is proceeding methodically. Erecting of those armour plates which were not delivered for the mid-September launch are in hand. Various trades are making good progress in store rooms, magazines and shell rooms.

27 October *Engine Works*

The last set of turbines has been shop steamed and is now being examined and closed-up ready for storage.

27 November *SDO*

The plans of the steel structure are practically complete and the plans now being issued including: paravane arrangements, magazine arrangements and the final sections of the ventilation arrangements. Gas organisation arrangements are in hand. Plans are being prepared for revised internal shoring at launch to allow for the shipping of boilers.

27 November *Shipyard*

Riveting and welding of bulkheads on main deck forward is well in hand and minor bulkheads are now being erected, in way of portions of main deck inside 25-feet bulkhead where armour has recently been laid. NC protection to gun machinery compartments in way of 5.25-inch guns is being erected, and splinter protection plates are being fitted in way of a B and Y barbettes. Surveying and flooding of compartments above lower deck continues. Shipwright is making good progress on laying of wood on upper deck aft, laying off and fitting out of storerooms, magazines and shell rooms. Cabins in mess spaces are being lined off and good progress being

October 1939. Although dated October, this photo must have been taken earlier as no launchways are in evidence. Fixed in three places with eye bolts and shackles, the rudder is about to be lifted up and into position on the cast steel stern frame. The rudder framework, manufactured at Beardmore's Parkhead Forge, comprised a cast steel frame which weighed 29.3 tons, which was then filled with slab cork, plated over and riveted. It required modification at Rosyth to strengthen it and change the area ahead of the stock. The rudder was of 360ft^2, operating up to 35° either side. The man standing might be the foreman shipyard engineer.

18 October 1939. All eight Admiralty three-drum boilers, built in the boiler shops at Clydebank, sitting by the fitting-out basin near the 150-ton derrick crane that would have shipped them had the ship been launched. With the launch delayed and work building up in the boiler shop, there was no option but to clear the boilers out of the shop and store them as seen here. A protective canopy has been built to shield them from the worst of the weather. In the end the decision was made to ship the boilers with the hull still on the building berth. Since the declaration of war on 3 September, the *Queen Elizabeth*'s Cunard colours have been painted out in grey. The top section of her aftermost funnel has still to be fitted.

18 October 1939. Two condensers, one each for 'A' and 'B' engine rooms, being moved near the fitting-out basin for temporary storage until the ship has been launched. The bottom of the condenser is parallel to the keel; the slight rake on the top surface is to match the rake of the propeller shaft and turbine. The white items at left look like boiler room fans. *Duke of York* is visible in the background as is one of two elevators used to lift men and small items of equipment to various levels of hulls under construction. The sandbags appear to be part of a lookout position probably for Air Raid Precautions (ARP) personnel in the event of air attack as the shipyard would have been a priority target for the Luftwaffe. In the event heavy air raids did not occur until March 1941.

24 October 1939. Great activity is evident in this photograph looking west down the River Clyde. No 2 berth in the foreground has the depot ship *Hecla*, *Duke of York* is on No 3 berth, No 4 berth is being prepared for the fleet carrier *Indefatigable* to be laid down on 3 November and lastly the *Queen Elizabeth* in the fitting-out basin in the process of having Cunard colours painted out in grey. A small hopper barge is visible at her stern. The quarterdeck of the battleship is being planked with 2½in-thick Borneo white hardwood. Her boilers can be seen by the fitting-out basin underneath a temporary shed.

made by electrical, plumbing and engineering departments, on their various installations. Work is now proceeding on stripping vessel over aft boiler room, with a view to shipping boilers before launch.

30 November *Engine Works*

Work is progressing on pipe arrangements and certain systems are almost completed. Platforms and gratings are well in hand. Auxiliaries in the wing machinery spaces are being put on board prior to shipping of main boilers which are now being prepared for shipping. The fitting of oil fuel suctions and heating connections is progressing.

1 December *Board*

The deferring of the launching of this vessel until the *Queen Elizabeth* is removed from our basin has slowed down progress with construction. With the delivery of main armament expected as late as mid-summer 1941, we were satisfied that the vessel would be ready for the armament even with the launching deferred. It is now expected that the armament will be delivered early in 1941, and to meet such earlier date we have arranged to ship the boilers with the vessel on the building berth. With boilers in position, decks can be closed and protective deck armour placed in position. It is proposed to launch the *Duke of York* immediately the *Queen Elizabeth* has left the basin. [*Queen Elizabeth* left the shipyard on 26 February 1940.]

13 December *SDO*

Work is now concentrated on equipment plans which are in an advanced stage. Paravane arrangements, offices and store rooms, magazine arrangements and the final sections of the ventilation are being issued. Plans of rigging and mast details are being prepared to suit revised radio direction finding equipment [RDF i.e. radar].

13 December *Shipyard*

Work is proceeding on riveting and welding of bulkheads on main deck forward, and also on minor bulkheads in the way of portions of main deck armour which have recently been laid. Splinter protection is being erected in way of A, B and Y

September 1939. The turbine and gearing set for the port outer shaft comprising the HP (at left) and LP and astern turbines (at right) with condenser below (not visible). The turbines are as yet unlagged. The cruising turbine is at the far end of the HP turbine. Note the much larger bolts securing the upper casing of the HP turbine (400lb/in^2) compared with the LP (about 25lb/in^2). The turbines have been set up for light steaming: the large diameter exhaust pipe at top left being part of the temporary arrangement, as it would normally connect to the top of the LP turbine. This low-powered trial turned the machinery over and checked clearances and balancing, after which the turbine set was dismantled into several parts and transported the short distance to the fitting-out basin, to be shipped after launch. The coupling for the propeller shaft is visible at the near end below the timber staging.

barbettes. Cabin and mess spaces are being lined off. Electrical, plumbing, and engineering departments are making good progress on their various installations. Diesel generators with auxiliaries are shipped. First boiler was shipped in after port boiler room on 8th December and the second boiler on 10th December. Subcontractor has commenced installing after capstan. General progress of vessel is satisfactory.

15 December *Engine Works*

Diesel generators [two at 300 kW each] and three boilers have been shipped in aft boiler rooms.

27 December 1939. A three-drum boiler being lifted onto the ship by sheers on the upper deck. Of the three strakes of armour that will form the ship's belt, the lower one is already in place while the timber fixed to the ship's side indicates where the other two strakes will be located. Behind the timber, the ship's shell is complete, the armour belt not being a structural part of the hull.

27 December 1939. An atmospheric view of the boiler raised up to upper-deck level against a backdrop of cranes, guy ropes and the funnels of *Queen Elizabeth*. It will be lowered into position in the boiler room below in a series of well-planned, slowly and carefully enacted moves.

22 December *Board*

Four of the eight boilers are now in position aboard this vessel and the erection of bulkheads and closing of decks above these boilers is in progress. Two further boilers will be in position by the end of this week and the remaining two will be shipped before the end of this month. Work on the several pipe systems, the electrical outfit, plumbing, etc is progressing satisfactorily. The present expectation is that this vessel will be launched on 28th February. Tidal conditions on the 29th also suitable for the launching if, for any reason, launching on the 28th is not suitable. In keeping with wartime regulations, the ceremony will be confined to a short religious service and the naming of the vessel entirely without the usual attendant launching function.

1940

31 January *Shipyard*

Minor bulkheads on upper deck are 95% completed. Plymax bulkheading in way of same is about 50% completed. Splinter protection being fitted in way of A, B and Y barbettes. Supports to 5.25-inch guns are being erected, faired and riveted. Wood planking is being laid on upper deck aft, and good progress is being made by shipwright in magazines and shell rooms and by finishing trades in storerooms. Re-erecting of loose work in way of boiler rooms is nearly completed, and it is expected that this work will be faired and riveted by the middle of February. The launch arrangements are well forward.

2 February *Engine Works*

Diesel generators and auxiliaries in wing machinery spaces and all eight main boilers have been shipped. The fitting of oil fuel suctions and heating connections etc is progressing.

Early February *Board*

All eight boilers are now in position onboard this vessel and the re-erection of loose ship construction in way of the boiler rooms is nearing completion. With earlier delivery of armament now promised, it is essential that this ship will be afloat in our basin early for the shipping of the main machinery, armament etc. Accordingly, it is now arranged that the launching will be performed on 20th [*sic*, actually 28th] February at about 4:30 PM (summer time). In keeping with wartime regulations, the ceremony will be confined to a short service followed by the naming and launching of the ship.

21 February *SDO*

Revised data for launching with increased armour weights and outfit has been prepared. It is under consideration to alter the

27 December 1939. The heavy planing machine at work in 'A' gun mounting space. This machine was manufactured by Thomas Shanks & Co engineers and manufacturers of heavy machine tools at their works in Johnstone not far from Clydebank shipyard. It weighed approximately 70 tons, so had to be erected in parts. The purpose of this machine was to plane level the structural steel surfaces that the main-armament turrets revolved on. A high level of accuracy was pivotal in operation of the main armament. Evidence provided by these photographs indicates that this was a two-stage process the planing machine being first used while the ship was on the building berth to rough plane the roller path that will support the 1582-ton revolving weight of a 14in quadruple mounting. After launch, the planing machine will again be used, this time to fine plane the bed on which the roller path casting supporting a series of tapered steel rollers will be laid such that the whole mounting will revolve smoothly on a perfectly level surface parallel to the other mountings and main directors. This surface can be seen at the right side of the machine while the adjustable cutting heads are at the extreme left-hand side. Note the winch at top left and piles of timber props most likely to be used for internal shoring of the hull prior to launching.

January 1940. Working from the outside to the middle, the quarterdeck is being planked. According to the specification the wood is Borneo white hardwood. The planks are generally 2½in thick by 7in wide and 24ft long. They are bolted with a nut on a threaded stud welded to the deck and the holes subsequently plugged. What is odd about this photo is the apparent light colour of the wood. On closer inspection, the original scans being very high resolution, it appears that the deck is covered with a thick frost. Where the deck has been covered at bottom right, and the cover removed, the true tone of the wood can be seen. The standing ways have been left in place after the launch was postponed from September.

general arrangements to suit flagship, and this will involve sundry modifications to plans as already prepared.

26 February *Shipyard*

Plymax bulkheading to 'tween decks is about 60% completed. Re-erection of loose work in way of boiler rooms is completed and riveted as far as necessary. Plating in way of engine rooms etc. is being secured with a view to strengthening for launch. Bridge structure is being erected. Good progress is being made by shipwright and joiner departments on lining-off and fitting-out of storerooms, magazines and shell rooms. The various piping installations are proceeding normally and progress is being made with vent trunking. Launch arrangements are well forward.

28 February *Engine Works*

All sea connections and stern-work is complete ready for launch. All turbines and gearing are ready for shipping.

28 February *Committee*

The launching of this vessel, long overdue and now necessary for the maintaining of our promised completion, is scheduled for about 4.45 this afternoon. The launching will be performed by Her Majesty in the presence of His Majesty. In keeping with wartime regulation, this function will be largely informal and simple. All eight boilers are in position and the decks in way of the boiler rooms are now plated. The main propelling machinery is ready for shipping aboard. It is now expected that the armament will be delivered during the early months of 1941.

Launching

Launching is a potentially hazardous operation for getting a hull from a slipway to the water. Over the years many mishaps have occurred, from collapse of the launchways and serious damage to the hull to the ways catching fire to capsize once afloat. Shipyards evolved successful launch techniques based on calculation and experience, making preparations long in advance of the anticipated launch date. Clydebank's practice had been honed by the successful launches for *Queen Mary* and *Queen Elizabeth*, with twice the launch weight of *Duke of York*. An appropriate declivity (slope) of both the building berth and the launchways plus adequate height of tide was necessary so that as the hull travelled down the launchways, its aft end picked up buoyancy and lifted before the hull's

Large openings inside the hull meant that the structure at launch was less rigid than in service. To mitigate undue deformation of the hull from the heavy loads imposed by the launchways and the poppets during the travel, heavy timber shores were fitted inside various compartments and spaces throughout the hull to distribute the loads. The original drawings dated 11 months before launch shown here give some indication of how this was done.

No 554.
INTERNAL SHORING FOR LAUNCH.
SCALE 1/8" = 1 FOOT.
SHEET 2 – SECTIONS.

Right above, Shoring 01: Title piece.

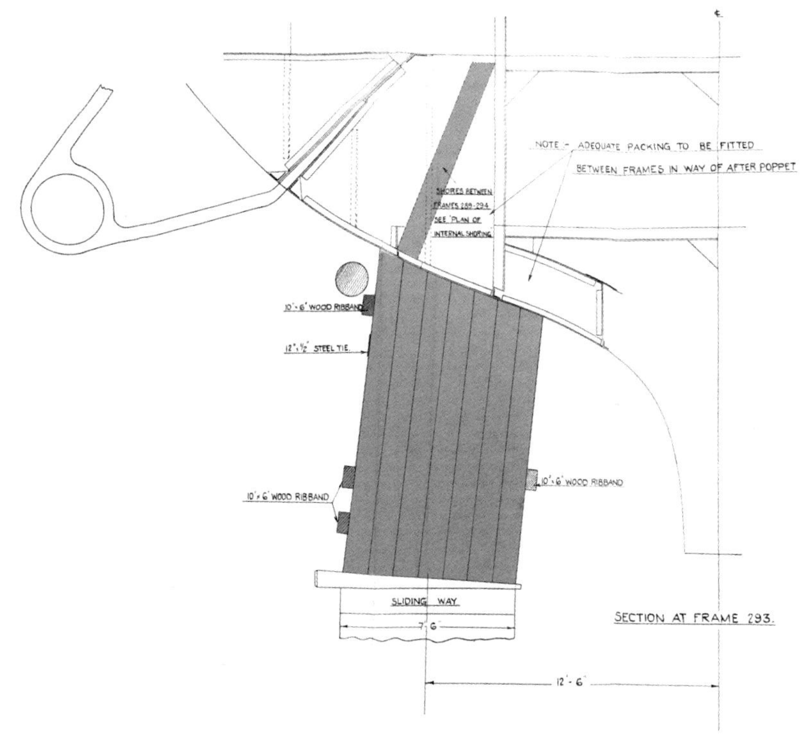
NOTE – ADEQUATE PACKING TO BE FITTED BETWEEN FRAMES IN WAY OF AFTER POPPET
10'×6' WOOD RIBBAND
10'×6' WOOD RIBBAND
10'×6' WOOD RIBBAND
SLIDING WAY
SECTION AT FRAME 293.
12'-6

Right, Shoring 03: This drawing shows the after poppet at Frame 293 and the shore in the compartment above. It also shows the inner shaft and the shaft bracket for the outer shaft with its lower palm. See also the photo on p69.

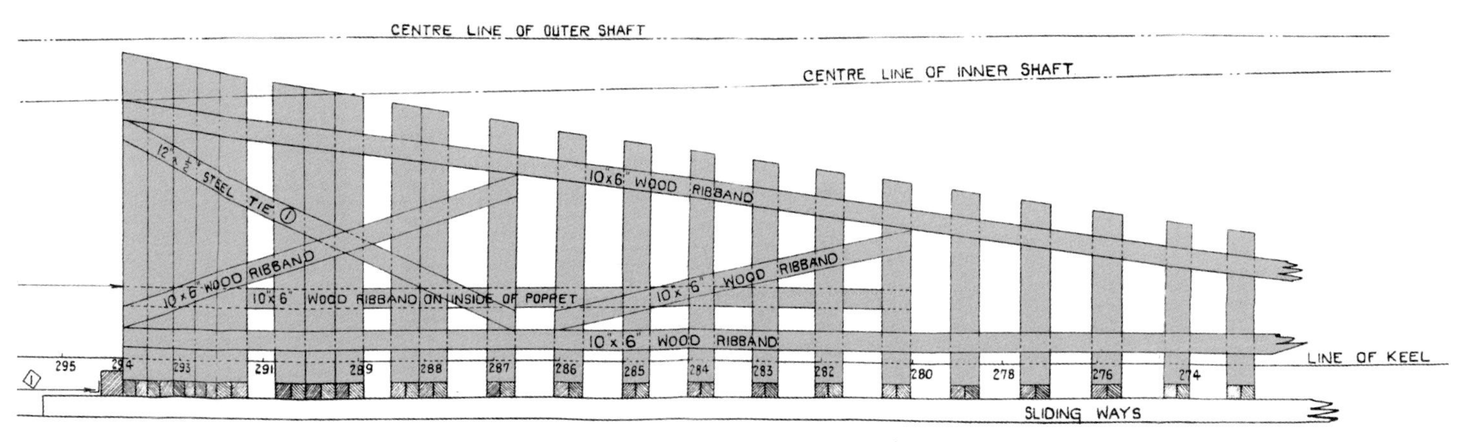
CENTRE LINE OF OUTER SHAFT
CENTRE LINE OF INNER SHAFT
10x6" WOOD RIBBAND
12"x½" STEEL TIE
10x6" WOOD RIBBAND
10x6" WOOD RIBBAND ON INSIDE OF POPPET
10x6" WOOD RIBBAND
10x6" WOOD RIBBAND
LINE OF KEEL
295
294
293
291
289
288
287
286
285
284
283
282
280
278
276
274
SLIDING WAYS

Below, Poppet 01: This original drawing (shaded for clarity) shows the construction of the port after poppet. The starboard one was similar. Note the frame numbers on the drawing indicating very careful positioning. The internal structure of the hull above the poppet was reinforced with timber shores to ensure there was no deformation of the structure when the weight of the hull was transferred to the poppets. The sliding ways bear on the standing ways as seen in the photo on p104.

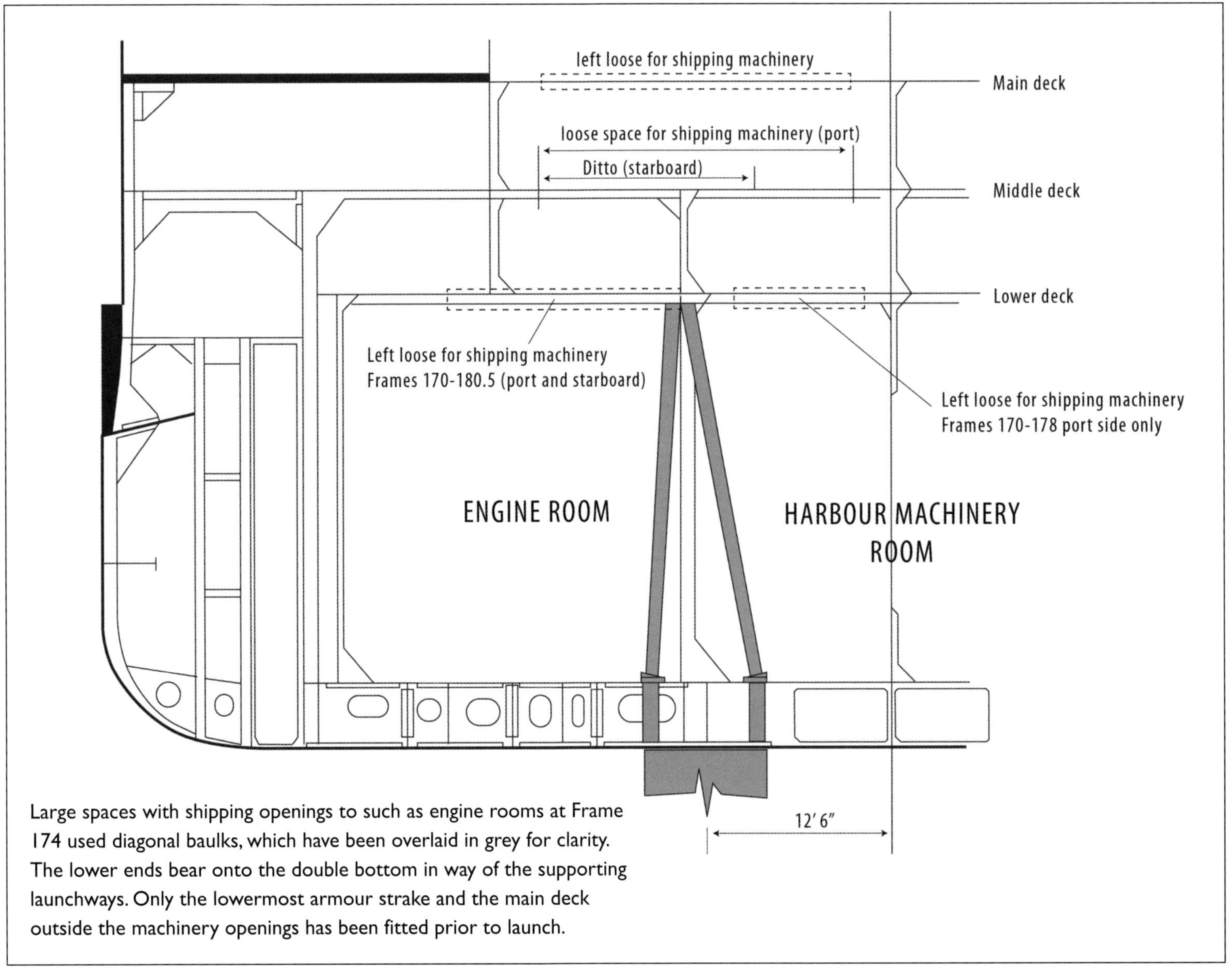
left loose for shipping machinery
Main deck
loose space for shipping machinery (port)
Ditto (starboard)
Middle deck
Lower deck
Left loose for shipping machinery
Frames 170-180.5 (port and starboard)
Left loose for shipping machinery
Frames 170-178 port side only
ENGINE ROOM
HARBOUR MACHINERY
ROOM
12′ 6″

Large spaces with shipping openings to such as engine rooms at Frame 174 used diagonal baulks, which have been overlaid in grey for clarity. The lower ends bear onto the double bottom in way of the supporting launchways. Only the lowermost armour strake and the main deck outside the machinery openings has been fitted prior to launch.

centre of gravity passed over the end of the standing ways, a potential tipping point. Once the stern lifted, the fore poppet formed a pivot point taking a heavy load. That structure not only had to be strong enough, but also served to transfer the weight at the fine ends of the hull to the wider launchways. Moderate launchway pressure (hull weight divided by area of the sliding ways) was a key factor, as was a suitable weight of drag chains to slow the hull after it had entered the water and avoid it hitting the other bank. A high tide was important but even so river bed dredging might be necessary to avoid any part of the hull touching the bottom. Launching arrangements of major warships had to be approved by the Admiralty.

A note made by Admiralty officials attending the launch and subsequently included in the Ships Cover read:

Arrangements for the launch followed the usual Clydebank practice for vessels of this size. A preliminary consideration of transverse strength indicated that the vessel could be carried on two ways with no anxiety whatever on account of the overhanging side armour weights. The lowest tier was in position together with all deck armour clear of machinery spaces. The fore poppet was of the usual Clydebank design with steel brackets riveted to the shell, and a shelf plate to take the heads of the timber poppets. The vessel was fully shored internally in way of the poppets and over the midship region with particular attention to the anticipated position of maximum pressure on the hull as it passed over the way ends. The vessel was launched successfully, and a subsequent examination of the structure and shoring indicated that no undue stresses or distortion had been experienced.

Duke of York was launched by HRH Queen Elizabeth who is seen here with King George VI making their way to the launch platform. Sir Stephen Pigott, Managing Director of the shipyard, is immediately behind the Queen while Winston Churchill, then First Lord of the Admiralty, is behind the King. The Chairman of John Brown & Co Ltd, Lord Aberconway, is to the right of the King. All work stopped in the yard to enable employees, at that time about 10,000, to watch the launch. Note the railway lines set into the ground for moving material, both standard gauge and narrow gauge.

The estimated launch weight of No 554 in tons was made up of:

Hull structure	9573
Incidental fittings	762
General fittings	312
Paint & cement	10
Armour	5097
Protective plating	1371
Machinery	600
Internal shoring	150
Shipyard plant	150
Water ballast	593
Total	18,615

The massively-constructed forward poppet on the port side photographed by the shipyard photographer but also the subject of a movie film crew and other unidentified personnel. It was one of four poppets, two located forward and two aft, whose purpose was to support the ends of the hull during the launching run, always the most critical event in the building of a ship. The design of the poppet comprised heavy baulks of timber (typically 12in square) within a steel frame, with brackets riveted to the shell. Once the ship was in the water the wooden structures could float free and be recovered. The poppet structures were all fixed to the hull above the waterline so could be removed without the assistance of divers. The light-coloured ribband shows where the sliding ways bore on the standing ways. Note the raised strakes of plates running to the bow, a feature evident only at this area of the hull, with those seams which will be underwater smoothed off with composition. Note also the anchor point in the foreground with a pulley which will be connected to a winch on the ground and, at the other end, to a crane or lifting beam.

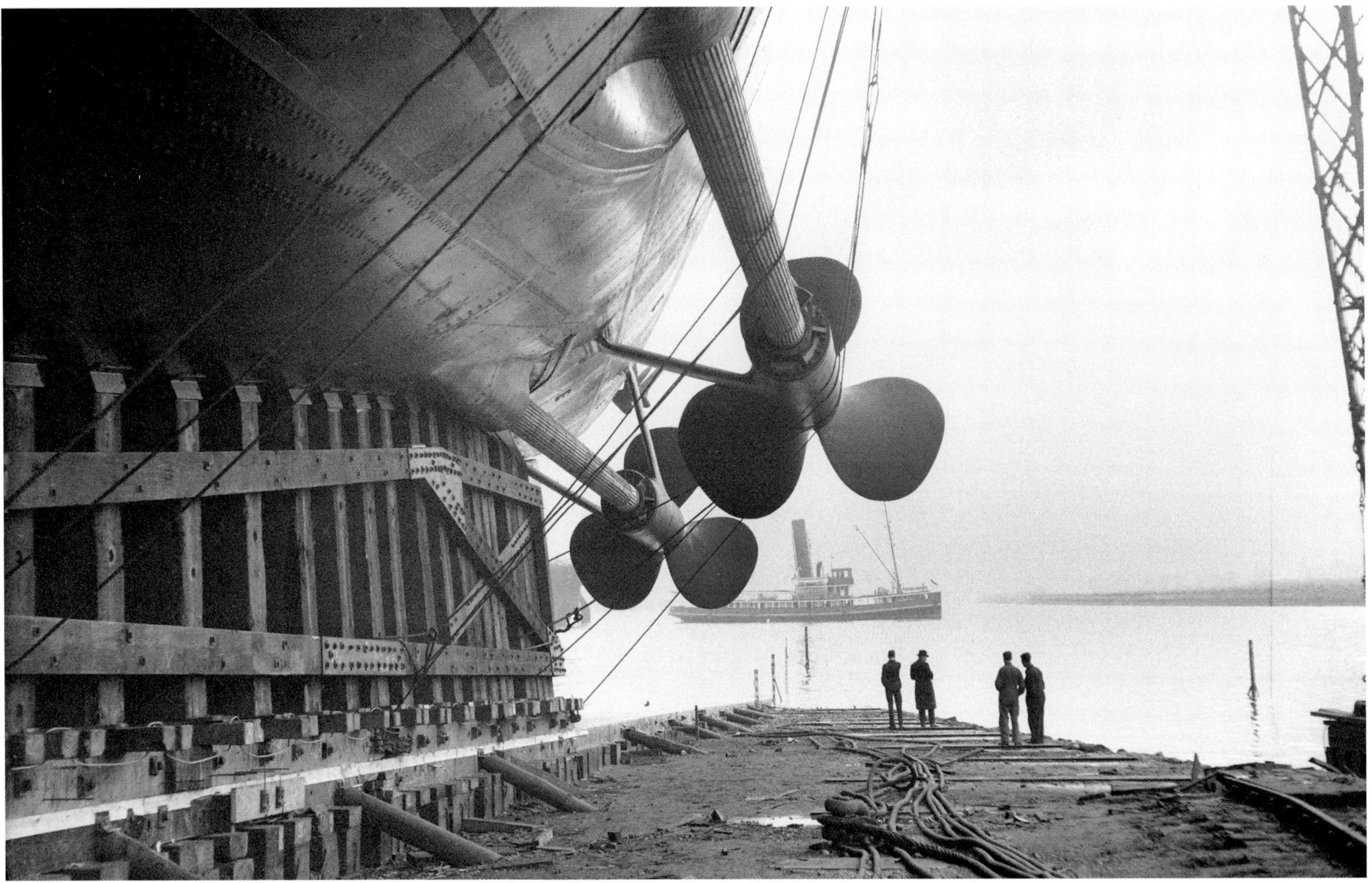

This was about 500 tons more than *King George V* and about half the finished weight of the ship. The actual weight at launch was 18,852 tons plus 480 tons of poppets and sliding ways.

Launching particulars

Overall length of ship as measured	745ft 0⅝in
Draught forward	12ft 11in
Draught aft	19ft 11in
Declivity of launchways	5/16in per foot (1 in 32)
Length of standing ways	821ft
Length of sliding ways	576ft 6in
Aft end of sliding ways to end of standing ways	244ft 6in
Average pressure on ways	2.24 tons/ft^2
Max pressure as middle of hull passed over way end	6.03 tons/ft^2
Depth of water over ways end	9ft
Travel to stern lift	605ft
Maximum load on fore poppet	4000 tons

The shipyard measured time and travel during launch and breakage (deflection) of the hull – 1.5in along the length when afloat. They also set up stress measuring points; three on the upper deck and one on the tank top close to 'B' mounting.

The port after poppet inboard of the inner shaft sitting attached to the sliding ways, resting on the standing ways 7ft 6in wide spaced 25ft apart on No 3 berth. (See also the poppet drawing on p101.) The tug *Paladin* is standing off the ways with a ship in tow. Note the wire ropes running from the poppet up and over the shafts, which enable the poppet structure to be pulled clear of the hull after launch. All four three-bladed 14ft 6in diameter propellers have been fitted prior to launch, each transmitting 27,500 shp at 236 rpm and weighing 14 tons, This image adds a great sense of scale with the figures standing close by and also illustrates the vulnerability of the propeller shafts to torpedo attack in particular. In December 1941 sister-ship *Prince of Wales* was lost primarily because the explosion of a torpedo against the port outer shaft broke the shaft bracket causing the shaft to distort and run free, opening up watertight glands and bulkheads inside the hull. The progressive flooding as a result was the single most important cause of her sinking.

The ship would hog during launch with ends drooping slightly, causing tension in the upper deck. The Cambridge recording instrument showed no more than a modest 1.65 tons/in^2 for the tank top, but as the shipyard had forgotten to renew the recording film in the upper-deck instruments, none of those were recorded. Modern shipyards use building docks so simply floating a ship out is a much less stressful operation.

The bow showing both forward poppets and how they transfer the weight of the narrow forebody out to the launchways. They also form a pivot point as the after end of the hull gains buoyancy. According to the date on the negative this was the day of the launch although there is clearly some work to be done removing the staging at the bow and hauling up the Jacob's ladder and there is no evidence of the launch platform off the port bow. So it was obviously taken sometime previously, possibly in early February 1940. Although the design of the *King George V* class was criticised for a lack of sheer forward, the hull did have pronounced flare as seen here.

Below: At 4.45 pm on Wednesday 28 February 1940, the launching triggers were released and over 18,800 tons of *Duke of York* began the short journey into the River Clyde. She is seen here part way down the slipway gathering speed to the tune of 'Rule Britannia' played by the shipyard band. Note the drag chains in the foreground which will be pulled into action to slow the ship down once she is in the water. The depot ship *Hecla* is just visible on No 2 berth.

Flying the Union flag and John Brown's house flag, *Duke of York* is brought from the river into the fitting-out basin where she will spend the next 18 months. At least four coal-fired tugs were in attendance with *Flying Eagle* at the port bow and *Paladin* alongside. The hull had been painted six months previously in anticipation of the original launch date and is now looking rather worn and faded. The forward draught reads 13ft, whereas the highest mark shown is 35ft. The fore poppet brackets are well above the waterline, so were removed soon after.

·A·R·P· DUTY POST
FIRE FIGHTING
Nº10

The *Duke of York* was launched at the height of the so-called 'Phoney War' when little by way of armed conflict was happening on land. Nevertheless the shipyard had to be protected like other major industrial enterprises in the UK. This sandbagged ARP post, one of many in the yard, was set up by the port forward poppet. Air attack finally came 13 months after this photograph was taken with widespread devastation in the town of Clydebank but only minor damage in the yard. Note that the bulkhead structure in the foreground is welded rather than riveted.

6 March 1940. One week after launch, fitting out what is still largely a steel shell is well under way. Some of No 554's turbines and gearing appear to have already been shipped, as decks are now being plated over where previously left loose. Staging has been erected down the starboard side in readiness for fitting the side armour plates. In the background, the collier *Bushwood* is being converted to a degaussing vessel.

Fitting Out

1 March *Board*

Her Majesty the Queen, in the presence of the King, graciously performed the naming and launching of this vessel at about 4:45 PM on 28th February. With the delivery of armament now promised at the beginning of 1941, it is essential that the work on the vessel must proceed without further delay. All eight boilers are in position and the propelling machinery is ready for shipping onboard. Only the lower strake of side armour was in position at the launching, but all the remainder is available for proceeding with the [middle and upper] side strakes and the remaining deck armour. [The lower armour strake was largely below water so had to be fitted before launch.]

26 March *SDO*

It has been decided to fit the vessel as a fleet flagship and the necessary modifications to arrangement, piping, ventilation and structural plans are in hand.

26 March *Shipyard*

Vessel was safely launched at 4:45 PM on 28th February.

Immediately after launch, ironworker proceeded with work of dismantling steel structure in way of poppets, opening up of decks etc., in way of machinery rooms forward. General structural work is proceeding and splinter protection in way of A, B and Y barbettes, supports to Nos. 2 and 3 5.25-inch guns, boiler room casings, vents and bridge structure. Finishing trades are engaged on storerooms, magazines and shell rooms which work is proceeding satisfactorily. Commencement also has been made on erecting of ship's side armour.

29 March *Engine Works*

All shafting, main thrust block, main and auxiliary machinery has been shipped in B engine room also auxiliaries in harbour machinery room. Shafts are being shipped in A engine room and pipe arrangement work in engine and boiler rooms is proceeding.

29 March 1940. The after superstructure is now being built up with some machinery installed. Visible as dark squares are the three after funnel uptakes (the large opening at centre and the pair forward and next to bulkhead 187) and the two after boiler room air downtakes at either side. The catapult machinery will be shipped in the open space to the right. Across the basin are two 'Hunt'-class destroyers, *Fernie* and *Garth*.

29 March *Board*

With this vessel now in our basin, the shipping of machinery is proceeding and a start has been made in the shipping of the mid and upper strakes of the ship's side armour. This armour on the starboard side will be put in position with the vessel on the east side of our basin following which the vessel will be moved to the west side of the basin for the shipping of the port side armour. [Actually fitted at east side after turning the ship.] She will then remain on the west side for the shipping

25 April 1940. This view taken from the 150-ton derrick crane looking aft shows that the quarterdeck has been planked up to and alongside 'Y' barbette. The other most notable feature is the deep shafts into the hull where the armament, main and secondary, will go, especially the 42ft-diameter opening for 'Y' mounting. The part of the superstructure with beams erected includes the various officers' galleys and shipwright's workshop.

25 April 1940. Looking forward, the most obvious feature is the massive ring bulkhead planing machine in 'A' barbette preparing the support for its gun mounting which will be one year away. Note the smaller planing machine at work in 'B' barbette. The hatchways at left where the two men are standing are for embarking ammunition, the nearest cordite for 'B' mounting, the further shells for 'A' mounting. There is little evidence to show that laying the wooden deck forward has begun, with no planking stored on deck or welded studs.

of the main armament and until completion. [See pp142–3 for actual movements.] It is now decided that the *Duke of York* will be completed as flagship similar to the *King George V*. This entails alterations to accommodation to provide for some 25 additional officers and about 75 of other ranks.

15 April *SDO*

It has been decided to fit the vessel as a fleet flagship and the necessary modifications to arrangement, piping, ventilation and structural plans are in hand. Proposals for stiffening of rudder, as a result of experience of other ships in service, are under consideration.

15 April *Shipyard*

Closing in machinery spaces has commenced, which will enable further progress to be made on bridge structure. Work is proceeding on 5.25-inch gun supports, casings in way of boiler rooms and 'tween deck structure in way of same. Good progress has been made on erecting ship's side armour, 20 plates being placed in position since vessel was launched.

17 April *Committee*

The main propelling machinery together with auxiliaries, thrust blocks and intermediate shafting, have been shipped in A and B machinery rooms, these forming the port and starboard outer sets, and the closing in on the decks is now in

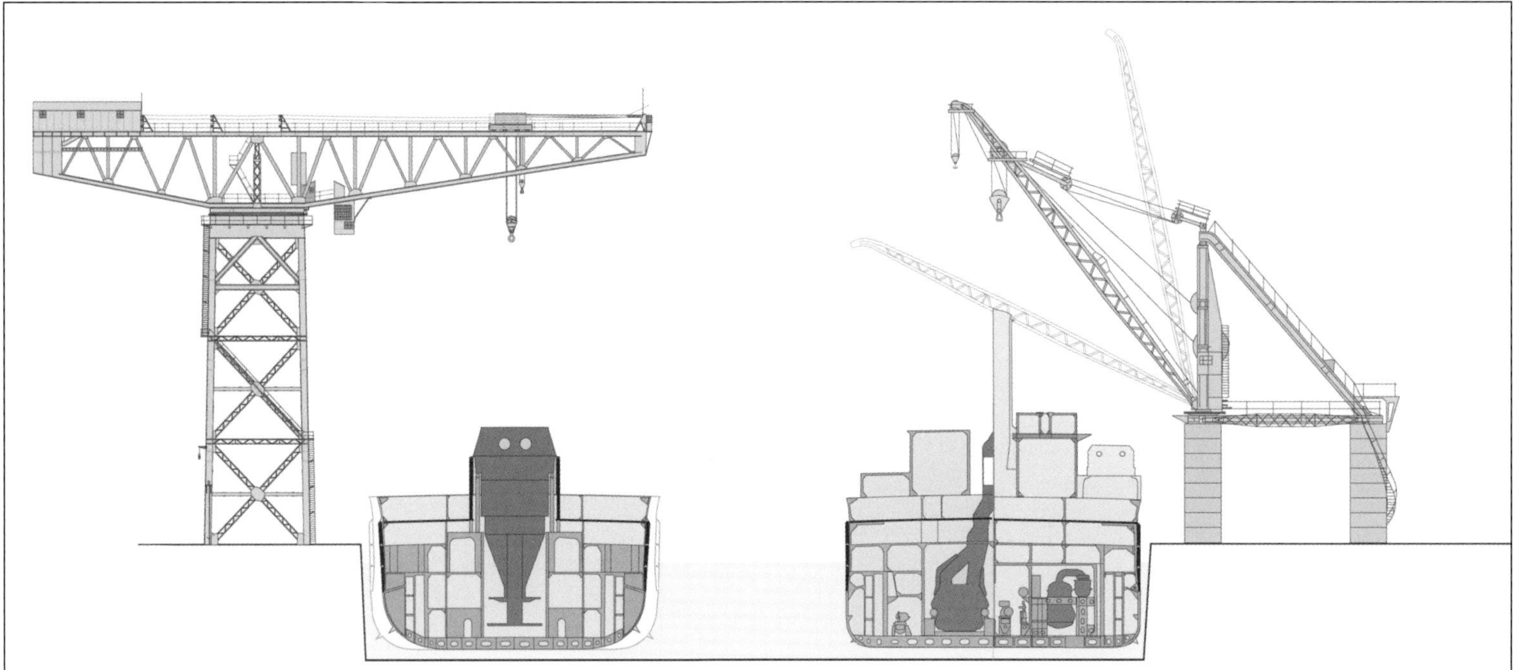

A cross section through the fitting-out basin at Clydebank looking to the head of the basin showing both heavy fitting-out cranes. At left, *Duke of York* under the 200-ton cantilever crane in position above 'B' turret. Of the two heavy cranes, this was the only one capable of lifting the 200-ton turntables of the 14in quad turrets. At right, the ship is under the 150-ton derrick crane which carried out the bulk of the heavy lifts including machinery (illustrated) and armour, the exception being the main gun mountings.

progress. Commencement has been made on the bridge structure and on the supports for the 5.25-inch guns.

26 April *Board*

The progress with this ship is satisfactory. Since launching on 28th February some 24 side armour plates have been put in position and commencement made on the bridge structure and on the seating for the 5.25-inch guns.

3 May *SDO*

Detailed plans for permanent degaussing of the vessel have now been received and will shortly be issued. Additional watertight subdivision in the form of intermediate bulkheads

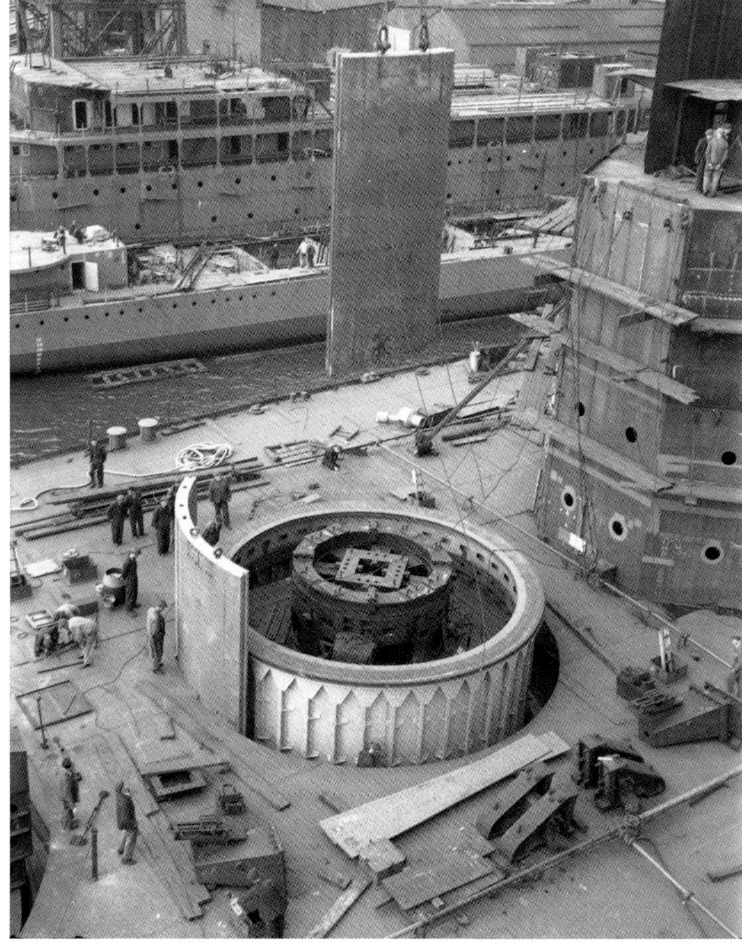

June 1940. This photograph shows the cemented armour Plate No 8 of 'B' barbette 520lb (12.7in thick) weighing 44 tons being lowered into position to join the two others already fitted. (See barbette armour drawing, p52 lower.) Altogether there will be eleven plates 20ft 5in high to form the armoured barbette. Note the substantial ring bulkhead already in position which will support the 898-ton twin mounting. The core of the barbette planing machine is inside the barbette with various other components from this device lying on deck. The depot ship *Hecla* and the newly-launched destroyer *Piorun* (ex *Nerissa*) are at the west side of the fitting-out basin. *Duke of York* has been turned 180° to be bows-out to allow the derrick crane to plumb 'B' barbette.

June 1940. All 'B' barbette armour in position; 29ft 6in inside diameter. Note the 'keys' which are slotted into the vertical channels locking each plate together are waiting to be cut flush with the finished top of the barbette. The different thickness of the armour can just be made out: the plate on the centreline is 2in thinner than those on the sides where the likelihood of a hit is greater. Immediately aft of the barbette are various items of equipment including kit lockers waiting to be taken into the forward superstructure where the main galleys are located. These images present many riddles to solve all of which made perfect sense at the time the photographs were taken. One of these riddles is the purpose of the two long 'booms' on the starboard side.

is being fitted on lower deck aft and temporary bulkheads are being arranged on middle and main decks for junior and warrant officers whose cabins are on lower deck.

3 May *Shipyard*

Good progress has been made in closing-in forward machinery spaces, and loose work in way of aft engine room is being stripped for the purpose of shipping main machinery. Ironworker is engaged in erecting bridge structure which work is being faired and riveted. Finishing trades are engaged on lining-off mess decks and middle deck amidships and forward of which work good progress is being made. 40 armour plates on the middle and upper tiers of starboard side armour are now in position, leaving 12 to complete.

3 May *Engine Works*

Main and auxiliary machinery thrust blocks and all shafting have been shipped in A and B engine rooms. Work on pipes and connections is proceeding in engine and boiler rooms.

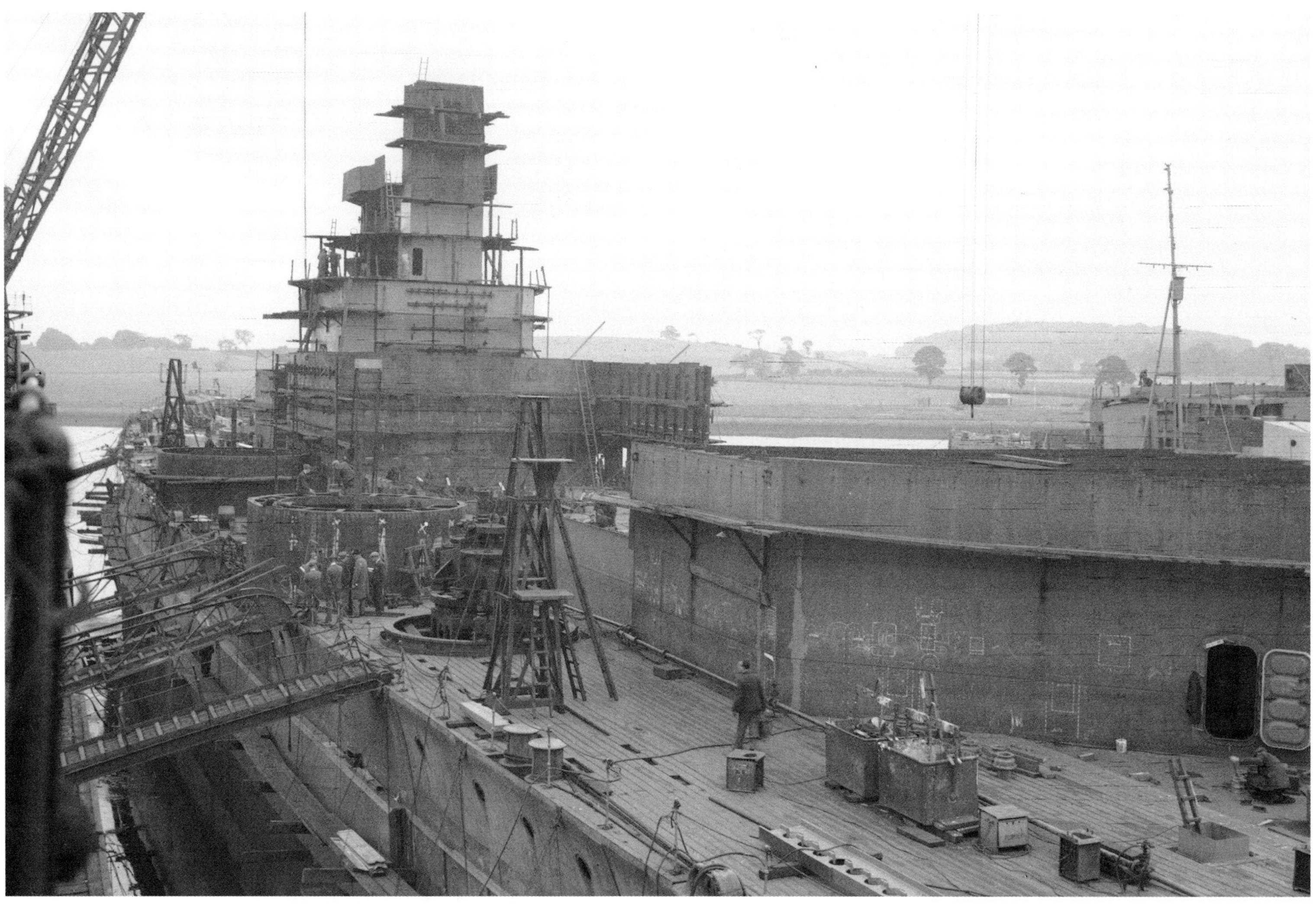

June 1940. With the ship turned bow outwards into the Clyde, this view shows work well advanced on the forward superstructure. Note that she is lying some way off the quay side with staging rigged down the hull side to allow fitting the armoured belt. Several top strake plates have yet to be added which will take the belt further aft to 'Y' barbette. Because of the manner in which these massive plates are keyed together, the first plate fitted would be at the centre with subsequent plates fitted working towards either end. Also of interest is the barbette planing machine in P4 5.25in position. Note the two steel towers with access ladders fore and aft of the 5.25in casemates. These towers appear frequently in various positions but are probably for measuring any deflection in the hull as weights are added.

29 May *SDO*

Plans have been issued for additional watertight subdivision in the form of intermediate bulkheads on lower deck aft. Plans giving particulars of additional stiffening required for rudder have been received from Admiralty. Preparation and issue of detail drawings in connection with cabins, messing and other arrangements throughout the ship is proceeding.

29 May *Shipyard*

A commencement has been made on loose work re-erection in way of aft engine room. Boiler casings in way of forward boiler rooms are being erected, faired and riveted. Hangar bulkheads are in position, faired and being welded. Progress is being made on supports for Nos. 2 and 3 5.25-inch guns with work faired, riveted and machining commenced. Work of finishing trades is continuing, and making satisfactory progress on magazines, shell rooms and store rooms. Shipping of auxiliary machinery is making good progress. Steering gear, after capstan, turbo and diesel generators are in position and secured. Installation of cold chambers [refrigerated stores] is in hand. Shipwright is engaged on deck planking. Y barbette armour protection is in position together with certain of the main deck armour plates in way of forward boiler room. During the last four weeks, 1028 tons of armour has been erected and secured.

31 May *Board*

Progress with this contract is satisfactory, the starboard side armour is now completed and the position of the ship in our basin has been reversed to allow the fitting of the port side armour which work is now in progress. The armour of Y

April 1940. A 600lb middle strake side armour plate weighing about 30 tons being fitted to the starboard forward end, for which the ship has been pulled back along the east wharf to be within the operational radius of the 150-ton derrick crane. Close examination of the image shows that two wire ropes have been passed through holes in the shell from inside the hull corresponding to tapped holes in the armour plate. Once pulled into position using these ropes, twelve armoured bolts will then fasten the plate to the ship's shell plating. Note the channel machined into the edge of the plate which allows for the plate to be joined to the adjoining plate using a 'key'. The top and bottom edges are tongued and grooved to fit the plates above and below. The timber bolted to hull keeps the armour from abutting the shell plating and causing a corrosion trap from salt water ingress, with the space filled by composition.

barbette is in position and main deck armour over boiler and engine rooms has been placed in position. Main and auxiliary machinery thrust blocks and intermediate shafting lengths are now aboard and in engine room.

24 June *SDO*

Plans for the degaussing installation have been issued. Preparation and issue of drawings in connection with cabin, messing and other re-arrangements throughout the ship due to change over of fleet flagship is proceeding.

24 June *Shipyard*

Erecting, fairing and welding of loose work continues and is nearing completion. Boiler casings to forward boiler room are erected, faired and being welded. Erecting, fairing and welding of bridge structure is proceeding and side bulkheads of hangars are erected and faired. Finishing trades are making good progress on accommodation, also on mess spaces in lower, middle deck where fitting of lockers etc., is proceeding. Installing of steering gear, after capstans, turbo and diesel generators is proceeding. Ironworker is engaged on attaching deck connections to barbette outer armour. Since last report, 1900 tons of armour has been erected on the vessel.
Armour to 18 May 1940 – 7255 tons fitted
To 18 June 1940 – 9156 tons fitted
To 3 July 1940 – 9899 tons fitted.

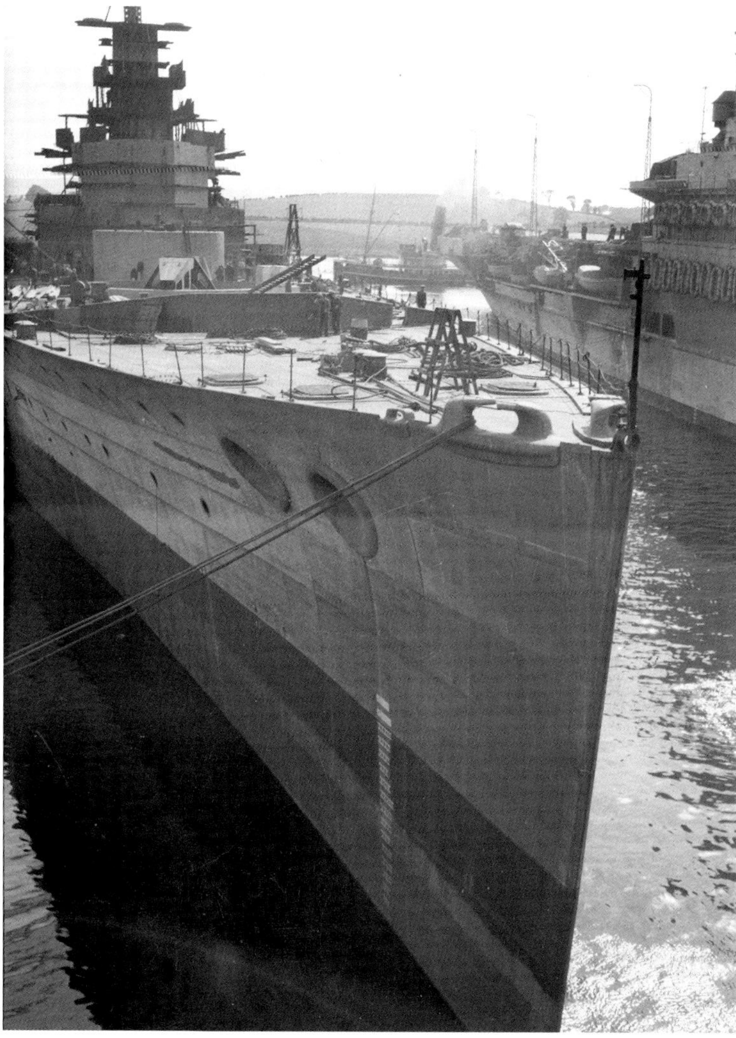

Late July 1940. By now, attention had shifted to the new fleet carrier *Illustrious* which arrived at Clydebank on 24 July 1940 for an emergency repair, not departing until 5 August. The unexpected arrival of this ship, built at Barrow by Vickers-Armstrongs, required many men to be taken off other contracts in the yard, a problem that would plague manpower allocation with a stream of vessels arriving throughout the war period for emergency repairs. To accommodate *Illustrious, Hecla, Nizam* and *Piorun* had to be moved elsewhere as with two capital ships in John Brown's basin there was room for little else. Note work progressing on *Duke of York*'s bridge structure and completed 'B' barbette. The fore poppet launching brackets have now been removed. Tug *Paladin* standing off.

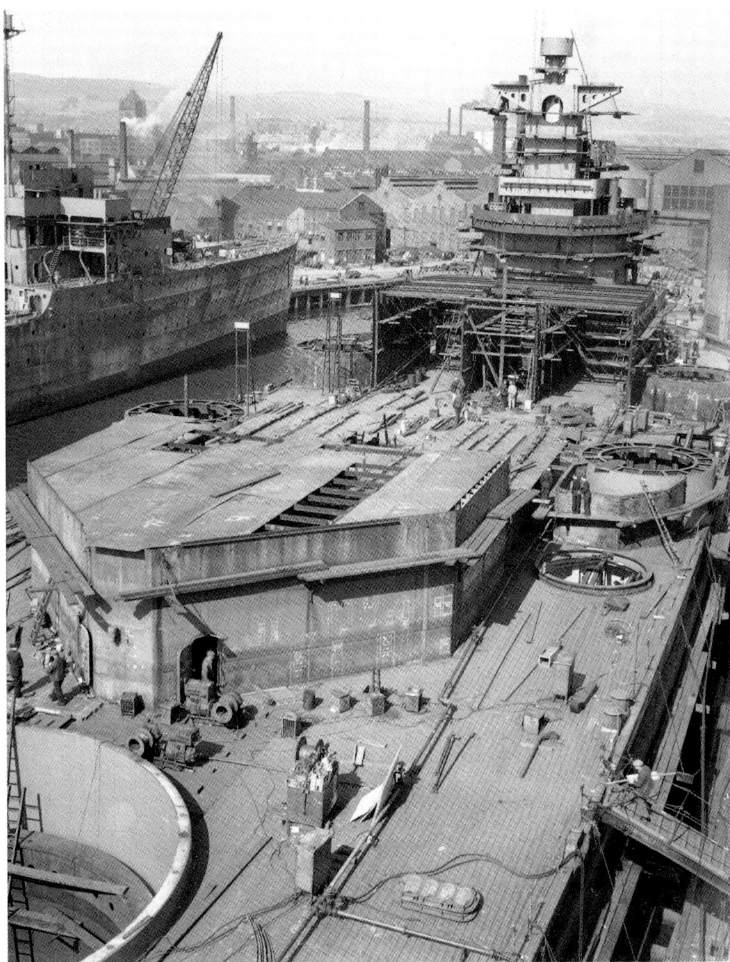

Circa August 1940. Abreast 'Y' barbette looking forward, undated but probably August 1940. 'Y' barbette armour has been fitted and all three main superstructure blocks are making progress, especially the forward block which has topped out at the pom-pom director position. The size of the hangars to house two Walrus aircraft is apparent. The depot ship *Hecla* is to the left.

28 June *Board*

Work on this contract is proceeding satisfactorily to schedule for completion in June 1941, based on expectation that the main armament will be delivered to our yard at the beginning of 1941. The side armour on the port side is now completing to be fully in place by mid-July. On the 24th instant we received personal request from the Engineer-in-Chief department for statement of the earliest date this ship could be rendered safe for making voyage with only two of the four sets of main engines working.

22 July *SDO*

Drawings of cabin, messing and other re-arrangements due to changeover to fleet flagship have been issued. This ship's side lining is to be removed from the vessel in order to obtain ready access to damage and also as a means of conserving aluminium supplies.

22 July *Shipyard*

Progress on this contract is proceeding to programme. All ship's side armour is in position and the few remaining main deck armour plates over aft engine room are being marked and fitted. Good progress has been made by finishing trades on 'tween deck work; fitting out of cabins with furniture, together with fitting on deck lockers throughout these spaces is proceeding satisfactorily. Plumbing and ventilation systems are making good progress on these spaces, the work being carried out systematically. Subcontractor has commenced work on cold chambers and on lagging of machinery spaces. It should be observed that the vessel was canted [turned 180°] in river after the side armour was placed in position.

26 July *Engine Works*

The section of uptakes between air heater and middle deck has been shipped on all boilers.

26 July *Board*

With the side armour now completely shipped in position and fixed, the vessel has again been turned in river and is again with bow at head of basin.

24 August *SDO*

A complete revision has been made of the openings through the upper deck in order to safeguard strength and the plan has been issued for lining-off purposes before obtaining confirmation from the Admiralty. The new scheme on DG [degaussing] installation has been received and is being investigated. This embodies M, S and Q coils and supplementary A coils all fitted internally. The question of the redesign of the rudders for this class has been thoroughly investigated with a representative of the Admiralty, and proposals have been forwarded showing an amended casting with additional stiffening on the fore end balanced part of the rudder, and with composite structure similar in principle to *Queen Mary*'s rudder, adopted for the main part.

24 August *Shipyard*

Loose work over machinery spaces is now erected, faired and being riveted. Ironworker is proceeding with completion of boiler casings. Work is also proceeding on hangar sides and on 5.25-inch gun supports. Good progress continues to be made in 'tween deck accommodation. Weather deck fittings, including deck winches, bollards and fairleads, are progressing according to programme. Subcontractors work on diesel generators, installation of cold chambers and lagging of machinery spaces is well forward. All side and deck armour is in position. Conning tower armour is erected. Preparations are well forward for final machining of A and B barbettes.

30 August *Engine Works*

Lining-up of main and auxiliary machinery is as far advanced as possible until further weight is added to ship [to get any deflection in the hull to its near final situation]. Pipe arrangement work is progressing and the remainder of the uptakes and funnels are complete ready for shipping.

30 August *Board*

The progress of work in our shipyard on contract vessels has been greatly disturbed by 'emergency' work such as that upon the aircraft carrier *Illustrious* which arrived on 24th July and departed on 5th August, the light cruiser *Fiji* for the period from 23rd of July until 2nd of August, the cargo vessel *Breconshire* for conversion to carrier for fuel and ammunition from 12th July until 24th August and the cargo vessel *Glengyle* for conversion to troop carrying which arrived on 27th June and is scheduled to complete on 7th September. Tradesmen to carry out the work of these emergency orders have been drawn from each of the contract vessels. Other than the delay resulting from [this] emergency work, the progress on this ship is satisfactory. The only other item of concern being the method of degaussing which has recently been altered from external to internal, this involving much piercing of bulkheads and coordinating with other installations throughout the ship's several compartments. [*King George V* had external degaussing cables.]

16 September *SDO*

For the purpose of defence against bombing attack, instructions have been received to complete the wing oil fuel tanks for flooding. Particulars regarding this and counter flooding arrangements have been issued to the yard. Lists of gearing to ventilation valves as-fitted in *King George V* have been received from Messrs Vickers-Armstrongs, and plans embodying these modifications and reductions have been completed.

16 September *Shipyard*

Good progress is being made by ironworker on hangar sides, beams and girders. Hangar is in position and a commencement has been made to erect shelter deck plating. Barbette roller paths are in hand. No. 1 [5.25-inch] gun support is being prepared for machining. Progress of work in magazines, shell rooms and storerooms is satisfactory. Messes on main deck are being lined-off preparatory to fitting kit lockers and mess tables. These are now on board and being placed. Work of plumbing, engineering, and electrical departments is proceeding methodically. Conning tower armour is erected and riveted. Final surveying and air-testing of compartments is in hand.

18 September *Engine Works*

Further weight having been added to the ship, the lining-up of main machinery and shafting is proceeding. Work is progressing on floor plate arrangements and on platforms and gratings.

27 September *Board*

Progress is generally satisfactory, also somewhat delayed by withdrawal of tradesmen for emergency work. At present the schedule calls for the delivery of main armament in January, February and March and completion about mid-June 1941.

30 October *SDO*

Plans showing holes in upper deck for vent openings as lined-off at ship have been sent to Admiralty for approval. A revised scheme of complement has been received indicating an increase in the numbers of personnel. This modifies the messing and sleeping arrangements. Plan of steam heating to hangar has been issued.

30 October *Shipyard*

Ironworker is continuing with work in way of bridges, hangars, engine and boiler vents, minor bulkheading on upper and shelter decks, upon which work satisfactory progress is being made. Final machining of roller paths, training racks etc. in way of A and B barbettes is completed. Progress is being made on magazines, shell rooms and storerooms by

November 1940. The foremast was assembled in one of the engine works bays and is seen here being transported from the shops the short distance to the fitting-out basin. The structure is being supported by the 10-ton capacity tower crane at one end and a steam crane at the other. This is a particularly awkward load to move, requiring great care and attention as the mast will be transferred to another crane for the final lift aboard ship. The crow's nest platform will later support the Type 273 radar aerial.

shipwright, electrical and sheet-iron departments. Forward capstan and certain of the winches have been received, enabling shipwright to proceed with fitting of timber beds for same. Subcontractor is making good progress with installation of cold chambers. Final surveying of wing oil fuel compartments outside protective bulkheads is completed. General progress of the vessel is satisfactory.

1 November *Engine Works*

Lining-up and chocking of main machinery [levelling machinery to seating with thin pieces of metal] and shafting is proceeding. Work is progressing on pipe arrangements and on platforms and gratings which have been completed in the boiler rooms. Forward uptakes are almost completed and forward funnel is ready for shipping.

1 November *Board*

The machining of the roller path for support of gun turret is completed in both the [forward] four-gun and two-gun barbettes and work is in progress on similar work in the after four-gun barbette. Generally, progress on this contract is good, but work has been handicapped by the withdrawal of tradesmen for necessary emergency construction and repairs. Latest advice indicates that the delivery by Vickers of the main armament will be delayed.

13 November *SDO*

A revised scheme of complement has been received indicating an increase in the numbers of personnel and the necessary modifications to general arrangement plans are being carried out. Collaboration with the Admiralty on the design of rudders has resulted on a revised plan for the spare rudder for this battleship class and this is now in manufacture.

15 November *Engine Works*

Lining up and chocking of main machinery and shafting continues and work on pipe arrangements and on platform and gratings is progressing. Pipe arrangement work is being completed and preparations are in the hand for basin trial on 26th November. Steam has been raised for auxiliary purposes and tests.

26 November *Shipyard*

Machining of Y barbette will be completed within eight days. Ironworker is continuing with work in way of bridges, hangars, engine and boiler vents, minor bulkheading on upper and shelter decks, upon which work satisfactory progress is being made.

29 November *Board*

Good progress is being made both with the hull and the machinery. The mainmast is now erected in position. Delivery of the main armament is promised in February and March and the procedure for receiving and shipping aboard the battleship is now being arranged.

10 November 1940. A striking view taken from the side of the Cowans Sheldon 150-ton derrick crane erected in 1904 in readiness for the *Lusitania* contract. Here it is carefully and very slowly lifting the foremast up and into position on the forward superstructure. Note the other 150-ton fitting-out crane in the background, the Arrol giant cantilever which, in 1938, was uprated to 200 tons to handle the heavy turntable of the quadruple 14in gun mountings.

18 December *SDO*

Plan of additional stiffening under turbo-hydraulic pumps in A and B action machinery rooms has been submitted to Admiralty. Arrangement of bulletproof protection to RDF offices has been approved. Proposals for facilitating escape from the lower deck cabins are being prepared for submission.

December 1940. Both the main and foremasts are now in position and good progress being made on the forward superstructure. The slits of the conning tower with its 160lb armoured sides are visible just below the windows of the admiral's bridge. The steelwork at the bottom section of the superstructure has various dotted lines in white paint denoting the position of various fittings such as 'stowed position for paravane'. The paravanes would subsequently be repositioned to behind the breakwater (see photo on p154). The curved pipes alongside 'B' barbette are air escapes from tanks lower in the hull. The ship is some distance off the quay wall to enable work to continue on the side armour and its cover plate which will fair the top edge into the hull, yet to be riveted into position. Note the absence of any guard rails on the staging. A planing machine is preparing the support for S3 5.25in mounting. The deck planking forward has now been laid.

18 December *Shipyard*

Further progress has been made in way of bridges, hangars and engine and boiler vents. Ironworker is also engaged in the completing of 'tween deck minor bulkheading. All barbette roller paths are now finally machined and progress is being made on the machining of the 5.25-inch gun supports. Good progress has been made on ventilation piping and electrical systems throughout the vessel, and work on accommodation is keeping pace with the general progress of the structure. Sub-contractors are continuing with the work of fitting diesel generators, turbo generators, capstan and refrigerating machinery. Installation of cold chambers and lagging in way of machinery spaces is making satisfactory progress. Fore and main masts are now in position and secured.

20 December *Board*

The Controller has stated that the completion of the ship is urgent and has asked that, with completion of repairs and alterations to the light cruiser *Fiji*, efforts will be concentrated on the completion of *Duke of York*.

1941

29 January *SDO*

Various proposals based on DNC's report of *King George V* trials have been transmitted for application in *Duke of York*. Consideration is being given to an extension of steam fire extinguishers, and it is understood that further facilities will be incorporated in the final fire-fighting scheme. Plan of additional stiffening under turbo hydraulic pumps in A and B action machinery rooms has been approved and issued to yard. Proposals for improving escape from lower deck cabins, by means of additional hatches, have also been sanctioned. It is under consideration to fit stowage for depth charges for use in aircraft and motor boats.

Undated. A twin Mark I 5.25in mounting on the dockside at Harland & Wolff's Scotstoun works (formerly part of the First World War Coventry Ordnance Works), guns elevated to 70°. The new paintwork suggests it is not one of *Duke of York*'s but more likely the first produced for *Prince of Wales* early in 1941. The weight including the frame was about 80 tons.

29 January *Shipyard*

Structural work in way of bridges is nearing completion and a commencement has been made by finishing trades i.e., electrical, plumbing and ventilation departments, on work in this vicinity. Good progress is also being made on magazines and shell rooms, and in store rooms throughout vessel. It is now estimated that 65% of electrical work is completed and arrangements are in hand for final surveying of compartments. In the cabin accommodation painting is completed, and joinery department is engaged on installing furniture. General progress of sub-contracting work is satisfactory.

31 January *Engine Works*

Alignment of all main shafting has been passed and chocking and lining up of main and auxiliary machinery continues. Pipe arrangement work etc., and riveting of uptakes on board ship is progressing.

Undated. Transporting the secondary armament from the place of manufacture to the shipyard was usually done by ship. A twin 5.25in mounting being loaded into a coaster at Scotstoun, just two miles upstream from Clydebank. The bridge structure (aft) suggests the coaster is Robertson's *Citrine* stern-first in to the dock so that the gantry crane would not foul the derrick mast between the two hatches. Although *Citrine* carried *Duke of York*'s mountings to Clydebank in the spring of 1941, the paintwork suggests this one is for her sister *Prince of Wales*, to be shipped to Birkenhead.

STRBD
4
STRBD
3

Late February 1941. The first of the eight 5.25in mountings to be fitted were S3 and S4 delivered from Harland & Wolff's ordnance works at Scotstoun by the coaster *Coral* on 4 and 19 February. Top left can just be seen the support for the after funnel. The cover plate has now been fitted to the top of the side armour. Note mushroom vents lying by S4 to be fitted, apparently waiting for an opening to be cut through the steel deck as the wooden decking is already cut.

26 February *SDO*

Proposals for fire-fighting arrangements have been submitted to Mr Pengelly [H S Pengelly, battleship constructor] for approval. A scheme for stowage of additional depth charges for use in aircraft and motor boats has also been submitted to Admiralty. Instructions have now been received that remote power control has to be arranged for pom-poms on B and Y turrets but wiring only is to be carried out in meantime. A proposal for messing and sleeping an additional 90 ratings on middle deck forward has been approved and issued.

26 February *Shipyard*

Work of finishing trades is progressing normally in way of hangars, and on bridges. Machining of 5.25-inch gun roller paths is completed. The two aft starboard 5.25-inch gun mountings are in position at ship [manufactured by Harland & Wolff at Scotstoun and arrived by coaster *Coral*]. Work is also proceeding on catapult machinery seatings. It is expected to have the pads in question completed by the middle of March. Finishing trades are making good progress on magazines, shell rooms, store rooms and accommodation. Air-testing and final surveying of compartments below lower deck is in hand.

28 February *Engine Works*

Lining up and chocking of main and auxiliary machinery continues. Pipe arrangement work is progressing and the forward uptake has been completed. Preparations are in hand for the assembly of the funnels on the quayside ready for shipping.

28 February *Board*

We are now being pressed by the Admiralty for earliest completion of the ship and with this object a conference was held at Clydebank on the 25th instant presided over by [Vice] Admiral Wake [Admiral Superintendent of Contract Built Ships] and attended by representatives of the armaments supplier and the various subcontractors. It is the aim of the Admiralty that the work at Clydebank will complete by the end of July and that the ship will be ready for service by the end of August.

Vickers now state the following deliveries–
Y turret by 18th of April
B turret in May
A turret by 20th of June.

From the final delivery at ship until the completion of gun trials, the sister vessels have required five months time which, with *Duke of York*, would mean end of November. [This turned out to be a fair forecast.]

Between 2 and 23 March 1941. A tranquil evening shipyard scene that belies the carnage inflicted on Clydebank by the Luftwaffe blitz of 13/14 March. On the east wharf *Duke of York* is assuming something of her finished profile with the destroyer *Piorun* alongside. The monitor *Roberts* is by the 200-ton cantilever crane on the west wharf. There appears to be little to see underneath the forest of derrick cranes in the East Yard, but the cruiser *Bermuda* and the fleet carrier *Indefatigable* are there, soon to be joined by the destroyers *Redoubt* and *Relentless* which were laid down in June.

The town of Clydebank was devastated by air raids on the nights of 13 and 14 March 1941 with minimal damage to the shipyard. This photograph was taken on Dumbarton Road, a stone's throw from the shipyard which lay on the other side of the tenements at right.

Clydebank Blitz. [On the two nights of 13 and 14 March, Clydebank was severely bombed by the Luftwaffe.]

25 March *Board*

Although damage within our shipyard and engine works is comparatively light, much dislocation and delay has resulted from the effect of the nine-hour raid on the night of 13/14th March and two other raids of 7¼ hours in total during the night of 14/15th March. On both Friday, 14th March and Saturday 15th of March, the total number of workers did not exceed 500 but throughout the following week the number rapidly increased to about 70%. Starting this week, the numbers have increased to some 80%. The electricity supply was not broken off but gas was not available until the 17th instant and serviceable supply of water not until the evening of the 19th instant within our works. Transport was completely dislocated for several days but by the evening of the 19th, train and bus services were operating very near to normal and by the morning of the 24th instant the tram service also was restored. First aid repair has been effected to the brass shop and in this shop work is progressing normally. Similar repair is effected to the roofing of the engine shop tool room and is in progress with the shafting shops, where the gearing hobbers and shafting lathes are being rapidly reconditioned. Feeding of our employees has been and remains a most difficult service. Mobile canteens within the yard serving tea and sandwiches and communal serving at the Town Hall have been the only possible means of feeding, observing that the restaurants in Clydebank which supplied meals to our workers have been without exception demolished by the bombing and, while it has been arranged that these restaurants are being reconditioned by first aid at the earliest possible reopening, such service will not now suffice the needs. Accordingly, canteens within our yard are being set up to give more substantial feeding, but these can only be of temporary nature. It now appears inevitable that a permanent canteen must be arranged with our works, when we have learned of experiences of other canteens. [Fortunately *Duke of York* was not hit.]

Duke of York [separate paper included in reports for March]
The latest intimation by the Admiralty is that this ship be advanced to leave the Clyde at the beginning of September and that Vickers Armstrong state that their work on the main armament will be completed by end of September. On Tuesday the 25th, the *Duke of York* was transferred to the west side of the basin to enable the mounting of the port side 5.25-inch gun turrets and to receive the 14-inch gun turrets now promised in April, May and June. Alterations and additions as indicated necessary by the sea voyage of *King George V* are being carried out on *Duke of York*.

End March/early April 1941. The layout of the anti-aircraft armament becomes clearer with S1 and S2 5.25in mountings fitted, and four platforms for eight-barrelled pom-poms surrounding the foremast, with the fore funnel yet to be fitted between them.
A 15in gun lies on the dockside top left for *Roberts*, plus a jumble of pipes top centre. Nearby is a railway wagon belonging to the London, Midland & Scottish Railway whose suburban line was closest to the shipyard.

DUKE OF YORK UPPER DECK VENTILATION
FRAMES 99–140

Drawing Key

1 16 x 16in exhaust from POs' washplace.
2 14½ x 14½in exhaust from stoker POs' mess.
3 10 x 10in supply to seamen's washplace.
4 17 x 17in supply to POs' mess.
5 12 x 11in supply to 5.25in magazine.
6 17 x 17in supply to seamen's mess and store.
7 14½in exhaust from pump room.
8 10 x 10in exhaust from store.
9 13in supply to 'B' magazine.
10 16 x 16in exhaust from POs' & seamen's mess.
11 17 x 17in supply to 'A' shell room.
12 17 x 17in supply to 5.25in magazine.
13 17½in supply to 'B' shell room.
14 17 x 17in supply to seamen's mess.
15 12 x 11in supply to POs' washplace.
16 17 x 17 in exhaust from bakery.
17 10 x 10in supply to No 1 wireless transmitter room.
18 12 x 8in exhaust from CWS alternator room.
19 12 x 8in supply to CWS alternator room.
20 9 x 8in supply to pantry.
21 10 x 10in exhaust from No 2 wireless transmitter room.
22 17 x 17in supply to 5.25in magazine.
23 17½in supply to 'B' shell room.
24 13in supply to 'B' magazine.
25 17 x 17in supply to seamen's mess.
26 17 x 17in supply to seamen's mess.
27 12 x 11in supply to 5.25in magazine.
28 12 x 11in supply to CPOs' washplace.
29 16 x 16in exhaust from ordnance artificers' mess.
30 12 x 11in supply to ordnance artificers' mess.
31 12 x 11in exhaust from seamen's washplace.
32 12 x 10in exhaust from store and pump room.
33 17 x 17in supply to 'A' shell room.
34 16 x 16in exhaust from CPOs' washplace.
35 14½ x 14½in exhaust from CPOs' mess.
36 10 x 10in supply to seamen's washplace.
'B' turret had a separate ventilation supply system through 5in diameter holes in the rear of the gunhouse floor, exhausting through holes in the gunhouse rear armour plate.

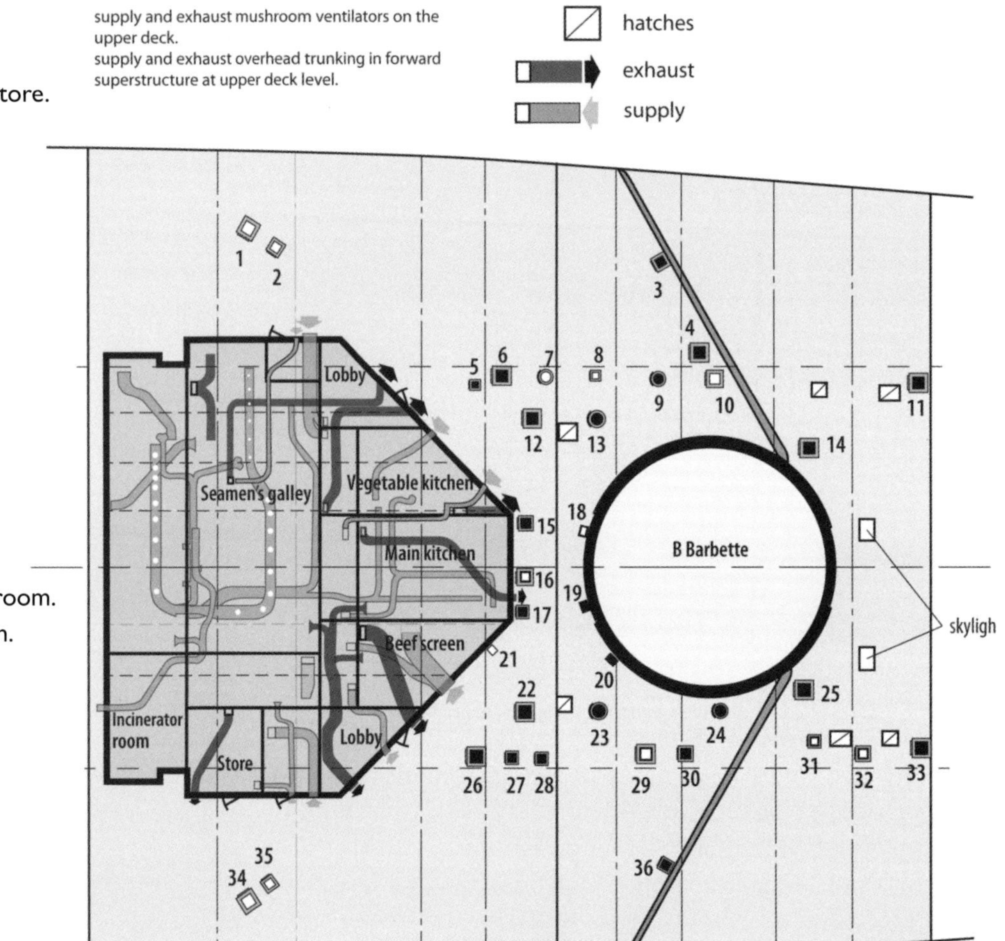
Ventilation between frames 102 and 148 showing:
supply and exhaust mushroom ventilators on the upper deck.
supply and exhaust overhead trunking in forward superstructure at upper deck level.
supply
exhaust
hatches
exhaust
supply
Lobby
Seamen's galley
Vegetable kitchen
Main kitchen
Beef screen
Incinerator room
Store
Lobby
B Barbette
skyligh
bulkhead 148
bulkhead 119
bulkhead 102

End March/early April 1941. Great activity is evident in this high level photograph on the west side of the basin. 'A' and 'B' barbettes are all but complete but yet to be painted. Mushroom ventilators are scattered about and planking is still underway. Note the wiring looms being fitted on the admiral's bridge with cable reels abreast 'B' barbette. The seat for the main gunnery director is being prepared. On the wharf side, anchor chain, ventilation trunking and parts of the bridge structure are waiting their turn to be lifted onboard. (See drawing opposite of vents in this area.) The British & Burmese passenger cargo vessel *Burma* is berthed alongside *Duke of York* to provide dining and sleeping accommodation for men unable to get home. This was a consequence of the severe aerial bombardment of Clydebank on the nights of 13 and 14 March when many houses were destroyed.

26 March *SDO*

Proposals for stiffening of breakwater and making the connection of barbettes to upper deck watertight, arising from report of weather damage to *King George V*, have been issued to the yard. Copies of as-fitted piping plans of *King George V* have been received from Vickers as a guide in the preparation of similar plans for No. 554. As-fitted plans of ventilation arrangements are in hand, and the scheme of damage control diagrams is being investigated.

26 March *Shipyard*

Seatings in way of catapult are in hand, and rings for turntable are being machined. Work in magazines, shell rooms, and store rooms is proceeding satisfactorily, and the finishing trades are making good progress on mess spaces and cabins. Galley gear has recently been received and is being installed. Air testing and final surveying of compartments is proceeding. All starboard 5.25-inch gun mountings are shipped and

machining of the first 2pdr. gun seatings has commenced. [The first of six eight-barrelled mountings, No 112, was shipped from Vickers-Armstrongs at Barrow in February.]

28 March *Engine Works*

Lining-up and chocking of main and auxiliary machinery continues and modification to keeps of turbine feet is in hand. Pipe arrangement work is progressing and the after uptake is being riveted. Funnels are being assembled on the quayside and both outer funnels are being riveted.

29 April *SDO*

Proposals for additional valves, etc. required for fire-fighting services have been received from Admiralty, and the necessary details are being prepared for the yard. Details of various fittings and stowages are being issued as required. The preparation of plans and particulars for the damage control arrangements indicating counter flooding systems is in hand.

End March/early April 1941. Taken at the same time as the previous two photos, this shows progress on the after part of the ship. Note the after funnel housing and uptakes on the boat deck and one of the funnels just visible with staging beside the tower of the 200-ton crane. Equipment in wooden crates is lying on the catapult deck and on the wharf side. The circular bases for the turntables for the trolleys for moving aircraft are being fitted. (See Aircraft Arrangement drawing on p217.) Inside 'Y' barbette, the upper arc is the roller path, the lower arc the training rack; ready for shipping 'Y' mounting in late April. The accommodation vessel *Burma* is visible alongside.

29 April *Shipyard*

Good progress is being made by finishing trades on fitting-out of magazines and shell rooms etc., also such installations as ventilation, electrical and plumbing are proceeding satisfactorily. Testing of rapid flooding, main suction, residue suction and Pneumercator systems [a system of measuring the depth and volume of fluid in tanks] is proceeding. Subcontractor work on deck covering, such as tiling, Aranbee [Rowan &

29 April 1941. Built separately in the funnel shop, the funnels were transported to the fitting-out basin and shipped by the 200-ton cantilever crane. To install the fore funnel, seen here about to be fitted, the ship had to be pulled out into the river as the crane was approaching its maximum working radius. Although S1 is not visible, all four starboard 5.25in mountings have now been shipped.

May 1941. 'Y' quadruple 14in gun mounting was the first to be installed, as its heavy weight then allowed the propeller shafting below to be aligned. The lower parts with the ammunition trunks had arrived from Barrow in the coaster *Sea Fisher* on 4 April, followed by the turntable and gunhouse on 20 April. By May the guns had been installed, leaving the gunhouse sides, rear and roof to be fitted, the latter supported by the heavy columns. The men in dark uniform jackets are probably RN ordnance artificers, most of the others will be Vickers-Armstrongs' men.

Boden's patent deck covering] etc. is in hand. We are now in receipt of six out of the eight 5.25-inch gun mountings [from Scotstoun], and we are also in receipt of the final delivery of Y mounting, which according to programme should be installed on board vessel by the 7th of May. [Components were shipped in coaster *Sea Fisher* from Barrow, arriving at Clydebank 4 April.] General progress of vessel satisfactory.

27 May *SDO*

Proposals for stiffening mushroom vents from weather damage and also from damage by gun blast have been issued. The as-fitted plans of piping and ventilation arrangements are in hand. Advance information has been received that a new form of clump for paravane is to be fitted to the stem, and plans will be developed accordingly. Additional capacity for reserve feed water is being provided at sides of A and B engine rooms by the appropriation of the cofferdams inside protective bulkhead.

27 May *Shipyard*

All small steel erections on bridges, hangar top and on boat deck are proceeding as necessary, including searchlight platforms. Fitting-out of magazines, shell rooms and store rooms is proceeding satisfactorily. Progress is being made in installing and testing the various piping installations of plumbing and engineering departments. Good progress is also being made on general ventilation of ship. Tiling, latex deck covering, lino and linoleum and corticene coverings are proceeding satisfactorily. A commencement has been made by shipwrights' department to line-off weather deck stowages, which work is progressing. Progress is also being made on the installation of turbo and diesel generators, refrigerating machinery, steering gear and galley. Installation of cold and cool rooms is nearing completion. Final surveying of compartments is proceeding at the rate of 25 per week.

30 May *Board* **[Loss of *Hood*]**

Immediately the loss of HMS *Hood* was known steps were initiated by the Admiralty to expedite the completion of *Duke of York*, and we confirm that, given sufficient additional workmen, work on this ship could be fully completed by the end of July. Subsequently it was found that Vickers could not have the armament work sufficiently advanced by end of July and it is now proposed that we will schedule for *Duke of York* leaving Clydebank and the Clyde at the end of August. It has now been arranged that a meeting will be held on Wednesday the 28th instant [May] at the Admiralty office, Glasgow, to discuss our requirements for men to accomplish completion of *Duke of York* by the end of August, while progressing also the monitor *Roberts* and the aircraft transport *Athene*. If this programme is to be accomplished, it will be necessary that workmen be transferred to Clydebank from other shipyards. Possibly these additional men will be supplied from Fairfield. After leaving Clydebank and the Clyde the ship must be in dry dock for about three weeks for structural alterations, during which time Messrs Vickers work on armament will be completing.

Report on Above Meeting 28 May
Work of completion will be accelerated to enable this ship to leave the builders' basin about the end of August, Messrs Vickers having given an assurance that their work will be suitably advanced at that date. This ship must be in dry dock for a period of approximately three weeks for the rebuilding and strengthening of the rudder and for the fitting of paravane attachment at the bow. During this period, Vickers will continue work on gun mountings, the schedule calling for the entire completion by mid-October.

Deferring completion of *Roberts* from July to September will free tradesmen for work on *Duke of York* and *Athene*. Further tradesmen are required to accomplish the completion of *Duke of York* and *Athene* and it was arranged that the following will be released by Fairfield for work at Clydebank: 60 shipyard engineers, 40 electricians and 10 plumbers.

7 June *SDO*

A list of proposed alterations suggested by the Commander-in-Chief, Home Fleet, and discussed at conference held on 23rd May, has been received, and the necessary action is being taken on items affected. Particulars received of the new type of paravane clump to be fitted to the stem have been issued to the yard. Estimates for the condition of the vessel going down river have been made and indicate a draft of about 31 feet. All information in connection with damage control arrangements has been agreed with ship's officers and is completing. Condition of the vessel dry docking is being prepared.

11 June *Engine Works*

Modification to keeps of turbine feet has been completed in both engine rooms. Chocking of main machinery is completed except for cruising turbines. Pinions are being shipped. Pipe arrangement work is well in hand and boilers are being water tested.

11 June *Committee*

The loss of HM Battle cruiser *Hood* in the Atlantic action against the battleship *Bismarck* and the loss of HM light cruiser *Fiji* in action in the Mediterranean are incidents which have brought to the workers of Clydebank a fuller realisation of war conditions and have aroused feelings of both regret for the loss of Clydebank-built ships and deep sympathy for the loss of life entailed with the sinking of these ships. As offsetting

Early June 1941. A waterline view looking aft on the port side from midships, with the bows now out and a trim by the stern, as 'Y' mounting has been shipped but not 'A'. The after part of the ship is substantially complete with P3 and P4 secondary mountings and catapult extension in place. There are still many items to be fitted however in what was soon to be additional pressure to complete the ship on time if not ahead of it, following the loss of *Hood* on 24 May. Note the four holes drilled in the casemate below P3 to form a rectangular opening which was obviously an afterthought as this would normally have been made while the plates were in the shops. The emergency conning position is being fitted around the after funnel.

in small degree this feeling of loss, is the interest in the announcement that the destroyer *Piorun* (ex *Nerissa*), launched from No. 7 berth about one year ago, was the first ship to sight and engage the *Bismarck* on the evening of 26 May. Also from this No. 7 berth will be launched today the destroyer *Paladin* of the same class as the destroyer *Piorun*. [Actually the former was 'P' class, the latter 'N' class.] Since the latest meeting of this committee on 31st March, two enemy air raids have been experienced, that of the 7th April causing the destruction of our mould loft and that of the 7th of May causing damage by landmines to the jetty on the East side of our basin and damage by two exploded and two unexploded bombs to No. 2 berth upon which preparations were in progress for the building of two destroyers, Numbers 589 and 590 [*Redoubt* and *Relentless*]. Following the sinking of *Hood* we were instructed by the Admiralty to concentrate upon the completion of the battleship *Duke of York* and the aircraft transport *Athene* both for completion by the end of August or early September. To maintain this schedule, all finishing trade workers have been withdrawn from other contracts and movement is in progress to obtain further shipyard engineers and electricians. [See graph of labour employed on ship, p22.]

27 June *Engine Works*

Chocking of cruising turbines has been completed and all pinions have been shipped. Pipe arrangement work is progressing. Boilers are being 'boiled-out' and preparations are in hand to raise steam for auxiliary purposes on 1st July.

27 June *Board*

The work on this ship is being accelerated for completion and the passage down the Clyde now scheduled for Sunday 7th September. The delivery and installation of the main armament is the measure of this effort. Y turret is in position and with all four guns shipped. B turret is also in position and the two guns are delivered and in process of shipping. A turret

Early June 1941. The forward superstructure nearly complete including the pom-pom platforms on top of the hangar. The 40ft ammunition derrick has been swung out and the 30ft sounding boom has been fitted immediately abaft the accommodation ladder.

KEEP CLEAR
OF
PROPELLER

Early June 1941. Looking forward on the port side underneath the 200-ton cantilever crane. The ship looks all but complete although the forward main armament mountings, the forward pair of port 5.25in mountings and all the close-range armament and directors have yet to be fitted.

was received at Clydebank on the 21st [shipyard diary says 24th June] instant and is now being shipped aboard, but all four guns are yet to be delivered. The last of these guns is now promised for 23rd July and if this programme holds, these should be in position onboard by the end of July. The basin trial, recently scheduled for 15th of July, will doubtless be delayed by about a fortnight as this may interfere with gun handling. However, we still aim at completion of this ship by the first week of September. After a very short trial of machinery in the Firth of Clyde the *Duke of York* will drydock [at Rosyth] and must remain in drydock for about three weeks for structural additions and for the rebuilding of the rudder to give the increased strength demonstrated as necessary by experience with sister-ships. In preparation for basin trial, the boilers are now being boiled-out and steam will be available for auxiliary trials by 1st July. As additional to the slow turning of propellers in basin trial, it has been arranged that each set of turbines and gearing will be run un-coupled from the shafting up to full power service revolutions with the object of confirming such items as lubrication, balance etc. Degaussing to be carried out in our basin.

23 July *SDO*

Docking plans and specification have been handed to overseer for forwarding to Rosyth Dockyard. A scheme of splinter protection (60lb D) to the 14-inch and 5.25-inch magazines has been submitted and approved. The necessary material has been ordered and plans have been issued to the yard. Copies have also been forwarded to Rosyth. Information has been received from Admiralty regarding the fitting of six Oerlikon

Above, 5 June 1941. The turntable which rested on rollers supported by the ring bulkhead (where the man has both arms up) was the largest indivisible component of a quadruple 14in mounting at 200 tons. The turntable for *Duke of York*'s 'A' mounting is being loaded into Fisher's coaster *Sea Fisher* at Vickers-Armstrongs Elswick works showing the specially widened No 2 hatch. *Sea Fisher* arrived at Clydebank on 24 June.

Right, 5 June 1941. Manufactured by Vickers-Armstrongs at their Elswick works, the lowest part of 'A' mounting showing the shell transfer ring on top of the circular cordite loading openings is being loaded into *Sea Fisher*'s No 1 hatch.

guns complete with special circular ramps and 20lb thick protection screens. A plan has been issued to the yard for lining-off purposes and the necessary material has been ordered. Work on the as-fitted plans is proceeding.

23 July *Shipyard*

Sheet ironworker continues on the completion of small fitments in and around bridges. Progress has also been made

CALLENDER CABLE

July 1941. Looking more warlike with the first multiple pom-pom fitted abreast the foremast, plus the main gunnery director and 44in searchlights, but as yet no HA or pom-pom directors. At bottom left various ventilation trunking parts are waiting to be installed.

on catapult sponson. This work is nearing completion and it is expected that the static test of catapult will take place early next week. Fitting-out of shell rooms and magazines is being advanced to completion. [See drawings on p45 bottom and p47 top.] Between four and five compartments are being surveyed daily. Finishing trades continue to make good progress on the various systems, pipelines, trunking and electrical work. Three-fourths of electrical tests have now been carried out. Since the last report we have received the last two 5.25-inch mountings, which are now in position, and work connecting up is well advanced. A barbette ammunition trunk, working chamber and turntable is shipped and in position. Work of fitting gun house is in progress. B barbette – both guns are delivered and shipped and work fitting roof plates is in hand. Pom-pom mountings have been received and shipped. [The remaining five eight-barrelled mountings, Nos 126–130, from Barrow.] General progress of vessel satisfactory.

25 July *Board*

Holiday Period

Owing to the urgency of completion of *Duke of York* and the *Athene*, working of all necessary trades continued throughout the holiday period so holidays must be arranged for these workers at later date, possibly about mid-September. Generally, the accelerated progress on this ship is satisfactory.

All parts of the main armament are now delivered at Clydebank. Y and B turrets have guns mounted in position, while with A turret the ammunition trunk, working chamber and turntable are in position. The gun house is assembling and all four guns lying on jetty ready for lifting and placing in A position. There is much work yet to carry out on the hydraulic control system etc. On the 15th instant all four sets of propelling machinery were run disconnected at full revolutions to test the various systems including the shafting excepting the propeller shaft, and on the 17th instant the usual basin trial with propeller shafts connected and propeller turning was successfully carried out. As far as possible we are now assured that the working machinery will be satisfactory on trial and in service. Very recently it was decided by Admiralty that additional protection on bulkheads forming the outer side of magazines must be fitted and this work is now in progress. Completion before this ship leaves Clydebank is not possible and a conference will be held at Clydebank during the coming week to arrange procedure. Also, additional secondary armament is being arranged following service experience with sisterships and this additional work is in progress. ['Secondary' armament is strictly 5.25in, correct term should be 'close range'.]

July 1941. A great dockside photo of the first 54ft long 14in gun being lowered into B turret. Although each gun barrel weighed 79 tons, with the cradle and balance weights the total lifted was 125 tons. Note the derricks being tested. This is the first image which shows the camouflage pattern applied to the ship. This scheme was an attempt at making the ship blend in with the industrial landscape that she was part of, similar to the scheme applied to *King George V* when she was fitting out on the Tyne.

1 August *Engine Works*

All four sets of machinery were run for a period at normal revolutions [2257 rpm at the turbines, geared down to 230 rpm at the propellers] with the propeller shafts uncoupled. They were afterwards coupled up and the usual basin trial was successfully carried out on Thursday 17th July. Cleaning of boilers is now proceeding and preparations are in hand for completion.

9 August *SDO*

Details of scheme for test of rapid flooding arrangements have been approved and issued. Plan of additional underwater stiffening to framing at the forward end has been issued. Work on the as-fitted plans is proceeding.

9 August *Shipyard*

All work on the smaller magazines and shell rooms, including 5.25-inch, is completed, and progress on the main armament shell rooms is proceeding in conjunction with Messrs Vickers-Armstrongs. All store rooms are completed and handed over to ship's staff. General tests and inspections of vessel are proceeding satisfactorily. These include steering gear trial: inspection of DG equipment, galley and bakery trials, final PV equipment trial [paravanes could be streamed from the bow to catch mine moorings, visible stowed on deck in the photo on p154], inspection of sickbay, static test of catapult etc. Work on testing the various piping installations is proceeding satisfactorily.

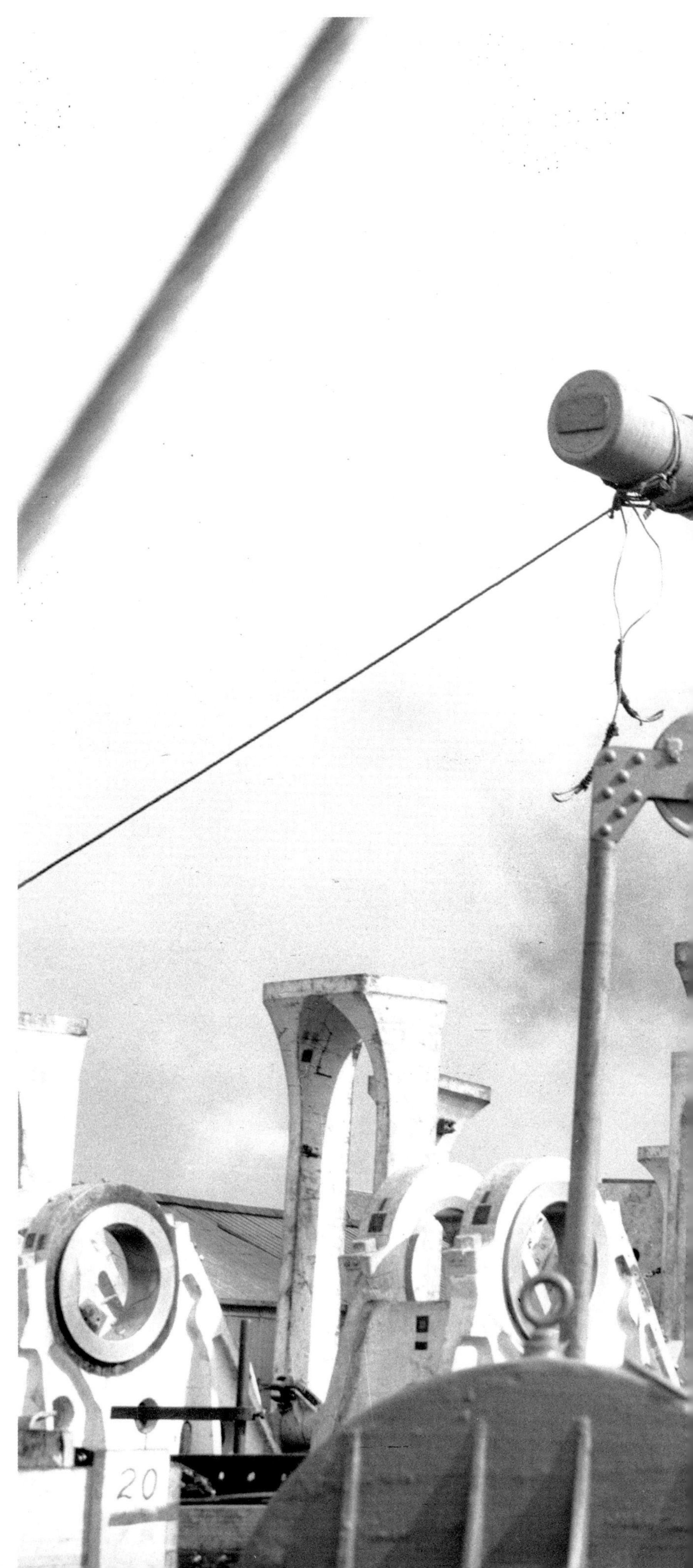
20

July 1941. A close-up view of the same event showing the left-hand gun of 'B' turret being fitted. Note that 'A' gunhouse is in course of assembly with floor plate, trunnions and columns in place. The 280lb non-cemented armoured rear wall of the gunhouse shows the holes for ventilation exhaust or cordite fire.

12 August *Engine Works*

Cleaning of boilers after the basin trial has been carried out, steam is being supplied for auxiliary purposes, and work is being completed for final acceptance on 19th of August.

12 August *Committee*

At the Admiralty conference held in Glasgow on 30th May and presided over by Vice Admiral Simeon [Deputy Controller of the Navy], it was directed that arrangements be made to complete both the battleship *Duke of York* and the aircraft transport ship *Athene* by approximately the end of August. To assist in accomplishing this it was directed that workmen of various trades would be transferred from Fairfield to Clydebank. Owing to unexpected difficulties this arrangement of transfer has not worked out satisfactorily, and while the completion of *Duke of York* subsequently arranged for 7th September as dictated by tidal conditions will be implemented, the completion of the *Athene* will not be completed until about mid-September. Earlier this month a proposal was made to us that with the completion of *Duke of York* further tradesmen would be transferred to Fairfield to assist in the progressing of work on the aircraft carrier *Implacable*. By letter to the Director of Warship [actually Naval] Construction at Bath, and by call upon the Controller in London, we have endeavoured to discourage such transfer and, alternatively, we have pressed to be allowed to concentrate more fully on ships building at Clydebank.

July 1941. The shipyard employed two photographers and three on occasions to record events. This photograph of the gun being lifted was taken at the same time as the last image but from the 200-ton cantilever crane. The cradle which elevated the gun and through which the gun recoiled 45in can be better seen. The rangefinder has yet to be fitted at the rear of the gunhouse.

A sequence of four photographs showing the last 14in gun to be lifted in on 1 August 1941.

The 200-ton crane unloaded the 14in guns delivered by rail from the maker's works and stored them within its working radius. The sequence starts with the gun slung and ready to be slewed over the ship. On the ground at left are parts of the ring bulkhead planing machine, at bottom right the jib of one of the two Clarke Chapman cranes and centre right some of the 240lb gunhouse roof plates.

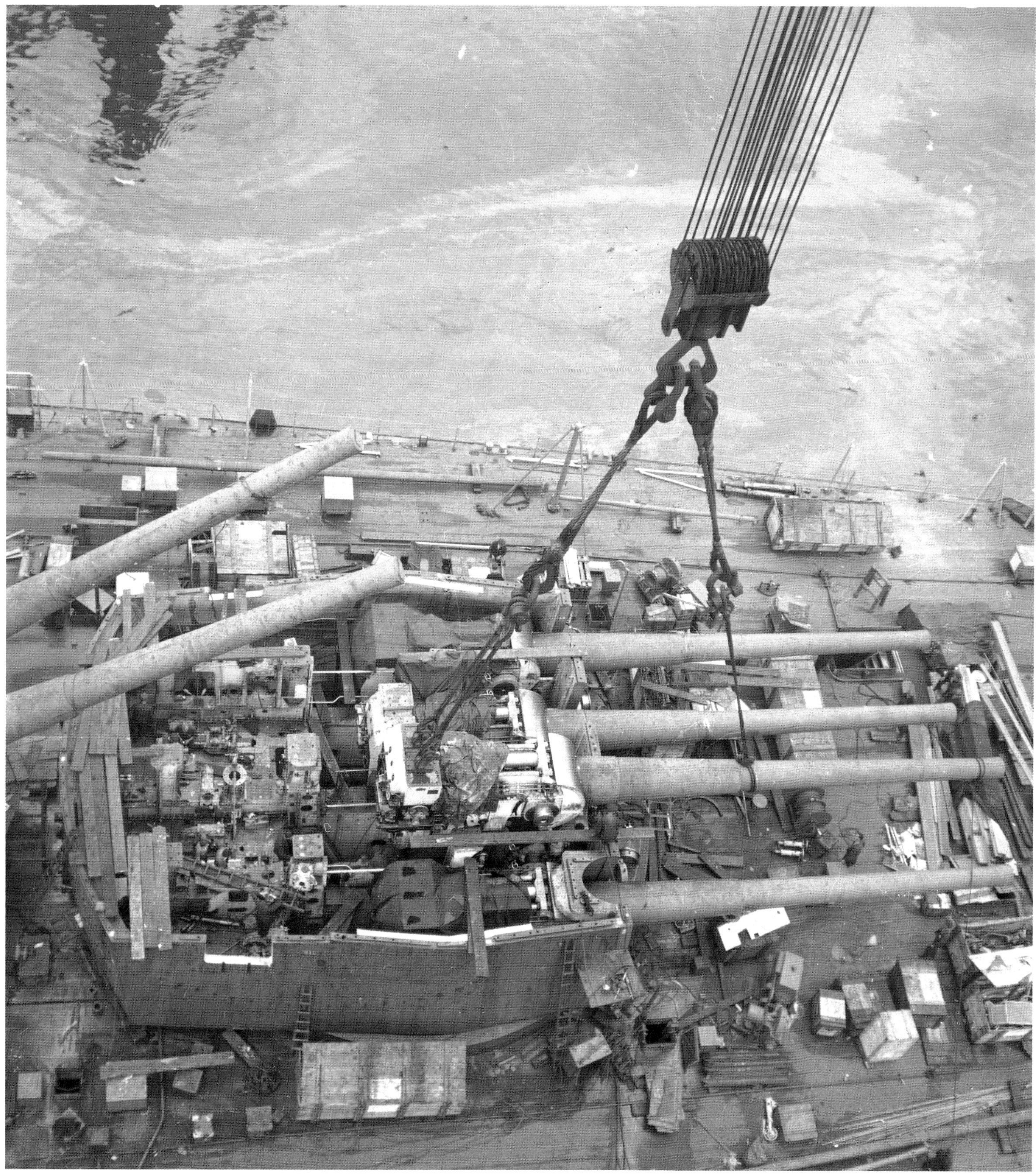

The last gun is slowly lowered onto its trunnions – a view that few Clydebank workers would have seen.

The fitters secure the last 14in gun in 'A' turret. The actual breech with its opening arm is in the centre, above and below are the balance weights which moved the centre of gravity of the whole assembly to nearer the trunnions and allowed the gun to elevate to 40°. The breech is detailed in the drawing on p47 bottom.

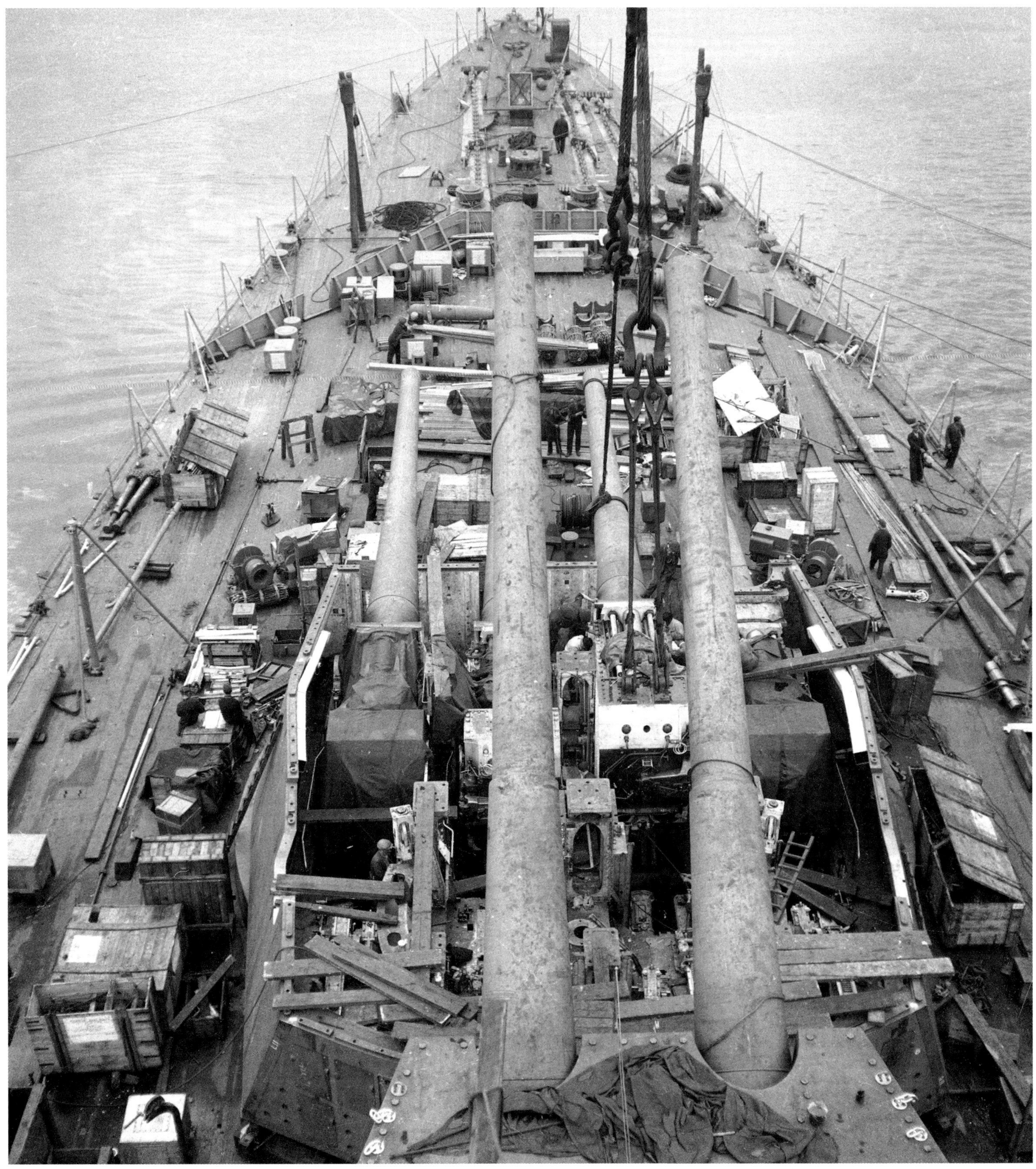

Looking down onto 'A' turret and the guns of 'B'. The clutter of equipment and stores on deck shows that much had yet to be done before the ship left Clydebank five weeks later.

25 August *SDO*

Arrangements have been made to fit fluid coolers to the hydraulic turret pumps in and A and B action machinery rooms. The coolers will be fitted by Messrs Vickers[-Armstrongs] and plans of the seats and piping have been issued. Additional installation and ventilation have been arranged for the switchboard room in view of the high temperatures obtaining in these spaces. A programme of tests and fire-fighting arrangements has been issued. The rigging model has been fitted in a case and handed over to the ship. The necessary copies of the as-fitted plans to go aboard the ship are well in hand. [These would be items such as piping plans rather than the general arrangement.]

25 August *Shipyard*

Good progress has been made on this contract on the cleaning up of various compartments with a view to final surveying. It is anticipated that, by the end of next week, all the living quarters on the main and middle decks will have been surveyed and taken over by the ship's personnel. We should also observe that in the same period it is anticipated that all shell rooms and magazines, with the exception of 14-inch, will also be completed and handed over.

29 August *Engine Works*

The working of the machinery and boilers of this ship under our supervision was taken over by the ship's staff on 20th of August.

29 August *Board*

This ship was commissioned in our basin on Wednesday, 20th August [and White Ensign hoisted], following final inspection by the Director of Warship Building [there was no such Admiralty post, probably Director of Warship Production S McCarthy] on 19th August. Good progress is being maintained in the completing of this ship and it is hoped that when the ship leaves our basin the only remaining work will be with Vickers who are yet to complete the system operating the 14-inch gun turrets. The work of mounting splinter-proof armour on the bulkheads adjacent to all magazines and shell rooms is completing and cleaning up of all the various compartments will be completed early for final survey of the ship. With the propelling machinery, preparations are in hand for the ship to proceed to sea after a short trial in the Firth of Clyde.

Movements in Fitting-out Basin

The shipyard kept a diary of ship movements from its start in 1871. The entries record events including arrivals, departures and launchings, providing an insight into the business of fitting out ships. The movements include not only ships being built but also ships coming in for repair and ships delivering items for the shipyard. These extracts cover No 554 from launch to departure, with the authors' comments in square brackets.

Feb 28 1940: No. J.1554 "Duke of York" launched 4-15 pm. H M King & Queen present. [J Numbers were the Admiralty's security designation for ships during the war.]

Apr 30: Pulled out for erection of armour 8 am to 3-30 pm. [Berthed bows in on the East side of the fitting out basin, allowing the 150-ton derrick crane to lift individual plates to the middle strake of the starboard side armour – see photo on p113 left.]

May 3 & May 6: Pulled out for [side] armour.

May 28: Taken out for canting 4-05 am – 5-30 am. [Turning ship 180° bows out to allow port side armour to be shipped, requiring tugs.]

Jun 13: Moved out for armour 8 am.

Jun 19, Jul 5, Jul 9: Moved out for armour. [Partly into river, probably to allow the crane to plumb the ends of the belt armour.]

Jul 12: Moved out for canting. [Now bows in at East wharf.]

Nov 10: Out for foremast 1-25 pm in 2-55 pm.

Feb 4 1941: SS "Coral" with gun mountings for No. 554 arrived 12-10 pm. Left 2-15 pm. [S4 5.25in from Scotstoun.]

Feb 19: SS "Coral" with gun mountings for No. 554 arrived 2-50 pm. [S3 5.25in from Scotstoun.]

Mar 4: SS "Coral" arrived 2-50 pm, left 4-40 pm (Gun mtgs). [S1 and S2 5.25in from Scotstoun]

Mar 5 1941: Taken out 150ft for mountings No. 1 & 2. [Bow in to East wharf. S1 and S2 5.25in mountings.]

Mar 25: No. 573 [monitor *Roberts*] taken out to allow No. 554 to West wharf. No. 554 moved to West wharf 10-40 am. [Bow in.]

Mar 26: S.S. "Burma" [arrived] providing dining & sleeping accommodation for men unable to get home. [Many Clydebank houses were damaged following air raids 13–14 March. Possibly also housing some of the many subcontractors working on the ship. British & Burmese passenger-cargo vessel berthed outboard of 554 until 15 April.]

Apr 4: "Sea Fisher" arrived 8-50 pm. [With parts of 'Y' mounting from Barrow.]

Apr 7: "Sea Fisher" moved into river & then wharf for discharging & left.

Apr 16: "Citrine" arrived with mounting 5-50pm leaving 7-35 pm. [P3 and P4 5.25in from Scotstoun.]

Apr 20: "King Fisher" [actually *Sea Fisher*] arrived 11-45 am. [With parts of 'Y' mounting from Barrow.]

Apr 29: Moved out for shipping [fore] funnel. [To bring its position

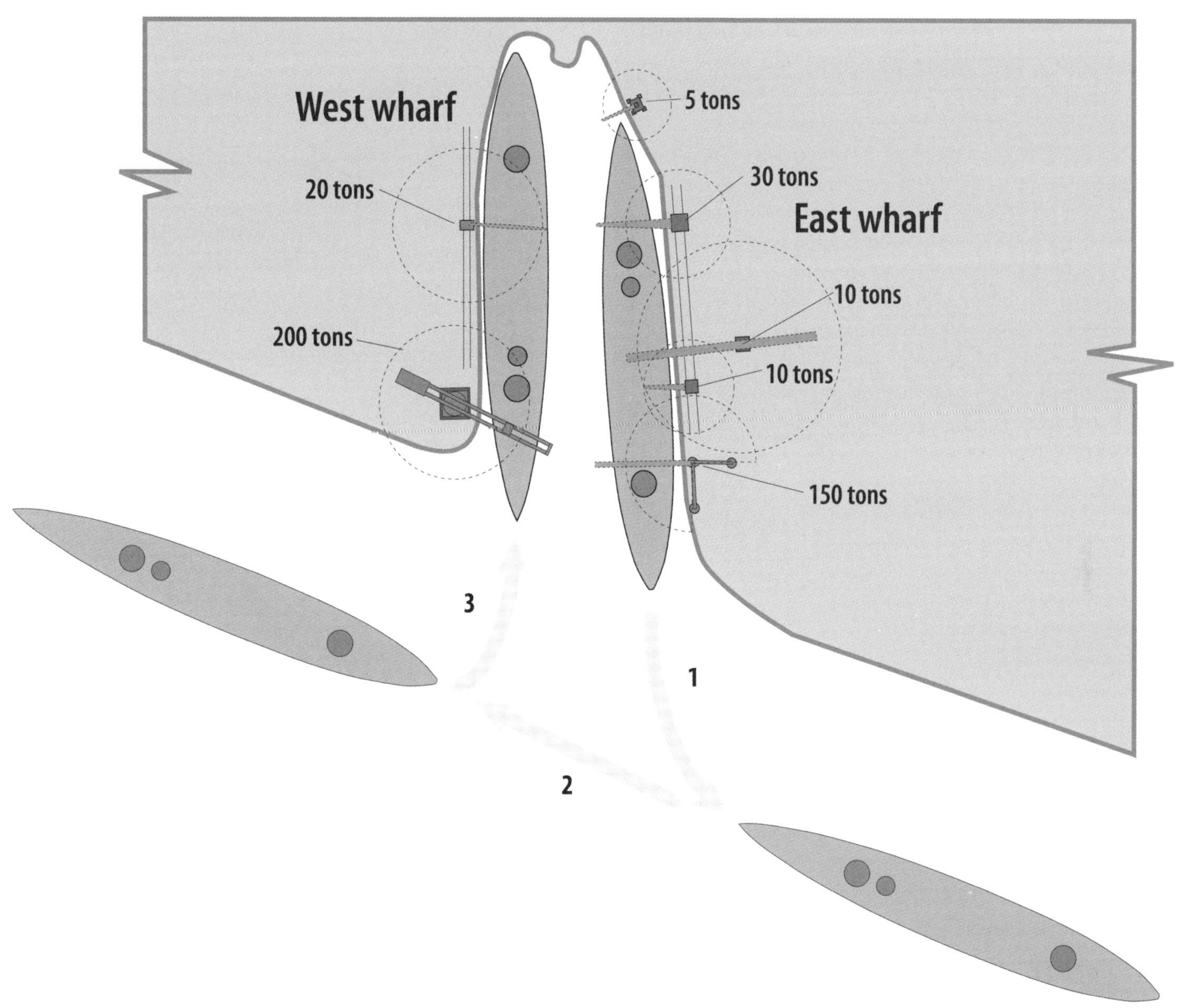
West wharf
20 tons
200 tons
5 tons
30 tons
East wharf
10 tons
10 tons
150 tons
3
1
2

on the ship under the fixed 200-ton cantilever crane at the south end of the wharf.]

May 18: No. 573 moved from East to West of basin 3-15 to 4-50 pm. [Probably by tugs holding her in the river.] No. 554 pulled across basin 3-49 pm to 4-25 pm. [Bow in, probably using dockside winches and wires from West to East wharf, to allow *Roberts* to ship her 15in gun mounting.] "Empire Ness" arrived at 10-25 am. [With 'B' mounting from Elswick.]

May 31: No. 573 moved from West to East 3-57 to 4-07 pm. No. 554 moved from East to West of basin 3-27 pm to 4-02 pm. [To ship 'B' mounting.] "Empire Ness" left for Princes Dock 11-20 am.

Jun 14 & 18: Moved into river for shipping material. [Bow out, probably for 'B' mounting.]

Jun 19: "Citrine" arrived 11-55 am with mountings leaving at 3-05 pm. [P1 and P2 5.25in from Scotstoun.]

Jun 24: "Sea Fisher" arrived 8-30 pm with mounting leaving at 3-40 pm. ['A' mounting from the Tyne]

Jul 12: Moved out for guns & canted. [Bow in, probably to enable port 5.25in mountings to be shipped.]

Aug 2: Moved out for shipping gear 4-40 pm to 9-30 pm. [Probably for multiple pom-pom mountings.]

Aug 9: No. 573 moved into river for Deperming [degaussing] No. 554 1-20 pm to 4-55 pm. [The gear had just arrived in *Schievan* and *Young John*.]

Aug 17: No. 554 canted for Deperming 5-25 pm to 7-55 pm.

Aug 29: Moved out 100ft for shipping guns. [Bow in to bring them under the crane at East wharf, probably the last multiple pom-poms.]

Sep 7: No. 554 left for T/B [Tail of the Bank Clyde anchorage] at 11-45 am.

Completion and Departure

9 September *SDO*

The passage of the vessel down the river was safely accomplished on 7th September, the mean draft being 31 feet maximum draft 31ft 2in, and the displacement 38,850 tons. The vessel was kept in the central channel without difficulty throughout and a plot of the course was obtained. A final weight observation was carried out before the vessel left. All the as-fitted plans necessary for the working of the vessel have been completed and handed over to the ship.

Addendum 9 September

Engine and ventilation trials were carried out during voyage and minor adjustments made as necessary. Details of additional stiffening to HP cruising turbine seats have been sent to dockyard.

9 September *Shipyard*

This contract left Clydebank basin at 11:45 AM on Sunday 7th September, and safely proceeded to the Tail of the Bank. Proceeding through the boom, she successfully carried out preliminary trials on the Firth of Clyde, returning to anchorage about 7 PM. It is anticipated that vessel will leave Tail of the Bank for her docking port on 9th September.

22 September *Shipyard*

This vessel proceeded safely to her docking port and was successfully docked on 10th September [entered the flooded No 1 dock]. Special stiffening of rudder and erecting of [paravane] clump on stem is in hand. Work is also proceeding satisfactorily on hull inspection and on the fitting of the remaining gearing to valves.

The following series of photographs shows *Duke of York* in the first days of September 1941 before she left John Brown's shipyard for Rosyth. She had commissioned on 20 August, hoisting the White Ensign and formally becoming HMS *Duke of York*. On leaving the yard she was probably about 99 per cent complete with the last items of equipment such as Oerlikon guns to be fitted at Rosyth. She would also be ammunitioned there and made ready to join the Home Fleet at Scapa Flow.

Visible in this view looking aft is, at left, the open watertight hatchway below which is a ladderway leading most immediately to the sick bay and CPOs' smoking and reading room on the main deck. The large box-shaped objects are mushroom ventilators while the tarpaulin is covering a 3-ton paravane winch. A few shipyard workers are still present but it is mainly members of the ship's company getting the ship ready for departure including the sentry with a Lee-Enfield rifle over his shoulder.

26 September *Engine Works*

Main and auxiliary machinery of this vessel worked very satisfactorily on the passage to HM dockyard where the ship is now in dry dock.

26 September *Board*

The passage of this vessel from our Clydebank basin down river to the Firth of Clyde was carried out without incident on Sunday 7th September, and entirely to schedule. After a short preliminary trial on the Firth of Clyde and the usual tests and adjustments, the *Duke of York* departed from the Clyde on 9th September and made the voyage around the north of Scotland at speed of about 20 knots, arriving at Rosyth and entering dock on the evening of 10th September. On the 11th instant she was dry-docked [drydock emptied] and work proceeded on the various items of work. The chief item of this work in drydock is the reconstruction of the rudder, and the completion of the rudder is the measure of the undocking. Meanwhile undocking is scheduled for 16th October [actually the 17th] and for the commencement of the official trials at the end of October. We have received from Sir Bruce Fraser, Controller of the Navy, a letter complimenting the builders on the work of completion. Also a similar letter from the Secretary of the Admiralty on behalf of the Admiralty.

9 October *SDO*

Records of breakage and deflection taken during the vessel's construction have been prepared and forwarded to the Admiralty, the final reading being 2½ inches sag. Plans for additional ready-use diesel oil tanks have been prepared and issued as also supplementary ventilation trunks to the spare armature rooms.

9 October *Shipyard*

This contract is at present in graving dock and the completion of work of same is proceeding satisfactorily. It is anticipated that she will leave the said graving dock for trials, etc., on October 29th.

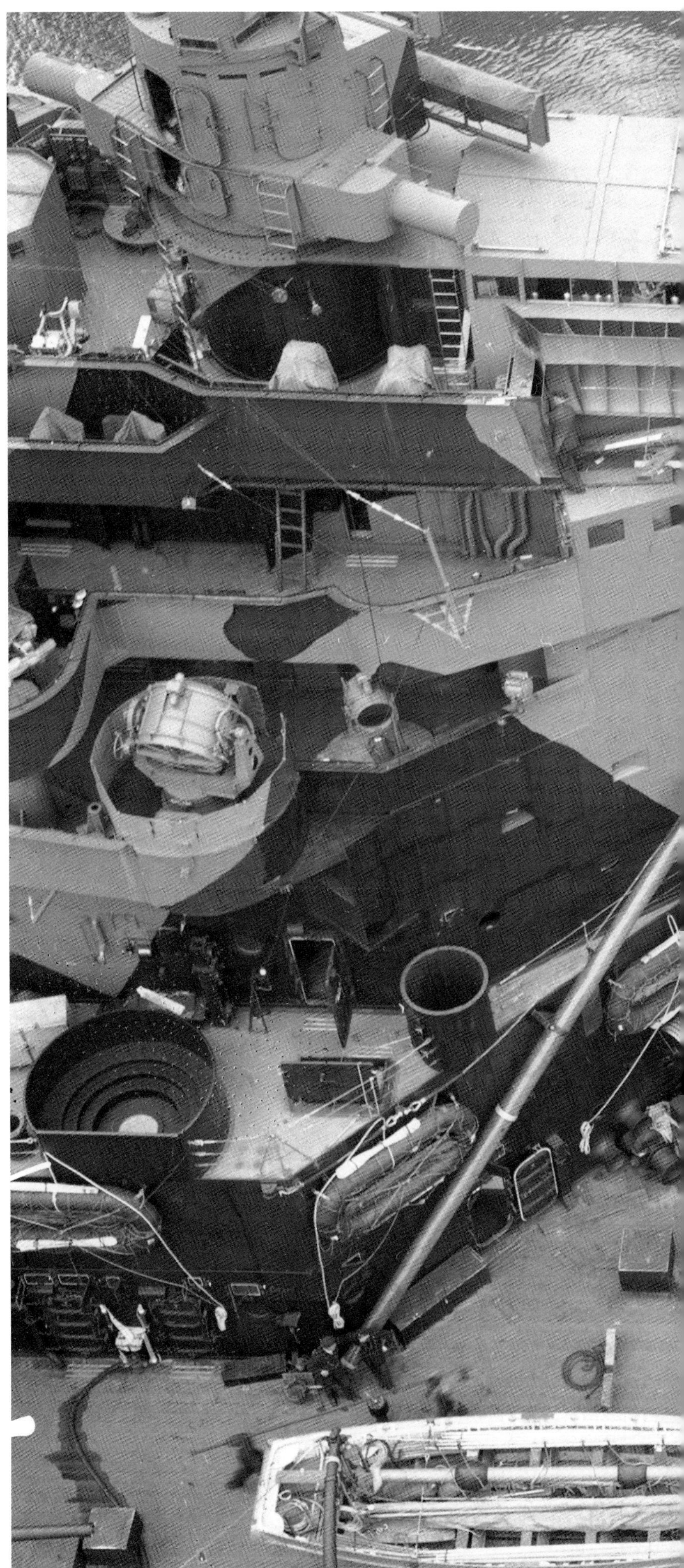

A good view looking down on the forward bridge structure and turrets. The *King George V* class had more and better ventilation than any battleship before. This view shows the layout of ventilators both square and round (see ventilation drawing on p122). The cordite embarkation hatches for both 'A' and 'B' 14in mountings are open and just visible, although no cordite would be embarked until the ship was at Rosyth. On the signal deck at left are one 44in searchlight, one 20in and one 10in signalling projector. Note the stern of the monitor *Roberts* at top right.

27 October *SDO*

All ship's copies of the as-fitted plans have been handed over and a receipt obtained. Plans for Type 271 RDF have been forwarded to Rosyth for fitting purposes [on foremast, although the improved Type 273 was actually fitted].

31 October *Engine Works*

All work has been completed ready for sea trials.

31 October *Board*

The completion work on this ship at Rosyth has proceeded satisfactorily. All work is now completed and the ship is ready to proceed on trials at sea which commence on 2nd November. The Clydebank trial party must attend for these trials, which will terminate at Scapa Flow. The workers at Clydebank are pleased that the *Duke of York* was selected by Glasgow for Warship Week.

24 November *SDO*

Drawing office work in connection with the as-fitted plans is now practically complete.

24 November *Shipyard*

Trials of *Duke of York*

The *Duke of York* left her anchorage above the Forth Bridge at daylight on Sunday, November 2nd, and proceeded at 9 knots until beyond May Island. This low speed was due to the danger from mines in the shallow water. Once clear of May Island, speed was increased to 20 knots and the 4-hours trial at the maximum cruising power of 28,000 SHP was commenced at 12:15 p.m. During the trial, gun trials were carried out on A and B turrets. The cruising trial was satisfactorily completed at 4:15 p.m. The ship remained at sea all night cruising at 20 knots. Speed was increased at daylight on Monday, November 3rd, and engines were worked-up to full power by 9:30 a.m. Gun trials were continued with Y turret. About 10:15 a.m. immediately after Y turret had fired all four guns on the beam with the 50% increased pressure in the recuperator cylinder [the recuperator stored energy from firing a gun to run it out for the next round], one of the bulkhead glands on X intermediate shafting heated up, and the full power trial had to be abandoned. The ship returned to Scapa Flow about 5 p.m, landed the Controller and DNC and

The after 14in turret showing the access ladder to the turret roof, pom-pom mounting and Carley floats. The pom-pom ready-use lockers (ammunition boxes) are immediately behind the mounting. The wedge-shaped extensions are to allow the 42ft turret rangefinder to slew 5° either way. Although a camouflage scheme has been applied over the ship, the main armament turret roofs have so far not been given a top coat.

anchored for the night. Next morning Tuesday, November 4th, the ship proceeded to sea at daylight and engines were worked-up to full power by 11 a.m. and the four-hour full power trial was satisfactorily completed at 3 p.m. The full power astern trial and full power ahead steering trials were completed by 3:30 p.m and the vessel returned to anchorage at Scapa Flow about 5 p.m. The *Duke of York* was finally handed over at 10 p.m on Tuesday, November 4th.

Two views looking down at both forward Mark V HACS directors fitted with Type 285 radar to control the 5.25in secondary armament. Each director had a five-man crew. The cupola between both directors contains a pom-pom director. Two further pom-pom directors are visible at admiral's bridge level. A total of five pom-pom directors were fitted on the forward superstructure and one aft at the mainmast. The rectangular forward main director with its 22ft FM.7 rangefinder has been fitted with Type 284 gunnery radar, for ranging and spotting shell splashes, one aerial array for transmitting, one for receiving. Smoke issuing from the fore funnel shows that some boilers have been flashed up.

28 November *Board*

From the report given by Mr [DW] Smithers, Principal Ship Overseer, all are highly pleased with the ship and copies of letters from Captain Harcourt, commanding the ship, and from Sir Stanley Goodall, Director of Naval Construction, are of interest. Also, Sir Bruce Fraser, the Controller, has in conversation expressed high praise. Vickers work on the hydraulic control of the 14-inch guns has given some trouble and our latest information is that leakage of water from these pipes is still being experienced in one turret.

5 December *SDO*

Drawing office work in connection with the as-fitted plans is now complete. [Apart from the general arrangement.]

8 December *Committee*

Since the committee meeting on 11th October, the battleship *Duke of York*, the aircraft transport ship *Athene*, the monitor *Roberts* and the destroyer *Onslow* have been completed and delivered, while the destroyer *Paladin* is at present on trials and the escort ship *Airedale* will be ready for trials at Christmas time. Clydebank has successfully carried out an unusually heavy programme during these recent months and expressions of appreciation received from Admiralty and the special mention directed to be entered in the board minutes are greatly valued by all at Clydebank. The cost investigation by the Admiralty of warship builders' accounts has shown that high profits were made by all builders on contracts completed during the first year of the National Emergency. While the Admiralty has not registered objection to the conditions which then obtained, the reaction is a demand for the adoption of the revised system of tendering for new contracts and it may be that the builders will be asked to re-tender for more recently placed contracts where a fixed price has not yet been agreed.

Looking forward from the boat deck over the catapult and aircraft and boat cranes to the forward superstructure.

A view amidships showing the starboard forward 5.25in mountings S1 and S2. The ship has been well fitted with Carley Floats and cork Flotanets with ten of the former and eight of the latter visible in this part of the ship. Neither gave any protection from the elements; survival depended on being picked up quickly. Note the prominent armoured belt, with draught marks extended to 42ft; damaged ships could be deeply flooded. The dockside travelling crane has a capacity of 10 tons.

Opposite, Good view of the forecastle showing four paravanes situated immediately behind the breakwater and an ammunition derrick lying forward of its deck fixing on the starboard side. The wooden deck is unpainted. This view also shows the sloped armour over the bulge of the monitor *Roberts* to good effect. The paravanes were subsequently moved to make way for Oerlikon guns.

19 December *Board*

The delivery of the *Duke of York* to the Admiralty was fully reported at the November board meeting. When on 10th December it was made known that the sister vessel, the *Prince of Wales*, had been sunk by enemy action, much surprise was shown by those responsible for the design of these battleships. As yet nothing has been made known to explain the sinking of this highly subdivided structure excepting the suggestion that the torpedoes used by the Japanese were set for operating at such depth as would strike the ship below the side armoured belt. At normal displacement the side armour extends some 12 feet below the water surface. Resulting from the loss of the *Prince of Wales*, the Admiralty is now hastening the completion of the sister-ships, the *Howe* building by Fairfield and *Anson* building by Swan Hunter. Clydebank has been asked to assist Fairfield by the loan of tradesmen and so far some 80 engineers have been transferred.

The boat deck showing stacked at right, a 45ft motor launch, a 27ft whaler and a 14ft sailing dinghy. Partly visible to the left is a 25ft motor boat. A 13ft 6in balsa punt is stowed on top of the engine room exhaust vent. Note the empty 20mm Oerlikon gun tub at bottom left. *Duke of York*'s 45ft fast motor boats would not be delivered to the ship until after she had left Clydebank. All the motor boats were petrol engined. The 'O'-class destroyer *Onslow* is at the west side of the fitting-out basin.

G17

27

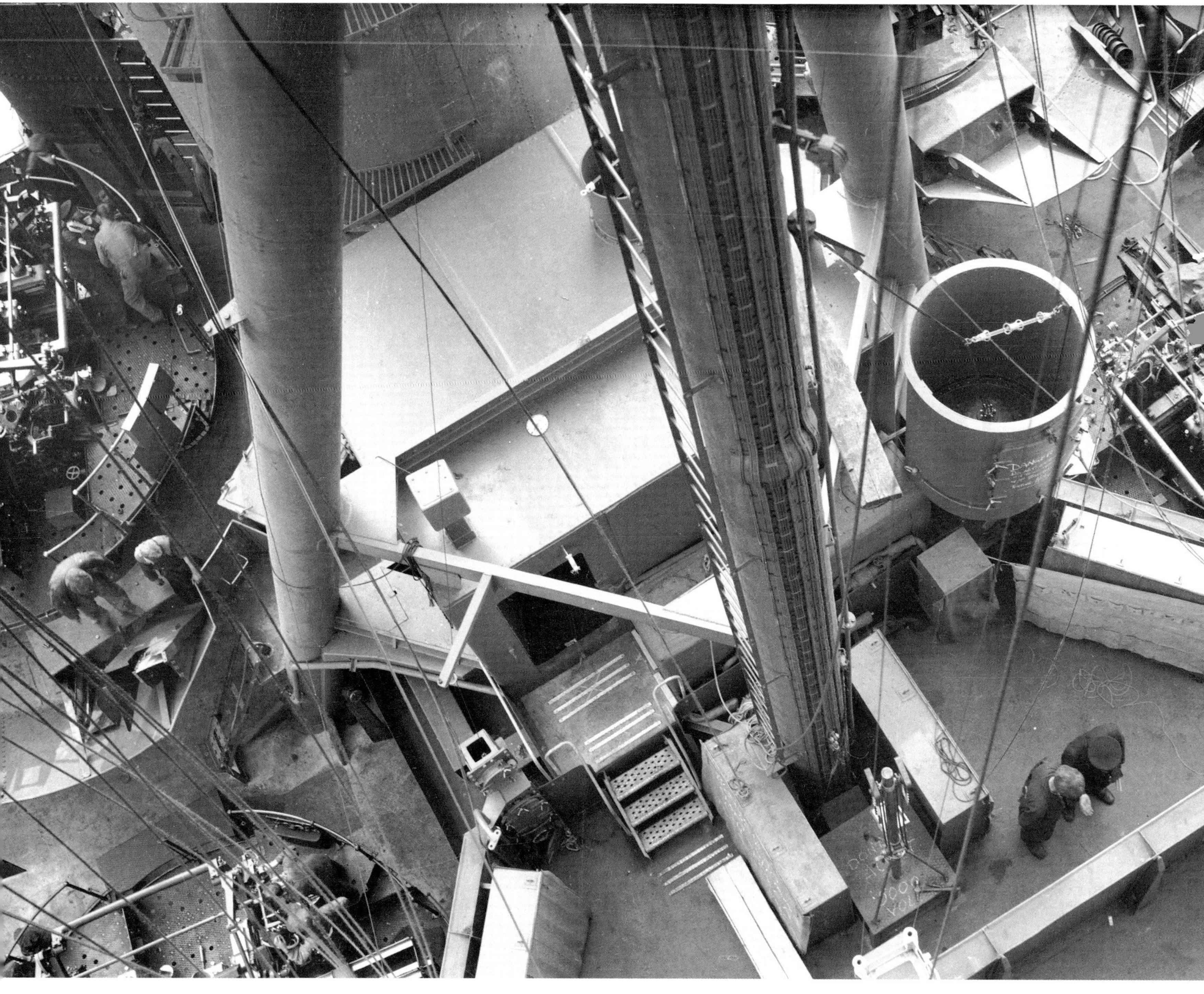

This image, probably taken from admiral's bridge level, looks down the foremast to the signal deck where four flag lockers can be seen. A semaphore is positioned between the two flag lockers by the base of the foremast. No 2 RDF (Radio Direction Finding or radar) office lies between the foremast struts and immediately in front of the funnel. Its three-step access ladder can be clearly seen. The circular tub is where the main wireless aerial cable terminates. There are numerous cable runs clipped to the mast.

Opposite, A close-up of No 5 Mark VI eight-barrelled 2pdr pom-pom mounting on the starboard side abreast the forward funnel. The mounting weighed 16 tons. Note the strut for the foremast and the multiple signal halyards.

1942

30 January *Board* [report by Stephen Pigott, MD Clydebank] It has now been made public that this ship carried the Prime Minister, Lord Beaverbrook, the First Sea Lord and others to the United States for conference with the American government. Early this week she returned to the Tail-of-the-Bank and on Monday evening I had the privilege of a meeting with Captain Harcourt, commanding the *Duke of York* and the first officer [not a naval title], Commander Mackintosh. They reported that on a trial run before leaving and with the vessel under escort, an estimate was made of maximum speed of 28¼ knots on a displacement of about 43,000 tons. The crossing from the Firth of Clyde to the American port of Norfolk, Virginia, was made at high-speed, both the Prime Minister and Lord Beaverbrook being anxious to arrive in America at the earliest possible time. Very heavy seas and gale conditions were encountered and the ship stood up exceedingly well to these conditions, the severity of which is demonstrated by the condition that when she arrived at Norfolk, there was scarcely a particle of paint left on the ship's structure: in the words of Captain Harcourt, it was almost as if the steel had been sandblasted. The main decks forward and amidships in way of the catapult were constantly shipping green seas, while the bridge was almost constantly covered by spray. The breakwaters on the forward deck, which had been reinforced as a result of experience on *King George V*, stood up exceedingly well, the doors or passage-pieces being the only parts affected and these disappeared with the sea. The ventilators, as strengthened, demonstrated no weakness; in fact, the ship's structure withstood the test exceedingly well. Some troubles have developed in the hydraulic system for operating the main gun turrets and Vickers' representatives went on board the ship on the morning of Tuesday the 27th to investigate troubles experienced with hydraulic pumps. Clydebank was not asked to send any representatives, which is evidence that there was nothing requiring attention.

The after end of the boat deck and base of the mainmast. With the exception of the 45ft motor boats, the complement of boats is complete with fitting adjustments in progress. The starboard after Mark V HACS director with 'yagi' or 'fishbone' aerials of the Type 285 radar pointing upwards, sits above No. 1 RDF office. To the left of this is the armoured after 14in director. Note the Oerlikon gun tub and just ahead, interestingly, what appear to be components of the simple device fitted at the foot of the ship's bow to stream paravanes. The casting with two distinctive holes and associated steelwork were not foreseen at the time of the ship's launch thus these components must await drydocking to be fitted.

This view gives a good idea of the layout of the aircraft arrangements and the aircraft cranes, manufactured by Clarke Chapman of Gateshead, which also handled the boats. These arrangements consisted of two hangars, one on either side of the fore funnel each housing one Walrus amphibian aircraft. Mounted on trolleys, the aircraft were pulled manually out of the hangar and onto a turntable and then turned 90° to be launched either to port or starboard. (See also drawing on p217.) The catapult mechanism by McTaggart Scott of Edinburgh was located on the deck below and employed a cordite charge to propel the aircraft into the air at a speed of 50 knots. The rectangular boiler room downtakes are on either side of the after funnel.

PEN THIS SIDE
G M

The same area photographed from the wharfside. Note the extension to the catapult which projects over the ship's side and the open hangar doors.

Another view of the after 14in director and, immediately behind, the No 1 RDF office on top of which are two Mark V directors and the pom-pom director controlling the mounting on 'Y' turret. The box-like structure below the pom-pom director is a shelter for the director crews. *Onslow* is fitting out at the west wharf of the basin, a single 4in HA gun replacing her after set of torpedo tubes.

Opposite, The after funnel with searchlight platform. Note the heat shield extending round the funnel at platform level. The forward part of the platform was the emergency conning position with a gyro repeater, rudder indicator and steering telegraph. In the 1944 refit this platform was extended forward. The 44in searchlight, port and starboard, was served with a portable davit for lifting in and out.

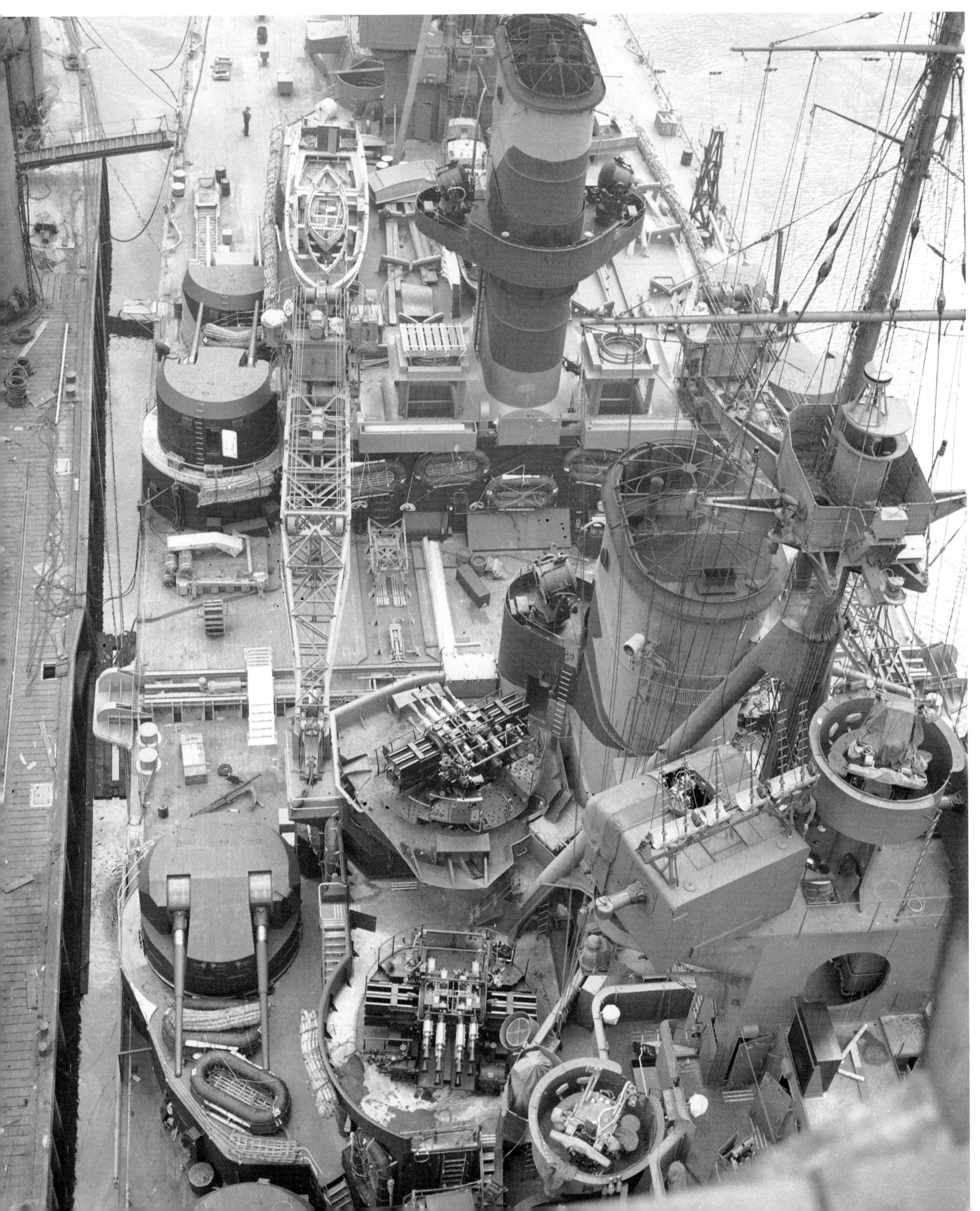

Looking over the bows of the monitor *Roberts*, *Duke of York* is a hive of activity with workmen and crew applying the final touches. The guns of 'B' turret are at maximum elevation while the two refuse chutes are being fitted on the ship's side. The travelling crane behind her bow could lift 30 tons.

Opposite, Another good shot from a shipyard crane looking onto the midships area. It shows the foremast starfish with temporary canvas screen and crow's nest lookout position, replaced by Type 273 radar at Rosyth. Note that the forward funnel is broader than the narrower after funnel

Since keel laying on 5 May 1937, it had taken 52 months to bring *Duke of York* to this stage of completion, considerably longer than the original contract specified. The pressure of war on Britain's armaments industry forced several major delays, partly due to other priorities but also to late supply of both 14in and 5.25in armament. No 3 berth on which *Duke of York* was built had since been used to construct the monitor *Roberts* and just over three weeks after *Duke of York*'s departure, the first steel for the last British battleship, *Vanguard*, will be laid down there.

Casting off from the east wharf on Sunday 7 September 1941, *Duke of York* prepares to be taken stern-first out of the fitting-out basin assisted by tugs. The buildings in the background are at right, shipyard offices and workshops and at left, engine and boiler shops. At top right note the tall columns of keel blocks positioned to support the bow of the aircraft carrier *Indefatigable*.

With the assistance of four coal-fired tugs (*Flying Eagle* and *Flying Falcon* visible at the bow), *Duke of York* is manoeuvred out of the fitting-out basin and into the River Clyde at the start of her passage to the Tail of the Bank (River Clyde estuary). The destroyer *Paladin* is at left fitting out, the entrance to the river Cart in the background.

FALCON

Assisted by tugs, (visible are *Flying Falcon* at bow and *Paladin* amidships) this atmospheric smoke-filled shot shows *Duke of York* positioned in the river channel passing the fitting-out basin and heavy cranes, with the East Yard in the background at right.

Forward turrets and bridge as the ship passes the covered West Yard berths. Some the crew are mustered by the guns of 'A' turret while three officers enjoy a magnificent view standing on top of the compass platform, one probably the pilot. Her mean draft is 31ft, as she has only a few hundred tons of oil fuel aboard. At her foremast-head, one of her two Type 281 air-warning radar aerials has been fitted. The seaboat in the davits is a 32ft cutter.

PALADIN

Midships with *Paladin* in company, which also acted as a personnel tender.

With tugs *Flying Spray* and *Flying Kite* holding her stern, *Duke of York* begins the journey down the Clyde. The tall building in the distance at right is the gun treatment shop, part of the Royal Ordnance Factory Dalmuir, where some of the 16in guns for *Lion*-class battleships would have been manufactured had the contracts for the ships not been suspended and later cancelled.

About the Photographs

In the late 1880s, the management at Clydebank shipyard, then known as J & G Thomson & Co., employed a photographer and set up a photography studio with the aim of making a record of ships under construction. At that time they were building ships of various types including some of the record-breaking passenger vessels working on the transatlantic routes. It is possibly for that reason that the Inman liners *City of New York* and *City of Paris* are among the first to be recorded. When John Brown & Co Ltd purchased the shipyard in 1899 they maintained the photographic department which typically would have a staff of three. While it was common practice among shipbuilders to make a photographic record of ships at launch and on trial (but rarely during construction), most shipyards hired commercial photographers to take the shots rather than set up an in-house department. The move to set up photography at Clydebank proved to be prescient as the shipyard would go on to build some of the most significant ships, merchant and naval, of the steam era. It is entirely down to this foresight that the authors are able to present this photographic record of this important British warship whose four sister vessels built elsewhere have no more than a handful of surviving building photographs between them – indeed *Anson* has none. Photography of ships at Clydebank ceased in 1971 when the shipyard became an oil-rig construction yard but fortunately the collection was saved and is presently under the expert care of the National Records of Scotland in Edinburgh. The collection consists of tens of thousands of glass plate and celluloid negatives and is unequalled in the UK in its coverage of shipbuilding and marine engineering manufactures. The first negatives exposed were 10x12in and 12x15in glass plates and the last almost 100 years later 5x4in celluloids. The *Duke of York* collection numbers over 600 and is a mixture of glass and celluloid. Combined with the reports written at the time also reproduced here, it presents an all but complete record of building a major riveted warship during the high period of British industrialisation. The omissions are that only one photograph was taken of the ship's machinery and no photographs were taken inside the ship at all. One further issue with the *Duke of York* negatives is that they appear to have been catalogued in the shipyard sometime after they were taken, with the result that some of the dates marked on the negatives are completely wrong, or are vague e.g. June 1939, or not given at all. The authors hope that they have managed to overcome the latter issue through careful study of the images and their chronological sequence even if some precise dates remain uncertain.

In July 1940, the wages ledgers for John Brown & Co list the following photographers, D B Lindsay, J R Gibson, James Graham and George Groves. Four boys were named as Ian Bennie, J H Miller, Alex C Hendry and D Calder. The photographers were paid £3 3s 9d per week and J R Gibson £5 11s. The boys were paid 12 shillings per week. David B Lindsay began working as a photographer at Clydebank in the 1890s becoming the chief photographer. By July 1940 he was most likely semi-retired. (UCS1/49/14)

Camouflage

In the last phase of fitting-out, a camouflage scheme was applied to *Duke of York*. The progress of construction photographs show that this appeared about mid-June 1941. The scheme lasted until October of that year and was painted out with an overall coat of Home Fleet Grey on arrival at Rosyth. No colour charts of this camouflage have survived but there is some correspondence which indicates the sequence of events leading to the adoption of a scheme.

In June 1940 the Admiralty asked the Ministry of Home Security to approach various shipyards including John Brown & Co., to arrange for the camouflaging of ships under construction in their yards, particularly where they were likely to spend more than three months in the yard. Little seems to have happened until May 1941 when the idea was revived, probably given some urgency following the bombing of Clydebank the previous March.

Lieutenant Commander John Yunge-Bateman from the Directorate of Camouflage (Naval Section), an artist as well as a naval officer, duly visited the yard in May as a result of which the following instruction survives although unfortunately without the sketch or the proposed colours.

> The ship J.1554 to have her paintwork modified in accordance with the scheme sketched out on the plan and left with the Principal Ship Overseer [H T Johnson]. The colours to be those arranged with the foremen painter on that day, samples of which were inspected and approved; both sides to be painted to the same pattern. The custom of painting ships Admiralty Grey just prior to handing over to be discontinued and no ships in fitting-out basins to be painted Admiralty Grey.

It is likely that the colours used were matched to the surrounding buildings with consideration of how they might look from the air. This implies grey-brown colours with the addition of black or a very dark shade of the grey-brown. The pattern suggests industrial buildings such as saw-tooth roof lines and is not dissimilar to the scheme applied to *King George V* when fitting-out on the Tyne in 1940.

The drawing shown here has resolved the scheme into

four shades of grey to show how the scheme was applied to the ship.

With thanks to Richard Dennis who kindly made his research on the camouflaging of this ship available to the authors.

Sir Stanley Goodall, Diary Extracts

Sir Stanley V Goodall KCB, OBE, naval architect, was the Director of Naval Construction from July 1936 until January 1944 and thus responsible for the design of British warships during that period. His professional diaries covering the latter part of his working life are held by the British Library (Add MSS 52790). Comments made about and during the time of the building of *Duke of York* are reproduced here to offer context and additional insight into the events of the period. The late supply of main-armament gun mountings and labour shortages are standout themes. With limited space, Goodall's entries are clipped and make extensive use of abbreviations and these have been written out here in full by the authors with persons and terms identified and explained in brackets and ship names in italics.

6 May 1936

Controller [Vice Admiral Sir R G Henderson] sent for me re tenders for battleships: I said I was lukewarm I didn't want Fairfield because I don't trust Barr [G W, Fairfield's Managing Director] but would be satisfied with any two of John Browns, Vickers-Armstrongs, Cammell Laird or Swan Hunter. I said we could give information to firms to enable them to start in July, lay down January. If tenders invited, orders would be placed in February, lay down in August, this would push back all succeeding ships because of bottleneck and make us keep the dud Royal Sovereigns longer. [Orders for the first two *King George V* and *Prince of Wales* were placed on 29 July without competitive tendering.]

[Goodall was appointed Director of Naval Construction on 25 July and at this time was standing in for DNC Sir A W Johns who was ill.]

30 May 1938

At Clydebank. Battleship [*Duke of York*] not on as far as expected. Pigott [Stephen, Managing Director of Clydebank shipyard] wants *Beatty*'s [later renamed *Howe*] armour. I said 'Take that up with Hannaford' [C, production constructor]. [The contract for *Duke of York*'s side armour was subsequently switched from Sheffield to Glasgow where Wm Beardmore & Co was also contracted for *Howe*.]

27 September 1938

At Glasgow. Inspected *Beatty* & *Phoebe* [cruiser] also destroyers at Fairfield. Discussed acceleration [of construction] with Barr. Saw liner *Queen Elizabeth* launched [at Clydebank], don't know cause of hitch. With Financial Secretary of Admiralty, Sir Geoffrey Shakespeare in overalls inspected *Anson* [renamed *Duke of York*] & *Fiji* and discussed moving *Queen Elizabeth* [presumably to free up shipyard capacity for warships].

31 May 1939

At launch of *Fiji*, thought welding bad [Goodall was an advocate of using welding more widely]. Looked at *Duke of York* which was getting on well.

17 February 1941

Pengelly [H S, battleship constructor] back from visiting battleships, says *Duke of York* can't keep her date. *Howe* [building at Fairfield] could if men available.

24 May 1941

Boyland [S E, Deputy Director of Naval Construction] phoned for speed of *King George V* on trials, gathered *Hood* sunk. Later heard *Prince of Wales* damaged. Came in after dinner, went to Dockyard Dept re sending *Prince of Wales* to U.S.A. Said I hoped not. With DDNC & DCW [Director of Contract Work, C Hannaford] decided to send message to Hudson [G, Warship Production Superintendent, Scottish] to get Johnson [H T, Admiralty overseer at Clydebank] & Hall [V W, overseer at Fairfield] to discuss accelerating *Duke of York* at expense of *Howe*.

Having reached the Tail of the Bank and cast off tugs, *Duke of York* is moving under her own power very slowly at 6 knots, heading for the boom and Rosyth.

These poor quality but rather dramatic photographs of *Duke of York* were taken during full power trials. It shows how wet she was forward even in a moderate sea, the consequence of having very limited sheer. This condition was applied to the design to allow 'A' turret to fire on forward bearings at low elevation. Rectifying this accounts for the pronounced sheer applied in *Vanguard*.

25 May 1941

Sunday. Deputy Controller held meeting re accelerating *Duke of York* all depends on gun mountings, he will see Controller this p.m. [only her 'A' 14in and two 5.25in mountings had yet to be fitted].

4 August 1941

Bank Holiday. At Glasgow long talk with Troup [Vice Admiral J A G, Flag Officer in Charge, Glasgow] fussed over labour & repairs. To Clydebank had talk with Pigott re labour; then look at *Duke of York*.

6 September 1941

U 570 [captured 27 August] at Iceland sending Pamplin [G W, submarine constructor]. Stirred up DDNC re *Duke of York* rudder [needed stiffening when drydocked at Rosyth] and received only chits in reply.

1 November 1941

Went to Rosyth met Controller, [Vice Admiral Sir Bruce Fraser] walked thro' workshops, then on board *Renown*. Embarked in *Duke of York* 1800. Solberg (U.S.N. constructor) at dinner, very interesting.

2 November 1941

At sea. Gun trials progressed. Weather calm. A hitch on F.P. [full power] preliminary trial due to a leaky turbo condenser, and inexperienced officer in charge not reporting this till salt water was present throughout the whole system. Ventilation of L.P. room [low power electrics] bad, action machinery space not good, otherwise all right. A lot of water in A magazine (hydraulic leak).

3 November 1941

At sea. 4 gun packed back [over pressurising the recuperator to test gun recoil and run-out] salvo from Y turret shook ship and hotted up one propeller shaft due to clearance being insufficient. This put off F.P. trial to Tuesday. Ship went well when at F.P. vibration very little, focsle [forecastle] wet, must alter *Vanguard*. *King George V* was leaving as we arrived [at Scapa] so I missed C. in C. [*Vanguard* was subsequently given very pronounced sheer forward.]

4 November 1941

With Controller inspected Lyness Yard [repair base on Island of Hoy with floating Dock AFD.12]. [Date of Admiralty acceptance of *Duke of York*.]

Log Books

Although it is not the intention of this book to cover the service career of *Duke of York*, some reference to what became of her immediately after leaving the shipyard is of interest until official completion on 4 November 1941. Examining a complex ship like *Duke of York* in such detail as this book attempts, inevitably ignores her function as a fully-manned warship. The language of the log books, although somewhat clipped, reveals the true function of the ship. Excerpts from the period of her departure from Clydebank until her becoming part of the fleet on 7 November at Scapa Flow are included here to make that transition.

Abbreviations

A/c	aircraft
a/c	altered course
Buoy	references to buoys such as Buoy 23, indicates passing a buoy in a swept channel.
BW	Both Watches
Ex	exercised
Fx	Forecastle
Pvs	Paravanes
PW	Port Watch
Rounds	Inspection of the ship by the officer of the day.
s/c	set course
SW	Starboard Watch
Z-z	Zig zag

Clydebank to Rosyth 6 September to 10 September

Saturday 6 September 1941

CLYDEBANK

0900 Hands employed cleaning ship. Exercised 5.25" trial and Pom Pom's crews and AA lookouts.
1100 Up spirits.
1200 Hands to dinner.
1315 5.25" trial crew to drill in S2 turret.
1700 Exercised fire quarters.
2010 Darkened ship.
2030 Closed X doors and scuttles.
2100 Rounds.

Sunday 7 September 1941.

CLYDEBANK TO TAIL OF THE BANK.

0750 BW Hands employed cleaning ship.
0900 BW Hands part of ship and securing for sea. Closed X doors and scuttles.
1100 Draught for'd 30' 9" mid 31' 0" aft 31' 1½".
1147 Slipped, hauled out of dock by tugs.
1200 Proceeded ahead course and speeds as requisite.

1215 Dalmuir Bend.
1226 Dalmuir Sewage Wharf.
1238 Kilpatrick Oil Wharf.
1258 Bowling.
1320 Dumbuck.
1328 Garrison Light.
1350 Cardross.
1421 Garvel Point.
1432 Cast off tugs.
1435 Princes Pier, courses and speeds as requisite leaving Clyde.
1517 Passed through boom.
1600 Evening quarters.
1615 Cumbrae Light abeam.
1640 Increased to 22kts.
1810 Special Sea Dutymen.
1812 Cable party.
1842 Hands fall in entering harbour.
1859 Came to port anchorage with 6 shackles cable in 17 fathoms. C2 berth off Greenock.
1910 Commenced anchor trials.
2000 Anchor trials completed.
2010 Darken ship.
2100 Rounds.

Monday 8 September 1941

TAIL OF THE BANK
0630 Ammunition lighter arrived but not required. Called the hands.
0700 Breakfast. Dress of Day No.3.
0750 Both watches securing for sea. Cable party muster on Fx.
0800-0820 *Flying Scotsman* [tug] alongside.
0842 Weighed and proceeded to DG Range [degaussing].
0907 Runs commenced.
1140 Trials completed.
1215 Secured by starboard bridle to buoy.
1235 Tugs *Flying Eagle* and *Flying Falcon* secured aft. Commenced swinging ship for adjusting compasses.
1330 Clear lower decks. Capt. addressed ship's company.
1530 Completed compass adjustment.
1545 Cast off tugs.
1615 2 ammunition barges secured stbd. side – port watch ammunitioning ship.
1620 Oiler *Montenol* secured port side.
1915 Stbd watch relieved port watch and continued ammunitioning ship.
2230 Completed ammunitioning ship.

Tuesday 9 September 1941

TAIL OF THE BANK TO ROSYTH.
0300 Oiler *Montenol* cast off. Embarked 732 tons oil fuel.
0445 Port watch prepare ship for sea.
0500 Special Sea Dutymen.
0558 Slipped from buoy.
0600 Pointed ship. Courses and speeds as requisite in Clyde approaches.
0640 Passed boom. *Penelope*, *Lightning*, *Vivacious*, and *Icarus* in Company.
0734 Cumbrae Light abeam speed 10 knots.
0738 Stream Pvs.
0746 Increased to 20 knots.
0800 Z-z [zig-zag] in searched channels throughout day.
0945 No 1 Pom Pom completed trials.
0950 No 3 Pom Pom commenced trials.
1012 No 3 Pom Pom completed trials
1018 No 5 Pom Pom commenced trials.
1104 No 5 Pom Pom completed trials.
1105 No 4 Pom Pom trials commenced.
1125 No 4 Pom Pom trials completed.
1135 No 2 Pom Pom trials commenced. No.38 Z-z commenced.
1205 SW prepare to take in Pvs.
1255 Pvs in.
1245 Orsay Light abeam 3.4 miles
1315 Commenced 5.25" trials.
1320 Commenced Z-z No.12.
1520 Cease Z-z.
1525 Skerryvore Light bearing 069°.
1600 Z-z No.12 resumed.
1720 Convoy bearing 010° going on opposite course.
1800 Ceased Z-z. 20 kts at 154 rpm.
1810 No.12 Z-z resumed.
1920 Ceased 5.25" trials.
1935 Ceased Z-z.
1953 Vaternish Light bearing 110°.
2040 Eilea Trodday abeam 0.8mi.
2123 Rudh Re Light abeam 5.5mi.

Wednesday 10 September 1941 at Sea

0032 Cape Wrath abeam 5mi.
0249 Dunnet Head. Courses as requisite through Pentland Firth.
0344 Duncansby Head abeam 1.5mi.
0608 Commenced Z-z astern of destroyers. Speed of advance 17 knots.
0722 2 extra Spitfires join original 2.
0727 Rattray Head bearing 194°
1014 Convoy bearing 190°.
1145 Ceased Z-z.
1214 Increased to 20 knots.
1338 *Penelope* and *Icarus* parted company.

36-3	2	Renown	9.9.41	24.10.41	26-3½	26-8	25-10½	26-8	Repairs to Bulge	[illegible]
38-6"	1	Duke of York	10-9-41	17-10-41	29'-6"	31'-6"	28'-10	30-10	Stiffening to rudder Bow Dump for P.V.'s	[illegible]
	F	C + a	11/9/41	17/9/41	3'-6"	9'-9"	3'-6"	9'-9"	Changing Propeller	H.J. Coleman

An extract from the Docking Log at Rosyth indicating dates, draughts and that work on the ship's rudder was in progress.

1400 Reduced to 9 knots.
1524 Passed through outer boom.
1536 Passed through inner boom.
1604 Passed Oxcars boom.
1619 Pilot aboard.
1630 Passed under Forth Bridge. Courses and speed as requisite for Rosyth dock.
1708 Entered lock
1800 Entered dock [Drydock No 1]. Draught fwd 29' 6" aft 31' 6".
1820 Ship in dock.
2000 Dockyard Patrol landed.
2015 Darkened ship.

At Rosyth

Thursday 11 September 1941

0630 Hands employed undarkening ship.
0800 Hands employed cleaning ship.
0900 Hands cleaning ship. Guns crews to drill.
1400 9 ratings discharged to hospital.
1530 Rev. R R Evans RN joined ship.
1745 Cover guns.

Friday 26 September 1941

0630 Open X doors, hands employed cleaning ship.
0800 Hands employed painting ship.
1015 Midshipmen Allen, Wingate and McFadyen joined ship.
1100 RMs [Royal Marines] landed. Captain went ashore to inspect RMs.

Saturday 27 September 1941

0630 Undarken ship, open X doors, hands employed cleaning ship.
0800 Hands employed painting ship.
0900 Gun drill.
1105 Torpedo officer and party returned from Belfast.
1125 8 ratings joined ship.
1500 Sub Lt. Sampson joined ship.
1700 No. 5 and 6 warrants read, exercised fire quarters.
2030 Cleared mess decks and flats. Closed X doors.

Thursday 16 October

0730 Hands cleaning ship.
0830 Small fire in compartment under 'Saltash' director extinguished.
0840 Fire fighting party landed for instruction.
1030 HMS *Isle of Thanet* entered basin.
1055 Prisoner and escort landed for Glasgow.
1100 2nd long leave party returned.
1300 Both watches hands employed preparing for ammunitioning and part of ship.
2150 Glasgow escort returned.

Friday 17 October

0830 B watch hands employed ammunitioning ship. Gunnery drill.
0835 Commenced embarking aviation spirit [petrol] and lub oil.
1030 Ceased embarking aviation spirit.
1130 Port watch to stations leaving harbour. Port watch cable party muster on foc'sle.
1200 Commenced shifting ship with assistance of 5 tugs out of dock to west wall.
1300 Berthed alongside. Cast off tugs. Draught fwd 28' 10", aft 30' 10".
1330 Ammunition lighter *Polly M* and *Bison* fast alongside.
1345 Hands resumed ammunitioning ship.
1820 Lighter *Bison* cast off.
1840 Lighter *Polly M* cast off.

Saturday 18 October

0805 Ammunition lighters alongside. Hands ammunitioning ship.
0915 Oil lighter cast off. Embarked 2870 gallons lub oil, 2000 gallons aviation spirit, 450 gallons of motor boat petrol.
1300 Hands Starboard Watch ammunitioning ship.
1400 For'd ammunition lighter cast off.
1555 After ammunition ship cast off.

This photograph, probably taken on 27 October 1941, shows *Duke of York* shackled to No 14 buoy in the River Forth, the ship having left Rosyth Dockyard that morning. With tugs at her port side and puffers and an ammunition lighter at her starboard side, an anti-torpedo boom is being arranged down her port side. Her new Type 273 surface-warning radar has been fitted to the foremast. Rosyth Dockyard is to the left of shot and the North Sea beyond the Forth Bridge is at right. Ammunitioning and fuelling were completed on 1 November. The ship sailed the following day to begin trials. (Imperial War Museum)

Sunday 19 October

0730 Hands cleaning ship. HC [Holy Communion] in chapel.
0815 Prayers on foc'sle.
0825 Hands ammunitioning ship.
1530 Ceased ammunitioning ship.
1700 Exercised fire quarters. HMS *Gleaner*, *Wallace* and *Quantock* entered harbour.
1800 HMS *Vanity* left wall for anchorage.

Monday 20 October

0830 Both watches hands employed ammunitioning ship. Gunnery drills. Fire fighting party landed for instruction.
0910 Ammunition lighter *Bison* secured alongside and small oiler.
1030 to 1100 Respirators worn by ship's company.
1115 Ammunition trucks (3) alongside [probably for close-range guns].
1300 Hands embark ammunition. Gunnery drills.
1320 Oiler cast off.
1615 *Bison* cast off.

Tuesday 21 October

0810 *Berwick* proceeded to sea from anchorage.
0900 Hands employed in store parties and special ammunition parties.
1030 Lost by accident one vice Patt 4349.
1215 Notice re 'complaints' read to ships company by Lt. Cdr Easy over broadcaster.
1400 Hands employed as in forenoon. One Walrus aircraft hoisted inboard.
1800 Embarked catapult charges [cordite].

At Sea. From Rosyth to Scapa Flow

Tuesday 2 November

To Scapa. At Sea
0600 Port Watch hands securing for sea and unshackling.
0655 Special sea dutymen.
0734 Slipped, pointed ship and proceeded.
0757 Speed 9 knots course as requisite in Firth of Forth.
0805 Passed under Forth Bridge.

0821 Passed inner boom.
0827 Passed outer boom.
0829 Oxcars Light abeam.
0902 Inchkeith lighthouse abeam.
0906 Passed through Inchkeith boom.
1010 No.1 buoy abeam *Punjabi*, *Tartar*, *Escapade* screening ahead, *Berwick* astern.
1034 Streamed Pvs speed 18 knots.
1100 Action stations exercised. Commenced working up to full speed on cruising turbines.
1120 No.22A buoy abeam. Set course to 024˚ speed as requisite.
1330 Gun trials of 14" turrets throughout the day.
1455 No.28 buoy zig-zagged as requisite in searched channels.
1608 No.30 buoy abeam a/c 327°.
1800 Exercised action stations.
1847 Port watch 5.25" defence stations close up.
1937 No.35 buoy abeam, 1943 No.34 buoy, 1945 Noss Head Lighthouse abeam.
2000 a/c as requisite for passage through Pentland Firth.
2039 Stroma light abeam.
2120 s/c 326° speed 19 knots.
2135 Commenced Z-z No.12.
2350 Passed 2 fishing vessels to starboard.
2359 Defence watch closed up. Four pom-poms closed up.

Monday 3 November

TO SCAPA. AT SEA
0100 Zig-Zag No.12 continued.
0730 Commenced working up to full power. 0800 a/c 090°. Position 59° 08' N, 4° 45' W.
0810 *Impulsive* relieved *Punjabi* as escort.
0825 Sule Skerry lighthouse abeam.
1000 Carried out gun trials as requisite.
1100 Abandoned full power trial, worked down speed.
1200 Zig-zagging as requisite.
1305 Sighted Sule Skerry brg 221°.
1518 *Victorious* passed to port with escort of 3 destroyers.
1524 In paravanes. Course and speed as requisite for entering Scapa Flow.
1609 Passed through Hoxa gate.
1616 Passed through Nevi Skerry boom.
1636 Came to anchorage with 9 shackles in 17 fathoms. In B1 berth.
1639 Finished with engines, reverted to 4 hours notice for steam.
1740 Oiler *Gold Ranger* secured port side.
1930 *King George V*, *Kent*, *Berwick* and *Suffolk* sailed.
2100 Rounds. Inspection by officer of the day.
2245 Ceased oiling.
2300 *Gold Ranger* cast off.

At Scapa Flow

Tuesday 4 November

TO SEA FOR EXERCISES OR AT SCAPA FLOW
0720 Cable party on foc'sle. Remainder hands securing ship for sea.
0730 Hoisted pinnace and second P boat.
0823 Weighed anchor.
0835 BDV [boom defence vessel] *Barnstone* crossed bow.
0900 Passed through Nevi Skerry boom and proceeded course and speed as requisite for leaving Scapa Flow. *Onslow* and *Impulsive* in company.
0907 Passed Hoxa boom, course and speed as requisite for Pentland Firth. Worked up to full power.
1023 Z-z No.12 as requisite.
1300 Sule Skerry bearing 266° 10mi.
1400 *Norman* relieved *Onslow* as escort.
1457 Repel aircraft stations.
1500 Completed full power trials. 28 kts at 232 rpm.
1510 Commenced steering trials. a/c as requisite.
1530 Commenced working down. Course and speed as requisite for entering Scapa Flow.
1638 Recovered paravanes.
1706 Passed through Hoxa Gate.
1734 Came to starboard anchorage 9 shackles in 17 fathoms in B1 berth.
1800 *Cumberland* entered harbour.
1900 Sub Lt's Henwood, Lintle, Wrathall and Hannen plus Midshipman Haming-Lee joined ship.

Wednesday 5 November

0700 Hands cleaning and securing ship for sea.
0830 Cable party of PW on Fx.
0810 Both Walrus's arrived. 0933 first embarked. 0957 second embarked.
1003 Weighed anchor. Courses and speed as required flying off aircraft.
1040 Launched A/c to port.
1125 Launched A/c to stb.
1200 Hands to dinner.
1323 Came up to buoy, shipped cutter.
1340 Secured to East buoy. Reverted to 4 hours notice for steam.
1700 Hoisted VA2's [Vice Admiral 2nd Battle Squadron] barge.
1915 Steam for slow speed ordered, closed up anchor watches and helmsman. Force 6 WSW wind.
2050 Emergency party prepare sheet anchor for letting go.

H.M.S. "Duke of York", Monday 3rd day of November, 1941.

From Rosyth, To Scapa or At Sea

Time	Log (Stating type) Patentmeter	Distance Run through the Water: Miles	Tenths	True Course	Mean Revolutions per minute	Wind: Direction (true)	Force (0-12)	Weather and Visibility	Sea and Swell	Corrected Barometric Pressure in Millibars	Temperature (°F): Dry Bulb	Wet Bulb	Sea	LEAVE GRANTED TO SHIP'S COMPANY / REMARKS	Initials of the Officer of the Watch
0100	303.9	18	-	360°	135.2									Zig-Zag No 12 continued.	
0200	322.9	19	-	360°	144.1									~~0200 reduced~~	
30		9	5	360°										0230 a/c 300°	
0300	341.9	9	5	300°	143.7										
30		9	5	—"—										0330 a/c 240°	
0400	371.8	9	5	240°	146.1	N	4	bc/7	23	Unshipped	47	43	45	0400 ———	[illegible]
30		9	5	—"—										0430 a/c 180°	
0500	391.0	9	5	180°	142.4										
0600	411.4	19	-	—"—	143.2										
0700	430.9	19	-	—"—	152										
30		9	5	—"—										0730 a/c 120° Commenced working up to	
0800	451.68	10	3	120°	152.4	N	4	bc/7	20	—"—	50	46	52	Full power. 0800 a/c 090° 0810 "Impulsive"	[illegible]
														relieved "Punjabi" as escort.	
0900	477.35	26	1	090°	210									0826 Sule Skerry [illegible]	
1000	508.0	28	-	000°	230.8									Carried out gun trials as requisite.	
57		26	7	180°										1055 a/c 180°	
1100	531.2	1	3	180°	218.9									1100 Abandoned Full power trial, worked	
														down speed.	
1200	556.2	21	7	180°	168.5	NNE	2	c/8	21	—"—	49	45	45	Zig-Zagging as requisite	[illegible]

Distance run through the Water	Position	Latitude N.	Longitude W.	Depending on	Currents experienced		ANCHOR BEARINGS	
490.8	0800	59 08	4 45	Land fix	Tidal		Draft.	at 1636
Zone Time kept at noon	1200	59 40	3 59	—"—			Ford. 31' 6"	A buoy 162°
Z-1	2000	–	–	–	Number on Sick List	10	Aft. 33' 6"	Fara Lt. 230° / N point Fara 281°

Time	Log	Miles	Tenths	True Course	Mean Revolutions per minute	Wind: Direction (true)	Force	Weather and Visibility	Sea and Swell	Barometric Pressure	Dry Bulb	Wet Bulb	Sea	Remarks	Initials
														Embarked 551 tons oil fuel.	
1300	578.9	21	8	180°	169.4									1305 Sighted Sule Skerry brg 221°	
30		11	7	—"—										1330 a/c 146°.	
1400 55	602.6	11	7	146°	184.6										
		21	4	—"—										1455 a/c 088°.	
1500 24	631.3	1	9	088°	183.4									1518 "Victorious" passed to port with escort	
				—"—										of 3 destroyers. 1524 In P.V.'s Co. & Sp. as	
1600	652.1	17	4	As req. entering	132.1	NNE	2	c/8	11	—"—	50	46	51	req. for entering Scapa Flow.	[illegible]
36		7	1	Scapa.										1609 passed thro' Hoxa gate. 1616 passed	
1700					53.0									thro' Nevi Skerry boom. 1636 Came to S with	
														with 9 shackles in 17 faths. in B1 berth.	
1800						NNE	2	bc	-	1029.9	47	46	51	1639 Finished with eng. reverted to 4 hours	[illegible]
														notice for steam. 1740 Oiler "Gold Ranger"	
1900														secured port side.	
														"King George V", "Kent", "Berwick", & "Suffolk" sailed.	
2000						NW	1	c	-	1029.4	47	46	51	2000 ———	[illegible]
2100														2100 Rounds.	
2200															
														2245 Ceased oiling.	
2300														2300 "Gold Ranger" cast off.	
2400						N	2	o	-	1028.7	49	47	51	Mid. ———	[illegible]

A page from *Duke of York*'s log book showing movements on 3 November 1941 during trials.

Thursday 6 November

0830 Gun drills all forenoon.
0900 *Montrose* with VA2 secured port side.
0905 VA2 boarded with staff. VA2 flag hoisted [Vice Admiral A T B Curteis].
0915 RA (D) [Rear Admiral Destroyers L H K Hamilton] visited VA2.
1010 *Montrose* cast off. RA (D) departed.
1115 *Norman* entered harbour.
1225 *Arethusa* left harbour.
1525 The death of C W Lang (A/B) occurred by drowning.
1635 Ordered steam for slow ahead. Commenced anchor watches. Helmsman closed up.
1720 All boats hoisted.

Friday 7 November

0900 Exercised action stations.
1030 Fall out action stations. Drifter took coffin ashore.
1145 *Trinidad* entered harbour.
1315 *Norman* entered harbour.
1500 Reverted 4 hours notice for steam. Anchor watches and Qm [quartermaster] fall out.

Left Scapa Flow for Clyde on 9 December arriving there on 12 December.
13 December embarked Prime Minister Winston Churchill for passage to Annapolis, USA where she arrived on 22 December.
Shake-down cruise to Bermuda began on 3 January 1942 arriving on 5 January.
Departed Bermuda 17 January for Clyde arriving Greenock on 25 January (Churchill flew home).
Arrived Scapa Flow 30 January for a further one-month period of working up.
Service career began on 28 February when she left for Hvalfjord in Iceland arriving there on 2 March.

Duke of York entered No. 1 dry dock at Rosyth on 10 September and left on 17 October 1941.

Like all new ships, drydocking was an essential part of the completion process. Various fittings fixed to the hull such as bracket connections for the poppets, fixings for drag chains all associated with the launch and difficult to access while the ship was afloat could be removed, although *Duke of York*'s had already been removed at Clydebank. The lower part of the hull was cleaned and given a fresh coat of Clark's anti-fouling paint while the camouflage applied in June 1941 in the shipyard was replaced with an overall coat of Home Fleet Grey 507B. Trials with *King George V* had pointed to a weakness in the design of the rudder and the drydock log records that the rudder was stiffened and also that the bow clump used for streaming paravanes was modified.

DUKE OF YORK

Plans

SHIP DRAWINGS HAVE three purposes: a medium for the designer to define intent; a means of transmitting information, e.g. from drawing office to workshop; and a record of what was done, useful both for the ship operator and for designing future ships. All three functions are illustrated: DNC's design intent e.g. Structural sections, pp33-4; John Brown's production definition e.g. Frame 176 drawing, p63; and a store of information e.g. As Fitted plans. Modern computer-aided design and draughting systems achieve the same functionality; only the medium is different, digital electronics instead of paper. The selection in this book features all three types, and can be directly related to the photographs.

1941 General Arrangement Plans (M1686–1696)

The Admiralty specified which drawings were to be supplied by the shipbuilder upon completion. Many are details such as piping plans, but the ones of widest interest are the As Fitted General Arrangements. Now in the National Maritime Museum, all eleven plans are reproduced, with the occasional pencil annotation.

One profile (inboard).
Eight deck plans.
Two cross section plans.
All were drawn to the same scale ⅛in = 1ft or 1:96.

It is not the intention to discuss the design of *King George V*-class battleships and thus the comments that follow here are aimed at noting specific areas of interest or offering some general points. The plans are largely self-explanatory and show the ship in all of its complexity from settees and ice cream machines to turbo generators and the fire-control stations.

The As Fitted drawings for *Duke of York* were produced by John Brown & Co and signed off by their Chief Draughtsman and the Admiralty's Principal Ship Overseer, H T Johnson, on 28 May 1942. One set was sent to the Admiralty, the set used in this publication, and one set was sent to the ship to be retained there throughout her life. The drawings, produced in the shipyard drawing office at Clydebank, were developed from the *King George V*-class design drawings which were prepared by the Naval Construction Department, then in Whitehall, and from plans of equipment supplied by sub-contractors such as capstan machinery. As with all As Fitted drawings of Admiralty ships, they are magnificent examples of draughtsmanship, identification and communication. However, these drawings do not show all external details of the ships and for that other sources must be consulted, e.g. Sketch of Rig p218. The drawing convention employed is to identify all major elements of the ship's layout and fittings but not to depict the external details of how the ship looked. Each of these drawings is almost 8ft long. The drawings were probably the work of a single senior draughtsman made over a period of several months. The draughtsman was required to visit the ship before it left the shipyard, and note where changes had been made from the design drawings. He would also have had copies of the progress photographs to assist him.

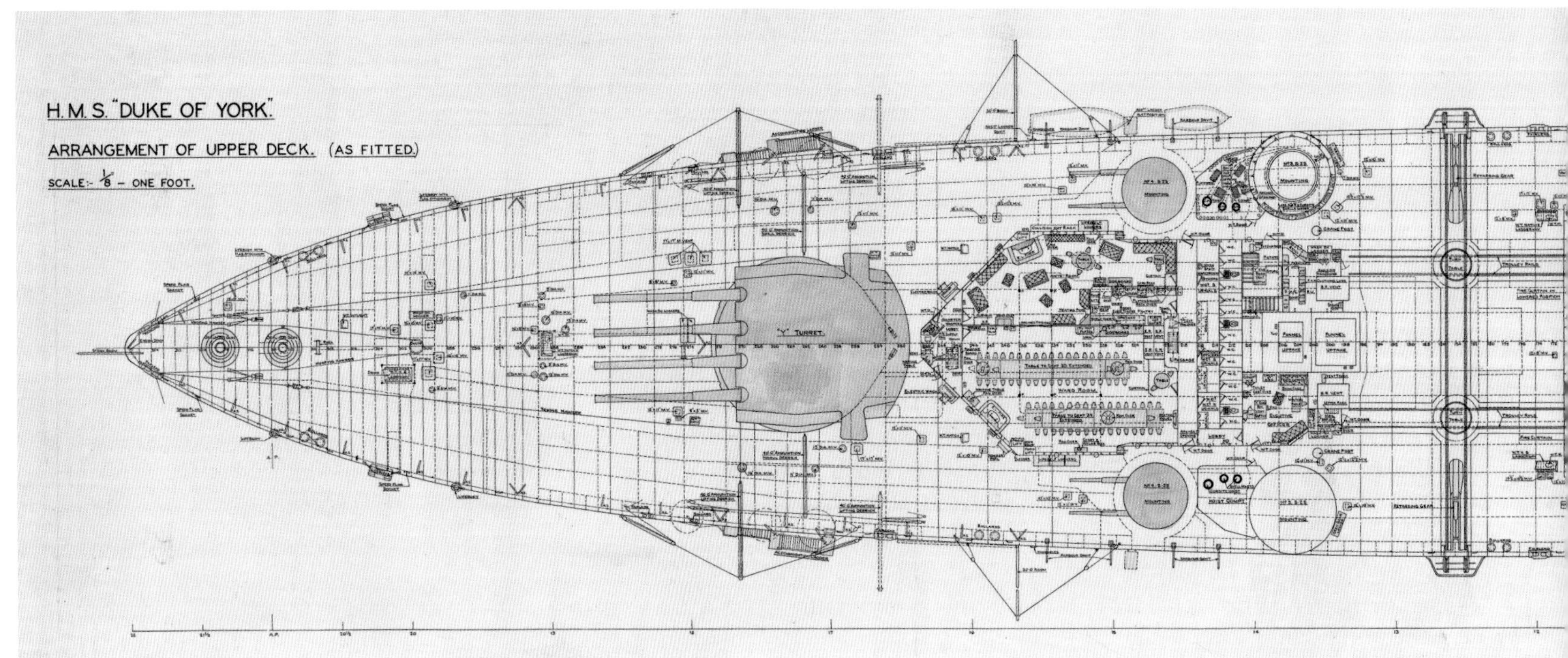
H.M.S. "DUKE OF YORK".
ARRANGEMENT OF UPPER DECK. (AS FITTED)
SCALE:- 1/8 – ONE FOOT.
'Y' TURRET.

Above, Upper Deck

While this drawing conforms in general to the convention mentioned above, it does show much more detail than the associated profile with all fittings visible on the upper deck represented down to stanchions, hatches, vents and furniture in the officers' wardroom. It also shows some elements of the rig in place such as various booms with their anchor points for ropes etc. identified. The drawing is somewhat cluttered by showing dotted the run underneath of beams, longitudinals and bulkheads. (© National Maritime Museum, London M1687)

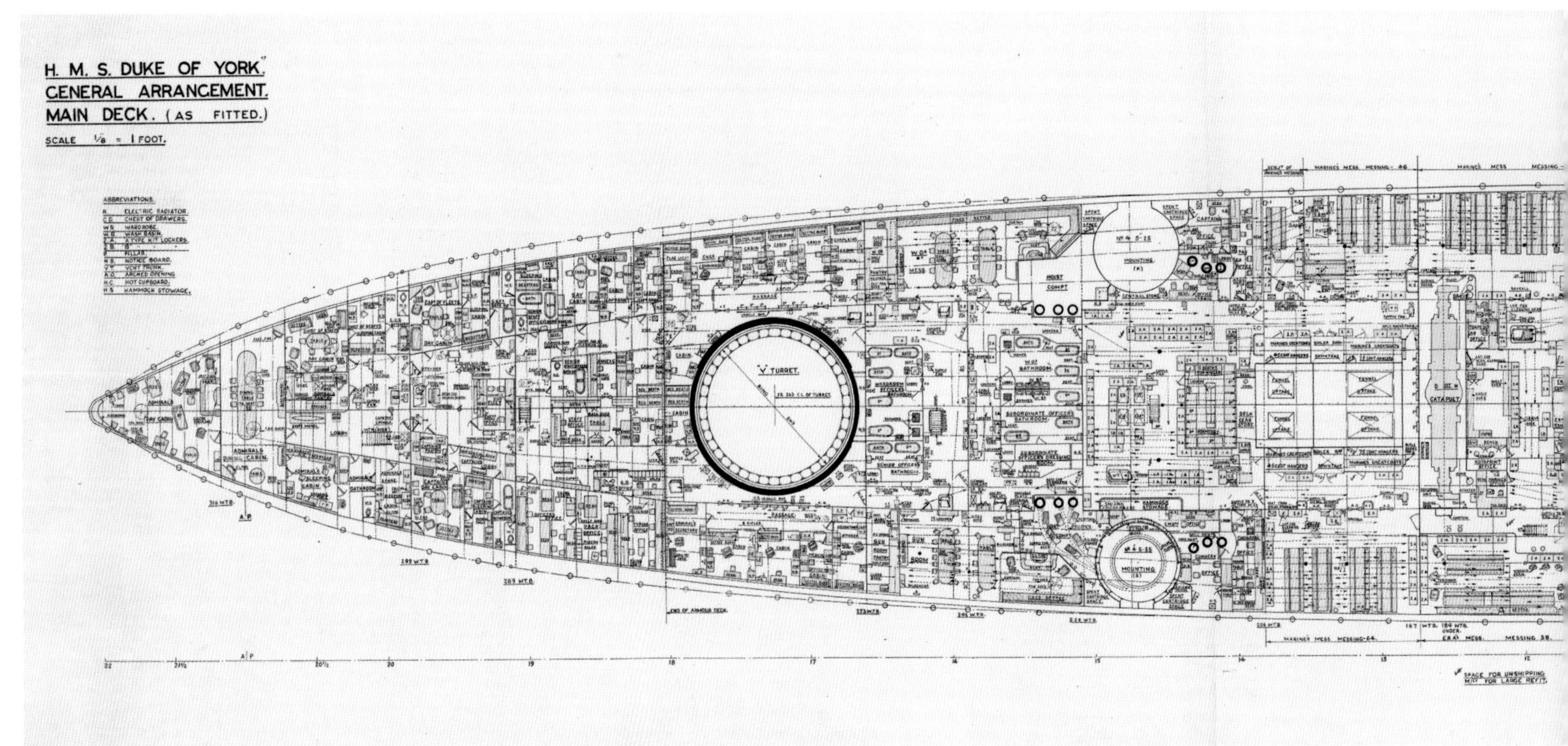
H. M. S. DUKE OF YORK."
GENERAL ARRANGEMENT.
MAIN DECK. (AS FITTED.)
SCALE 1/8 = 1 FOOT.
'Y' TURRET.

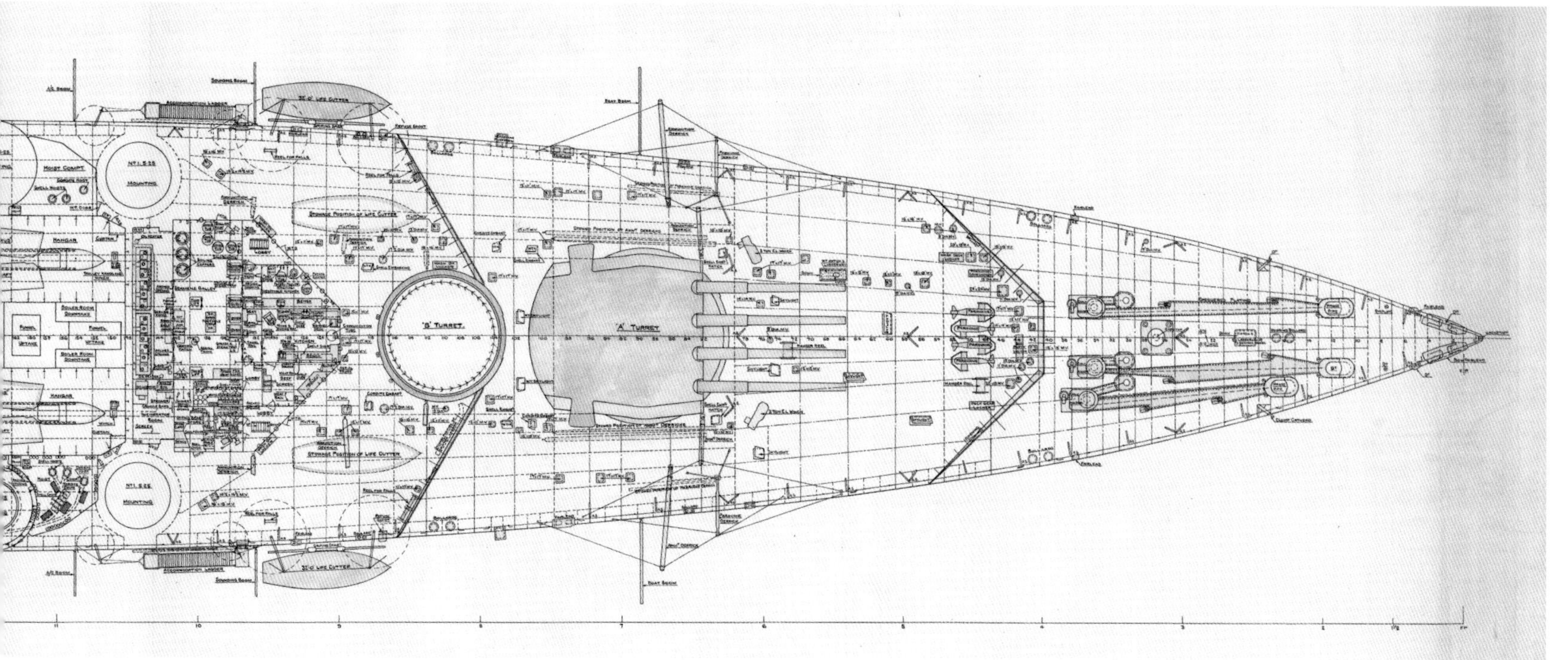
'B' TURRET
'A' TURRET

Below, Main Deck

There is a wealth of information in this drawing which depicts how life was lived on this ship from the seamen's heads (WCs) forward to the admiral's day cabin right aft. The armour deck was located at this level which varied in thickness from 5in to 6in extending from just forward of 'A' barbette to just aft of 'Y' barbette. The barbette armour seen here in scale gives a real appreciation of its thickness, 11–13in, in the context of the surrounding structure. Note the prominently defined armoured tubes for 5.25in shell and cordite hoists, the communication tube and wireless aerial trunk. Medical spaces including a dental surgery are right forward.

Although a list of abbreviations is given, it is by no means complete, e.g. W.T.C. = watertight compartment, M.V. = mushroom vent, R.U. = Ready use, S.P.O. = Stoker Petty Officer. (© National Maritime Museum, London M1688)

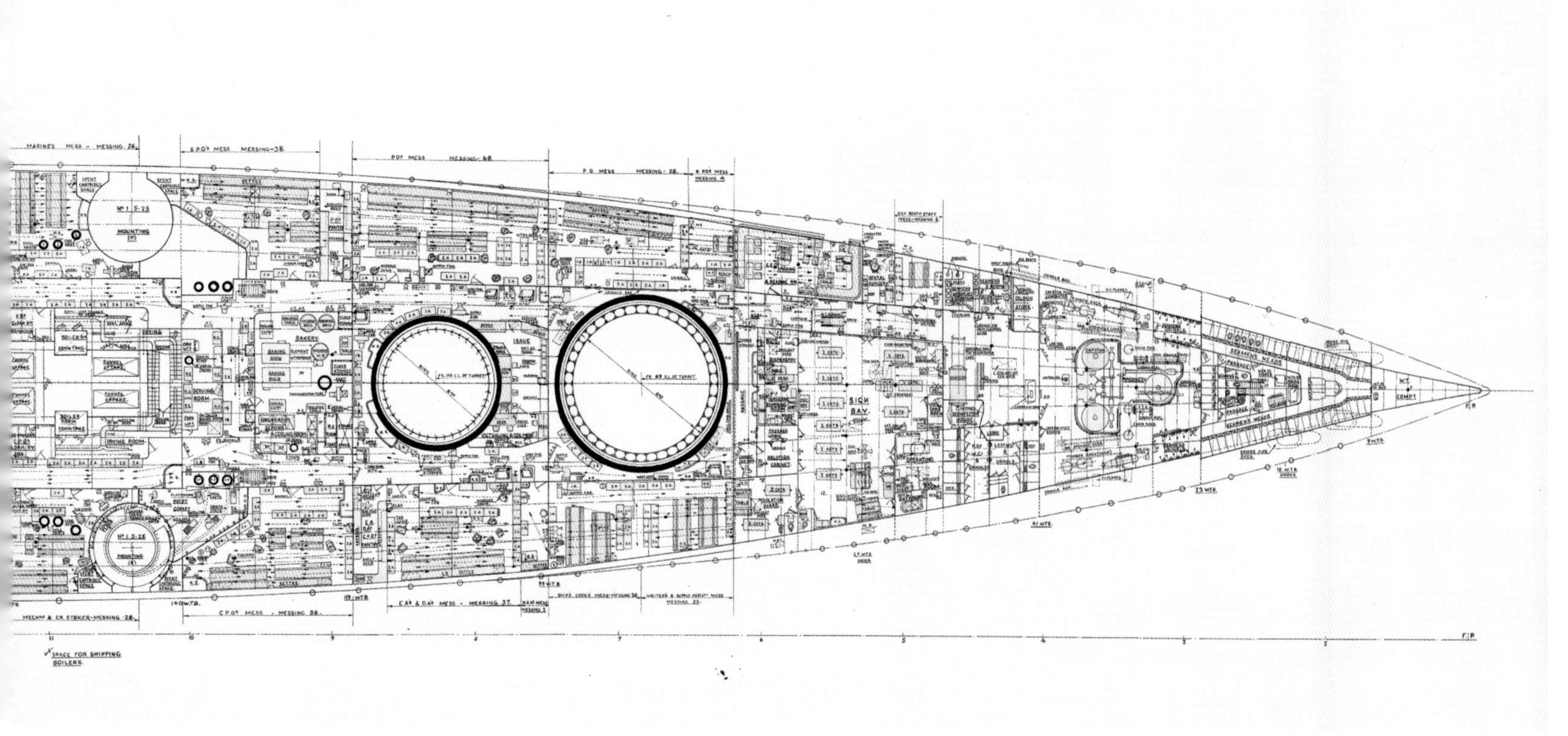
SICK BAY

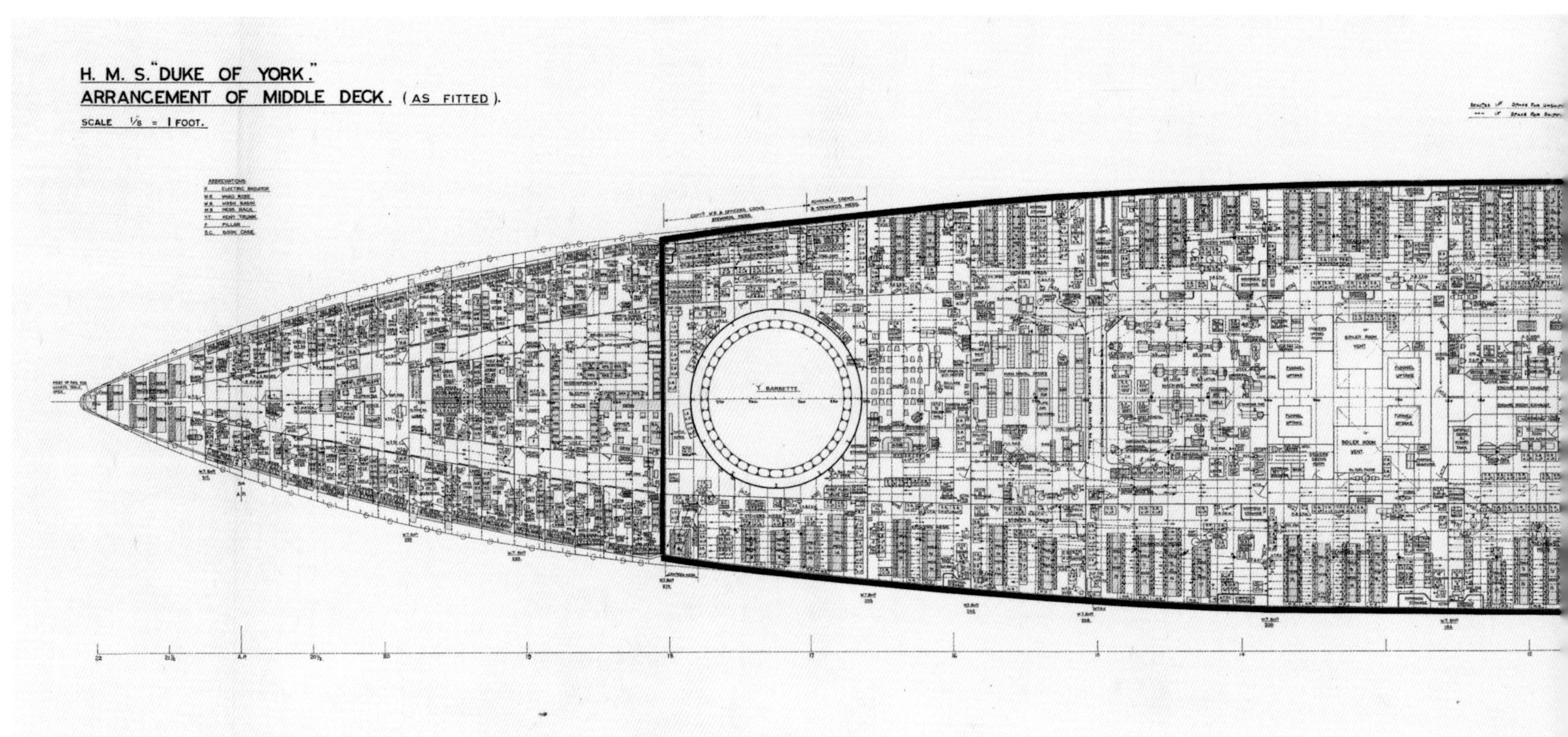
H. M. S. "DUKE OF YORK."
ARRANGEMENT OF MIDDLE DECK. (AS FITTED).
SCALE 1/8 = 1 FOOT.
Y BARBETTE

Above, Middle Deck

This is the lowest deck where fore and aft access is possible. Compartments below this level can only be accessed through vertical hatches and ladderways. Where the barbette armour stops, the armoured box formed by the side armour and the end armoured bulkheads takes over. This deck is primarily about living accommodation for crew with messes for all ranks arranged down either side and forward and aft of the armoured bulkheads. A typical mess comprised tables with benches for eating and recreation plus kit lockers and hammock stowage bins. Hammock spaces are indicated by <- - ->. They were also slung in passageways, guaranteeing a disturbed night for the unfortunate occupants. Naval stores and machine shops occupy the central axis along with boiler room vents and uptakes. (© National Maritime Museum, London

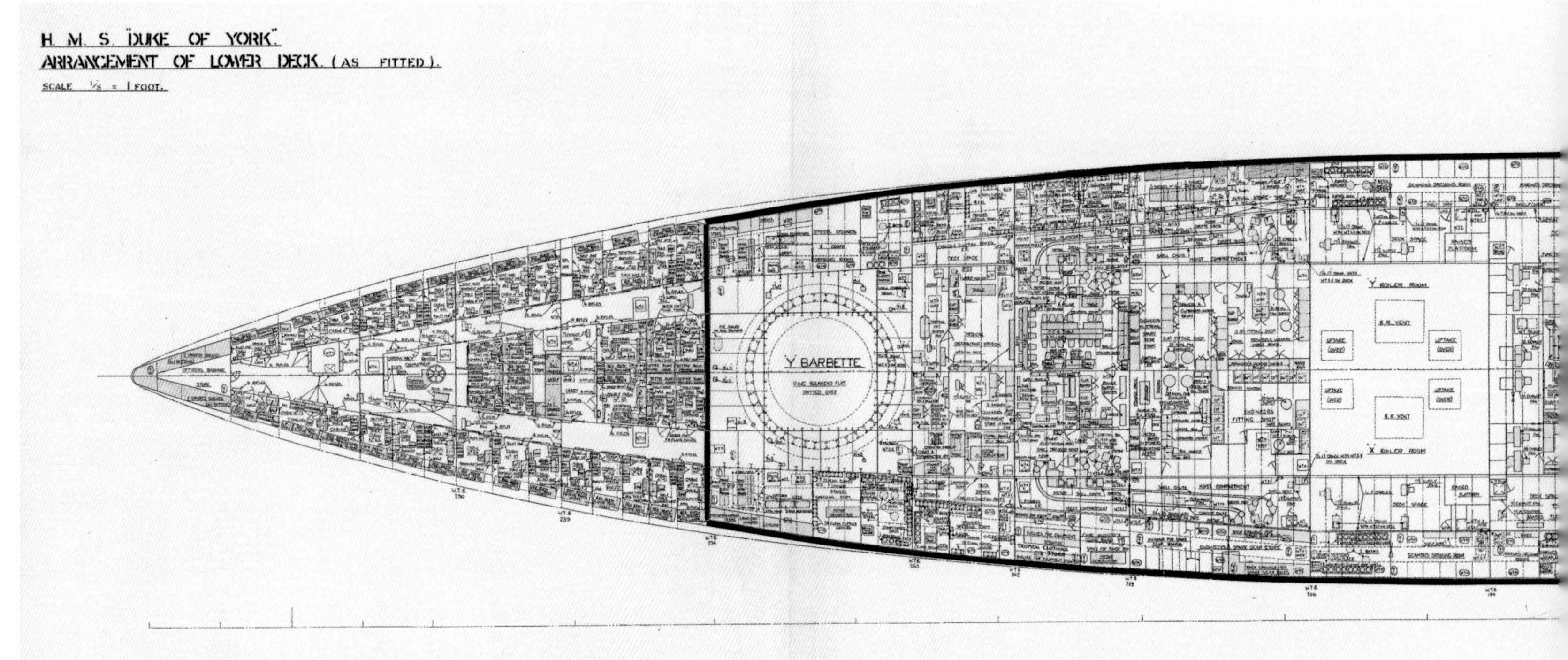
H. M. S. "DUKE OF YORK."
ARRANGEMENT OF LOWER DECK. (AS FITTED).
SCALE 1/8 = 1 FOOT.
Y BARBETTE
Y BOILER ROOM
X BOILER ROOM

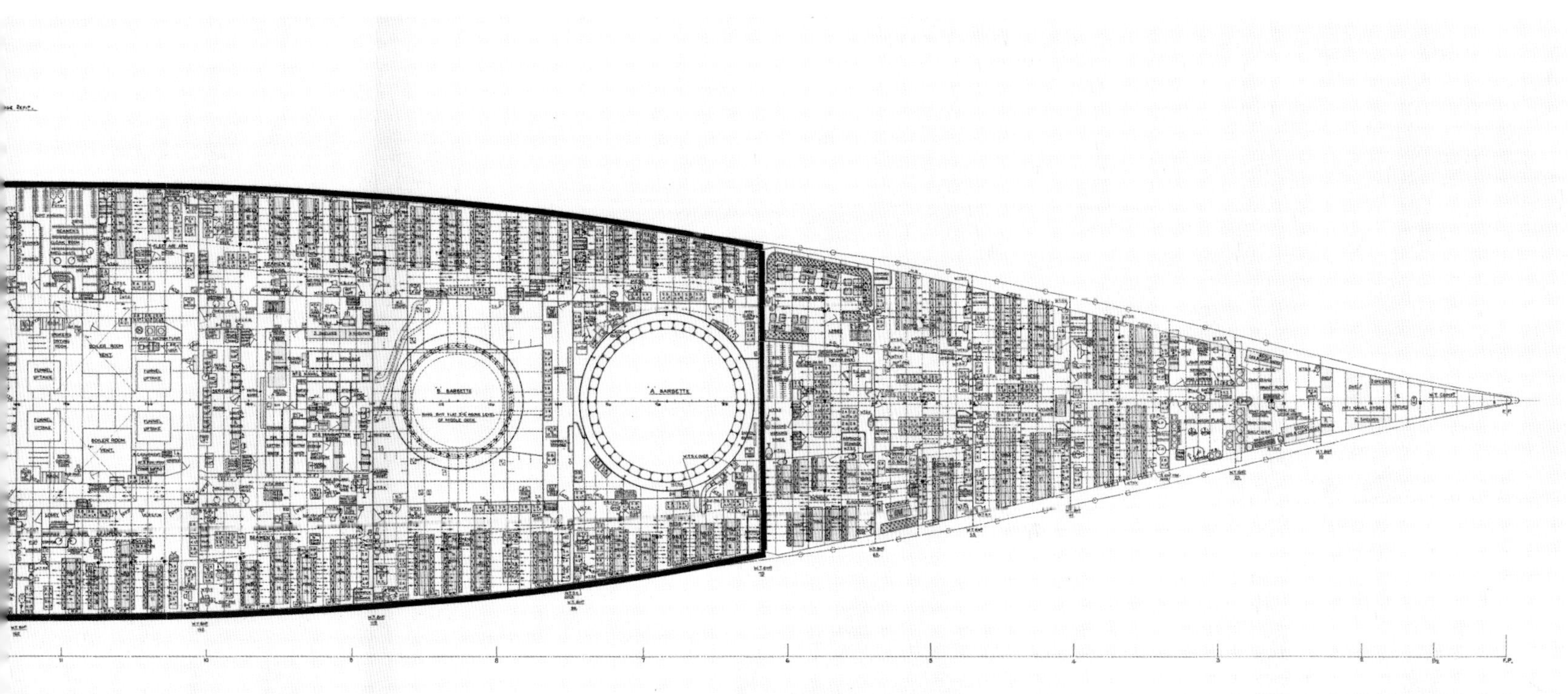

Below, Lower Deck

The armoured box continues down to this level which is otherwise more fully occupied with the mechanics of the ship including the upper part of the four boiler rooms. The lengthy run of the 5.25in shell and cordite chutes show the route taken by both, from embarkation and supply down through the respective hoists to the magazines on the platform deck and hold below. Officers' accommodation aft of armoured bulkhead 274 shows cabins increasing in size the further aft they go. Forward spaces include the Royal Marines band music room and six prison cells for defaulters. (© National Maritime Museum, London M1690)

PRISON Nº 1
PRISON Nº 2
PRISON Nº 3
PRISON Nº 4
PRISON Nº 5
PRISON Nº 6

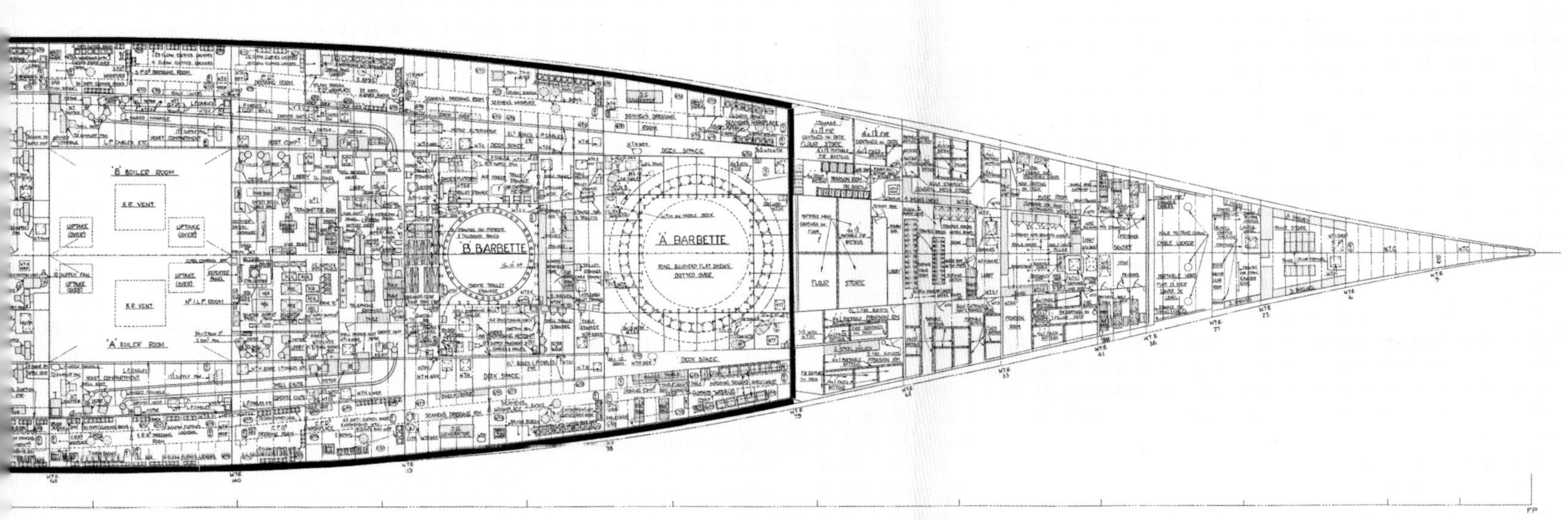
'B' BOILER ROOM
'A' BOILER ROOM
'B' BARBETTE
'A' BARBETTE

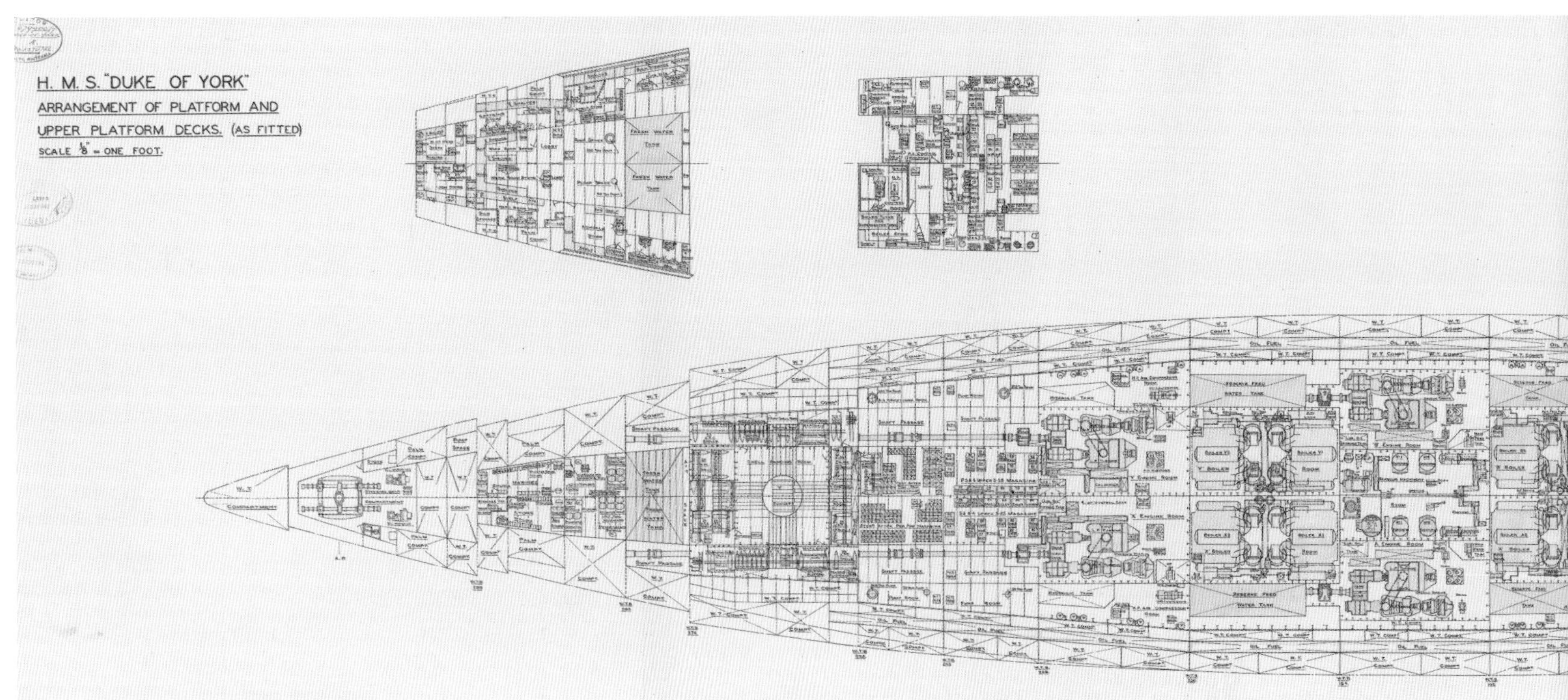
H. M. S. "DUKE OF YORK"
ARRANGEMENT OF PLATFORM AND
UPPER PLATFORM DECKS. (AS FITTED)
SCALE 1/8" = ONE FOOT.

Right above, Platform Decks

Below the armour belt and to accommodate tall installations in areas such as boiler and engine rooms and the supporting structure of the main armament mountings, what is termed the Platform Deck is in reality a series of intermediate decks at varying levels constructed around the former. They also show where much of the real business of the battleship lay, the well-protected layout of the main, secondary and close-range armament magazines. Propulsion occupies the bulk of space between the magazines with boilers and associated engine rooms arranged on the unit system to minimise disruption in action conditions. This area is enlarged in the three machinery layout drawings on pp212–13. The transverse bulkheads are pierced only by shafts, pipes and cables with watertight glands, with no watertight doors (unlike merchant ships). (© National Maritime Museum, London M1691)

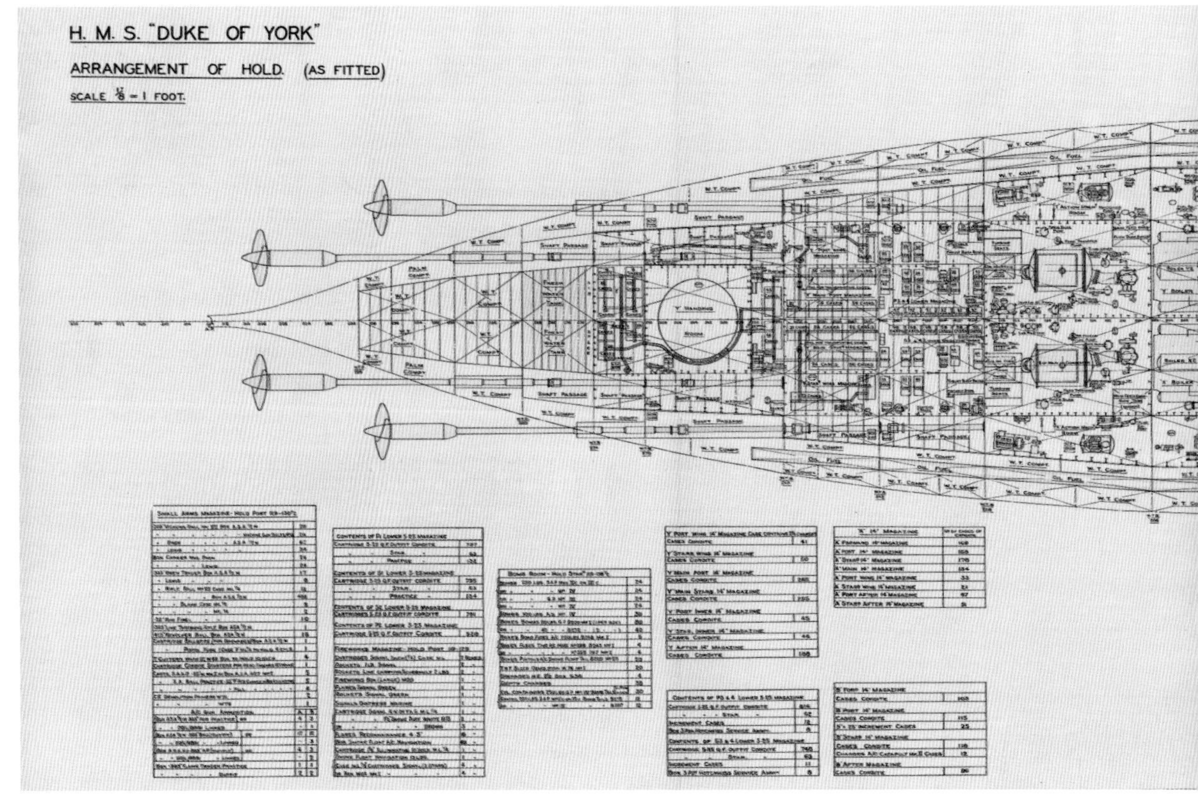
H. M. S. "DUKE OF YORK"
ARRANGEMENT OF HOLD. (AS FITTED)
SCALE 1/8" = 1 FOOT.

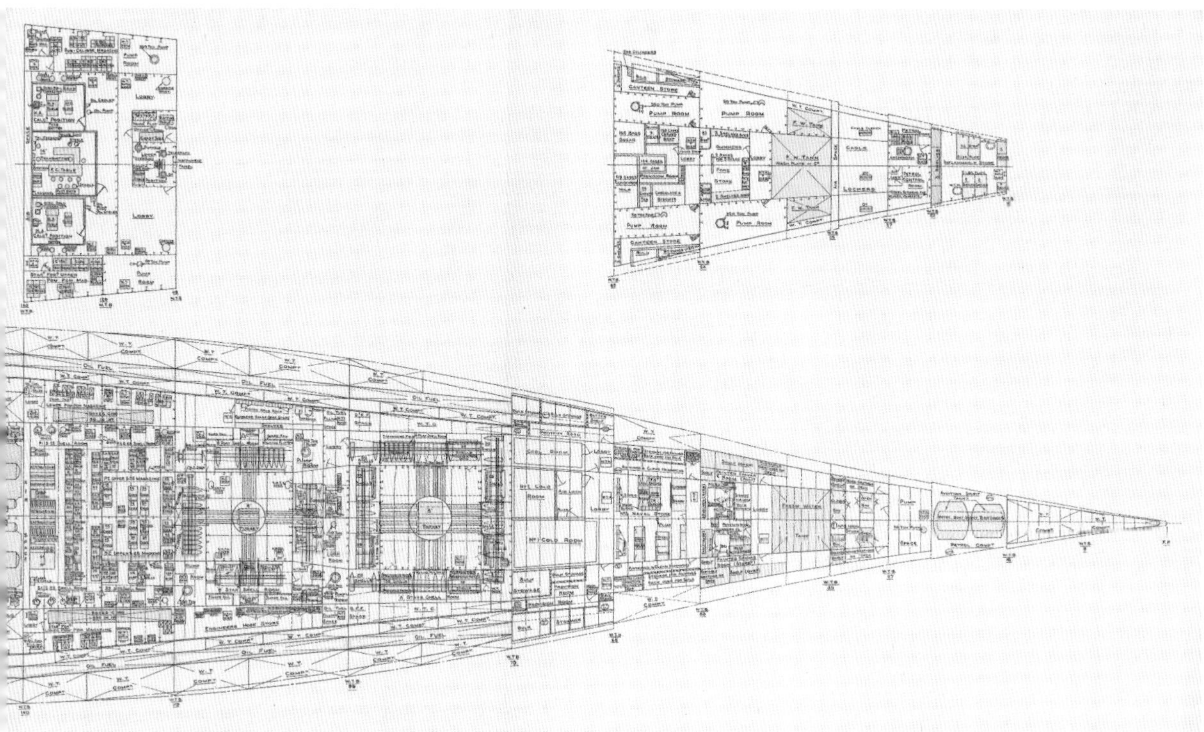

Below, Hold

Immediately above the double bottom, this is foundation level for the boiler and engine rooms. The magazines with cordite cases are on this level, with detailed tables of stowage: e.g. 'B' magazine 432 cases (216 full charges), 54 250lb or 100lb aircraft bombs and 38 depth charges. It is also where the ship's eight generators are located. As at Platform Deck level, the width of the side protective system is evident. Oil and water tank capacities are tabulated. *Prince of Wales*' Achilles heel is shown by the line of the outer propeller shaft tunnel which permitted extensive flooding once the torpedo-damaged shaft bracket and resulting whirling shaft had destroyed the watertight glands in the bulkheads. (© National Maritime Museum, London M1692)

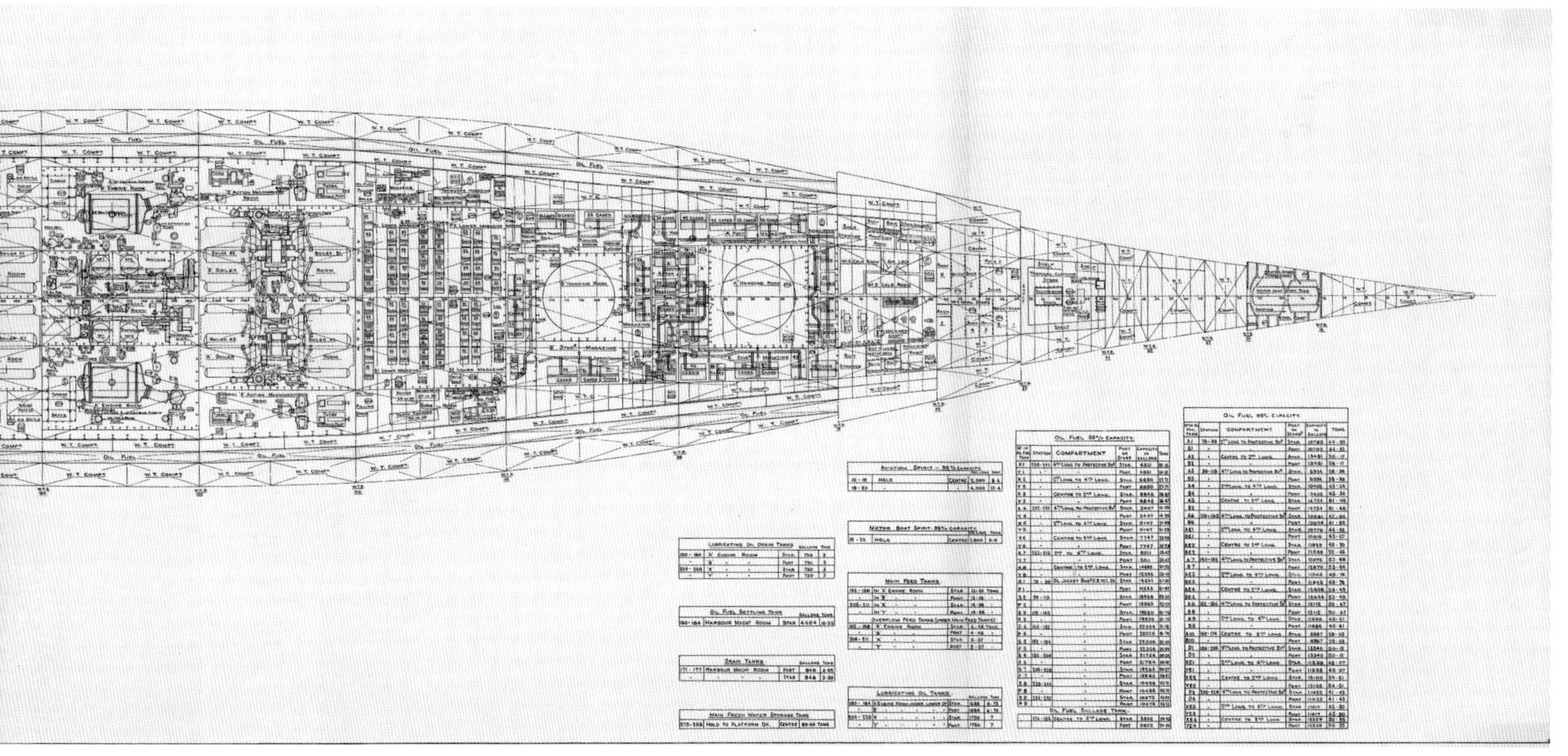

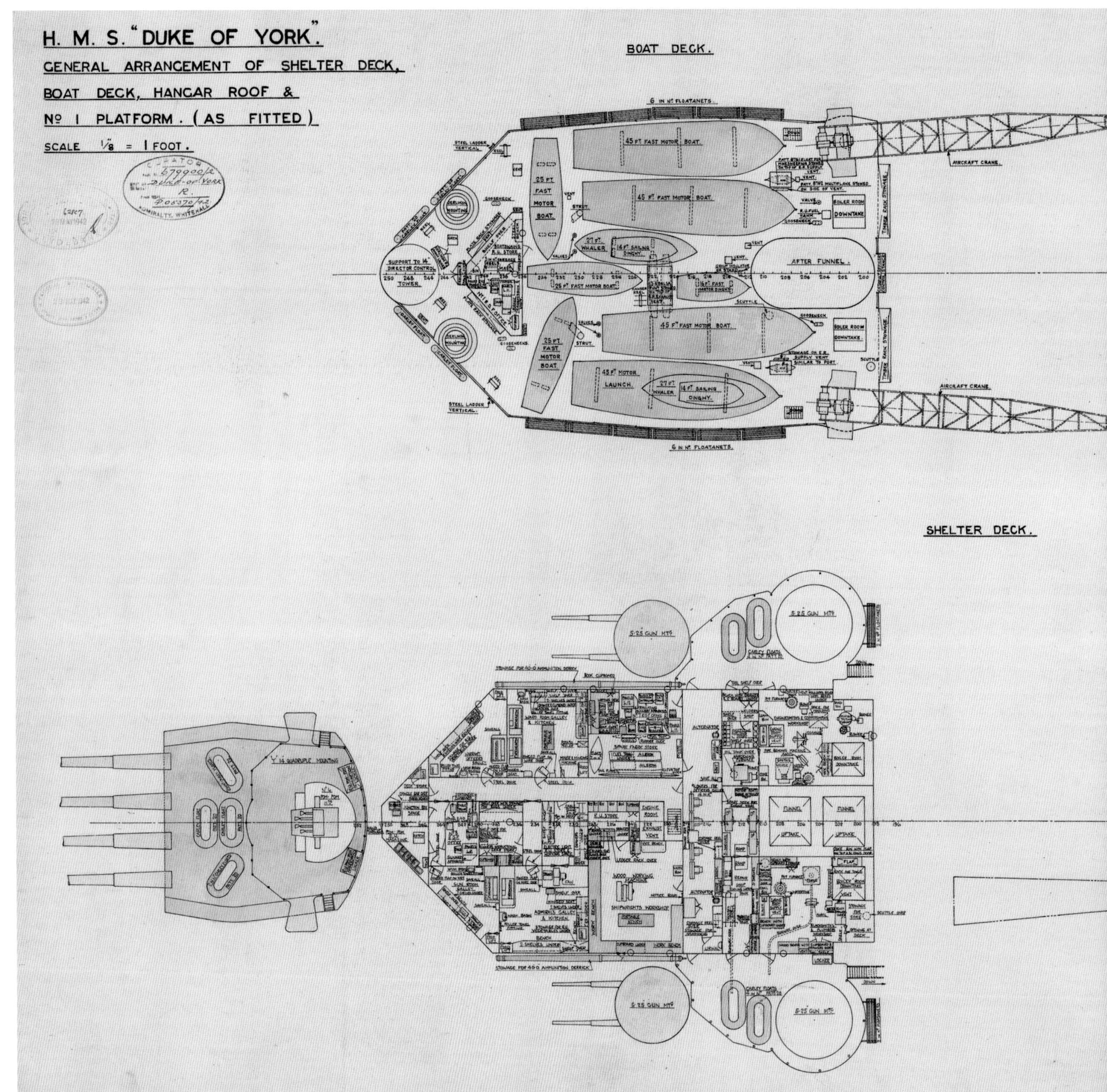
H. M. S. "DUKE OF YORK".
GENERAL ARRANGEMENT OF SHELTER DECK, BOAT DECK, HANGAR ROOF & Nº 1 PLATFORM. (AS FITTED)
SCALE 1/8 = 1 FOOT.
BOAT DECK.
6 IN Nº FLOATANETS.
45 FT FAST MOTOR BOAT
25 FT FAST MOTOR BOAT
27 FT WHALER
14 FT SAILING DINGHY
25 FT FAST MOTOR BOAT
45 FT MOTOR LAUNCH
AFTER FUNNEL.
SUPPORT TO 14" DIRECTOR CONTROL TOWER
AIRCRAFT CRANE
BOILER ROOM DOWNTAKE
STEEL LADDER VERTICAL
SHELTER DECK.
5·25 GUN MTG
CARLEY FLOATS
FUNNEL UPTAKE
SHIPWRIGHTS WORKSHOP

Shelter Deck, Boat Deck, Hangar Roof and No I Platform

The ship's superstructure is in two sections starting with the Shelter Deck and going upwards. Between both superstructure blocks are the aircraft arrangements. The ship's cranes were so positioned to work both aircraft and the ship's boats. This involved lifting the ship's Walrus aircraft from the sea onto a trolley and rails for transfer to the hangars on either side of the forward funnel, and lifting and stowing the ship's boats. The plan shows that congested area with several boats nested. Much of the close-range AA armament was grouped in this area

UKE OF YORK."

(AS FITTED).

1 FOOT.

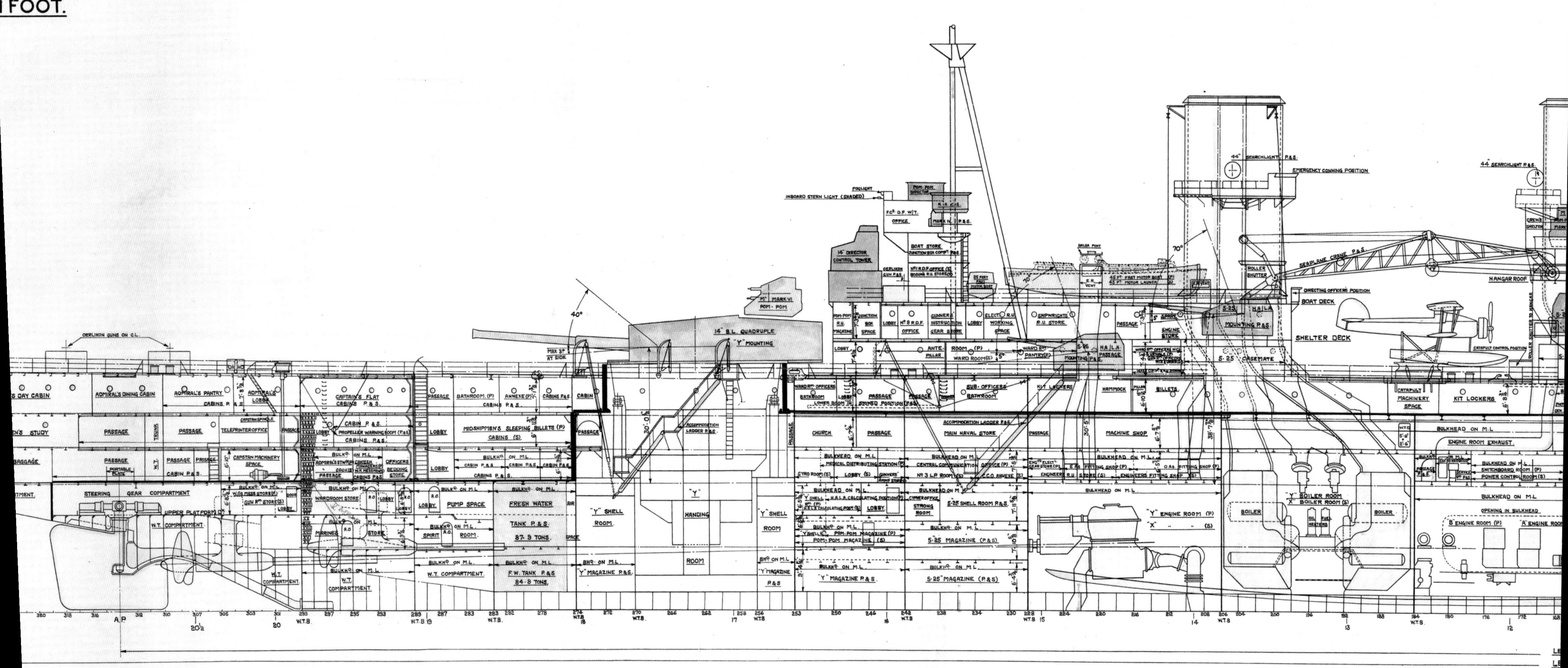

OERLIKON GUNS ON C.L.
INBOARD STERN LIGHT (SHADED)
POM-POM DIRECTOR
14" DIRECTOR CONTROL TOWER
BOAT STORE
POM-POM MARK VI
14" B.L. QUADRUPLE "Y" MOUNTING
44" SEARCHLIGHT P&S.
EMERGENCY CONNING POSITION
SEAPLANE CRANE P&S
HANGAR ROOF
DIRECTING OFFICERS POSITION
BOAT DECK
SHELTER DECK
5·25 CASEMATE
CATAPULT CONTROL POSITION
ADMIRAL'S DINING CABIN
ADMIRAL'S PANTRY
CAPTAIN'S FLAT
MIDSHIPMEN'S SLEEPING BILLETS (P)
TELEPRINTER OFFICE
CAPSTAN MACHINERY SPACE
STEERING GEAR COMPARTMENT
UPPER PLATFORM
PUMP SPACE
FRESH WATER TANK P.&S. 87·9 TONS.
F.W. TANK P.&S 84·8 TONS.
"Y" SHELL ROOM
"Y" HANDING ROOM
"Y" MAGAZINE P.&S.
CHURCH
MAIN NAVAL STORE
MACHINE SHOP
KIT LOCKERS
HAMMOCK
BILLETS
CATAPULT MACHINERY SPACE
5·25 SHELL ROOM P.&S.
5·25 MAGAZINE (P.&S)
"Y" ENGINE ROOM (P)
"X" " " (S)
"Y" BOILER ROOM
"X" BOILER ROOM (S)
BOILER
BULKHEAD ON M.L.
ENGINE ROOM EXHAUST
"B" ENGINE ROOM (P)
"A" ENGINE ROOM
A.P.

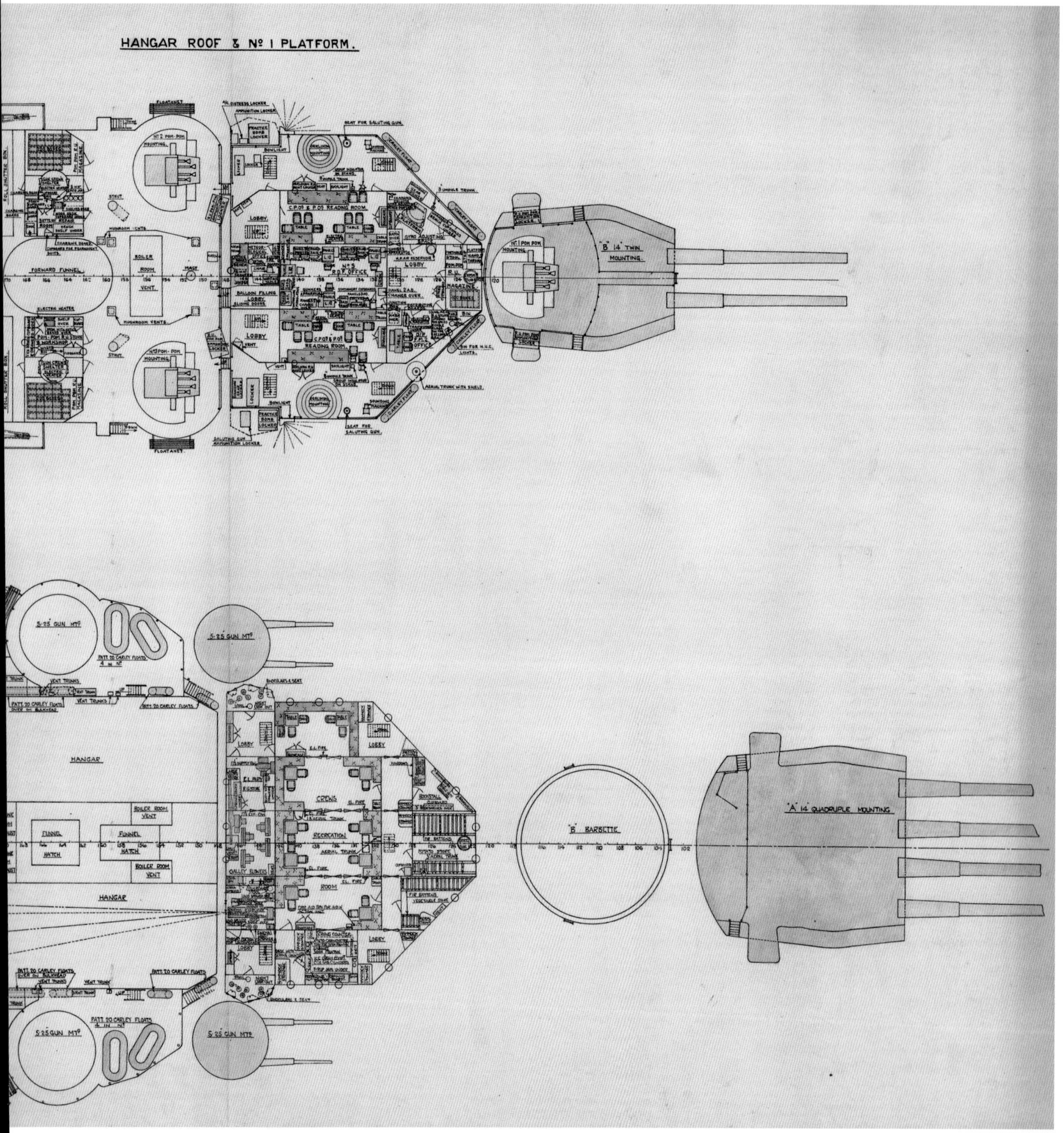

comprising four eight-barrelled pom-poms and a further two atop 'B' and 'Y' turrets, with associated ready-use magazines and lockers. The forward and after superstructure blocks each had two single 20mm Oerlikon gun tubs which together with the two tubs on the upper deck aft amounted to the total of six. This arrangement of the ship's superstructure made it possible for a significant upgrading of the ship's fighting qualities to be made as seen in the As Fitted 1945 drawings. Just forward of the hangar are the powerful galley ventilation fans (see also ventilation drawing on p122). (© National Maritime Museum, London M1695)

Sections

The two drawings showing cross sections along the ship's length complement the profile and plan views, showing for exampl of the machinery spaces. Sloped deck camber is visible, providing drainage and strength. Frame 294 shows an outer shaft bra being fitted in the photo on p69. (© National Maritime Museum, London M1693 and M1694)

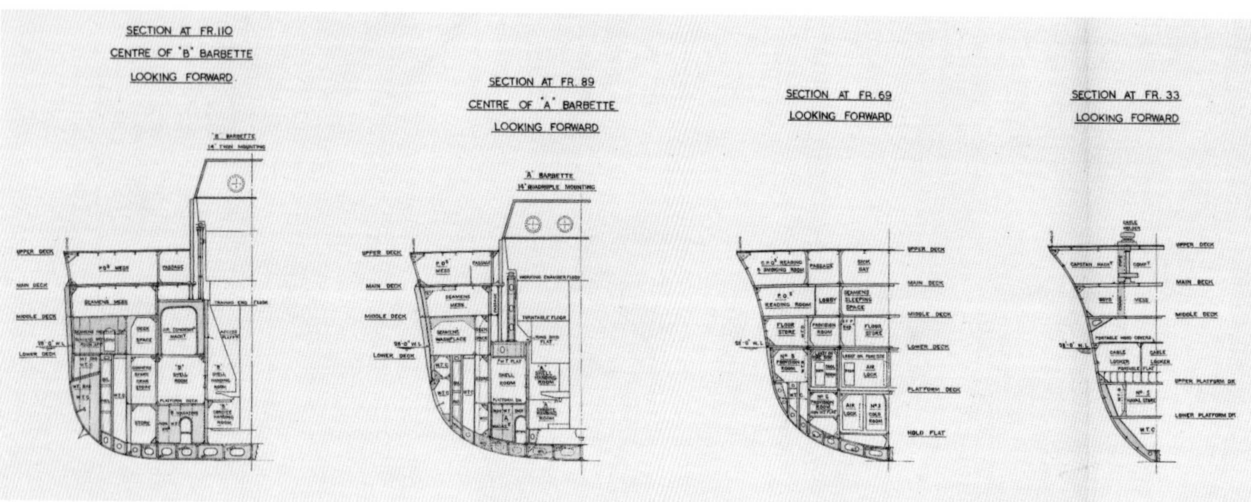
SECTION AT FR.110
CENTRE OF 'B' BARBETTE
LOOKING FORWARD
SECTION AT FR. 89
CENTRE OF 'A' BARBETTE
LOOKING FORWARD
SECTION AT FR. 69
LOOKING FORWARD
SECTION AT FR. 33
LOOKING FORWARD

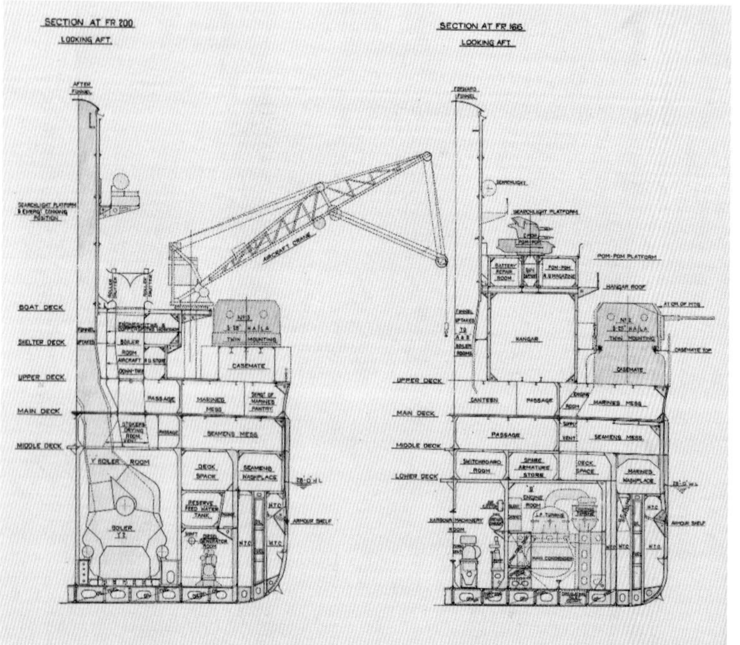
SECTION AT FR 200
LOOKING AFT
BOAT DECK
SHELTER DECK
UPPER DECK
MAIN DECK
MIDDLE DECK
HANGAR

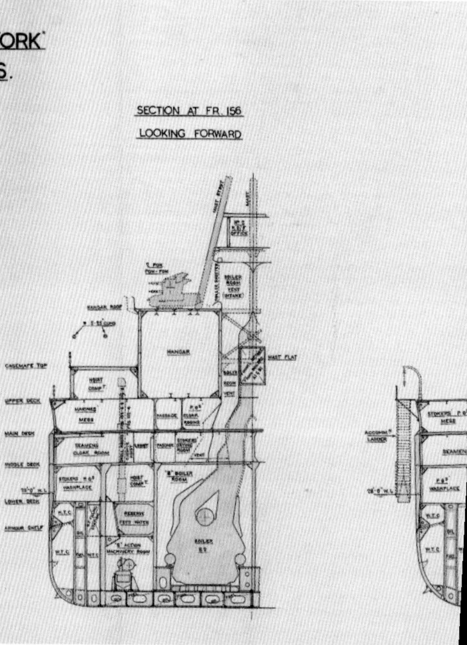
YORK'
IS.
SECTION AT FR. 156
LOOKING FORWARD

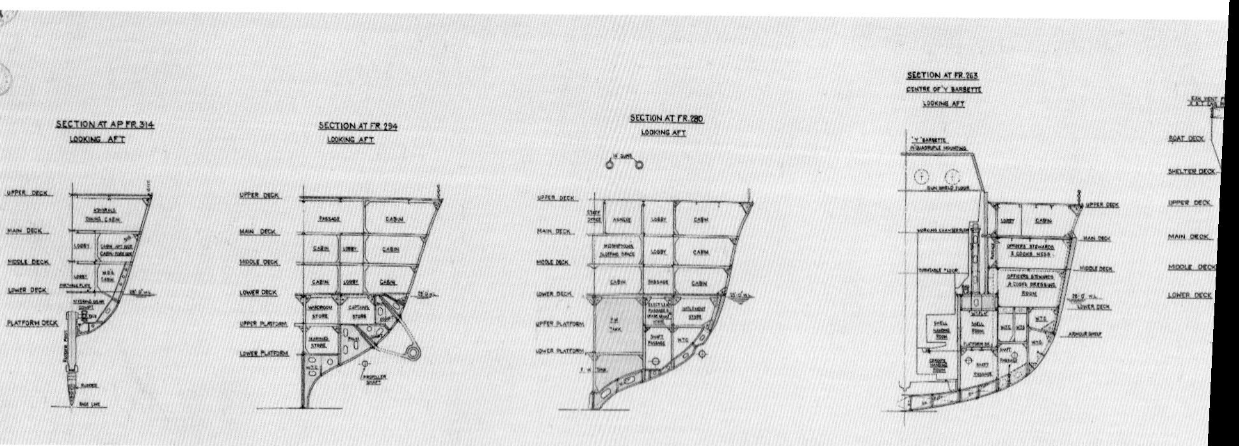
SECTION AT AP FR.314
LOOKING AFT
SECTION AT FR.294
LOOKING AFT
UPPER DECK
MAIN DECK
MIDDLE DECK
LOWER DECK

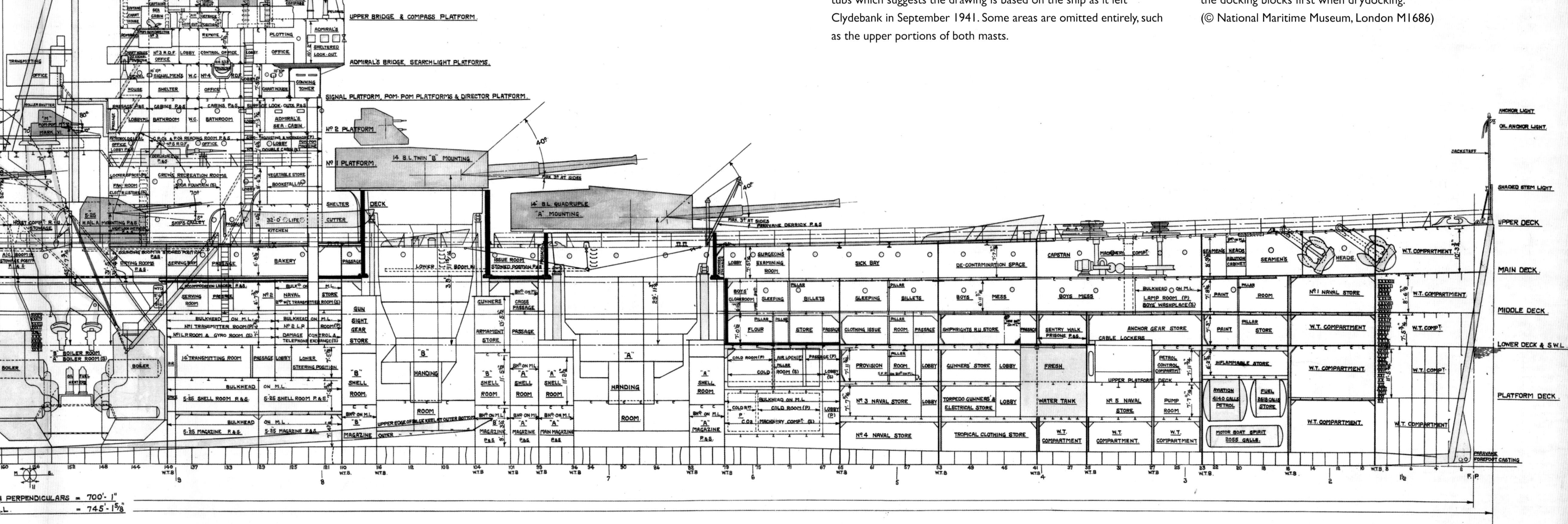
UPPER BRIDGE & COMPASS PLATFORM
ADMIRAL'S BRIDGE, SEARCHLIGHT PLATFORMS
SIGNAL PLATFORM, POM-POM PLATFORMS & DIRECTOR PLATFORM
Nº 2 PLATFORM
Nº 1 PLATFORM
14" B.L. TWIN "B" MOUNTING
14" B.L. QUADRUPLE "A" MOUNTING
BAKERY
SICK BAY
CAPSTAN
ANCHOR LIGHT
UPPER DECK
MAIN DECK
MIDDLE DECK
LOWER DECK & S.W.L.
PLATFORM DECK
PERPENDICULARS = 700'- 1"
= 745'- 1 5/8"

Profile

This drawing serves to show the main internal elements of the ship, with supporting frames, bulkheads and decks, identifying the main compartments and spaces. Although accurate in showing the foregoing, it is not highly detailed in depicting the external appearance of the ship, providing only an outline representation. Despite being date-stamped 28 May 1942, by which time the ship had been in service for six months with ample time for the drawing to be scrutinised, it shows Mark IV High Angle Control System (HACS) directors as fitted in *King George V* and *Prince of Wales* and not the Mark V versions actually fitted. Similarly, it does not show the 20mm Oerlikon guns fitted at Rosyth but does show the gun tubs which suggests the drawing is based on the ship as it left Clydebank in September 1941. Some areas are omitted entirely, such as the upper portions of both masts.

The plan shows the numbering of the frames from forward to aft, generally spaced 4ft apart, as well as the hull form stations numbered 1 to 21 with 11 at midships (Frame 157). Merchant ships number their frames from aft to forward. It also shows the forward and aft perpendiculars 700ft 1in apart as built at the designed waterline of 28ft. This was well below the full load draught of 33ft 3in, so giving a misleading impression of the already low freeboard and the submergence of much of the side armour belt. The draught marks are shown in Roman numerals, with the lower edge of the number being the height above the keel. The after marks are at the start of the cut up at Frame 299, as this is the point that will touch the docking blocks first when drydocking.
(© National Maritime Museum, London M1686)

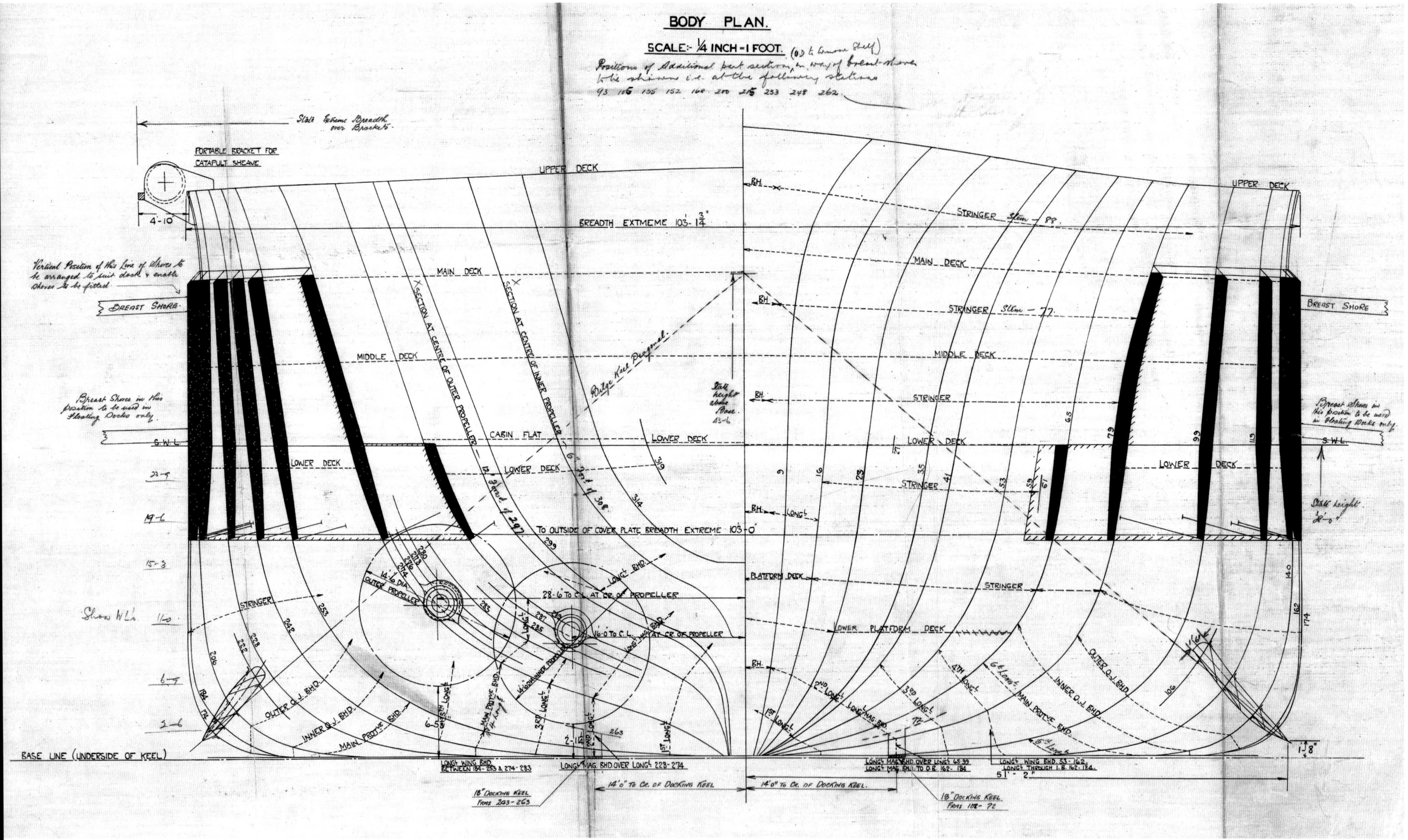

BODY PLAN.

SCALE:- 1/4 INCH - 1 FOOT.

Docking Drawing (right-hand side only)

The shipbuilder provided the shipowner with a docking plan to assist drydocking his ship. It showed internal structure positions where docking blocks and breast (side) shores should be best placed to support the ship. It also showed the position of openings in the hull below the waterline and how the rudder and propellers could be unshipped. The full drawing showed the elevation and plan views. The body plan reproduced here is drawn at specific structural frames, unlike the lines plan which was drawn at the standard ten or twenty stations in the length. For battleships with their heavy side armour and gun mountings, side docking blocks the length of the armoured citadel were needed to avoid the distortion which would arise if only centreline keel blocks were used. The sweep of the propellers and run of the bilge keel are also shown, which could be damaged during the docking process. (© National Maritime Museum, London M2064)

Outer Bottom Plating

These two drawings show the arrangement of the shell plating at each end of the ship, to a scale of ¼in to 1ft (1:48). Drawn originally for construction purposes, these As Fitted versions were useful should repairs be necessary, by showing the size, thickness, quality and arrangement of each steel plate. Such a plan was normally called a Shell Expansion and drawn with the keel at the bottom as a straight line, with the upper deck shown as a curve to represent the girth at each point along the length; Admiralty practice was different. (© National Maritime Museum, London M2062 and M2063)

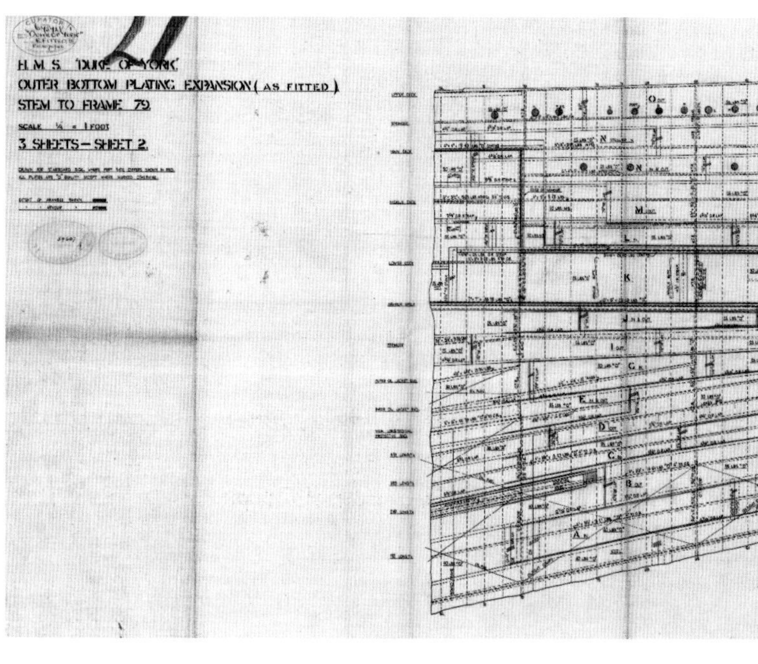
H.M.S. 'DUKE OF YORK'
OUTER BOTTOM PLATING EXPANSION (AS FITTED)
STEM TO FRAME 79
SCALE ¼ = 1 FOOT
3 SHEETS – SHEET 2

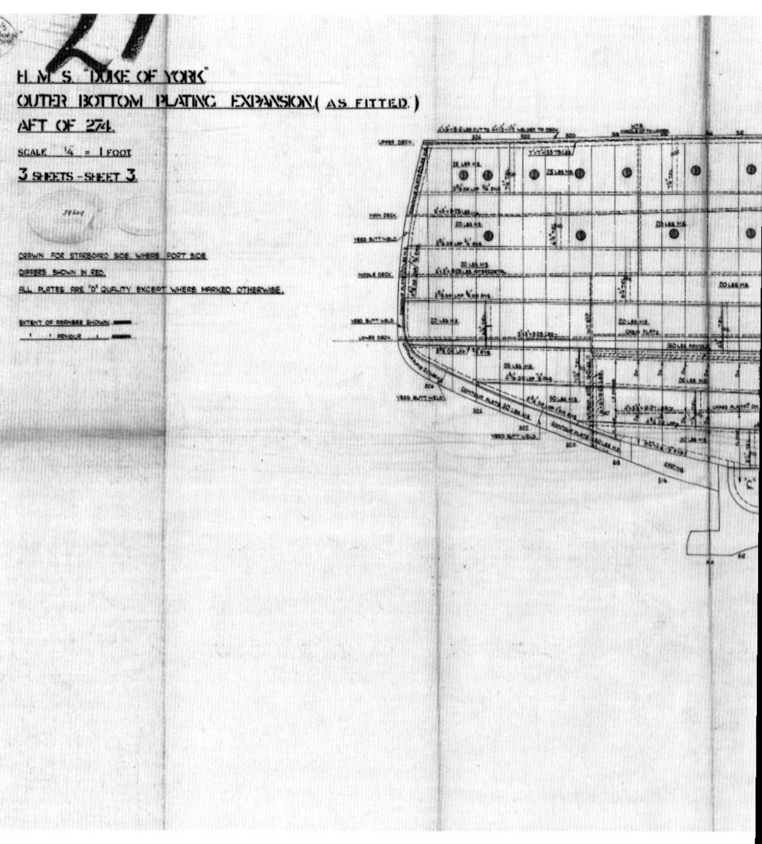
H.M.S. 'DUKE OF YORK'
OUTER BOTTOM PLATING EXPANSION (AS FITTED)
AFT OF 274.
SCALE ¼ = 1 FOOT
3 SHEETS – SHEET 3

The Shell Expansion is a two-dimensional drawing of a three-dimensional object, so like a map of the globe has a degree of distortion. For large ships like 554, the shipyard modelmaker made a (15ft long) half block model of wood from the lines plan, which was coated with varnish to take ink lines. Starting from the midship section drawing showing width and thickness of the shell plates, the draughtsman used strips of paper to mark out the strakes as they tapered towards the end of the ship. For 554 plates were typically 30–40ft long and 5–7ft wide in the main body of the hull; each plate's seams (fore and aft joints) and butts (transverse joints) were drawn on the model. The size of each plate could be lifted off and after a suitable 'green' margin had been added, the steel order prepared. The draughtsman then prepared the shell expansion drawing, using strips of paper to lift off the position of each seam round the girth of the model at frame positions along the length. After approval, the drawing was sent to the mould loft to prepare the full-size sections and templates, and to the plating workshop and to the shipwrights.

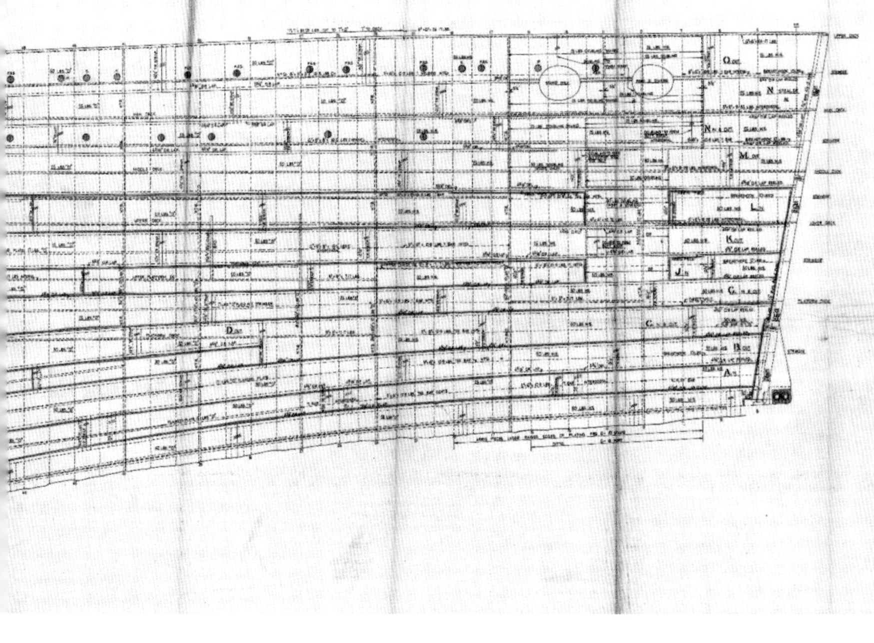

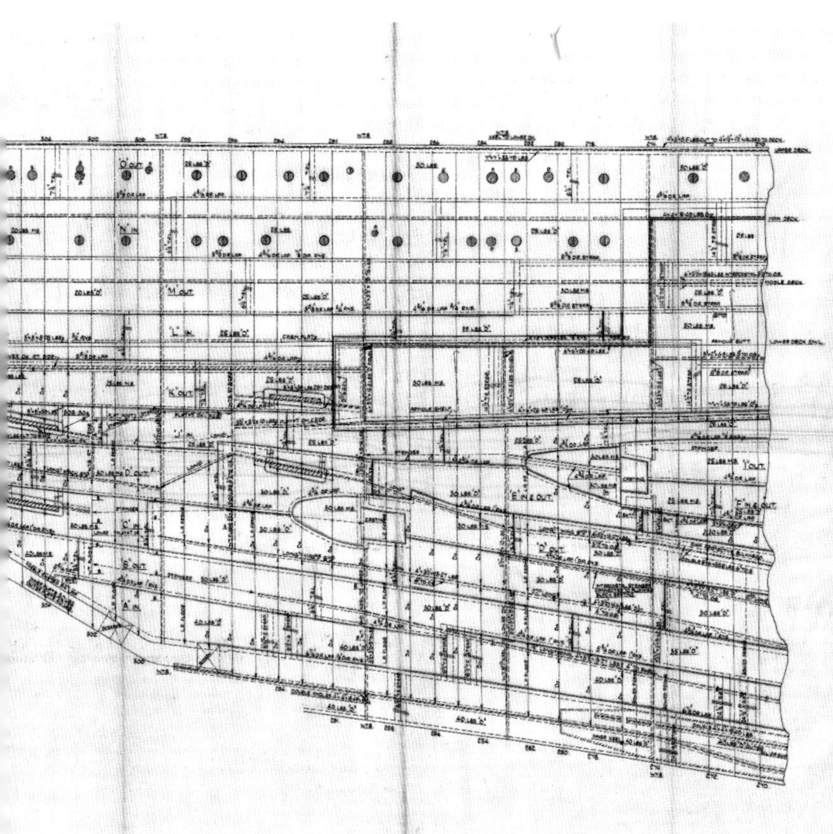

Nearly all the joints were riveted, either overlapped (marked LAP) or butt-strapped to give a flush outer surface e.g. keel or behind armour (STRAP). The width of the joint and the number of rows of rivets is marked: D.R. = double row of rivets, T.R. triple, Q.R. quadruple (see drawing on p67 left). The red lines show where the overlapping seams are faired off with composition after caulking watertight, to give a smoother surface underwater; most of the butts were strapped so needed no fairing. Blue lines denote the extent of side armour plating, fitted externally to the thinner plating behind. Supporting stiffeners and decks are shown as dotted lines. At the forward end, beneath the anchor hawsepipes, the plating is a double thickness of 25lb (1.22in in total) – see photo on p89. At the after end, the plating becomes more complicated, especially where the propeller shafts emerge and where the shaft brackets are fitted (see photo on p69).

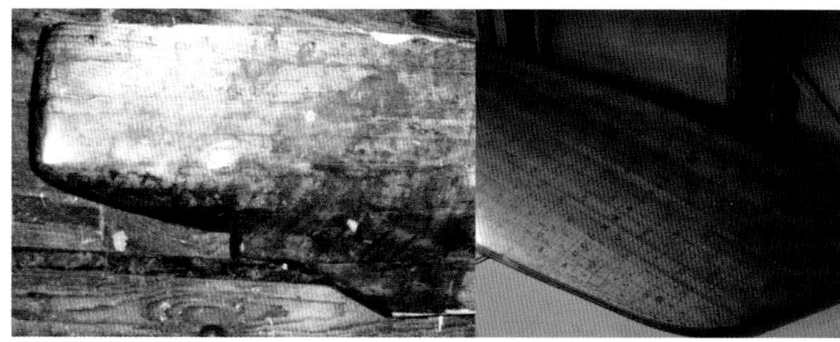

The highly degraded half block model of *KGV* shortly before it was discarded, alongside one of a liner which has been preserved, showing the complex plating detail that has been applied.

Although showing the drawing office at the Fairfield shipyard and the model of a liner, the Clydebank drawing office would have been similar. The two draughtsmen are inking in and numbering each plate on a half block model.

Bridges, etc

The four decks that comprised the forward superstructure block contained the main areas from where the ship would be fought. (© National Maritime Museum, London M1696)

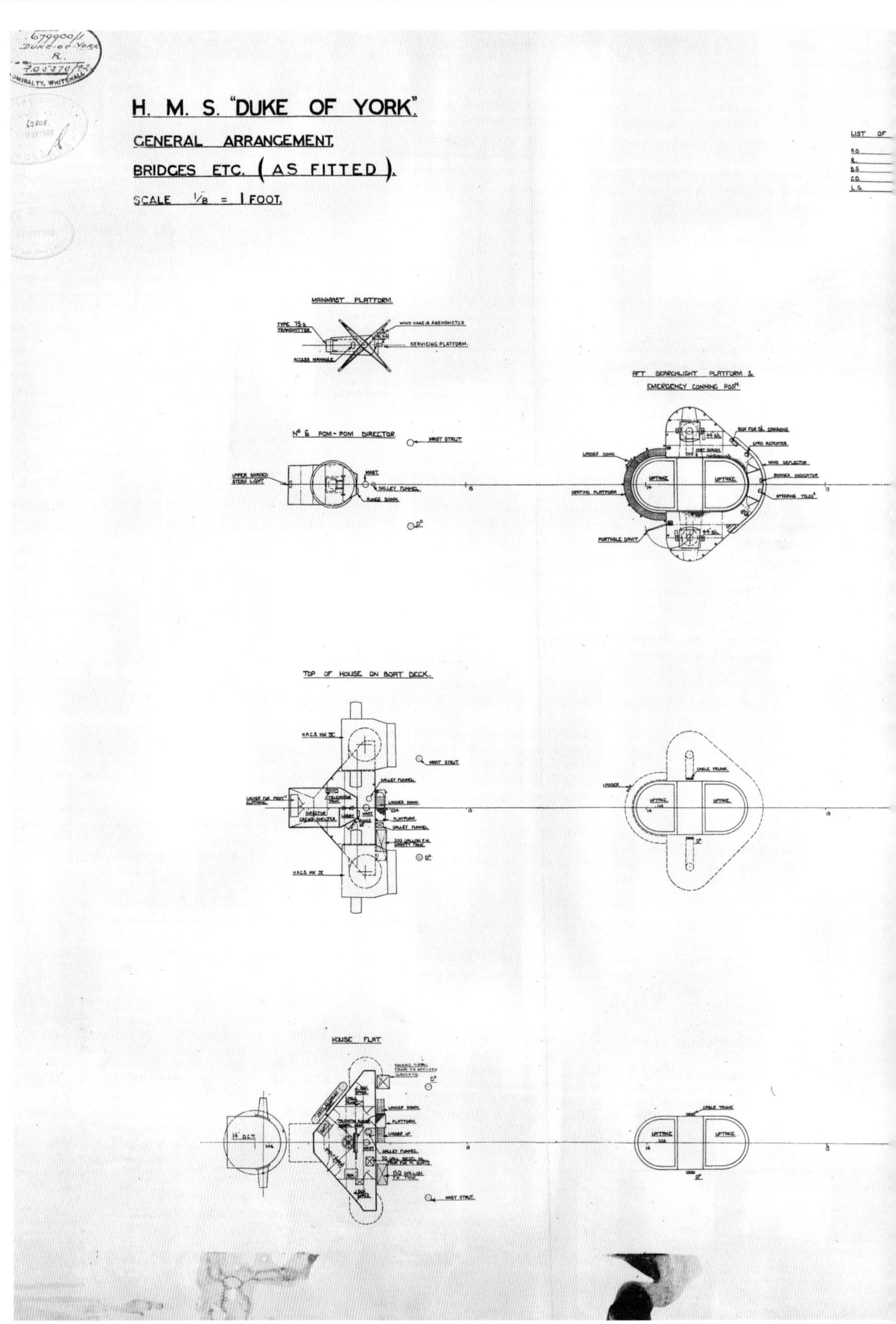
H. M. S. "DUKE OF YORK"
GENERAL ARRANGEMENT
BRIDGES ETC. (AS FITTED).
SCALE 1/8 = 1 FOOT.
MAINMAST PLATFORM
Nº 6 POM-POM DIRECTOR
AFT SEARCHLIGHT PLATFORM & EMERGENCY CONNING POSN.
TOP OF HOUSE ON BOAT DECK.
HOUSE FLAT

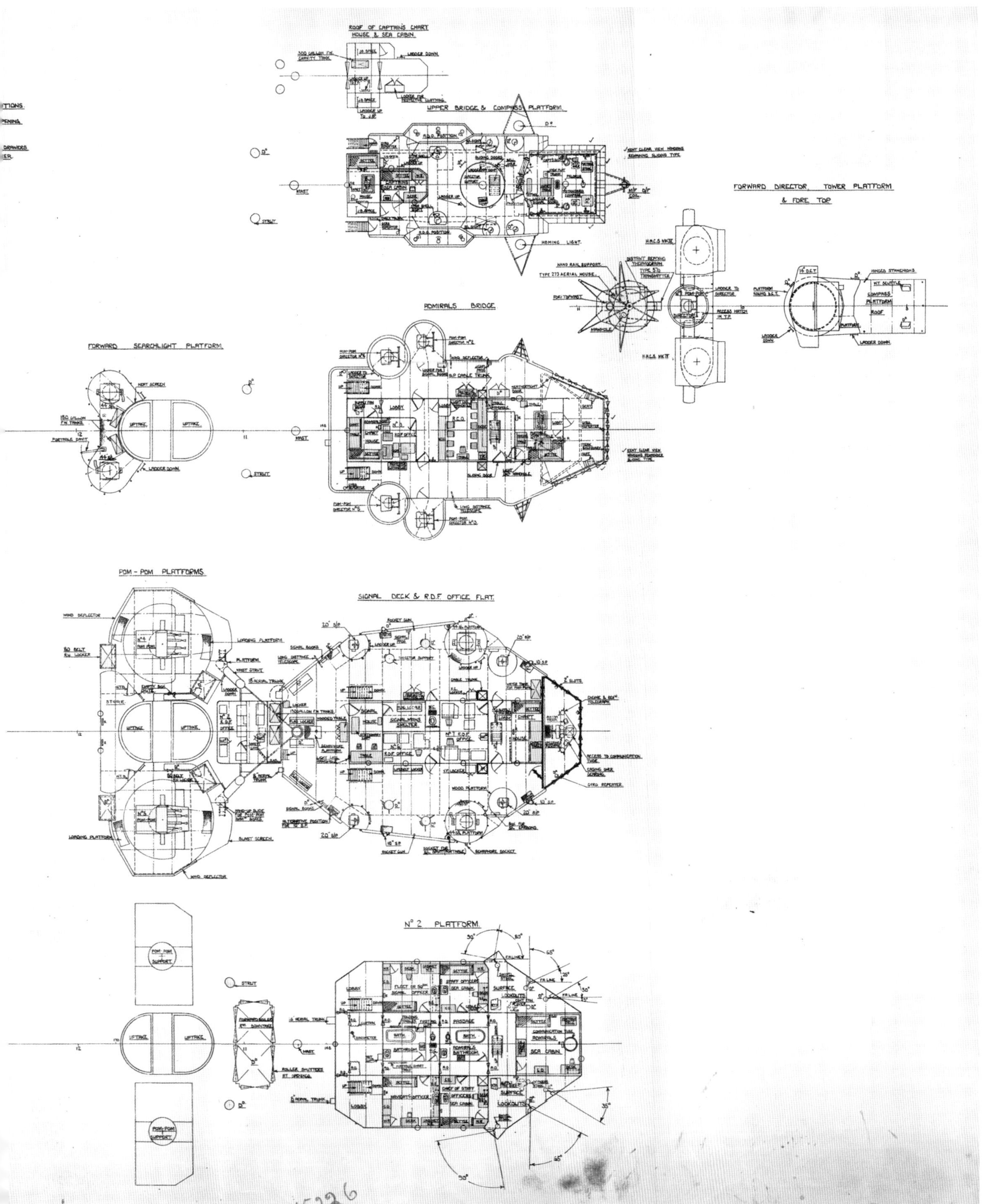
ROOF OF CAPTAINS CHART HOUSE & SEA CABIN.
UPPER BRIDGE & COMPASS PLATFORM.
FORWARD DIRECTOR TOWER PLATFORM & FORE TOP
ADMIRALS BRIDGE
FORWARD SEARCHLIGHT PLATFORM.
POM-POM PLATFORMS.
SIGNAL DECK & R.D.F. OFFICE FLAT.
N° 2 PLATFORM.

Machinery Space Plans

No As Fitted machinery plans have been found, although it was part of the contract that the machinery builder should supply them to the Admiralty. Fortunately *Duke of York*'s general arrangement plans are more detailed than for most warships regarding the machinery spaces, perhaps because the engine works drawing office was close to the shipyard's. Three Machinery Diagrams have been extracted and annotated. The machinery for the *King George V* class was on the unit system, i.e. each group of boilers and turbines was separated from the others. The forward machinery spaces described here driving the outer propeller shafts were very similar to the after spaces.

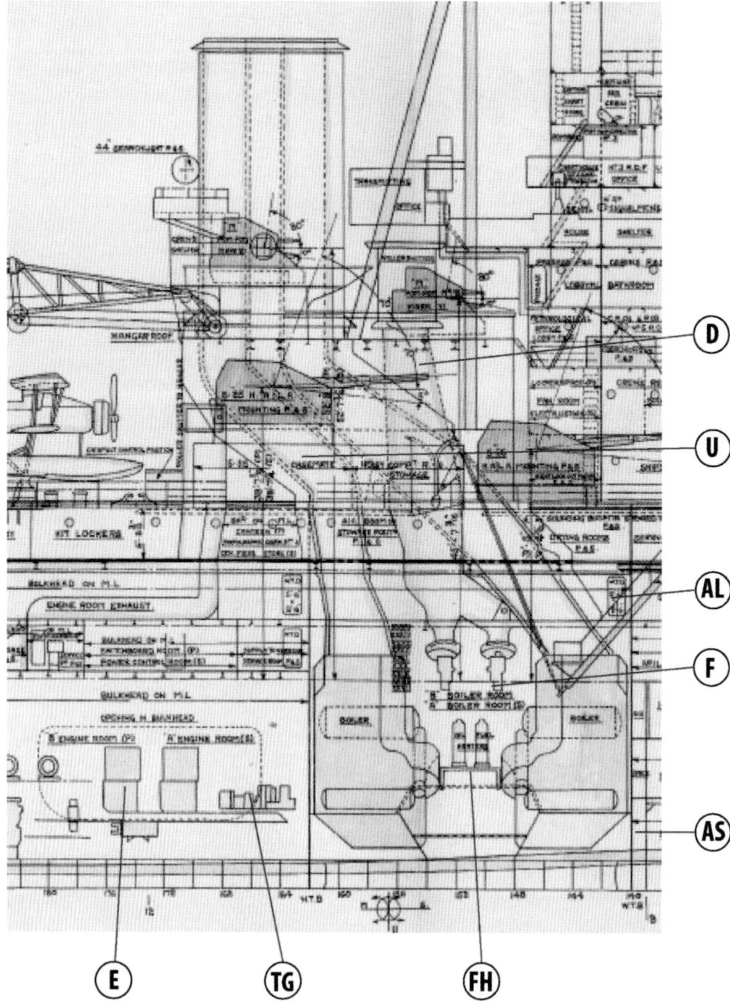
D
U
AL
F
AS
E
TG
FH

Boiler Rooms (Frames 140–162)

In each boiler room ('A' starboard and 'B' port) were two oil-fired Admiralty type three-drum watertube boilers. Triangular in cross section as seen in the photo on p98 right, the two lower drums were filled with water, joined by narrow steam generator tubes to the upper drum which collected the steam. In the brick-lined furnace space between the drums the oil burners produced enough heat to boil the water into saturated steam, which then passed through a further bank of tubes out of contact with water to create superheated steam at 695°F and 400lb/in^2. Each boiler room was pressurised to up to 0.35lb/in^2 which increased the air flow and improved combustion efficiency. Steam turbine-driven fans shown at (F) in the profile sucked air down the downtakes (D) next to the fore mast. There was an air lock (AL) for access from the middle deck. The uptakes (U) from the four boilers were trunked to the fore funnel.

Steam that had passed through the main turbines was condensed to water and then recirculated back to the boilers. The main feed pumps (FP) transferred the water back into the boiler, first passing through a feed heater (H). The latter used low pressure steam to preheat the water before passing into the water drums. Oil fuel service pumps (OP) drew fuel from the wing and double bottom tanks first into settling tanks (ST) to allow any water and sediment to settle on the bottom before being removed by the sullage pump (SP). The oil fuel was then passed through centrifuge separators (OS) to remove any last trace of contaminants, then fuel heaters (FH) to reduce its viscosity before reaching the boiler sprayers which atomised the liquid for more complete combustion.

The steam/water system was closed, but still needed occasional topping up with feed water, which came from the Main Feed Tank (MF). In turn this was supplied by the evaporators or distillers which turned seawater into fresh water by boiling and condensing, also supplying the domestic systems for washing, cooking and drinking. But if an evaporator failed (they could easily be fouled up by salt deposits), the Reserve Feed Water Tank (RF) could be drawn upon to make up shortages. The air space (AS) ahead of the forward boiler room prevented the heat from the boilers 'cooking off' ammunition in the adjacent 5.25in magazine.

Action Machinery Rooms

Each forward boiler room was flanked by an action machinery room. Each contained one 300 kW turbine-driven generator (TG) made by Allen of Bedford and a turbine-driven pair of hydraulic pumps (P) to power the 14in gun mountings at 1100lb/in^2. On the upper level was the associated hydraulic (treated fresh water) tank, the reserve feed water tank and a high pressure air compressor (4000lb/in^2) which was used for charging accumulators etc. At the lower level of the boiler rooms and AMRs were a number of 75-ton/hour emergency bilge pumps (BP), some steam turbine driven (T.D.), some electric motor (M.D.) They could pump water from flooded compartments as well as supplying the pumping, flooding and draining system and fire main.

Engine Rooms (Frames 162–184)

Steam from the boilers was passed to 'A' and 'B' engine rooms via pipes lagged with asbestos, which also included expansion sections to take up deformations from temperature changes. They also had cross connections to other boiler and engine rooms in case of damage. Driving each propeller shaft was one high pressure (HP) and one low pressure (LP) turbine, both of Parsons design, connected through a single reduction gearbox (G) to the shaft (see photo on p97) which revolved at a

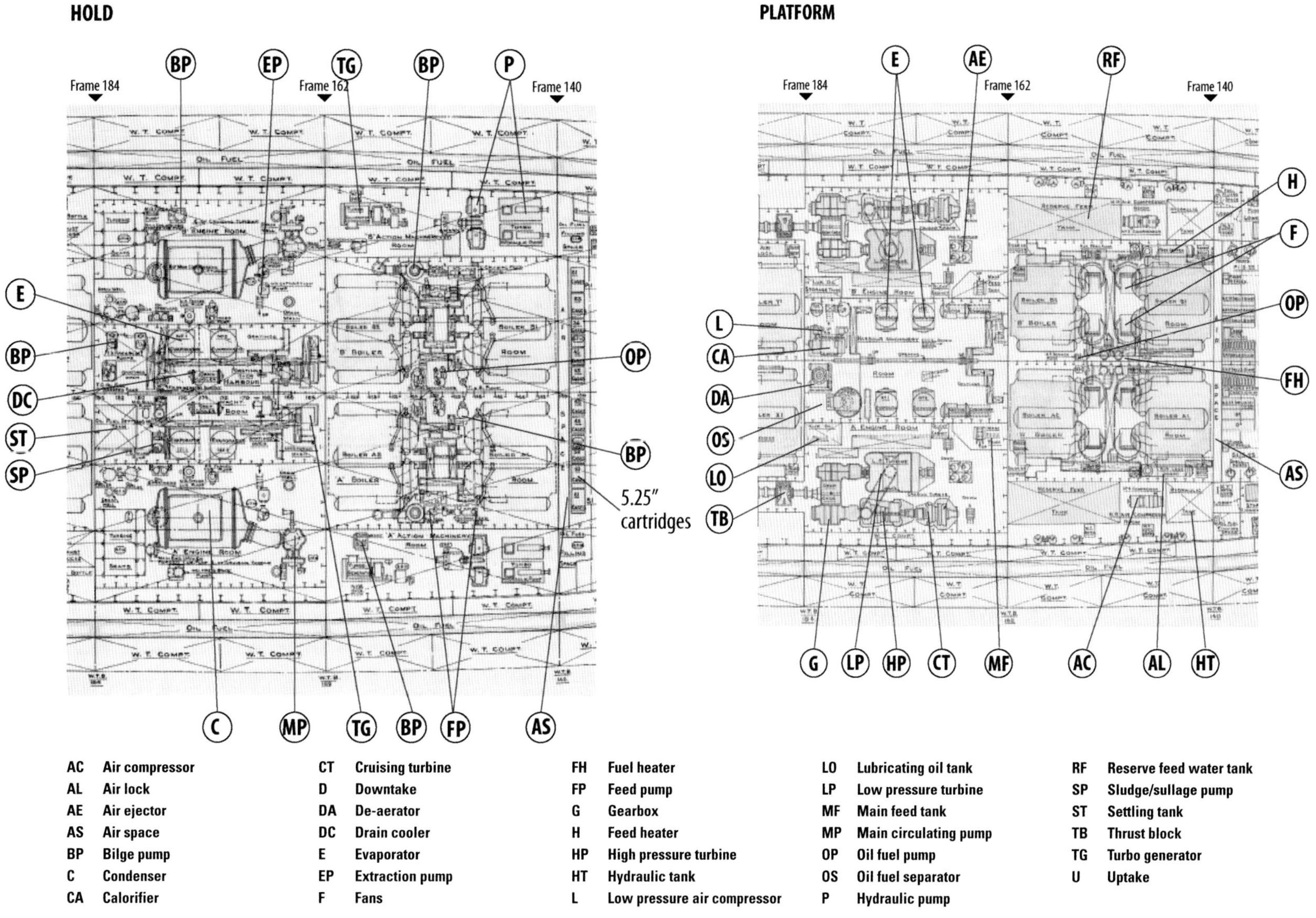
HOLD
Frame 184
Frame 162
Frame 140
5.25″ cartridges
PLATFORM
Frame 184
Frame 162
Frame 140
AC Air compressor
AL Air lock
AE Air ejector
AS Air space
BP Bilge pump
C Condenser
CA Calorifier
CT Cruising turbine
D Downtake
DA De-aerator
DC Drain cooler
E Evaporator
EP Extraction pump
F Fans
FH Fuel heater
FP Feed pump
G Gearbox
H Feed heater
HP High pressure turbine
HT Hydraulic tank
L Low pressure air compressor
LO Lubricating oil tank
LP Low pressure turbine
MF Main feed tank
MP Main circulating pump
OP Oil fuel pump
OS Oil fuel separator
P Hydraulic pump
RF Reserve feed water tank
SP Sludge/sullage pump
ST Settling tank
TB Thrust block
TG Turbo generator
U Uptake

maximum of 230 rpm. A cruising turbine was clutched to the forward end of the HP turbine for more economical steaming at up to 19 knots. Inside the HP turbine casing was the small astern turbine (turbines are uni-directional unlike steam reciprocating or diesel engines). The propellers converted the torque in the shaft into thrust which was transmitted to the hull through a Michell thrust block sited in the thrust recess just aft of Bulkhead 184.

Below the LP turbine was the condenser (C) (see photo on p96 left) operating at a vacuum of about 29in of mercury (14.2lb/in^2 absolute where standard atmospheric pressure is 14.7lb/in^2), which allowed more energy to be extracted from the expanding steam. The condenser was filled with a nest of cupro-nickel tubes (which did not corrode in salt water), through which circulated seawater. This cooled the steam to water allowing it to be fed back to the boilers. The main circulating pump (MP) drew seawater from beneath the hull through the condenser (also helped by a scoop when the ship was moving fast enough), discharging at its after end back to the sea. An extraction pump (EP) maintained the vacuum in the condenser while the air ejectors removed air to maintain the vacuum (AE). The condensate water was fed to the de-aerator (DA) in the harbour machinery room which removed any remaining air from the system. Steam turbines used much less lubricating oil than diesel engines so only small storage tanks were needed (LO) plus associated pumps, coolers and strainers.

Harbour Machinery Room

The harbour machinery room was sandwiched between the port and starboard forward engine rooms, illustrated on the profile. It supplied ship services when most of the main machinery was shut down, but some boiler power was still needed. Steam was supplied to four evaporators (E) which could produce a total of 240 tons per day of distilled water and to two 300kW turbo-generators, with the drain coolers (DC) being mini-condensers for auxiliary machinery draining back into the main feed tank. A calorifier (CA) supplied hot water for domestic services. A low-pressure air compressor (L) at 100lb/in^2 powered pneumatic tools and moved petrol from storage to ready use.

Given the complexity of the main and auxiliary machinery systems, it is no surprise that to operate and maintain everything the engineering complement numbered about 300 men.

1945 Profile and Visible Decks

As fitted March 1945

(© National Maritime Museum, London M1703 Profile, M1702 Upper Deck, M1697 Bridges, etc, M1698 Shelter Deck and Boat Deck)

During the short operational career of the *King George V* class, there was only one major refit which took place approximately three years into their service careers and lasted about five months on average. The refits were spread over 16 months based on availability of individual ships and dockyard capacity. The first of the four ships to be taken in hand was *Howe* in December 1943 followed by *King George V* in

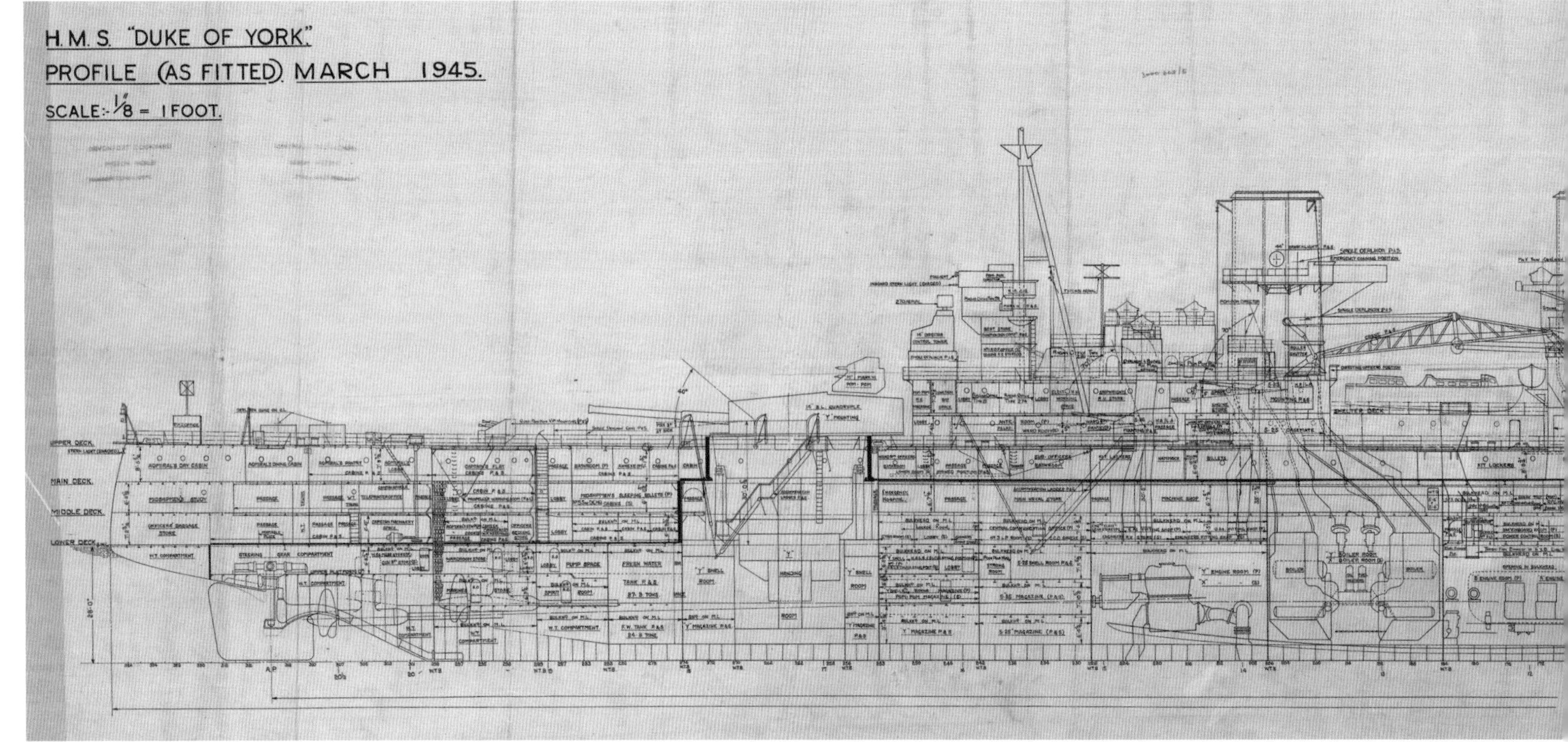
H.M.S. "DUKE OF YORK."
PROFILE (AS FITTED) MARCH 1945.
SCALE:- 1/8" = 1 FOOT.
UPPER DECK.
MAIN DECK.
MIDDLE DECK.
LOWER DECK.
SHELTER DECK

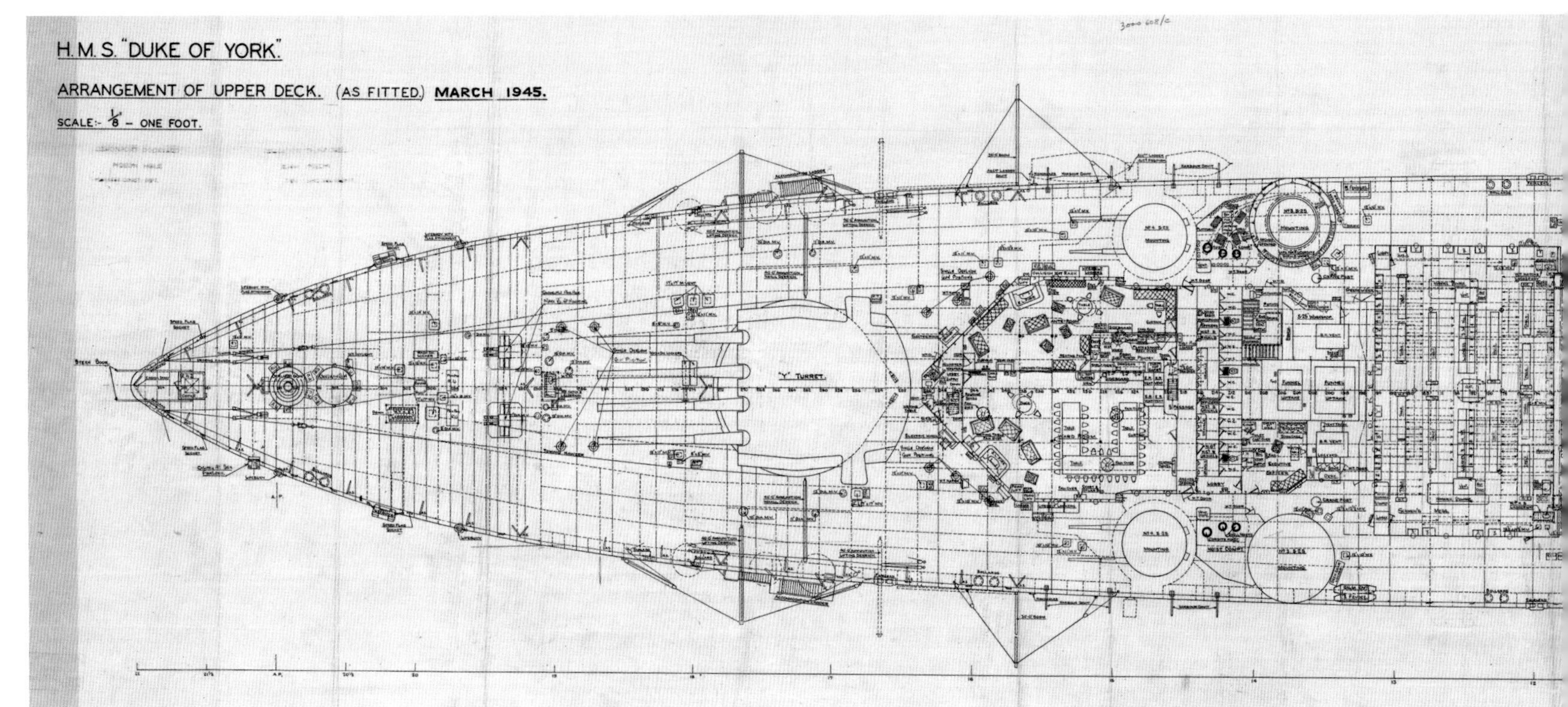
H.M.S. "DUKE OF YORK."
ARRANGEMENT OF UPPER DECK. (AS FITTED.) MARCH 1945.
SCALE:- 1/8" – ONE FOOT.
'Y' TURRET.

February 1944, *Anson* in June 1944 and lastly *Duke of York* in September 1944. *King George V* and *Duke of York* were refitted by Cammell Laird at Liverpool's Gladstone Dock and the other two at Devonport Dockyard.

The drawings selected here, profile and visible decks, show the *Duke of York* post refit in March 1945. The drawings are not entirely accurate and, for example, the profile perpetuates the error made in the 1941 As Fitted profile by showing Mark IV HACS instead of the Mark Vs that were actually fitted.

The general aim of the refit, in addition to addressing numerous updates and accumulated modifications, was to prepare the ships for service in the Far East in what was to become the British Pacific Fleet. The most obvious outcome of the refit was the midships structural

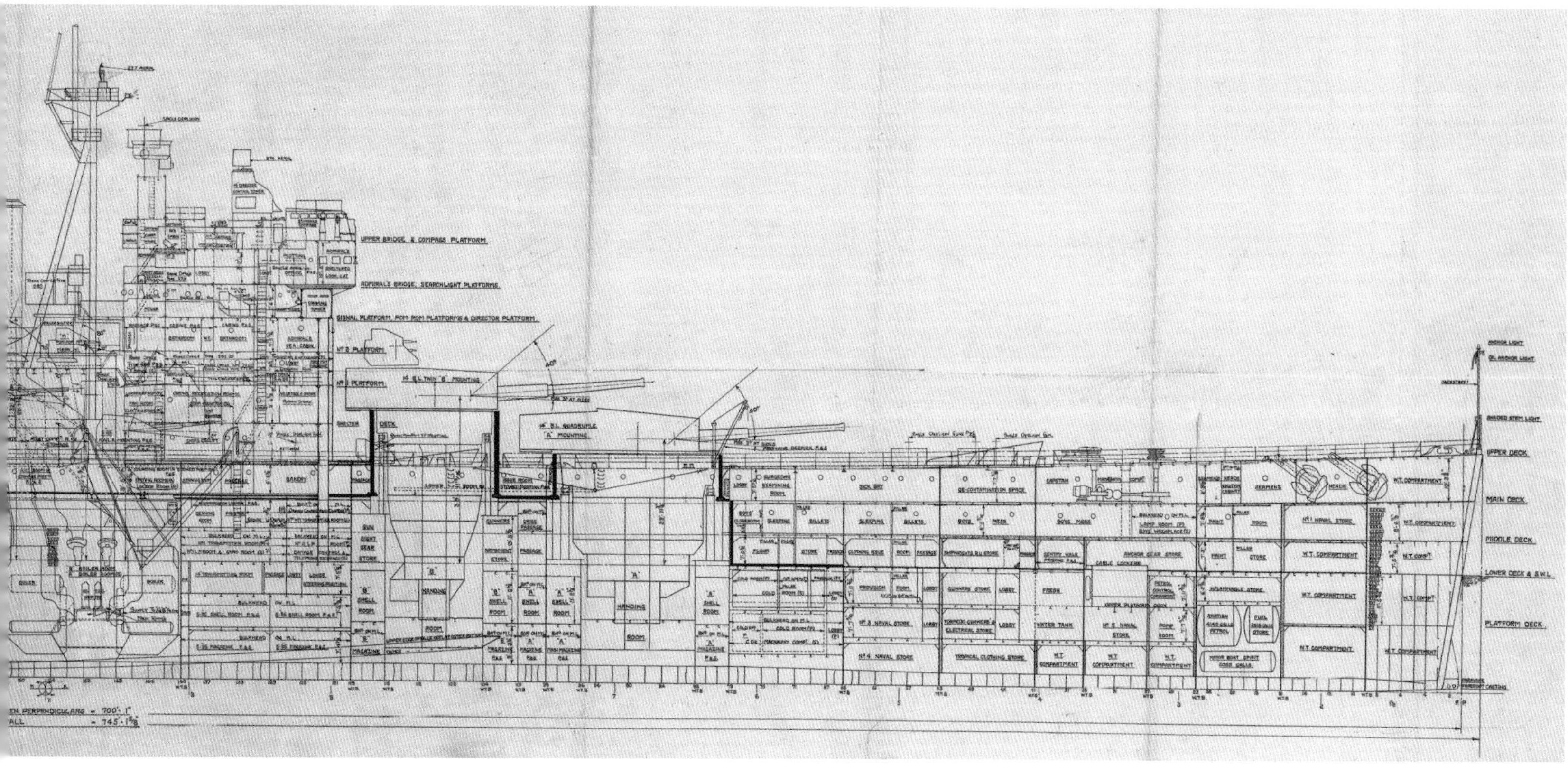

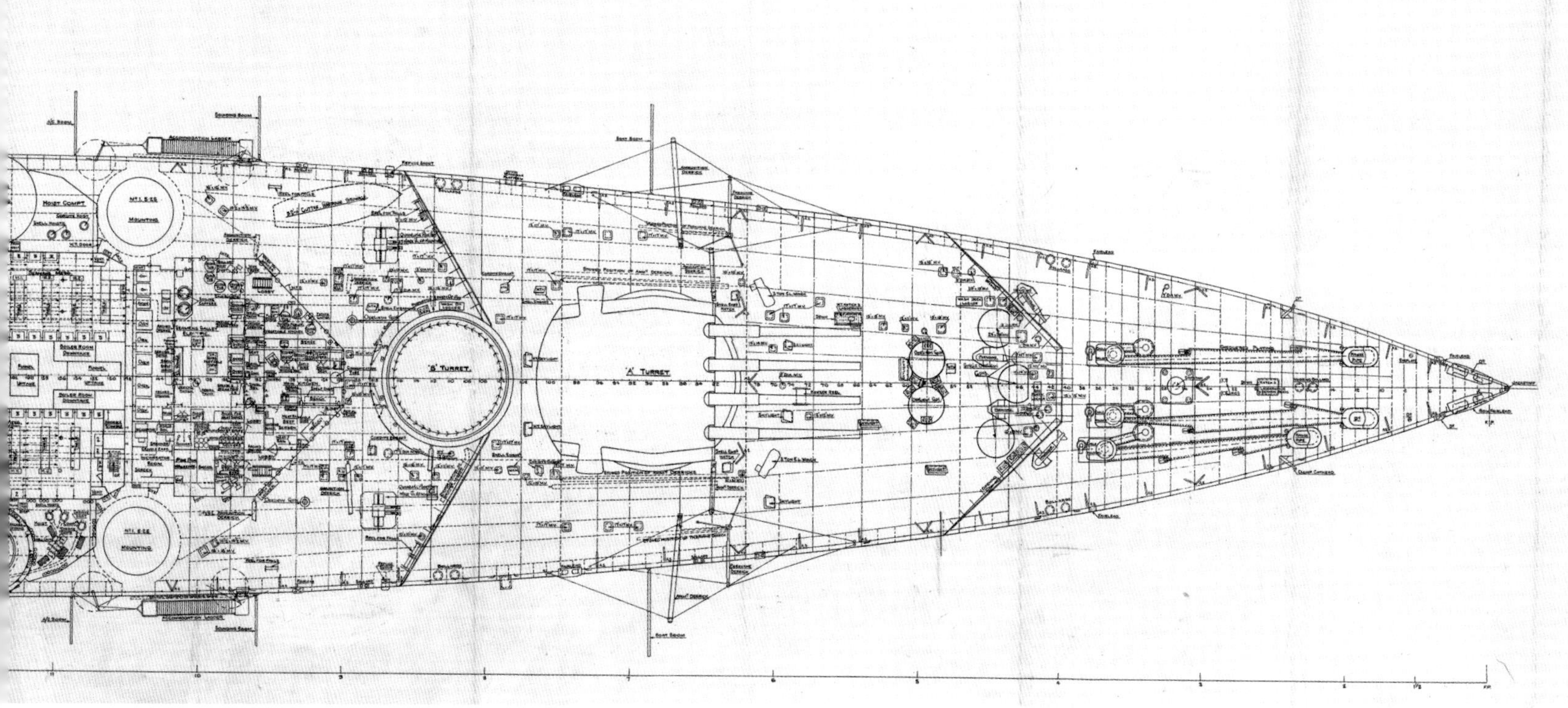
'B' TURRET
'A' TURRET

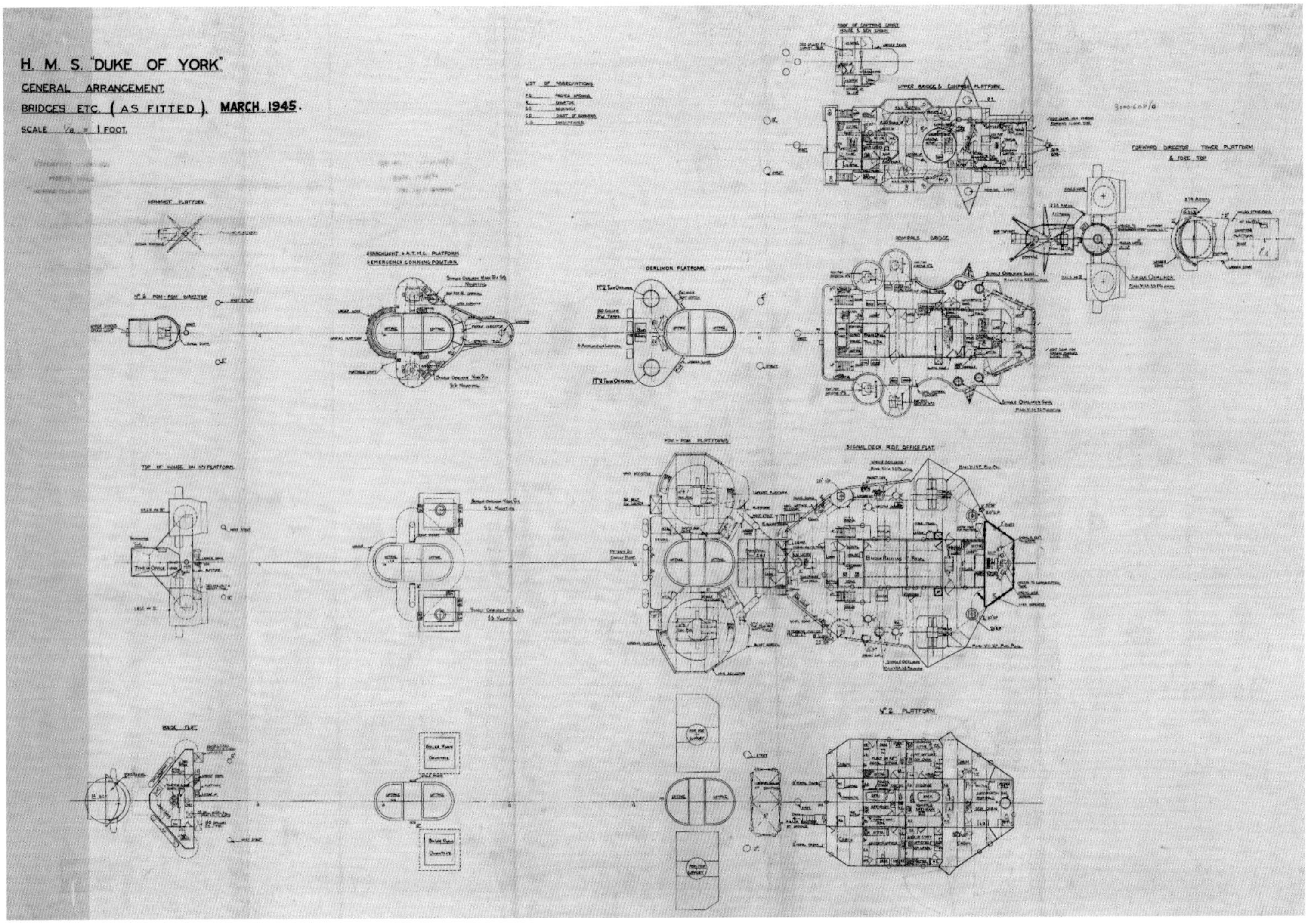

H. M. S. "DUKE OF YORK"
GENERAL ARRANGEMENT
BRIDGES ETC. (AS FITTED). MARCH. 1945.
SCALE 1/8 = 1 FOOT.

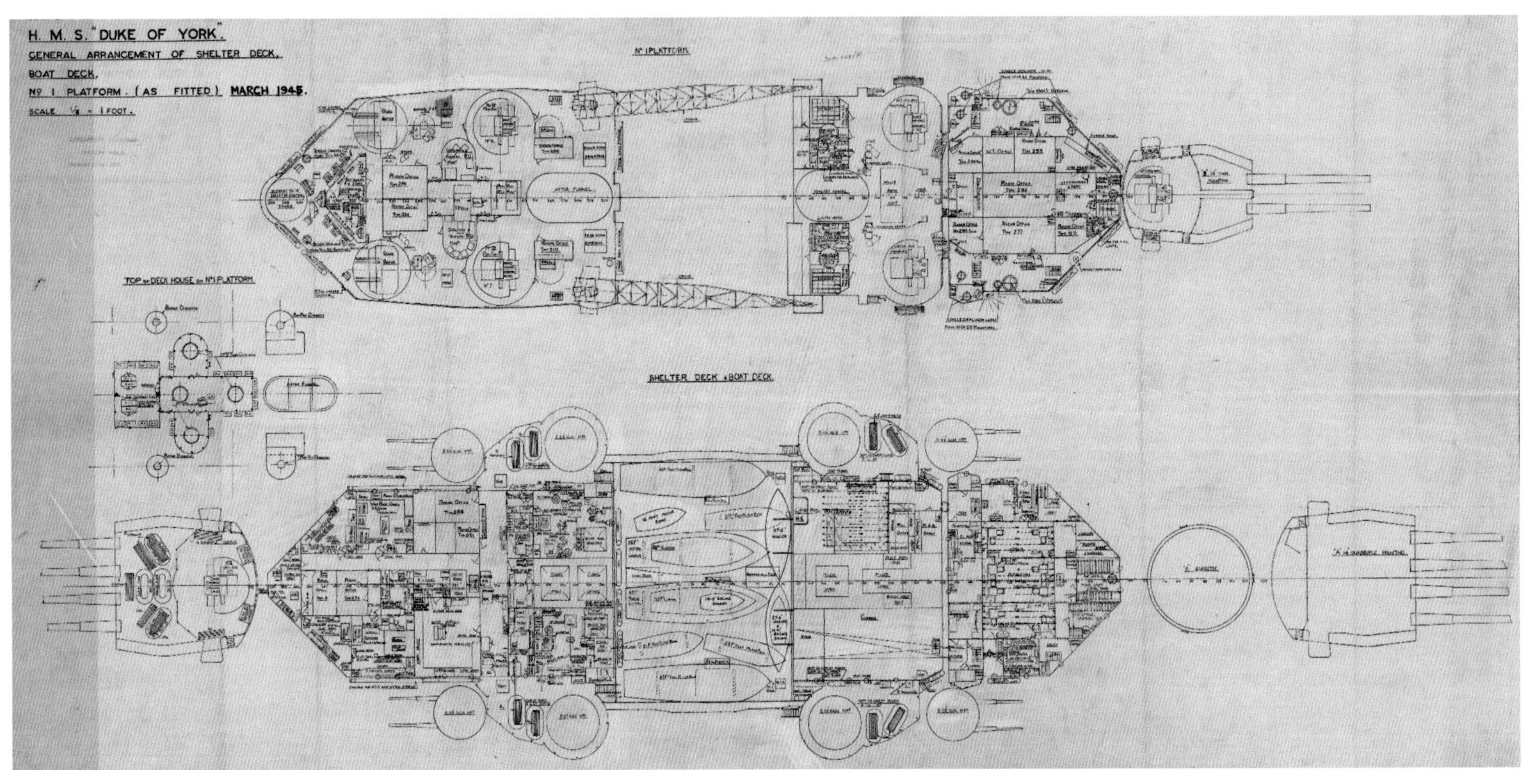
H. M. S. "DUKE OF YORK".
GENERAL ARRANGEMENT OF SHELTER DECK,
BOAT DECK,
No 1 PLATFORM. (AS FITTED) MARCH 1945.
SCALE 1/8 = 1 FOOT.
No 1 PLATFORM
TOP OF DECK HOUSE ON No 1 PLATFORM
SHELTER DECK & BOAT DECK

alterations made possible by the removal of the cross-deck catapult. The primary reason for its removal was the proliferation of flight decks at sea in the form of fleet carriers, light carriers and merchant/carrier conversions. As henceforth *King George V*-class battleships would always be part of a balanced fleet in which air cover would be a constant, aircraft arrangements were redundant. Radar reduced further the need for reconnaissance and gunfire spotting. The removal of the catapult and conversion of the hangar space created opportunities on the upper deck which allowed a number of issues to be addressed, namely the need for significantly more anti-aircraft barrels, additional crew accommodation and facilities.

The area between both funnels thus cleared was used to relocate the similarly-sized boat deck from its position abaft the after funnel to that location. The new boat deck was raised on a one-deck-high structure, the inside of which was given over to seamen's messes. The former aircraft hangar on the port side was also a seamen's mess with recreational space above while the starboard hangar became the Royal Marines' mess area with a cinema and stage above. The aircraft and boat handling cranes were now solely concerned with the ship's boats.

Given the dramatic growth of air power and the intensity of Japanese air operations in particular, the former boat deck was used to provide a major increase in the ship's anti-aircraft defence. Renamed No 1 Platform, a small cruciform structure was built on the former boat deck on top of which were fitted four twin 20mm Oerlikon mountings complete with ready-use ammunition boxes. The after part of this structure housed the Type 281 air-warning radar office. On No 1 Platform itself, immediately aft of the cranes, two eight-barrelled Mark VI pom-poms (on either side) were fitted. Abaft of this, two US-built four-barrelled 40mm Bofors mountings were fitted, one on either side. In total the redeployment of this area alone allowed for an additional thirty-two anti-aircraft barrels.

However, this would form only one part of the additional AA weaponry with the ship being liberally peppered with them including on both funnel platforms, the vacated pom-pom director above the director tower on the forward superstructure and clusters on the upper deck between 'Y' turret and the after superstructure. Many of these locations were inconvenient and costly in manpower to operate and maintain, borne out by the fact that on the cessation of hostilities the mountings were removed at the first opportunity. Eventually all 20mm Oerlikon mountings were removed.

Although the appearance of *Duke of York* was not significantly changed after the refit, the addition of the boat deck between the funnels added to the built-up look, as did the additions on the No 1 Platform. *Duke of York* was also fitted with a feature that would serve to distinguish her from the rest of the class – the extended emergency conning position on the after funnel. The other distinguishing feature, shared with *Anson*, was the extension fitted to either side of the forward end of the signal deck. Cantilevered over No 2 Platform, the extensions were added to support a four-barrelled Mark VII pom-pom on either side. Note the small RH2 VHF/DF office fitted right aft which was removed soon after the end of the war.

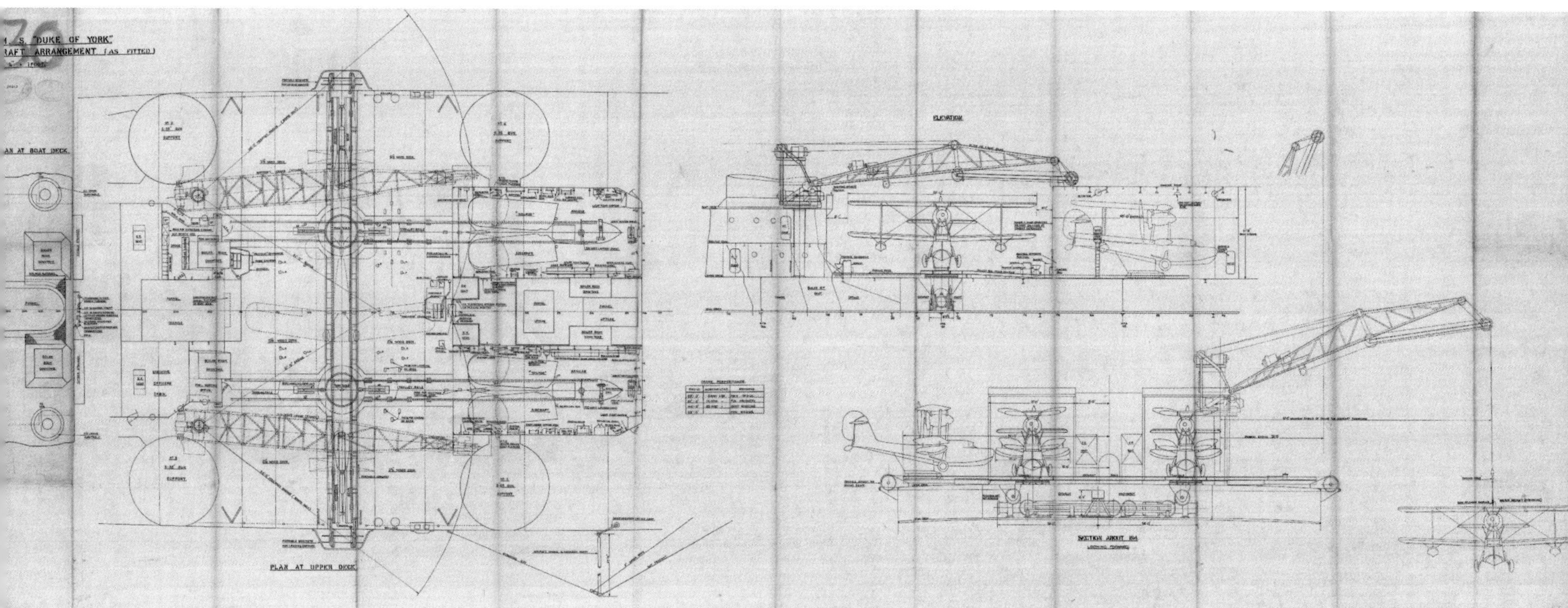
PLAN AT UPPER DECK

Aircraft Arrangements

The facility to handle just two Walrus amphibian aircraft took up a lot of space, 100ft in the ship's length, and almost its full breadth. Even with wings folded the aircraft were a tight squeeze in the 45ft x 21ft hangars. The aircraft were moved onto the catapult by a trolley on rails pulled by a winch. Each crane could lift the 5½-ton aircraft at 61ft radius, or a 10-ton boat at 44ft. The outboard sheaves could be removed for passing through locks such as the 110ft-wide ones at Portsmouth, Rosyth and the Panama Canal. In the 1945 refit, the catapult machinery was replaced by a laundry, and the catapult track by a mess for 100 seamen. (© National Maritime Museum, London M1685)

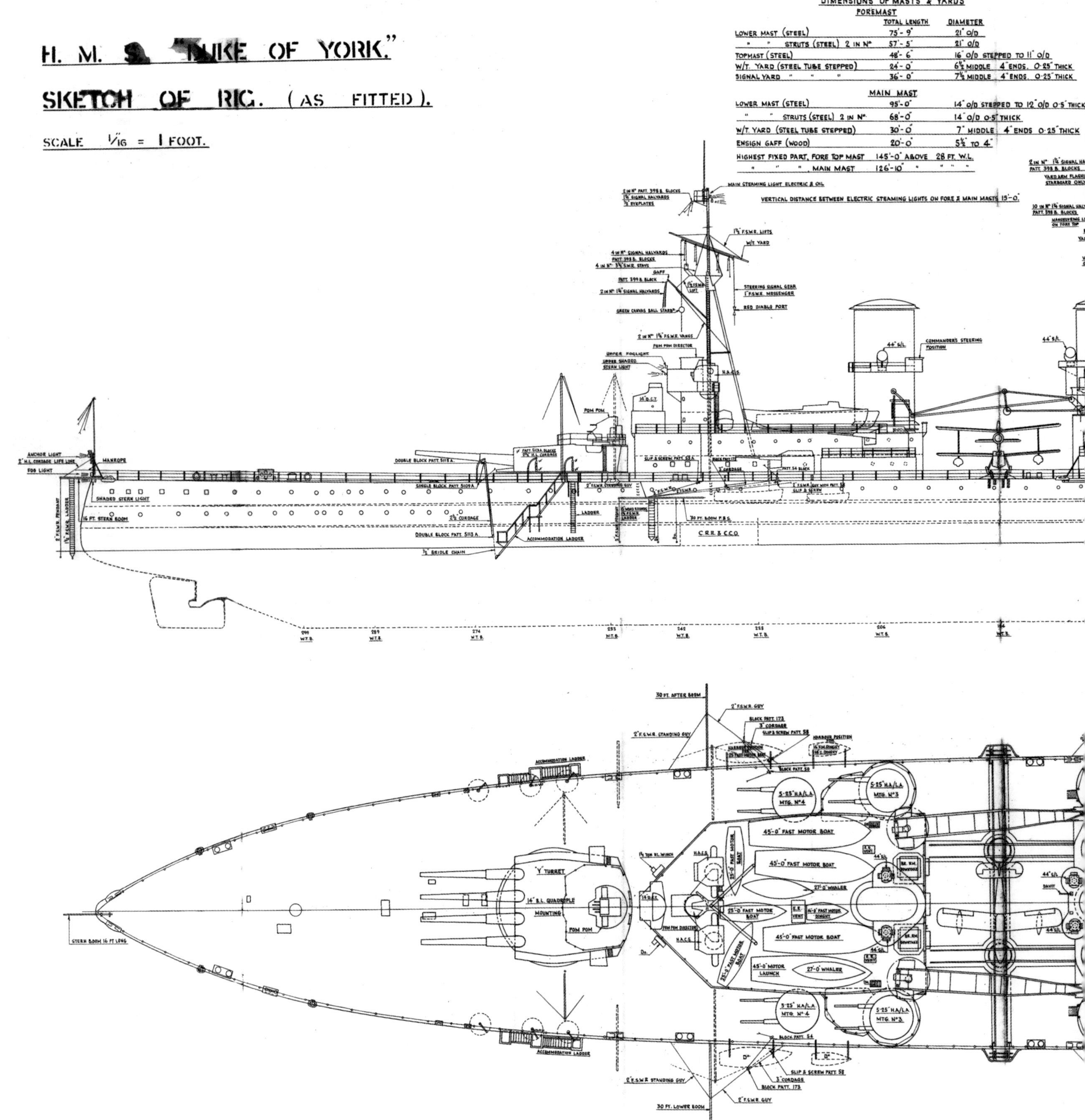

H. M. S. "DUKE OF YORK."
SKETCH OF RIG. (AS FITTED).
SCALE 1/16 = 1 FOOT.
DIMENSIONS OF MASTS & YARDS
FOREMAST
TOTAL LENGTH DIAMETER
LOWER MAST (STEEL) 75'-9" 21" O/D
" " STRUTS (STEEL) 2 IN Nº 57'-5" 21" O/D
TOPMAST (STEEL) 48'-6" 16" O/D STEPPED TO 11" O/D
W/T. YARD (STEEL TUBE STEPPED) 24'-0" 6½" MIDDLE 4" ENDS. 0·25" THICK
SIGNAL YARD " " " 36'-0" 7½" MIDDLE 4" ENDS. 0·25" THICK
MAIN MAST
LOWER MAST (STEEL) 95'-0" 14" O/D STEPPED TO 12" O/D 0·5" THICK
" " STRUTS (STEEL) 2 IN Nº 68'-0" 14" O/D 0·5" THICK
W/T. YARD (STEEL TUBE STEPPED) 30'-0" 7" MIDDLE 4" ENDS 0·25" THICK
ENSIGN GAFF (WOOD) 20'-0" 5½" TO 4"
HIGHEST FIXED PART, FORE TOP MAST 145'-0" ABOVE 28 FT. W.L.
" " " , MAIN MAST 126'-10" " " " "
MAIN STEAMING LIGHT ELECTRIC & OIL
VERTICAL DISTANCE BETWEEN ELECTRIC STEAMING LIGHTS ON FORE & MAIN MASTS 15'-0".
1½" F.S.W.R. LIFTS
W/T. YARD
COMMANDER'S STEERING POSITION
44" S/L
ANCHOR LIGHT
FOG LIGHT
MANROPE
SHADED STERN LIGHT
16 FT. STERN BOOM
ACCOMMODATION LADDER
LADDER
C.R.R. & C.C.O.
30 FT. AFTER BOOM
30 FT. LOWER BOOM
'Y' TURRET
14" B.L. QUADRUPLE MOUNTING
POM POM
45'-0" FAST MOTOR BOAT
27'-0" WHALER
45'-0" MOTOR LAUNCH
5·25" HA/LA MTG. Nº 4
5·25" HA/LA MTG. Nº 3
STERN BOOM 16 FT LONG

Sketch of Rig

From the days of sail, a Sketch of Rig had been drawn for Admiralty ships, the nearest to the outboard profile plan normally supplied for merchant ships. Seamanlike details included mast and yards and their dimensions, derricks, boat booms and even clothes-drying lines. A separate drawing was made of Visual Signalling and Wireless Transmission Rig, which also showed the newly-fitted radar aerials. (© National Maritime Museum, London M2065)

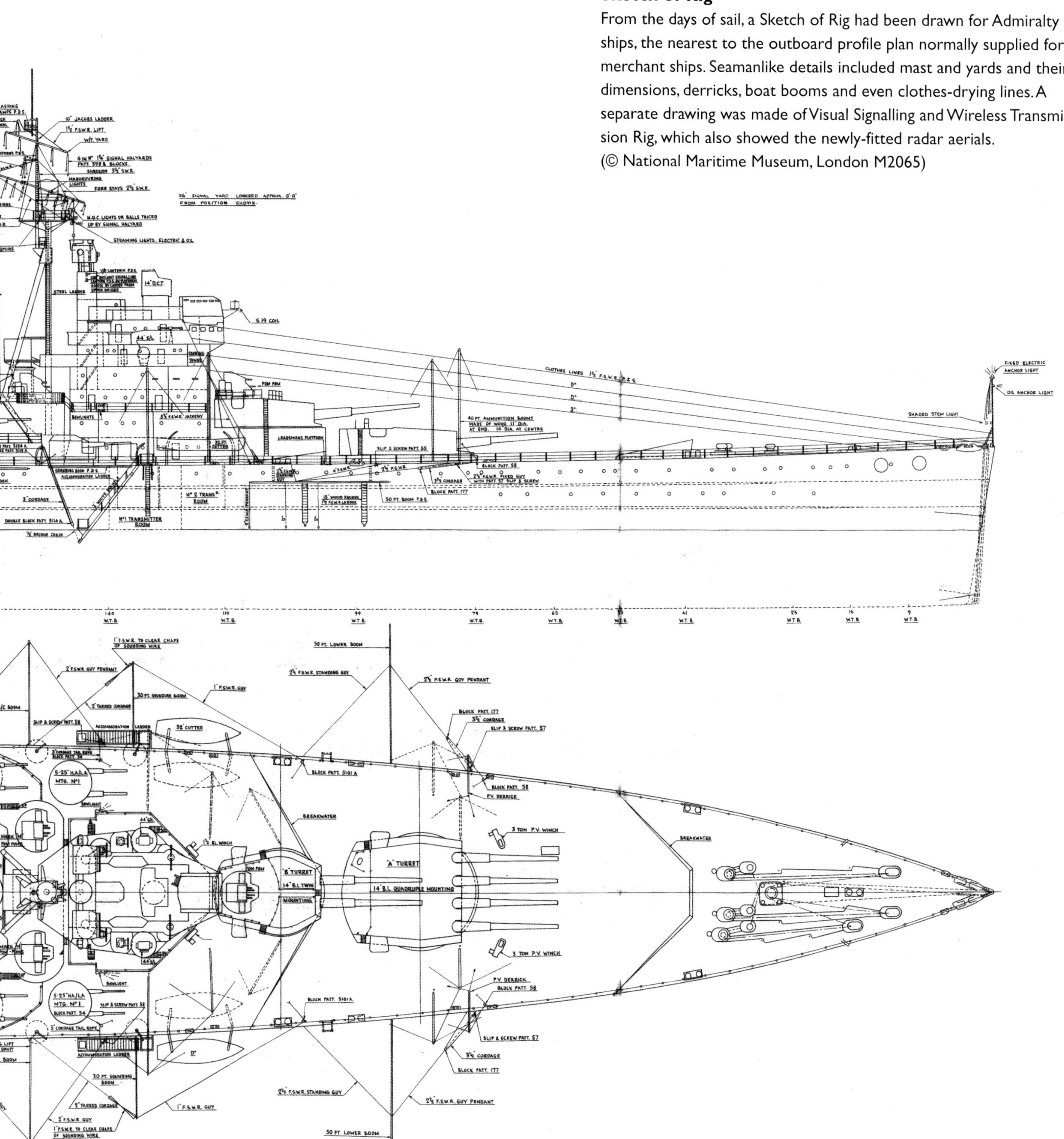
FLASHING LAMPS P. & S.
10" JACOBS LADDER
1½" F.S.W.R. LIFT
W/T. YARD
4 IN Nº 1¼" SIGNAL HALYARDS PATT. 398 & BLOCKS.
SHROUDS 3½" S.W.R.
MANOEUVRING LIGHTS
FORE STAYS 2½" S.W.R.
36' SIGNAL YARD LOWERED APPROX. 5'-0" FROM POSITION SHOWN.
N.U.C. LIGHTS OR BALLS TRICED UP BY SIGNAL HALYARD
STEAMING LIGHTS, ELECTRIC & OIL
V/S LANTERN P. & S.
STEEL LADDER
14" D.C.T.
S.19 COIL
44" S/L
CONNING TOWER
POM POM
BOWLIGHTS
3½" F.S.W.R. JACKSTAY
32 FT. CUTTER
LEADSMANS PLATFORM
SLIP & SCREW PATT 55
40 FT. AMMUNITION BOOMS MADE OF WOOD 11" DIA. AT END. 14" DIA. AT CENTRE
CLOTHES LINES 1½" F.S.W.R. P. & S.
D°
D°
D°
FIXED ELECTRIC ANCHOR LIGHT
OIL ANCHOR LIGHT
SHADED STEM LIGHT
BLOCK PATT. 58
2½" F.S.W.R. FIXED GUY WITH PATT. 57 SLIP & SCREW
3½" CORDAGE
BLOCK PATT. 177
50 FT. BOOM P. & S.
15" WOOD ROUNDS 1½" F.S.W.R. LADDER
4" F.S.W.R.
2½" F.S.W.R.
2½" F.S.W.R. STANDING GUY
Nº 2 TRANSR ROOM
Nº 1 TRANSMITTER ROOM
SOUNDING BOOM P. & S.
ACCOMMODATION LADDER
3" CORDAGE
DOUBLE BLOCK PATT. 5114 A.
½" BRIDGE CHAIN
3" WHITE MANILA
140 W.T.B.
119 W.T.B.
99 W.T.B.
79 W.T.B.
65 W.T.B.
W.T.B.
41 W.T.B.
23 W.T.B.
16 W.T.B.
9 W.T.B.
1" F.S.W.R. TO CLEAR CHAFE OF SOUNDING WIRE
2" F.S.W.R. GUY PENDANT
30 FT. SOUNDING BOOM
2" TARRED CORDAGE
1" F.S.W.R. GUY
50 FT. LOWER BOOM
2½" F.S.W.R. STANDING GUY
2½" F.S.W.R. GUY PENDANT
A/C BOOM
SLIP & SCREW PATT. 58
ACCOMMODATION LADDER
32' CUTTER
3" CORDAGE TAIL ROPE
BLOCK PATT. 54
5·25" HA/LA MTG. Nº 1
BOWLIGHT
44" S/L
1½" EL. WINCH
BREAKWATER
BLOCK PATT. 5101 A.
BLOCK PATT. 177
3½" CORDAGE
SLIP & SCREW PATT. 57
BLOCK PATT. 58
P.V. DERRICK
3 TON P.V. WINCH
"A" TURRET
14" B.L. QUADRUPLE MOUNTING
"B" TURRET
14" B.L. TWIN MOUNTING
POM POM
MARK "M" POM-POMS
BREAKWATER
3 TON P.V. WINCH
P.V. DERRICK
BLOCK PATT. 58
BLOCK PATT. 5101 A.
5·25" HA/LA MTG. Nº 1
SLIP & SCREW PATT. 58
BLOCK PATT. 54
3" CORDAGE TAIL ROPE
ACCOMMODATION LADDER
D°
SLIP & SCREW PATT. 57
3½" CORDAGE
BLOCK PATT. 177
30 FT. SOUNDING BOOM
2" TARRED CORDAGE
1" F.S.W.R. GUY
2" F.S.W.R. GUY
1" F.S.W.R. TO CLEAR CHAFE OF SOUNDING WIRE
2½" F.S.W.R. STANDING GUY
2½" F.S.W.R. GUY PENDANT
50 FT. LOWER BOOM

Breaking

AFTER *DUKE OF YORK* was paid off into reserve in November 1951, she was laid up at buoys in the Gareloch, just 12 miles from where she was built along with sisters *King George V* and *Anson*. *Howe* remained in Reserve at Devonport. At this point the ships were in full working order. They had not quite been abandoned, however, and the decision was made to 'cocoon' sensitive equipment which allowed for the rather unlikely option of reactivation should events require it. Cocooning involved covering delicate items of equipment such as directors and gun mountings in an airtight covering and dehumidifying the interior. This was done by covering the equipment completely in a fine netting which was then sprayed with a solution of plastic, bitumen and paint. Once dried, the air was pumped out, the result looking rather as if the equipment had been shrink-wrapped. Ships thus treated and laid up were referred to unofficially as the 'Mothball Fleet'.

The ships lay in this condition for years, more of an attraction than anything else, until 8 May 1957 when the Admiralty finally made the decision to scrap all four battleships of the *King George V* class. As all of the earlier battleships had already been scrapped, the ships of this class together with *Vanguard* were the last survivors of this type of warship. As *Vanguard* would soon follow to the scrapyard, the opportunity was missed to preserve an example of a warship type in which Britain had invested so much both in terms of the evolution of the type and of course in capital, human as well as financial.

At that time, few British warships were 'sold' for scrap, despite what many reference books say. Instead they were 'handed over' by the Admiralty to BISCO, the British Iron & Steel Corporation which was the British steel industry's raw material procurement agency. BISCO then allocated each ship to the most appropriate shipbreaker, on the basis of their capability, their current workload and their proximity to the lay-up port. Shipbreaking Industries' shipbreaking '(SI's) yard at Faslane was very close to the Gareloch moorings, so it was no surprise when the first of the four, *Anson*, was towed alongside at Faslane on 17 December 1957. *Duke of York* followed soon after on 18 February being allocated SI's Job Number 76. *King George V* was taken to Dalmuir on 20 January 1958 for part demolition by Arnott Young, her hulk being finished at Troon. *Howe* was broken up by Thomas Ward at Inverkeithing arriving there on 4 June 1958 from Devonport.

SI, formerly Metal Industries (Salvage), had taken over the wartime emergency port on the Clyde in August 1946. This had six 500ft long berths with 35ft depth of water alongside, with cargo handling cranes, an extensive rail network, workshops and other facilities. Additional facilities for shipbreaking were added as detailed in the book *Shipbreaking at Faslane* including a 60-ton floating crane and a beaching ground. By 1957, Faslane had broken up five capital ships but had lost both *Warspite* and the Brazilian *Sao Paulo* on tow for scrapping.

Under the standard BISCO contract, the shipbreaker was a sub-contractor who was required to demolish the ship, send its scrap steel to designated steelworks, recover valuable non-ferrous metals and find customers for re-usable items like anchor cables, accommodation fittings and machine tools. For this, BISCO reimbursed the yard its wages, cutting gases and craneage and paid 27s 6d remuneration per ton of steel recovered plus 20s (£1) per ton to cover overheads and profit. It also paid commission on sales of non-ferrous, armour plate and reusables, typically 5–10 per cent of value. BISCO collected the sales proceeds of all these materials (with steel at an internal industry price that did not involve the shipbreaker), deducted its costs and commission and returned the net balance to the appropriate Government department, at that time the Ministry of Supply, which was in effect a deferred sale price.

With work on *Anson* already in hand, serious demolition on *Duke of York* did not start until September, although equipment that had to be returned to the Admiralty was removed for potential further use. To facilitate this process, the main lighting circuits below decks were energised, but access to remote compartments required a torch. This enabled one of the authors to explore the ship and take photographs, after signing a chit that it was at his own risk.

Demolition started from the upperworks downwards, opening the ship up deck by deck, until the lower hull was lightened sufficiently for it to be beached for final demolition. Among the earliest removals were the ten 14in guns and the masts, while flammable material like timber was removed to reduce the risk of fire from cutting the steel structure with oxy-propane torches. Work continued steadily with three quayside cranes of 6–12 tons capacity removing about 800 tons a week. This work was carried out by ship burners, cranemen, slingers and labourers, with the resulting large sections being removed on rail wagons to areas where the shore burners could reduce the steel to furnace size of 5ft x 2ft for transport by rail to a designated steelworks. Equipment and machinery items were taken to stores for sale or to the non-ferrous workshop for breaking down into component metals. Unsaleable items like tiling and insulation were removed and buried in a remote area of the yard. Armour plates and gun barrels were made of valuable nickel steel so commanded a price about double that of regular mild steel, so such scrap was sent to the specialist steel makers in Sheffield such as English Steel Corporation. Armour plates up to 15in thick could be readily cut, either by manual torches or by semi-automatic cutters running on portable rails after removal ashore. The floating crane was useful for lifting outboard (port) side armour, out of the reach or the capacity of the quayside cranes, as well as for heavy items like rudders.

Photographs show that by January 1959, the 14in gun mountings and much of her superstructure had been largely removed, by which time some 5000 tons had been taken off the ship, reducing her draft by 3ft. The lower armour strake was usually underwater, but that and the two upper strakes were soon able to be removed. By August *Duke of York* was an unrecognisable hulk, but opened up with compartments identified in the photo on p252 top. Now lightened sufficiently, she was towed to the beaching ground on 17 November 1959, by which time 30,000 tons had been removed. It took four more months before the last section of double bottom was fully 'out of the water' on 16 March 1960. Material remaining ashore was processed and despatched, and the last trace of the once-mighty battleship gone for ever. About 353,000 man-hours had been needed to demolish the ship, only about 2 per cent of those needed to build her. Each man-hour cost on average 4s 11d (24.6p), wages making up about half the demolition cost.

SI recorded the outturn of material weights carefully, not only for BISCO records but also to help them estimate the likely outturn of similar ships they might bid for in future. Their figures showed:

	Tons
Steel scrap	19,998
Armour-quality scrap	12,083
Cast iron	247
Anchor cables	109
Boiler tubes	144
Miscellaneous steel	100
Total Ferrous	32,681
Gunmetal	668
Copper	275
Lead	280
Manganese	265
Brass	150
Aluminium	92
Cupro-nickel	60
Propellers	58
White metal	3
Miscellaneous non-ferrous	110
Total Non-ferrous	1961
Saleable machinery	128
Timber	51
Sundries	137
Total Ship Saleable	34,958
Oil fuel	328
Debris & rubbish	1762
Total from Ship	**37,048**

When compared with *Anson*'s outturn, SI found that *Duke of York* yielded about 1800 tons more steel. There is no explanation from the construction of the two ships; it is more likely that SI staff misallocated similar material from each of the two ships being demolished at the same time. Reducing *Duke of York* by about 900 tons and increasing *Anson* by 900 accords closer with the outturns from *King George V* and *Howe*.

SI could not draw up a profit and loss account for the whole ship as they did not know the prices of steel scrap that BISCO received. But BISCO's own figures at June 1961 show that the net value of the ship was £543,499, the highest of the four *King George V*-class battleships. However, reducing her steel by about 900 tons would bring her value down to about £533,000:

	Tons	**£/ton**	**£**
Steel scrap	20,305	11.2	227,415
Armour scrap	12,083	20.0	241,652
Non-ferrous	1978	151.5	299,586
Reusables and sundries	606	31.9	19,331
Total sales	34,972	22.5	787,984
Demolition costs		5.22	182,525
Towage, carriage etc			61,960
Total costs		6.99	244,485
Surplus		15.54	543,499

Unfortunately SI's accounts do not show the profit they made on *Duke of York* or *Anson*. The best that can be estimated is to take the company profit for 1958 and 1959 of about £120,000, a period when the two battleships made up about 75 per cent of the tonnage recovered, suggesting that each battleship made about £45,000 profit.

The following photographs were taken by Ian Buxton and where indicated by T W Ferrers-Walker.

At a time when a large number of Royal Navy warships were being disposed of for scrap, Ian Buxton was serving an apprenticeship as a naval architect at the Dumbarton shipyard of William Denny & Co Ltd. This well-known Clyde shipyard lay between where *Duke of York* was built at Clydebank and where she was scrapped at Faslane. Living in close proximity to the breaker's yard enabled Ian Buxton to make a number of visits to photograph the demolition of the ship over the period of two years. She was berthed alongside at Faslane on 18 February 1958.

Tom Ferrers-Walker took a keen interest in major Royal Navy warships being broken up, having been a been a young naval officer at the end of the Second World War. Shipbreaking Industries would advise him of ship movements so he could travel to Faslane from Birmingham, where he lived, to photograph them both in colour and black & white.

The two battleships, *Duke of York* right and *Anson* left, lie at their moorings in the Gareloch on 4 May 1957, where they have been maintained by SI's sister company Metal Industries (Salvage), soon to be moved alongside the yard at Faslane.

OF YORK

Duke of York alongside Faslane's No. 4 berth on 1 March 1958, her guns and directors still in their protective cocoons. In the background is the maintenance aircraft carrier *Perseus*. (T W Ferrers-Walker)

SI allowed approved visitors into the yard and on board ships, at their own risk. As a young naval architect, the author was able to take a number of photographs from *Duke of York*'s mastheads on 1 March 1958. Looking down from the foremast reveals the top of the 14in director topped by its Type 274 radar aerial. The 6in-thick roof plates on 'A' 14in turret are secured by bolts, allowing them to be removed to change guns when they were worn out.

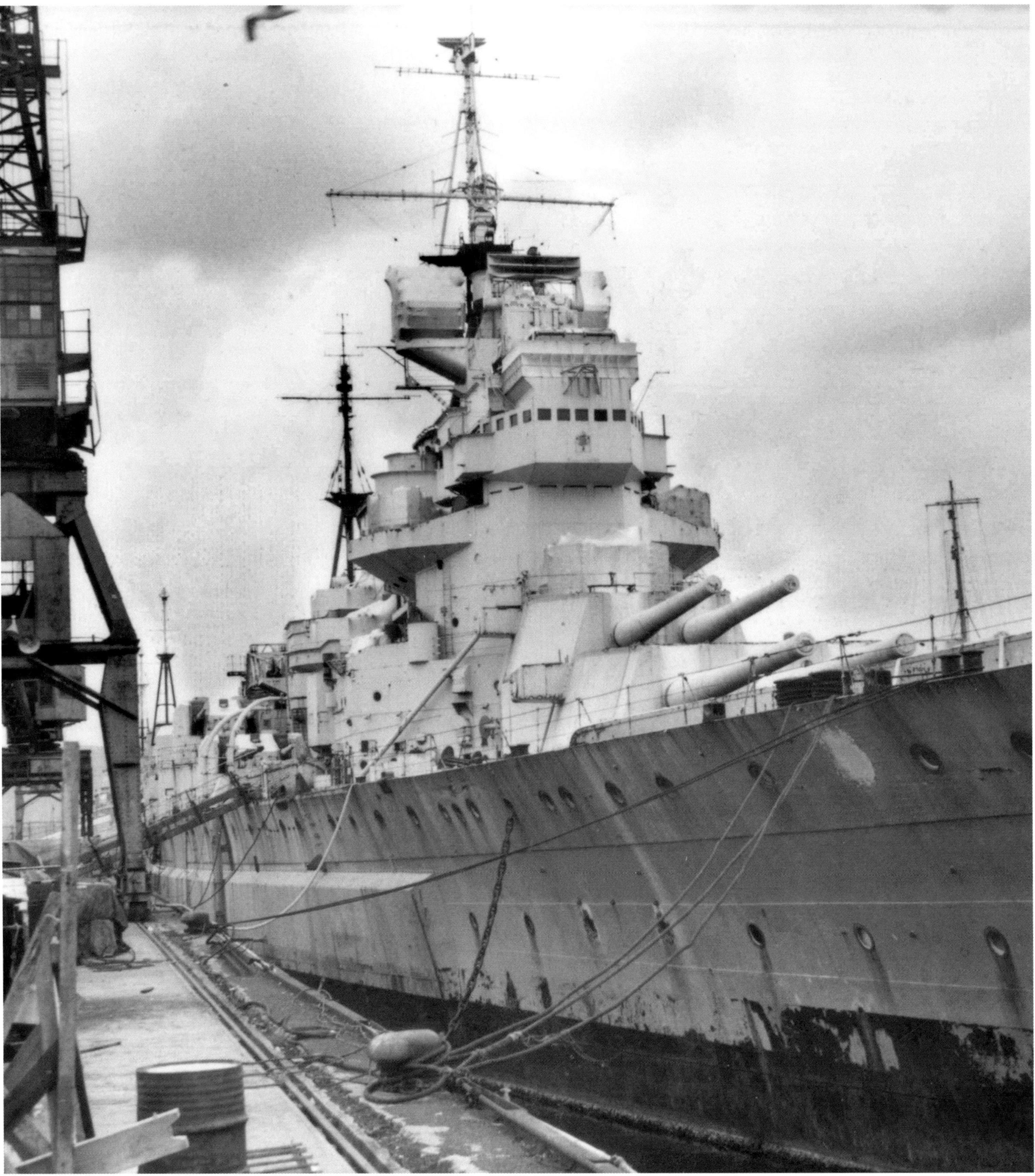

Above: Alongside Faslane's No 4 berth on 26 May 1958 with gangway access. The crane is one of the original Stothert & Pitt travelling cargo-handling cranes.

Opposite: This view on 1 March 1958 shows off *Duke of York*'s fine lines forward. Metal Industries (Salvage)'s salvage vessel *Salveda* is berthed alongside.

Looking aft from the foremast shows the two 44in searchlights and the emergency conning position on the after funnel – a feature that was different in each surviving *King George V*-class battleship.

A slightly different angle shows her port 10-ton crane now used for handling boats, but previously for aircraft as well at its previous higher rating of 12 tons. Alongside is the oiler *Rowanol*, probably removing some of the 328 tons of oil fuel that remained on board.

ROWANOL
LONDON

Looking forward from the mainmast shows the forward funnel and both Clarke Chapman cranes, as well as the two remaining searchlights (originally six). Compare the somewhat similar as-built view on pp152–3.

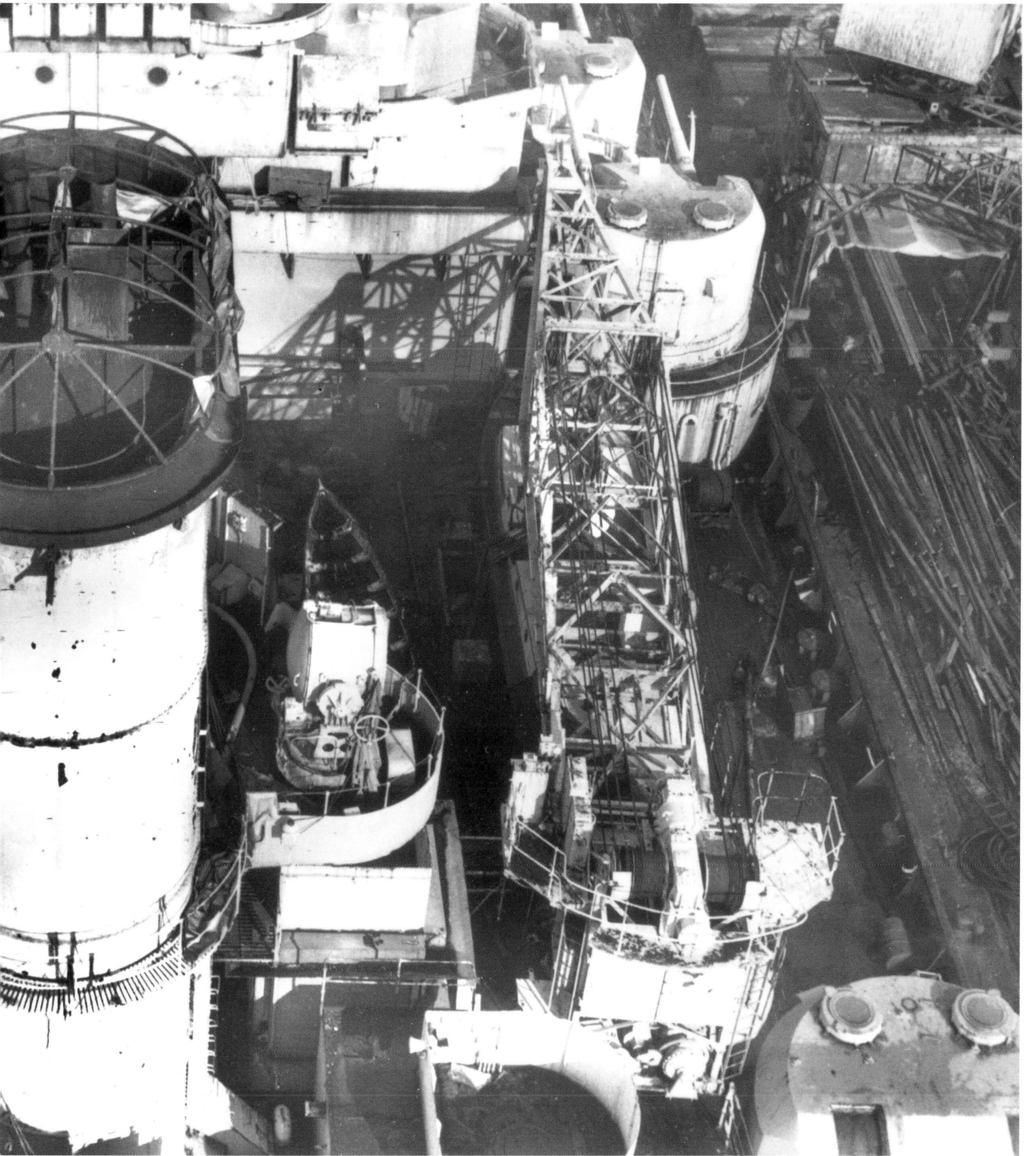

SURFACE GUARD
AIR GUARD
SUNRISE
SUNSET
ZONE
MOONRISE
MOONSET
D.C. STATE
RADAR STATE

Above: A view inside her upper bridge with most instruments still in place. (T W Ferrers-Walker)

Opposite: Looking straight down from the foremast shows the circular aerial of the Type 277P surface-warning radar, a cocooned Mark V director for the starboard forward 5.25in mountings and an empty platform previously housing a pom-pom director and then an Oerlikon gun.

SI put a launch at Ferrers-Walker's disposal on 26 May 1958 so he could take photos from the seaward side. This shot of the port bow shows that demolition had not yet commenced; items were still being removed for return to the Admiralty. (T W Ferrers-Walker)

A closer look at *Duke of York*'s superstructure showing some boats still aboard. (T W Ferrers-Walker)

A port-quarter view on 26 May 1958. The tug *Metinda III* is alongside with the liner *Asturias* ahead, part repainted black from when she doubled as *Titanic* in the film *A Night to Remember*. (T W Ferrers-Walker)

Opposite: A characteristic shipbreaking yard view taken from the hulk of *Asturias*. (T W Ferrers-Walker)

The rear of 'Y' turret showing the vent holes in the 7in-thick rear plate, topped by a cocooned eight-barrelled 2pdr pom-pom and its ready-use ammunitions boxes. (T W Ferrers-Walker)

Opposite: Looking aft from the forecastle, still intact externally on 20 May 1958, showing the three anchor capstans and with the hatch to the seamen's heads open. The crane on the quay is one of SI's 12-ton Scotch derricks. (T W Ferrers-Walker)

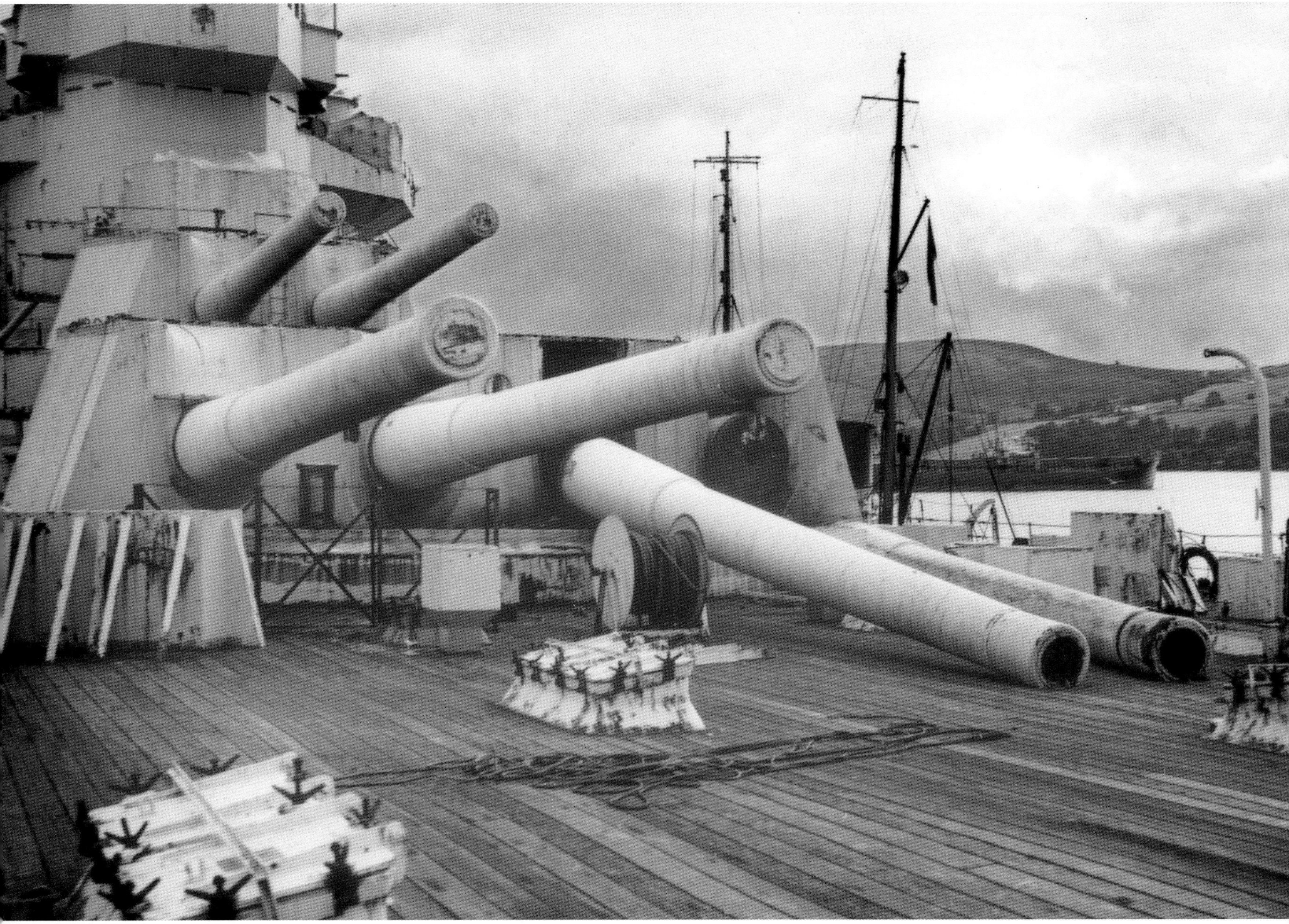

Two of 'A' turret's 14in gun barrels have been cut off on 6 August 1958, ready to be lifted off by Faslane's 60-ton floating crane. As the complete gun, breech and balance weight weighed 92 tons, each had to be removed in two pieces. (T W Ferrers-Walker)

Opposite: Port side looking aft, with 32ft cutter still under its davits, with P1 and P2 5.25in gun mountings behind. (T W Ferrers-Walker)

The view from outside the yard on the A814 road (now diverted above the Clyde Submarine Base) on 11 October 1958, with the battleship now moved to No 3 berth. Demolition is now under way, with cranes and boats removed. Vista House on right, then occupied by Metal Industries (Salvage) manager Tom McKenzie, later becoming a NAAFI club.

A sunny January day (the 24th) shows that much of *Duke of York*'s superstructure has been removed. To date, approximately 1330 tons of armour quality, 220 tons of non-ferrous and 2450 tons of mild steel scrap had been taken off.

Opposite: A rainy day at Faslane on 17 November 1958. The nickel-rich armoured gunhouse of 'A' turret has been removed, revealing the trunnion supports for each 14in gun and cradle. The deck planking has been removed for possible sale, lying at left. The foredeck is a mass of small hatchways (some for embarking ammunition) and mushroom ventilators. The hulk of *Anson* is ahead.

E3

Opposite: By 2 May 1959, *Anson*'s hulk has gone to the beach, with *Duke of York* moved to No 1 berth. She has been cut down aft to the 4½in armoured lower deck revealing the officers' cabin layout; the dark canyon is the main fresh water tank (coated with Rosbonite), with the remains of 'Y' mounting ahead. Amidships the level is that of the main (armoured) deck with some of the upper strake of side armour yet to be removed.

Right: Forward on 2 May the level is that of the middle deck, an area of stores and mess decks. The dark circular ring bulkhead supporting 'B' turret can be seen just ahead of the step up to the main deck. The tongue on the upper edge of the middle strake of side armour is just visible. The submarine berthed inboard is *Storen* (ex-*Vulpine*), recently returned from the Danish Navy. The frigates astern are *Whaddon* and *Wigtown Bay*.

By 30 June, much of the armoured main deck has been lifted off by the floating crane, ready to be cut into smaller pieces for sending to the specialist steelworks. The underlying plating and deck beams are still attached to each 5in or 6in thick armour plate. (T W Ferrers-Walker)

The hull is riding high on 30 June, still encrusted with barnacles – she was last drydocked at Liverpool in 1951. With about 18,000 tons removed, her draft is now about 20ft compared with 31ft when she arrived and 35ft at full load. The two sections of framing left standing are used to attach mooring wires. (T W Ferrers-Walker)

Virtually all of the revolving structure of 'A' gun mounting has been removed by 30 June. This view looking forward shows the shell room with its storage bins. The deck perimeter above is the platform deck with the heavily stiffened main protective bulkhead to the right. (T W Ferrers-Walker)

Opposite: This general view from the top of a crane on 7 November 1959 includes the bow of the cruiser *Newcastle*. Ahead of the transverse bulkhead 228 catching the sun are the two after engine rooms, next ahead 'X' and 'Y' boiler rooms (with the boilers already removed), then the two forward engine rooms with the harbour machinery room between them, with 'A' and 'B' boiler rooms ahead. Compare with the photo on p66; demolition was not the reverse process of construction.

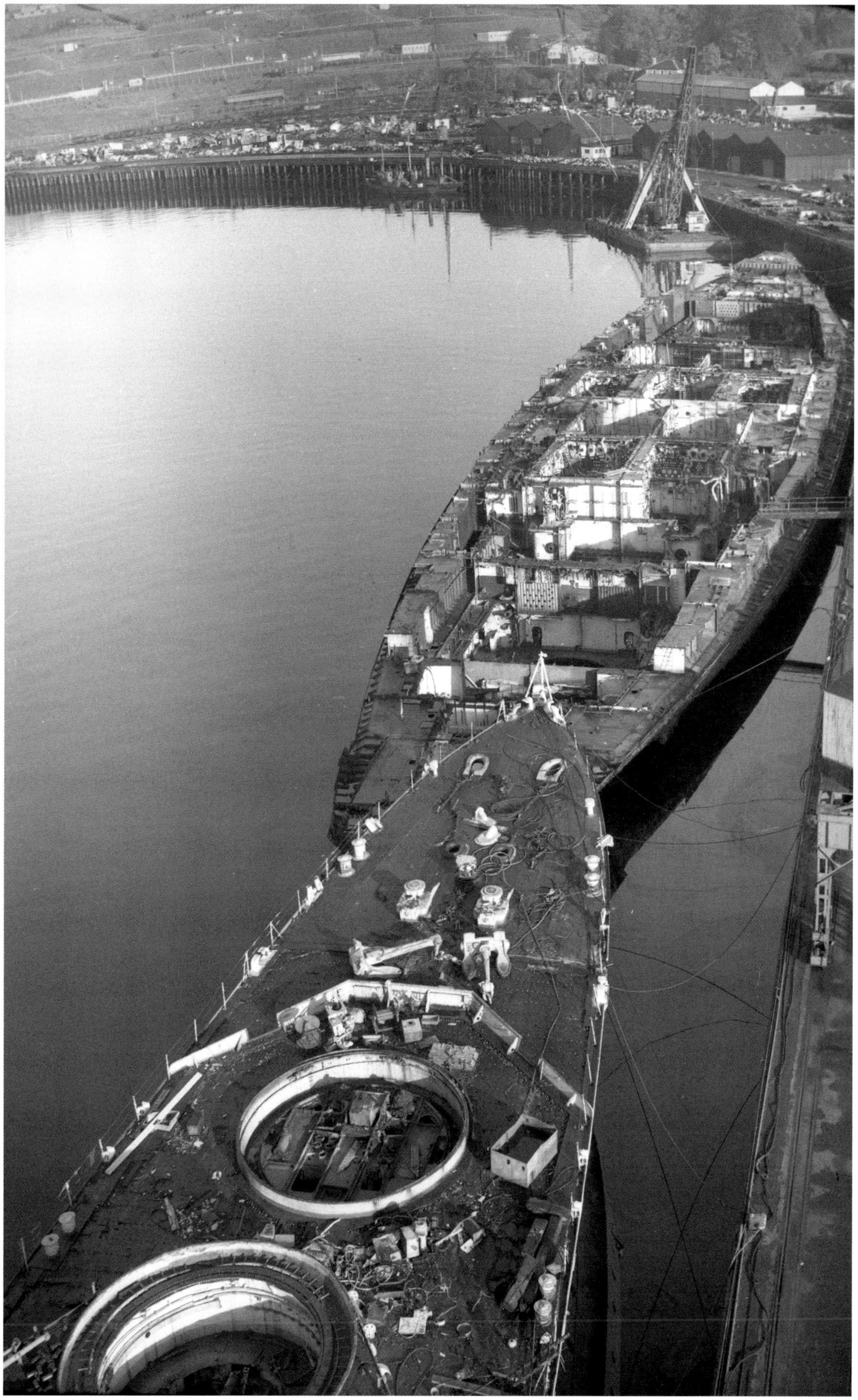

A closer view on 7 November from *Newcastle*'s bow. All the side armour has now been removed.

Y Engine room
After 5.25" magazine
Y Shell room
Y Magazine
Port inner shaft passage
Rum store
Upper platform deck
Pump space
Store
Marine's store
Y Boiler room
X Boiler room
X Engine room
Lower deck level
Watertight compartment
Fresh water tanks
Armour shelf
Admiral's store
Palm compartment
(shaft bracket support)

The hulk was moved to the beach at midday on 14 November 1959, which dried out at low tide allowing final demolition, seen here on 9 January 1960.

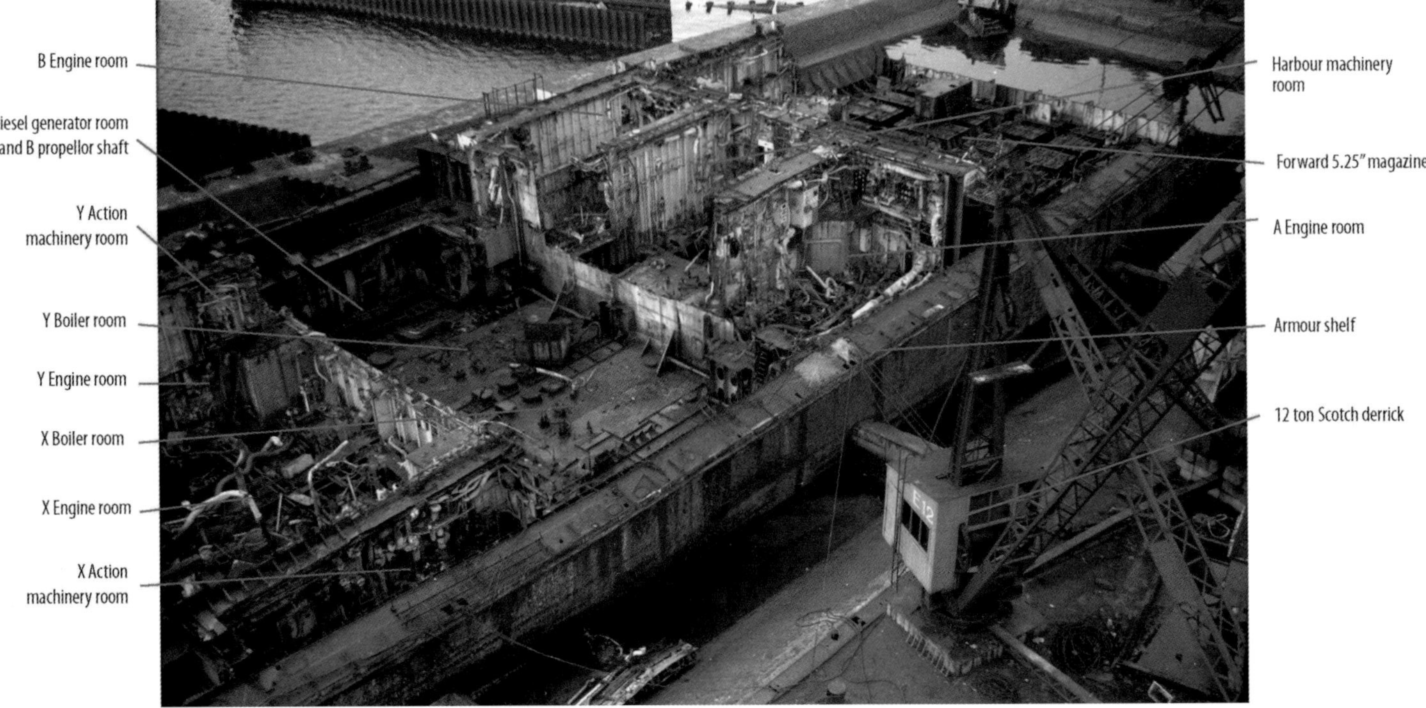
B Engine room
Diesel generator room
and B propellor shaft
Y Action
machinery room
Y Boiler room
Y Engine room
X Boiler room
X Engine room
X Action
machinery room
Harbour machinery
room
Forward 5.25" magazine
A Engine room
Armour shelf
12 ton Scotch derrick

With so much cut away, the hulk is no longer buoyant on 13 February. She was totally 'out of the water' by 16 March.

A view from the head of the beach looking aft on 9 January 1960. The side protection system is revealed. Outermost is a watertight compartment, then the higher narrow oil fuel compartment, then the inner watertight compartment, its inboard side being the double thickness protective longitudinal bulkhead, also seen in the final photo (right). Inboard is 'B' action machinery room showing two of the steam turbine-driven hydraulic pumps powering 'A' and 'B' gun mountings, with the now empty boiler rooms further inboard. The layout of the 5.25in magazine cases is clearly seen.

Conclusion

DUKE OF YORK and the rest of the *King George V* class were constructed as quickly as possible given the inevitable delays in the armour and armament industries, both of which had been run down for over a decade. The start of the war exacerbated the situation with new and unexpected demands placed on suppliers and shipyards alike. The four and a half years required to build *Duke of York* compares unfavourably with the similarly delayed but larger *Hood* which took three and a half years. Last of the line, *Vanguard*, built like *Hood* and *Duke of York* on the No 3 berth at Clydebank, would take longest of all, at close on five years.

Build times apart, there is little doubt that these battleships played a great part in maintaining Britain's position on the high seas during the Second World War acquitting themselves well, the exception being *Prince of Wales* which was unfortunate enough to be torpedoed in an area impossible to defend. Built for a war in which they played a significant role, the *King George V*s bolstered and lent credibility to an otherwise ageing fleet of capital ships. Their active careers were short, coinciding with the eclipse of the big-gun battleship. For five years after the end of the war some were maintained in the active fleet before being laid up for the next seven and then scrapped in less than two. For such a major investment in capital and labour they had short lives. Unfortunately, despite the unparalleled history of development and deployment that preceded this class of battleship, it was not possible to preserve any ship of the type in Britain, in contrast to the preserved status of the eight battleships in the United States.

Most of Britain's warship builders published glowing reports of their contribution to the war effort. However, Sir Stanley Goodall, who as DNC reviewed their activities at first hand, often confided differing views to his diary. Some, like Scotts, he thought less of while others such as Yarrow he admired for just getting on delivering ships without complaint. Although he was sometimes critical of Clydebank, e.g. too slow to adopt more welding, the Admiralty viewed John Brown as their 'go to' shipyard for major warship projects. *Vanguard*'s contract was placed with them without consideration of other builders, they were asked to build the prototype prefabricated anti-submarine frigate *Loch Fada*, and they completed ships where other yards had failed, e.g. the destroyers *Milne* and *Roebuck*. DNC asked them to prepare the design for converting *Queen Mary* and *Queen Elizabeth* to aircraft carriers, although this was not taken up as they would carry too few aircraft to justify the long conversion time. They were entrusted with the management of the Dalmuir facility for fitting out escorts and tank landing ships and they would have been the lead yard if the large *Malta*-class aircraft carriers had been built. They took on major repair jobs, often at the expense of new building. Their engine works delivered on time not just machinery for their own hulls but for many others built elsewhere. Managing director Stephen Pigott was a frequent caller at Goodall's office where such projects were discussed. They had the prestige of completing two of the Royal Navy's last four battleships not to mention many of the nationally-significant liners including the great Cunarders *Queen Mary* and *Queen Elizabeth* of a few years earlier. Not surprisingly they were placed in the top three of British warship builders and well placed to deliver the merchant ships in great demand post-war.

By all accounts, *Duke of York* was a soundly-built ship that sailed through her trials and was delivered at a critical time for the Royal Navy. She performed well in service, notably at the sinking of *Scharnhorst*. The *King George V*s were the smallest battleships of their era, all the others having significantly higher full load displacements as completed. That inevitably limited the scope for more generous design features such as wider side protection and more oil fuel. After initial teething problems with her 14in mountings were overcome and many additional close-range weapons were fitted, they proved to be well armed. While some have criticised their modest calibre 14in guns compared to other navies with 16in, the latter calibre was not compatible with a balanced design of a ship of their size, speed and protection. Indeed when new battleship designs were being prepared later in the war, Goodall noted in his diary that the Admiralty gunnery division favoured continuing with 14in guns on the grounds that quick and frequent hitting with 14in at an early stage of the action would lead to success rather than a few heavy blows from 16in. Her armour protection was good for her size, using the superior British cemented armour developed between the wars. Her naval architectural properties concerned with stability, strength and hull form were never in doubt.

Although her standard displacement as completed at 39,000 tons was higher than the nominal figure of 35,000 tons, much of the extra was due to Admiralty additions, e.g. more protection around magazines. While her 27.5-knot sea speed was sufficient for most operations, her endurance was appreciably lower than US battleships. This was partly down to a modest naval staff requirement to meet shorter-range European operations, whereas the US ships needed to operate over greater distances in the Pacific, but also due to more conservative machinery design with relatively high specific fuel consumption (pounds of oil per horsepower per hour). The low freeboard resulting in a wet ship forward was another shortcoming which derived from an unrealistic staff requirement, later corrected in *Vanguard*. Accommodation was somewhat cramped, especially after crew numbers were increased with more close-range weapons and electronics, only partially ameliorated after the aircraft arrangements were removed. Many other relatively minor changes were made between 1942 and 1945 as service experience dictated. But none of these shortcomings can be laid at the door of her builders.

This book would not have been possible without the wonderful series of drawings given by the Admiralty for preservation by the National Maritime Museum. If there was an inevitability that drawings from such a nationally-significant body as the Royal Navy would be preserved, such assurances did not necessarily apply to the records of British industry, much of which disappeared into skips and bonfires as industries fell into decline. That the collection of photographs from such an illustrious shipbuilder as John Brown has survived is remarkable in itself. That these photographs, full of drama and atmosphere, can describe the complexities of a ship in conjunction with the cool authority of the drawings is as close as we will ever get to understanding the building of such a great ship at this range in time from the actual events depicted. So too, the less glamorous but as important end of life photographs taken by individuals fascinated by what these ships would reveal.

DUKE OF YORK

Appendices

Duke of York Tender

Although it was a foregone conclusion about who the builders of the five *King George V*-class battleships were to be, tendering, although not in this instance competitive, still had to be carried out to establish an accounting basis for the contract. What follows is taken from Clydebank's Tender Book, revealing the breakdown of costs for the parts of the contract for which the shipbuilder was responsible and does not include armament or armour for which the Admiralty contracted separately.

The tender price was calculated by cost estimators who used the guidance drawings made available by the Admiralty for the purpose, totalling £3,409,000. To the basic manufacturing cost to the shipbuilder of labour and material, profit at varying rates and charges have been added by the directors. Charges were the overheads associated with operating the shipyard, a percentage of which would be set against individual contracts. Allowance has also been made for projected increases in wages and materials. After minor adjustments the agreed contract price was £3,405,736 as shown on p27. The final price at March 1942 as determined by Clydebank records is discussed on p25 and estimated at £3,378,937.

The original delivery date of 15 January 1941 could not be kept although no penalties were applied as the delays which pushed back delivery to November 1941 were outside the control of John Brown & Co.

15 February 1937

Admiralty

Proposed battleship for HM Navy

Engines 4 set Parsons type geared turbines 100,000 SHP at 230 rpm 110,000 SHP at 236 rpm

Boilers 8 Small tube with superheaters. 400lbs WP and 250° Fahrenheit superheat.

				£	
Hull					
	Material			736,550	
	Wages	Ironworkers	242,400		
		Increase 5%	12,100	254,500	
		Remainder	385,870		
		Increase 15%	57,880	443,750	
				1,434,800	
	P&I	12%	75,390		
		Increase 10%	8,410	83,800	
	Charges	50%	314,140		
		Increase 10%	34,960	349,100	
					1,867,700
Electrical					
	Material			118,700	
	Wages		41,350		
		Increase 15%	6,200	47,550	
				166,250	
	P&I		4,960		
		Increase 15%	765	5,725	
	Charges		20,675		
		Increase 15%	3,100	23,775	
					195,750

Machinery				
Material			468,900	
Wages		159,000		
	Increase 15%	23,500	182,500	
P&I		19,080		
	Increase 15%	2,820	21,900	
Charges		79,520		
	Increase 15%	11,730	91,250	
				764,550
				2,828,000

Delivery – On Firth of Clyde 15 January, 1941

Hull	Basis price		1,832,300	
	Profit		183,700	
	Increased wages		150,000	
	Increase in materials	35,000		
	Contingencies	37,000		
	Yard equipment	15,000		
	Probable delay in delivery of Sub-Contracts & Admiralty supplies	30,000		
				2,283,000
Electrical	Basis price		190,500	
	Profit		9,000	
	Increased wages		10,000	
	Increase in materials	5,000		
	Contingencies		5,000	
				229,500
Machinery	Basis price		787,500	
	Profit		78,700	
	Increased wages		30,000	
	Increase in materials	15,000		
				911,200
				3,423,700
Tender Price	Hull			2,270,000
	Electrical			233,000
	Machinery			906,000
				3,409,000
	Contribution from F		14,700	
Insurance	(1) Underwriters to be liable for all claims up to £500,000. Admiralty to indemnify for any excess over that amount			23,500
	(2) As at (1) but cover to the extent of £2,000,000			25,000

P&I = Power and insurance.

Particulars

Displacement tons*
Standard** as designed 35,000, as completed 39,000
Displacement tons, full load as completed 43,000
Gross tons
24,475 (100ft^3 = 1 ton)

Length, ft
Between perpendiculars 700
Overall 745
Breadth, ft-in
Moulded 103-0
Extreme over catapult 112-4
Depth, ft-in
Keel to upper deck 50-9
Draught as completed, ft-in
Standard 30-7
Fully loaded 33-3
Air draught to top of foremast, ft 145

Machinery
Steam turbines max shaft horsepower 110,000, single reduction gearing 4 shafts, rpm 230
Cruising turbine machinery shaft horsepower 28,000
Speed, knots
Cruising turbines 19
Full power 27.5
Boilers
Eight, 400lb/in^2
Generators
Two diesel, six steam turbine, 300 kW each

Armament
10 x 14in 45-calibre breech-loading Mark VII guns.
2 quad Mark III, 1 Mark II twin mountings
16 x 5.25in 50-calibre quick-firing Mark I guns. 8 twin Mark I mountings
48 x 2pdr Mark VIII guns. 6 8-barrel Mark VIA mountings
6 x 20mm Oerlikon guns on single mountings

Aircraft
2 Walrus amphibians with DIIIH catapult (McTaggart Scott)

Capacities, tons
Fuel oil, 3588
Diesel oil, 185
Fresh water, 430
Reserve feed water, 256
Petrol, aircraft and boats, 28

Endurance, nautical miles (tons oil/hour)
Cruise power 6500 (12)
Full power 2500 (40)

Armour
Main belt: 15in C over magazines; 14in C over machinery
Main deck: 6in NC over magazines; 5in NC over machinery
Barbettes: 13–11in C
Armour bulkheads 79 and 274: 12–10in C
14in gunhouse: front 13in C, sides and rear 7in NC, roof 6in NC
5.25in gunhouse: 1in D1HT [steel]

Radar as completed
1 Type 281 air-warning, 1 Type 273 surface-warning, 1 Type 284 14in gunnery, 4 Type 285 5.25in gunnery, 6 Type 282 2pdr gunnery

---

* In September 1945 the Admiralty wrote to the commanding officer of *Howe* with what amounts to a rebuke concerning displacement:

> The British Press have attributed to you a statement that *Howe*'s displacement is now 45,000 tons compared with 35,000 tons originally. This seems to be due to confusion between standard displacement and deep displacement. These figures are as follows:
> A. Designed standard displacement 35,000 tons
> B. Present standard displacement 38,000 tons
> C. Present deep displacement 44,500 tons
> The difference between A and B represents weight of additional protection, A/A armament and radar.
> Difference between B and C represents fuel, reserve feed water and supplementary provisions and stores for leave purposes.
> This is a highly technical subject which Press may easily garble and on which public speculation is undesirable. Commanding officers would therefore be well advised to avoid or evade it.

The note was copied to the Commander of the British Pacific Fleet, Admiral Bruce Fraser, among others. Even today the Press is confused by tonnages, mistaking cruise ships' gross tonnage (a measure of volume) with its weight or displacement.

** Standard displacement = Full load minus fuel and reserve feed water.

War Complement (1941)

	Private ship	Fleet flagship
Admiral		1
Chief of Staff		1
Captain of Fleet		1
Captain	1	1
Wardroom Officers	41	73
Gunroom Officers	13	13
Warrant Officers	15	19
CPOs	122	131
Sergeants of Marines	10	9
POs	112	122
Seamen	612	636
Marines	190	212
Stokers	201	202
Boys	95	95
Officers' stewards, cooks	23	45
Writer and supply assistants	16	22
Ship's cooks	23	24
Fleet Air Arm	25	25
Sick Bay staff	6	6
Canteen staff	6	6
Total	1511	1644

Changes following 1945 Refit

Displacement tons March 1945

Average action	43,540
Deep	44,794 Draught 34ft 4in mean
Light	39,229

Fuel oil capacity 3879 tons

Close-range AA March 1945

20mm Oerlikon
38 x Mark II guns on single Mark IIIA or Mark VIIA mountings
8 x Mark II guns on twin Mark V mountings
Total 54 barrels

Pom-pom 2-pdr
8 x Mark VIII guns on octuple Mark VIA mountings
6 x Mark VIII guns on quadruple Mark VIIP mountings
Total 88 barrels

40mm Bofors
2 x Quadruple Mark II mountings
Total 8 barrels

150 close-range AA barrels in total

Radar fit September 1945

Type 242M	Interrogator for surface craft and low-flying aircraft. Located on foremast.
Type 293P	Surface warning and target indicating to 30,000 yards maximum. Located at top of foremast.
Type 274	Gunnery surface. Two sets, one on forward DCT and the other on after DCT. Ranges up to 50,000 yards.
Type 285P	Gunnery aircraft. Four sets, one for each 5.25in director. Range up to 30,000 yards
Type 281BQ	Aircraft warning. Transmitting and receiving aerials on mainmast. Range up to 160 miles.
Type 243Q	General interrogator for aircraft. Aerial fitted on mainmast.
Type 941	Aircraft identification. Aerial on top of Type 281BQ array and trained with it.
Type 277P	Surface warning. Rotating stabilised aerial on foremast. Range 150,000 yards maximum. Also used to provide warning of low-flying aircraft.
Type 282P1	Gunnery close range. Seven sets, one on each pom-pom director. Range 6000 yards maximum.
Type 251M	Aircraft homing beacon. Aerial on foremast.
Type 253P	IFF set. Two, one on each mast.
Type 91	Jamming enemy W/T transmitter. Aerial on mainmast.
Type FV1	Direction finding. Installed in Type 91 office in after superstructure.
Type 651	Jamming transmitter. To counter German guided missiles. Aerial on mainmast.
Type CXFR	Jamming transmitter.

Boats September 1945

Diesel
2 x 45ft motor picket boats
2 x 45ft motor launch
3 x 25ft motor boat
1 x 35ft motor boat
1 x 16ft motor dinghy

Sail/oars
2 x 32ft cutter
2 x 27ft whaler
2 x 14ft dinghy

Rafts and Floats
45 Carley rafts
22 Flotanets.

Complement as a private ship (September 1945)	
Officers	100
Seamen	900
Engine Room Department	300
Marines	300
Others	300
Total	**1900**

Source: *Duke of York* Battle Book and Ship's Book.

Refits

The wartime service career of *Duke of York* was subject to several refits as follows:

Briefly drydocked at Rosyth 20–26 October 1942

Rosyth 8 December 1942 to 14 March 1943. Drydocked No 1 dock 17 December to 3 March 1943

Included among other items fitting of additional close range AA – 20mm Oerlikons.

Drydocked at Rosyth 11–17 October 1943 and 11–24 January 1944

Liverpool (by Cammell Laird at Gladstone Dock) 26 September 1944 to 31 March 1945.

Refit and partial modernisation included removal of aircraft arrangements with area reconfigured as the Boat Deck. Former Boat Deck utilised as additional AA platform with twin Oerlikon and 40mm quad Bofors mountings. Improved radar fitted.

Drydocked Sydney 21–28 July 1945 (new Captain Cook dock)

Post-War Refits and status

Thereafter she received minor modifications, updates and removal or cocooning of close-range weapons.

Sydney, Captain Cook Dock, 15 April 1946 to 14 May 1946, drydocked 18 April to 13 May

Devonport, 26 September to 30 November 1946, drydocked No 10 dock 6–23 November 1946

Portsmouth, 3 November 1947 to 27 February 1948. Drydocked 9 December 1947 to 23 January 1948

Portsmouth, 10 May 1949 to 24 February 1950. Drydocked 11 May to 30 September 1949

Last drydocking Gladstone Dock, Liverpool 24 September to 23 October 1951

Flagship of the Home Fleet from December 1946 to April 1949

Flagship of the Reserve Fleet from July 1949 to September 1951

Up until this point *Duke of York* had been maintained and updated in working condition.

Reserve status. On 6 November 1951 left Mersey in tow for the Gareloch and lay-up.

Placed on the Disposal List with approval to scrap the four ships of the *King George V* class given by the Director of Dockyards on 8 May 1957.

Arrived at Shipbreaking Industries jetty on 18 February 1958 still capable of electrical power generation.

Dates from Ordering to Joining the Fleet at Scapa Flow

Order placed on 28 April 1937

Laid down on 5 May 1937

Launched on 28 February 1940

Commissioned on 20 August 1941 under Captain C H J Harcourt

Departure from John Brown's shipyard 7 September 1941

Completed 4 November 1941

Acknowledgements

With thanks to:
Staff at The National Archives, Kew
Staff at The Ballast Trust, Johnstone.
Staff at Glasgow University Archives, Thurso Street, Glasgow
Staff at the National Maritime Museum particularly, Andrew Choong and Jeremy Michell
The authors are indebted to staff at the National Records of Scotland and in particular Linda Ramsay and Eva Martinez Moya for making the photographs used in this book available.
Fairfield Heritage, Glasgow
Newcastle University, Marine Technology Special Collection. British Shipbuilding Database
Individuals:
Richard Dennis
Roy Metcalfe
Brian Newman
Fred Walker

DUKE OF YORK

Sources

National Records of Scotland

The records of John Brown & Co Ltd are held by the National Records of Scotland partly at Glasgow University Archives and at Thomas Thomson House in Edinburgh.

Photographs
UCS1/118/554 series.

At Glasgow University Archives
UCS1/49 Pay Books
UCS1/52/7 Pay Roll Books
UCS1/59/11-13 Employment Returns
UCS1/59/29 Employees by Contract
UCS1/59/50-52 Employees by Trade
UCS1/61/4 Admiralty Payments
UCS1/76/4-5 Contract Costs Registers
UCS1/77/264 Progressive Cost Books
UCS1/80/16-17 Hull Costs Books
UCS1/83/2 Wages Cost Books (ships 542–657)
UCS1/85/27 Finished Costs
UCS1/86/128-9 Comparison Costs and Estimate Books
UCS1/107/161 Schedule of Instalments hull and machinery

Monthly Reports
UCS1/5/35 (1937) to UCS1/5/46 (1941)

Plans
UCS1/554/1 Fore end framing (Frames 65 to stem)
UCS1/554/2-6 Transverse framing between protective bulkhead and armour shelf
UCS1/554/7 Ventilation arrangements (ten sheets)
UCS1/554/8 Body plan
UCS1/554/9 Lines

Boxed drawings
UCS1/554/10 Main deck
UCS1/554/11 Upper deck
UCS1/554/12 Platform and upper platform decks
UCS1/554/13 Profile
UCS1/554/14 Midship section

Ballast Trust
No. 554 Launching and Shoring Arrangements

National Maritime Museum

***Duke of York* rolled drawings**
General Arrangement as fitted 1941 M1686 to M1696
General Arrangement as refitted 1945 M1697 to M1706

Folded drawings in box ADBB0265
Sketch of Rig (M2065)
Docking Drawing (M2064)
Outer Bottom Plating (M2062 & M2063)
Aircraft Arrangements (M1685)
Embarking Ammunition (M2061)

Design drawings *King George V* Class
Structural Sections (M2067)

Ships Covers
***King George V* Class**
ADM/SC/547
ADM/SC/547A
ADM/SC/547B
ADM/SC/547C
ADM/SC/547D
ADM/SC/547E

Contract for HMS *Anson* (*Duke of York*) 233/584

The National Archives

ADM234/271 Handbook for 14 inch BL Mark VII Gun on Twin, Mark II and Quadruple, Mark III Mounting
ADM234/183 Handbook for 5.25 inch, Q.F., Mark I Gun on HA/LA Twin, Marks I and II Mounting
ADM53/114151-54 Logs for HMS *Duke of York* Aug-Nov 1941

Bibliography

Buxton, Ian, *Shipbreaking at Faslane* (World Ship Society, 2020)
Johnston, Ian, *Ships for All Nations: John Brown and Company Clydebank 1847 – 1971* (Seaforth Publishing, 2016)
__________ and Buxton, Ian, *The Battleship Builders: Constructing and Arming British Capital Ships* (Seaforth Publishing, 2013)

Index

Above: Last of the British battleships, *Vanguard* corrected some of the faults inherent in the design of the *King George V* class, not least in the greatly increased sheer. She was also a product of the John Brown shipyard at Clydebank. She is seen here in the fitting-out basin at Clydebank on 2 May 1946 prior to departure to run trials. Also in the dock is the cruiser *Tiger*, which will be subject to lay-up, redesign and completion thirteen years later, and the Port Line's *Port Wellington*. To the left of *Vanguard* the yard is being fitted with new 20- and 40-ton tower cranes to replace the 5-ton derricks installed before the First World War. This is an indication of the move to welded fabrication still to come. Note the steam turbine machinery castings and items of equipment stored at the head of the basin.

Right: *Vanguard* running trials on the Firth of Clyde.